Infertility
Psychological Issues and Counseling Strategies

Edited by

Sandra R. Leiblum

JOHN WILEY & SONS, INC.

New York • Chichester • Brisbane • Toronto • Singapore • Weinheim

Copyright © 1997 by John Wiley & Sons, Inc.

Library of Congress Cataloging-in-Publication Data:

Infertility : psychological issues and counseling strategies / edited
  by Sandra R. Leiblum.
      p. cm. — (Wiley series in couples and family dynamics and treatment)
  Includes bibliographical references.
  ISBN 0-471-12684-5 (cloth : alk. paper)
  1. Infertility—Patients—Counseling of. 2. Infertility-
-Psychological aspects. I. Leiblum, Sandra Risa. II. Series.
  [DNLM 1. Infertility—psychology. 2. Infertility—therapy.
3. Counseling. 4. Ethics, Medical. WP 570 I438733 1997]
RC889.I566 1997
618.1'78'0019—dc20
DNLM/DLC   96-23253
for Library of Congress

Series Preface

Our ability to form strong interpersonal bonds with romantic partners, children, parents, siblings, and other relations is one of the key characteristics that define our humanity. These coevolving relationships shape who we are and what we become—they can be a source of great gratification, or tremendous pain. Yet, only in the mid-twentieth century did behavioral and social scientists really begin focusing on couples and family dynamics, and only in the past several decades have the theory and findings that emerged from those studies been used to develop effective therapeutic interventions for troubled couples and families.

We have made great progress in understanding the dynamics, structure, function, and interactional patterns of couples and families—and made tremendous strides in treatment. However, as we stand poised on the beginning of a new millennium, it seems quite clear that both intimate partnerships and family relationships are in a period of tremendous flux. Economic and sociopolitical factors are changing work patterns, parenting responsibilities, and relational dynamics. Modern medicine has helped lengthen the life span, giving rise to the need for transgenerational caretaking. Cohabitation, divorce, and remarriage are quite commonplace, and these social changes make it necessary for us to rethink and broaden our definition of what constitutes a family.

Thus, it is no longer enough simply to embrace the concept of the family as a system. In order to understand, and effectively treat the evolving family, we must incorporate into our theoretical formulations, and therapeutic armamentarium, information derived from research and clinical practice on important emergency issues, such as ethnicity, culture, religion, gender, sexual preference, family life cycle, socioeconomic status, education, physical and mental health, values, and belief systems.

The purpose of the *Wiley Series in Couples and Family Dynamics and Treatment* is to provide a forum for cutting-edge relational and family theory, practice, and research. Its scope is intended to be broad, diverse, and international. All books published in this series share a common mission—to reflect on the past, offer state-of-the-art information on the present, and speculate on, as well as attempt to shape, the future of the field.

FLORENCE W. KASLOW

Florida Couples and Family Institute
Duke University

Preface

The decision to edit a book on infertility counseling was, like most things in life, overdetermined. As a young(er!) woman, 18 years ago, I found myself struggling to become pregnant. The wish to have a child had long been present, dating back to those intensely serious but profoundly pleasurable doll-play sessions of childhood. The time to do so arrived decades later and my difficulty in conceiving was definitely unexpected. After three years of committed but often frustrating enterprise, success! My son Jonathan is now 16 and deeply satisfying.

Thus, my interest in infertility, its exigencies and treatment, sprang from personal experience. As a psychologist with a research background, I sought to understand more about the impact of infertility and its treatment on the lives and psyches of affected couples. For the past 15 years, studying attitudes toward multiple pregnancies, donor insemination, in vitro fertilization, single and lesbian motherhood, and the sexual and personal relationships of infertile couples have been major foci of research for myself and many others. Some of this research has clarified how infertile couples differ from their more readily fertile counterparts, and how much of the emotional upheaval experienced is a result rather than a cause of infertility. Without a doubt, infertility leaves its mark.

For the past decade, I have served as the consultant for several of the infertility programs at the Center for Reproductive Endocrinology and Fertility at Robert Wood Johnson Medical School. We have seen many women, men, and couples who are reacting to an initial diagnosis of infertility or who are trying to decide which of the many technologically advanced parenthood options to pursue (and for how long). These women and their partners are clear about their desire to become parents. What they are often struggling with is determining when the cost—physical, psychological, and financial—of treatment exceeds the uncertain return. Often, these decisions are painfully difficult and involve choosing among a number of unsatisfactory alternatives. Often, the negotiation and the chronic nature of decision making create stress and upset relationships. Working with these couples has given me a better appreciation of how infertility stress can be the catalyst that either undermines fragile relationships or fortifies sturdier ones.

This book is inspired by many motives: to assist clinicians who may be unfamiliar with the current state of infertility medicine; to provide clinical examples illustrating the great variety of women, men, and couples requesting consultation for infertility-related issues; and to suggest assessment and treatment strategies that may be clinically helpful. A review of currently available assisted reproductive options is included. Updates on relevant research findings are presented by individual authors.

As with any major undertaking, a number of individuals are responsible for providing both the stimulus and support to complete this book. I want to acknowledge my gratitude to all the reproductive endocrinologists and gynecologists with whom I have worked at the Center for Reproductive Endocrinology and Fertility at Robert Wood Johnson University Medical School for the past 16 years, but especially to Ekkehard Kemmann, MD, the Director of the Center. Special thanks go to my colleagues and fellow clinicians, Deborah Cherniss, Jean Ciardiello, Yakov Epstein, Joan Hammond, Gilbert Honigfeld, Helane Rosenberg, Patricia Schreiner-Engel, Leslie Schover, and Elizabeth Williams. I have benefited greatly from their warmth as well as their wisdom. As with all my enterprises, I am indebted to my secretary, Dorothy Sima, for her unfailing efficiency and enthusiasm. And finally, I want to express my deepest gratitude to the two loves of my life, Jonathan Leiblum Kassen and Frank Brickle.

SANDRA R. LEIBLUM

Piscataway, New Jersey

Contents

PART ONE

Infertility: Medical, Ethical, and Psychological Perspectives

CHAPTER 1

Introduction

SANDRA R. LEIBLUM

> If the Lord Almighty had consulted me before embarking upon the
> Creation, I would have recommended something simpler.
> —Alfonso X of Castile

In the past few decades, the topic of infertility has captured media attention. The popular press regularly features the plight of infertile couples with glowing descriptions of the latest reproductive technology and documented reports about the miraculous pregnancies of women believed too old or too reproductively damaged to conceive. Along with the triumphs of modern reproductive medicine, the news media have noted the tragedies: unethical physicians who have used their own rather than anonymous donor sperm to fertilize eggs, accidental transfer of fertilized embryos into the wrong woman, selective reduction resulting in pregnancy loss. The field of reproductive medicine is percolating with the possibility of joy as well as the possibility of frustration and loss.

The proliferation of new reproductive techniques is staggering. Whereas in the recent past, the only alternatives available to the infertile couple were adoption or living without children, current options include an impressive range of medical interventions such as in vitro fertilization (IVF), intrauterine insemination (IUI), gamete intrafallopian transfer (GIFT), zygote intrafallopian transfer (ZIFT), and subzonal insemination (SUZI). Revolutionary technological breakthroughs are announced almost weekly. For example, through a newly developed micromanipulation method, intracytoplasmic sperm injection (ICSI), it is now possible to engineer the passage of a single sperm into a single oocyte: The sperm may belong to the husband or to a donor, the egg may belong to the wife or a donor, and the transfer of the fertilized ovum may involve the uterus of a single, divorced, or lesbian woman, or a surrogate of any sexual orientation or marital status. This has profound psychological implications for all parties, whether it be the infertile couple, the donor of sperm or egg, the surrogate, and certainly for the resulting infant.

Even as this chapter was being written, the latest technological innovation was announced. Physicians have successfully removed an ovary (but not the other parts of the reproductive system) from cancer patients undergoing chemotherapy or radiation and then, at a later date, may be able to partially re-place the ovary so that future conception can be attempted. One physician, Dr. Bernadine Healy, former head of the National Institutes of Health, declared, in commenting on this achievement: "It is one of those amazing areas where sci-ence marches on and almost the unthinkable becomes doable" (*New York Times*, December 12, 1995, p. 8).

Despite the bounty of reproductive options and the optimism they induce in individuals and couples struggling with the insult of infertility, there is a down-side to these new medical approaches. They typically incur unanticipated phys-ical and psychological stress and, many times, ultimate disappointment. Moreover, with the proliferation of ever-changing reproductive options, it is dif-ficult for most couples ever to relinquish their dream of having a biological child. As several authors have noted, couples who were considered sterile only a few years ago now may receive treatment and even encouragement about the possi-bility of successful conception, although the individual likelihood of success may remain low (Shushan, Eisenberg, & Schenker, 1995). The truth is that sub-fertility is distressingly commonplace and conception may remain elusive for many, many couples, despite the promises and optimism induced by the new re-productive alternatives. At present, of all couples undergoing assisted reproduc-tion, about 40% will be disappointed in their quest for a biological child.

There are also myriad ethical, legal, economic, moral, and psychological quandaries that the new reproductive technologies pose for the infertile couple and the professionals who treat them. As an attorney specializing in infertility issues has noted:

> Embryos have been lost, misplaced, and sometimes given to the wrong couples. Disputes between couples and between couples and programs over "their em-bryos" have occurred. Some programs face the question of disposal of frozen embryos when contact with the couples has not occurred for many years. (Robertson, 1996, p. 11)

Such questions as which couples or individuals should be accepted into—or screened out of—infertility programs, questions regarding the parental rights of surrogates versus donors versus recipients, questions about confidentiality, privacy, and disclosure are far from answered. Currently, there is a lively and heated controversy about the costs of assisted reproductive techniques (ARTs) and the price healthcare systems absorb (DeCherney, 1995; Shushan, Eisen-berg, & Schenker, 1995). These questions are often perplexing and challenging and are inextricably associated with the ever-increasing use of assisted repro-ductive technology.

Embryo donation illustrates this issue. There are thousands of frozen embryos potentially available for donation and a large number of recipients eager to re-ceive them. Moreover, there is a significant demand for infertility treatments that are less costly than IVF. Yet the donation of embryos poses many ethical, legal, and psychological questions (Robertson, 1995). Is embryo donation an example of adoption or gamete donation? What is the potential effect on off-spring of having siblings they will never meet? What is the effect on donors of knowing they have genetic offspring in the world whom they have not met? Should women even be told whether their donated embryos have successfully implanted in the uterus of another female? Should recipients be screened for embryo donation the way they might be screened as potential adoptive parents? These are just some of the questions presented by what, at first glance, would appear to be a felicitous solution to the supply-and-demand problem of excess embryos and infertile but receptive recipients.

Disclosure versus secrecy of origins is another controversial issue in ovum and sperm donation protocols as well as with embryo donation. What if a pro-gram believes in openness about these procedures while a recipient couple does not want to divulge this information? What does it signify to be born to parents with whom the child has no shared genetic ties? Should offspring be told they are the product of a donated embryo? Does the child's right to know his or her genetic origins supersede the parents' right to privacy? What is the impact on the couple of keeping such a loaded secret? What is the cost of having the se-cret leak out unexpectedly in less-than-ideal circumstances? These and other ethical and psychological issues are addressed by Cooper (Chapter 3) and Klock (Chapter 9) in this volume.

In the past, infertility specialists have tended to recommend that couples not disclose the use of donated sperm or ovum to their offspring. In fact, in a study looking at the beliefs of reproductive endocrinologists concerning the wisdom of disclosing or not disclosing the use of sperm donation (Leiblum & Hamkins, 1992), 56% of those queried believed that offspring need not be told about their conception while 21% endorsed a neutral position. Only 22% be-lieved that children should be told about the use of donor sperm.

In recent years, however, the pendulum has been swinging away from se-crecy as a preferred option. Mental health experts have taken the lead in advo-cating disclosure from the earliest years onward; they present a variety of compelling reasons for this recommendation. In part, this trend also reflects a growing appreciation of the role of genetics in intellectual and personality func-tioning and an acknowledgment that upbringing and family environment, while important, may not override the impact of genetic factors. Moreover, it is ar-gued—often passionately—that children have a right to know their genetic background and that this right overrides the right of their parents to secrecy. Klock (Chapter 9) presents a cogent analysis of the issues that must be consid-ered when dealing with this sensitive and very emotional issue.

As Jacob (Chapter 10) and others have noted, nearly all single and lesbian couples opt for openness regarding the circumstances of conception (Leiblum, Palmer, & Spector, 1995). This sentiment, however, is not universally shared by heterosexual couples who may have sought ovum or sperm donation as a way of protecting the infertile status of their partner. In this, as in many additional issues, mental health professionals are making a significant contribution to the policies and recommendations evolving in the field of reproductive medicine.

This chapter will provide a brief overview of the ways in which infertility has been regarded and treated historically and will highlight some of the special considerations that are involved in the current practice of infertility management. We will note the unique psychological dilemmas that ARTs pose for infertile clients and their therapists. The remaining chapters in this book will address topics that are of particular relevance to mental health professionals treating individuals and couples with the diagnosis of primary, secondary, or unexplained infertility.

A HISTORICAL PERSPECTIVE ON INFERTILITY

Infertility has always existed. Attempted solutions have ranged from faith in miracles and magic to a reliance on modern medicine. Historically, there have been descriptions of miraculous births from ancient times to the present. The Bible tells the story of Sarah and Abraham. Sarah, long-married and childless, consented to have Hagar, her maid, engage in sexual intercourse with Abraham, which resulted in the birth of a son, Ishmael. Finally, according to the Scriptures, Sarah became pregnant herself at the age of 90, and bore a son, Isaac.[1] Many of the major biblical patriarchs and their wives were infertile— Isaac and Rebecca, Jacob and Rachel. The common biblical solution for female infertility, was for the husband to take a second wife or a concubine since in Jewish law, it was a man's obligation to have children (although women had no such obligation) (Gold, 1988).

Every culture has had its set of customs and folklore for the relief of infertility (Johnston, 1963). For example, the ancient Hindus had a custom that sprang from the worship of the *lingam* (erect penis) and *yoni* (female genitalia). A hole in a rock or cloven tree symbolized the female birth passage and females who passed through such a cleavage were believed to have improved fertility. This same custom of passing through holes in trees to overcome infertility is still practiced in many places throughout the world.

In the ancient world, astrology and numerology provided numbers for the day and month that promised greatest likelihood of fertility. Similarly, the waxing and waning of the moon in its many phases were considered important. Numerologists of old considered libido to be associated with a full moon.

---

[1]While not as impressive, modern-day "Sarahs" do exist and are becoming more prevalent. Through the use of ova donated by younger women, peri- and postmenopausal women are able to successfully carry and deliver full-term babies. Recently, the *New York Times* reported the delivery of an infant to a 61-year-old Italian woman and her 34-year-old husband.

Noting this trend, a *New Yorker* cartoon featured an elderly woman requesting supplies from the prescription counter of her pharmacy: "Arthritis pain formula Anacin, Poli-grip, and a home pregnancy test."

Menstruation was thought to be under lunar control and, consequently, fertility as well.

Amulets or good-luck pendants were commonly used in early Arabic times and the Egyptians had great faith in these pieces. Statuettes of pregnant females or of males with large phalluses are found as fertility fetishes and symbols in many countries, including Africa, Central America, Indonesia, and Polynesia. Even today, superstitious rituals not infrequently accompany fertility procedures among both professionals and nonprofessionals (although individuals may be loathe to admit this).

The role of the male in reproduction was poorly understood and consequently, many primitive tribes considered conception to be exclusively a female undertaking. The Ingarda Tribe in Australia, for example, believed that the child was the product of some food the mother had eaten. The Trobian Islanders believed that pregnancy followed rupture of the hymen by whatever means and that intercourse was intended purely for pleasure and had nothing to do with procreation. Women, traditionally, have been blamed for the lack of successful conception and have been ostracized or even beheaded, when unable to produce children. In point of fact, it has only been very recently that physicians are willing to talk about the couple's infertility rather than the woman's (Laborie, 1993), and that men are routinely included in the infertility work-up.

Although medical schools arose in about the seventh century B.C., medical management of infertility remained magical, at best. For example, the eating of the eye of a hyena with licorice and dill was said to cause a woman to conceive, and this was "guaranteed within three days." (Johnston, 1963). Another belief was that if two hairs were pulled from the tail of a she-ass while being mounted, they would make a woman conceive even against her will if they were knotted together during sexual intercourse.

Soranus, a physician practicing in Alexandria in the first century was regarded as a "specialist" in gynecology and obstetrics by his contemporaries, and indeed, he made several major contributions to fertility management. Along with the invention of the vaginal speculum (which was then forgotten until the 1800s), he had several good ideas for enhancing the probability of conception such as remaining in bed after coitus.

Other recommendations for fertility management during the early centuries included body massage, fumigation, fomentations, douches, irrigations, and pessaries, as well as faith healing, relics, charms, and incantations.

The eighteenth century witnessed several scientific discoveries that advanced the medical understanding of fertility. In 1786, Lazzaro Spallanzani showed that spermatozoa were essential to fertilization and in 1827, Van Kolliker demonstrated that spermatozoa originated in the testicular cells and then fertilized the ovum which then underwent segmentation. Carl Von Baer, in 1827, discovered the mammalian ovum.

J. Marion Sims, an American gynecologist, performed the first successful case of artificial insemination in 1866. He inseminated a woman who had been unable to conceive for nine years. He also stressed the importance of demonstrating the presence of sperm in the semen through the use of the microscope.

In the nineteenth century, scientists studied the influence of the ovaries on menstruation, on the development of the genitalia, and the secondary sexual characteristics. In 1839, Augustus Nicolar Gendrin suggested that ovulation controlled menstruation and it was now generally acknowledged that the ovaries had more control over menstruation than the moon did. The relation of conception to menstruation became clearer and Sigmund, in 1871 advanced the belief that a woman menstruated because she failed to conceive.

Modern concepts of the physiology of menstruation date from the isolation of estrogen from the human ovarian follicle in 1923 by Edgar Allen and Edward Boisy. The function of the pituitary gland as the controlling agent over the ovarian function became well established through the work of Aschner in 1912, followed by the discovery of the gonadotropic activity of the anterior pituitary.

The modern era of infertility in medicine is generally acknowledged to have begun only in this century with the studies of Huhner on sperm survival in the cervical mucus. With greater scientific understanding of fertility and the factors that govern it, the rate of technological innovations has skyrocketed. In 1978, Louise Brown was born through the use of IVF. The past 20 years have resulted in dramatic advances in the understanding and manipulation of the various factors contributing to, and controlling conception and in the proliferation of a great number of infertility options (see McShane's summary of infertility diagnosis and assisted reproductive techniques in Chapter 2).

PREVALENCE OF INFERTILITY

While estimates vary, the prevalence of infertility is generally cited as being about 10% to 12% of couples of reproductive age, or approximately 1 in 6 couples. There are an estimated 5.3 million infertile couples in the United States, and an estimated 2.3 to 3 million couples seek treatment for infertility each year. While the majority of couples experiencing difficulty conceiving succeed with low-tech interventions such as drugs to regulate ovulation, more than 40,000 couples find themselves shunted to "high-tech" assisted reproduction, such as IVF, GIFT, and ZIFT. Since 1982, the number of infertility clinics in the United States has grown from 5 to 315 (American Society for Reproductive Medicine, 1995) and the numbers increase monthly.

It certainly appears that the incidence of infertility is increasing. According to the National Center for Health Statistics, the percentage of childless, infertile couples increased from 14.4% in 1965 to 18.5% in 1995 (*Newsweek,* September 4, 1995, p. 40). Experts have cited sexually transmitted diseases, especially pelvic inflammatory disease, exposure to environmental toxins, and delayed childbearing as factors in the increased prevalence of infertility. Recent articles have commented on the reduction in sperm quantity and quality over the last several decades (Wright, 1996). Treatment of infertility has become a growth industry that generates about 2 billion dollars annually.[2]

Moreover, there is certainly evidence that women today are more likely to delay childbearing compared with their predecessors. According to the Advance Report of Final Natality Statistics (1993), in 1991, 31% of all U.S. births were to women age 30 or older (up from 29% in 1989) with about 9% of all births to women over 35 (up from 8%). As noted earlier, women in their 50s are now attempting pregnancy and achieving motherhood using the donor oocytes of younger women (Sauer, Paulson, & Lobo, 1995). Nevertheless, the likelihood of having a successful pregnancy for women over 40 is quite low. Among the New York region's 12 busiest clinics, the success rate for women 40 or over varied from zero to 15% in 1993 (*New York Times*, Sunday, January 7, 1996). In a recent study (Smith & Buyalos, 1996), it was reported that the risk of spontaneous abortion in women over the age of 36 was significantly increased and, in fact, there was a fivefold increase in spontaneous abortion in women over 40 compared with women aged 31 to 35 (3.8% vs. 20%). Thus, although they may conceive, their likelihood of delivering is diminished.

The *actual* incidence of infertility in the population is impossible to state with absolute certainty because the diagnosis of infertility is difficult to make. Specialists have noted that infertility represents a continuum ranging from absolute sterility (complete infertility) through subfertility to normal fertility and perhaps, even superfertility. Complete infertility or sterility is believed to affect about 5% of couples attempting to achieve a pregnancy (Jansen, 1994). This may be due to azoospermia, anovulation, and female genital tract occlusion and will generate straightforward diagnoses.

Relative infertility is something else: it means making a sometimes arbitrary distinction between normal fertility and low fertility.[3] Infertility investigations may yield results that are inconclusive. Pregnancy seems possible but has not yet happened. Sometimes several abnormalities occur together. Although each may be considered mild taken individually, combined they interfere with conception.

---

[2]Many have claimed that the infertility "business" is a virtually free-market branch of medicine that has been largely exempt from government regulation and from the downward pressure on costs that insurance companies exert. This situation appears to be changing rapidly, with the increase in complaints from consumers about costs and the influence of managed care in limiting procedures. Nevertheless, many individuals have felt (and continue to feel) that assisted reproduction is only an option for the affluent who have good insurance or can afford treatments not covered by traditional policies. For the infertile couple, adoption or foster care has seemed to be the only alternative to childlessness.

[3]The causes of relative infertility include the following: ovulation disorders, oligospermia, endometriosis, peritubal adhesions, uterine cavity abnormalities, uterine cervix abnormalities, and sperm antibodies (Jansen, 1994).

Moreover, the cutoff point on the continuum where normal is differentiated from abnormal is arbitrary since there is no agreed-on standard definition of infertility (Wagner & Stephenson, 1993). When the definition of 12 months of unprotected coitus without pregnancy is used to define infertility, only 16% to 21% of couples meeting this definition actually remain infertile throughout their lives. Several studies suggest that while 30% of couples take more than a year to conceive, many couples are eventually successful with—or in spite of—infertility treatment.

Currently, two considerations are given importance when trying to decide whether or not to initiate treatment with advanced reproductive technology: the duration of infertility and the time remaining for conception (Jansen, 1994). These factors are considered more significant than the actual cause of infertility and should be considered when counseling infertile couples. In most cases, the infertile woman's age is considered the single most important factor in the outcome of infertility intervention. Fertility tends to be very low after the age of 45 and the slope of success becomes much steeper after the age of 37. The clinician working in infertility counseling should be aware of these issues.

COSTS OF TREATMENT

Infertility treatment with the new technologies is expensive. In vitro fertilization and other advanced treatment procedures are costly because they depend on the skills of highly trained personnel and require the use of expensive equipment (Collins, Bustillo, Visscher, & Lawrence, 1995). In 1986, the median charge for a single cycle of IVF was $4,688; more current estimates are $8,000 per cycle. According to a recent review article, the computed cost of a single live birth from IVF treatment was in excess of $40,000 (Neumann, Winstein, & Gharib, 1994).

Moreover, IVF and other advanced reproductive procedures are typically not a standard benefit in the majority of health insurance programs. Consequently, couples must often shoulder the cost of all or parts of the treatment. For many, the financial considerations involved in undertaking cycle after cycle of assisted reproduction, where the likelihood of success can be quite variable versus putting their savings into a more certain option such as adoption poses a real quandary. Sometimes, in fact, arguments over the allocation of resources becomes a source of considerable domestic friction (see Chapter 7 by Epstein and Rosenberg, who discuss this among other issues concerning the negotiations couples must make in resolving the multitude of financial issues associated with infertility).

THE SUCCESS OF THE NEW REPRODUCTIVE OPTIONS

Since the first IVF-embryo transfer birth in 1978 in England, approximately 100,000 such children have been born worldwide. Currently, it is estimated that about 27,000 IVF and similar procedures are performed annually with a success rate of approximately 19%. About 4,200 GIFT procedures are initiated annually with a success rate of 28%; about 600,000 intrauterine inseminations (IUI) are undertaken annually with donor semen with a success rate of 10%; and about 1,500 zygote intrafallopian transfer (ZIFT) are completed each year with a success rate of 24%. (American Society for Reproductive Medicine, Fact Sheet, 1995).

Although these numbers are impressive, there are two caveats. While an overall success rate of about 21% per cycle for IVF (and similar techniques) is typical, this still means that 79% of couples will fail in their attempts—not a negligible number. Moreover, there are physical costs and risks associated with the increasing utilization of IVF and other medically assisted reproductive interventions. There are effects on the individual—psychologically and physically—and effects on the couple. In Chapter 5, Leiblum and Greenfeld address the immediate and long-term impact of infertility on individuals, and Leiblum (Chapter 8) discusses the impact of infertility on the couple's sexual and emotional relationship. Daniluk (Chapter 6) explores the differences (and similarities) in how men and women react to the diagnosis of infertility.

An example of a physical risk associated with assisted reproduction is the likelihood of multiple gestation due to the use of ovulation-stimulating drugs and the transfer of multiple embryos. In their Fact Sheet on the side effects of gonadotropins, the American Society for Reproductive Medicine (1995) writes:

> Up to 20% of pregnancies resulting from gonadotropins are multiple, in contrast to a rate of 1% to 2% in the general population. While most of these pregnancies are twins, a significant percentage are triplets or higher. Higher order multiple gestation pregnancy is associated with increased risk of pregnancy loss, premature delivery, infant abnormalities, handicap due to the consequences of very premature delivery, pregnancy-induced hypertension, hemorrhage, and other significant maternal complications.

A recent French study looked at the incidence of multiple pregnancy and prematurity associated with the use of IVF in France between 1986 and 1990. They found that both multiple pregnancy and prematurity rates were elevated when compared with natural conception. The rate of multiple births (primarily twins, but also triplets) was 26.8%, and the preterm birth rate, 29.3% and low birth weight rate, 36.2%, were higher than the national average. Multiple pregnancies were the main cause of prematurity but the prematurity rate among single pregnancies resulting from IVF was also much higher than in the general population. (FIVNAT & Institut National, 1995).

Many infertile couples are not initially dismayed by the possibility of giving birth to twins or even triplets (Leiblum, Kemmann, & Taska, 1990). They want to complete their "family" as quickly as possible and they know they may have only a single "shot" at successful conception and delivery. Nevertheless, couples are usually naive about what raising multiples entails and must be informed about the economic and psychological realities. Just recently, for example, the birth of a set of quintuplets was reported in the newspaper, the 42nd surviving set in the United States.[4] Each newborn weighed less than two pounds. The financial burden to the parents, (as well as ultimately to society) to cover the cost of inpatient neonatal treatment to ensure their survival and well-being, as well as the cost of raising, rearing, and educating more than one child at a time, is staggeringly high.

There are also potential risks associated with infertility treatment—particularly extended treatment. Ovarian hyperstimulation syndrome can be a life-threatening complication of treatment with human menopausal gonadotropins. The long-term effect of hyperstimulation on the female reproductive system is not known with certainty. Moreover, while there are virtually no published reports detailing the psychiatric side effects of ovulation-inducing agents, clinicians working with women taking fertility medication often hear a variety of complaints. Certainly, hormonal treatments that affect the pituitary axis are likely to affect mood and cognition. Aside from the direct effect of medications, the associated indirect stresses are also considerable. The uncomfortable injections, the constant monitoring by medical personnel, the physical and psychological side effects of treatment, the high costs of treatment and lost time from work, the scheduling of intercourse, the disruption to professional and personal activities, and the ever-present possibility of disappointment are some of the definite costs of infertility treatment (Downey, 1993).

STRESS AND THE NEW REPRODUCTIVE OPTIONS

Stress (and distress) is intimately associated with the experience of infertility. There are multiple sources of infertility stress. Stress occurs as a result of the failure to conceive, the failure to identify a cause of the infertility difficulty, the pressure to account for one's infertile status to an inquisitive and often insensitive world, the blame directed at oneself or one's partner for having infertility problems, the indignities of infertility evaluation and treatment, and so on. Nevertheless, while it is clear that infertility diagnosis and treatment cause stress, it is not clear to what extent stress causes infertility difficulties and/or interferes with successful conception and delivery.

Several authors have postulated that stress can affect treatment outcome in both direct and indirect ways: by delaying or preventing ovulation and by influencing tubal transport, embryo implantation, or sperm production. Some of the hormones that are affected by stress include prolactin, opiates, dopamine, noradrenaline and adrenaline, oxytocin and prostaglandins. Opiates and catecholamines associated with stress can affect the hypothalamic gonadotropin

[4]All but two sets of quintuplets were thought to have been conceived through the use of fertility therapy. In fact, the increase in triplets and quadruplets is further raising the anxiety of insurance companies and health management organizations since they must cover the expensive costs associated with extreme prematurity.

releasing factor, which in turn impacts the follicle-stimulating hormone and luteinizing hormone.

In cases of unexplained infertility, the role of stress is particularly intriguing. Current figures suggest that about 5% of infertility is due to unexplained factors (Hull et al., 1985; Shushan, Eisenberg, & Schenker, 1995) although these numbers are subject to considerable controversy. Traditionally, psychogenic infertility has been defined as those cases of infertility where clinicians cannot find any organic or medical explanation for the failure to conceive. The percentage of such psychogenically infertile individuals, has decreased over the last few decades, from approximately 50% to less than 5% of all infertile persons with the development of greater sophistication in diagnosis. Nevertheless, while the vast majority (if not all) infertile couples do have identifiable somatic, neurological, or endocrinological problems that are interfering with conception, it is also possible that psychological factors contribute to difficulties in conception. Psychosocial factors may be of particular significance in situations of unexplained infertility (Wylie, 1993).

Recent research has investigated the role of stress on pregnancy rates and pregnancy outcome. In a recent prospective study, for example, Boiven and Takefman (1995) had women complete daily stress ratings during one complete IVF cycle. Their results suggested that the women who did not become pregnant reported more stress during specific stages of IVF and had a poorer biological response to treatment than women who were successful in becoming pregnant.

Both psychological support and/or counseling and coping techniques may help mitigate or diminish the stress of infertility diagnosis generally, and infertility treatment, specifically. Such interventions are potentially cost-effective from both a human and economic point of view. While there is a dearth of well-controlled studies on this important topic, Domar, Seibel, and Benson (1990) have described a multifactorial treatment program that includes education, relaxation, breathing exercises, cognitive restructuring, nutrition and exercise designed to help infertile couples cope with the stress of infertility treatment (see Chapter 4). A bonus of this time-limited and cost-effective group treatment program is a modest increase in pregnancy rate in graduates of this "Mind/Body" program. While improved pregnancy rates cannot be guaranteed, it is likely that couples benefit from learning coping techniques to deal with the demands and disappointments of infertility treatment.

WHEN PREGNANCY IS ACHIEVED

Although the goal of infertility treatment is pregnancy and delivery of a healthy infant, individuals and couples must be counseled that success does not automatically or necessarily ensure bliss. The old Chinese proverb is meaningful here: Beware of what you wish, for you may get it.

Women may be unprepared for the physical and/or psychological discomfort associated with pregnancy. In fact, pregnancy itself may be accompanied by excessive anxiety concerning the possibility of miscarriage. Further, recovery from a miscarriage is not easy for anyone but is particularly poignant for women who have been attempting conception medically (as described by Glazer in Chapter 12).

As stated earlier, the new reproductive technologies are associated with an increased incidence of multiple births, which carry their own risks of physical and psychological morbidity (Downey, 1993). Often, the pregnancies are complicated and treatment necessitates an extended period of bed rest. Once the babies are born, the pressure of caring for more than one infant—particularly for an older parent—can be physically, emotionally, and financially overwhelming.

Finally, both mothers and fathers may be unprepared for the time constraints and demanding realities of childrearing. As one father poignantly noted in thinking about life before children, "There was a time in our lives when sex was scheduled. . . . There were actually days, consecutive days, when Paula and I had to have sex. Sure, it was mechanical, unromantic, pressure-laden sex. But you know what? It still was sex." He concludes his reminiscences by advising couples, "Children, all children, are a wonderful blessing of innocence. Their beguiling smiles and contagious laughs can soften the hardest of hearts. But be warned, they are work; they are work; they are work!" (Reiss, 1996).

ALTERNATIVES TO BIOLOGICAL PARENTHOOD

While assisted reproductive technologies are often presented as the solution to the problem of infertility, many individuals and couples do not become pregnant after treatment with the new techniques. Once a woman embarks on IVF or GIFT, it is very hard to stop. For example, one study found that 90% of women assessed at least 8 months after completing IVF or GIFT treatment said they would resume infertility treatment if a new treatment became available (Leiblum, Kemmann, & Lane, 1987). Moreover, physicians are not always straightforward in recommending treatment termination. Critics of the infertility "business" even allege that clinics push patients toward costly high-tech solutions when they would be just as successful with simpler treatments, or when their odds of success are so low they should not be encouraged at all. Even physicians have argued that the effectiveness of ART compared with conventional treatment for the various conditions that cause subfertility is not overwhelming and that costs should be a factor influencing decisions about which infertility option to pursue or whether to pursue treatment at all (Shushan, Eisenberg, & Schenker, 1995).

Nevertheless, decisions about when to terminate treatment must eventually be made, either because of financial, health, or interpersonal considerations. When and how does one counsel discouraged and/or depressed couples? What are the alternatives for infertile couples who wish to parent a child?

In Chapter 11, Braverman suggests that while there is no truly satisfactory resolution to the inability to successfully reproduce, there are choices that couples should consider. While the grief associated with involuntary infertility is considerable, most couples are eventually able to move on and to consider other alternatives, whether surrogacy, adoption, or living without children. Individuals and couples should not be rushed to premature closure, however, since second-guessing is common, along with wondering "what might have been" if one more reproductive attempt was undertaken. Conjoint couples' therapy is often extremely helpful in this aspect of infertility counseling since couple conflicts over this issue are often divisive and destructive and may have long-term relationship consequences.

Adoption

As Brodzinsky discusses in Chapter 12, adoption is rarely a first or easy choice for infertile couples, particularly in the current societal climate. Couples read about genetic mothers changing their minds after relinquishing their infant for adoption and about litigious fathers suddenly appearing and claiming paternity rights. Some couples are loathe to undergo what feels like the inquisitorial process required for becoming adoptive parents while others worry about adopting children with physical or psychological scars from their genetic or foster parents. Nevertheless, adoption, as the oldest alternative for infertile couples, is also the most reliable—most couples who embark on the adoption quest are eventually successful in securing a child.

Child-Free Living

While most couples who have grappled with infertility yearn to become parents, some decide that if they cannot have biological children, they would prefer to live child-free. Less is known about the successful long-term adjustment of involuntarily childless couples than of couples who chose child-free living voluntarily but there are certainly many who have developed meaningful and gratifying lives. Moreover, it must be remembered that there are many individuals and couples who, although distressed about their infertility, decide to adopt a "wait and see" attitude rather than initiate treatment with the ARTs. Waiting sometimes helps clarify for the couple their most sensible option and should be supported.

ROLE OF THE MENTAL HEALTH PROFESSIONAL IN REPRODUCTIVE MEDICINE

Increasingly, mental health professionals are becoming involved in the field of infertility counseling and research. Individuals with clinical backgrounds are in a unique position to educate, inform, alert, and counsel both physicians and patients involved in the infertility process. It sometimes happens that in their zeal to achieve pregnancy in the couple who is insistent, reproductive endocrinologists and other physicians involved in infertility work, overlook or minimize important psychological considerations. For example in a recent case, a 46-year-old newly married mother of two grown children, wanted to use the eggs of her 22-year-old daughter, in order to become pregnant. Her new husband was 34 years old and was eager to have a biological child of his own. While the physician was sympathetic to the couple's request, he ignored the fact that the 22-year-old daughter (who was currently single) felt coerced—she was reluctant to "donate" her ovum but felt responsible for her mother's happiness. She also disliked her mother's new spouse and wanted to have a child of her own before assisting her mother in her reproductive venture but felt unable to refuse on the grounds that she had been financially dependent on her parents in recent years.

Only after extensive interviewing by the psychologist and support of her right to refuse egg donation was she able to assert herself.

Evaluating and counseling known and anonymous donors is but one of many instances where mental health professionals can make significant contributions to the field of reproductive medicine. Covington (1995) has identified five primary functions that may be performed by mental health clinicians working in this area:

1. Assessment and evaluation of patients, recipients and donors.
2. Intervention and treatment of psychological issues that are important from both an etiological and current functioning perspective.
3. Education.
4. Research.
5. Consultation.

Each of these areas requires clinical sophistication and training. Even with such training, however, infertility counseling is such a new area that the data needed to guide our treatment recommendations are not always available. For example, while there is consensus that clinicians perform a valuable role in the assessment and evaluation of patients and donors, there is far from unanimous agreement about what the basis for treatment exclusion should be.

A recent pilot study illustrates how complicated the issue of treatment inclusion or exclusion can be. All the members of the mental health special interest group of the American Fertility Society were sent questionnaires asking them about whether or not explicit policies were articulated in their infertility program or clinic with respect to suspension or refusal of treatment on psychological grounds (Leiblum & Williams, 1993). Results revealed that the majority of respondents did not have formal policies governing these decisions. Nevertheless, most programs could describe the use of informal considerations. Four criteria tended to be utilized by most programs as grounds for treatment rejection: substance abuse, physical abuse, severe marital strife, and coercion of one spouse by the other. More stringent criteria were applied if clients sought ovum donation than if they sought ovulation induction. In actual practice, clinicians and physicians often differ dramatically and vocally in evaluating candidates for admission or exclusion from treatment. For example, the cutoff age for accepting candidates for ovum donation varies from center to center. While some facilities are willing to accept women over the age of 50, others are not. What is a reasonable cutoff age? Typically, each case must be individually considered, taking into account the health, relationship, and resources of the individual couple or client.

Certainly, the role of the clinician in counseling individuals and couples seeking treatment with the new reproductive technologies is complicated. It often feels like negotiating rocky terrain without a map and without any certainty of arriving at a desirable destination. Nevertheless, mental health professionals have much to offer both their patients and the professionals with whom they consult. They are experts in the psychology of motivation, personality, and relationship dynamics. They know how systems work—health systems as well as family systems. They do not have a vested interest in whether or not a couple continues or terminates infertility treatment. And, they are aware of the obligations they have to all parties concerned—the recipients of infertility treatment, the donors, and the unborn children.

The field of infertility counseling has never been more exciting. The opportunity to work with physicians and patients is stimulating and meaningful. The opportunities for clinical research could not be greater. I hope this book will provide clinicians with the latest theoretical, research, and practice considerations to guide them in these endeavors.

REFERENCES

Advance report of final natality statistics, 1991. (1993). *Monthly Vital Statistics Report, 42*, 3.

American Society for Reproductive Medicine. (1995). Assisted reproductive technology in the United States and Canada: 1993 results generated from the American Society for Reproductive Medicine/Society for Assisted Reproductive Technology Registry. *Fertility and Sterility, 64*(1), 13–21.

American Society for Reproductive Medicine. (1995, August 3). *Fact Sheet: The Society for Assisted Reproductive Technology and the American Society for Reproductive Medicine Release 1993 ART Success Rates*. Washington, DC: Author.

American Society for Reproductive Medicine. (1995, October). *Fact Sheet: Side Effects of Gonadtropins*. Birmingham, AL: Author.

Boiven, J., & Takefman, J. (1995). Stress level across stages of in vitro fertilization in subsequently pregnant and nonpregnant women. *Fertility and Sterility, 64*(4), 802–810.

Collins, J., Bustillo, M., Visscher, R., & Lawrence, L. (1995). An estimate of the cost of in vitro fertilization services in the United States in 1995. *Fertility and Sterility, 64*(3), 538–545.

Covington, S. N. (1995). The role of the mental health professional in reproductive medicine. *Fertility and Sterility, 64*(5), 895–897.

DeCherney, A. (1995). Infertility: We're not taking new patients! *Fertility and Sterility, 64*(3), 470–473.

Domar, A. O., Seibel, M., & Benson, H. (1990). The mind/body programme for infertility: A new behavorial treatment approach for women with infertility. *Fertility and Sterility, 53,* 246–249.

Downey, J. (1993). Infertility and the new reproductive technologies. In D. E. Stewart & N. J. Stotland (Eds.), *The interface between psychiatry and obstetrics and gynecology* (pp. 193–206). Washington, DC: American Psychiatric Press.

FIVNAT & Institut National de la Sante Et de la Recherch Medicale U292 (1995). Pregnancies and births resulting from in vitro fertilization: French national registry, analysis of data 1986–1990. *Fertility and Sterility, 64*(4), 746–756.

Gold, M. (1988). And Hannah wept: Infertility, adoption and the Jewish couple. Philadelphia: Jewish Publication Society. Quoted in Schwartz, L. (1991). *Alternatives to infertility: Is surrogacy the answer?* New York: Brunner/Mazel.

Hull, M., Glazener, C., Kelly, N., Conwzy, D., Foster, P., Hinton, R., Coulson, C., Lambert, P., Watt, E., & Desai, K. (1995). Population study of causes, treatment and outcome in infertility. *British Medical Journal, 291,* 1693–1697.

Jansen, R. P. S. (1994). Elusive fertility: Fecundability and assisted conception in perspective. *Fertility and Sterility, 64*(2), 252–253.

Johnston, D. R. (1963). The history of human infertility. *Fertility and Sterility, 14,* 261–269.

Laborie, F. (1993). Social alternatives to infertility. In P. Stephenson & M. Wagner (Eds.), *Tough choices: In vitro fertilization and the reproductive technologies* (pp. 37–52). Philadelphia: Temple University Press.

Leiblum, S. R. (1996). Love, sex and infertility: The impact of infertility on the couple. *In Session, 2,* 29–40.

Leiblum, S. R., & Hamkins, S. E. (1992). To tell or not to tell: Attitudes of reproductive endocrinologists concerning disclosure to offspring of conception via assisted insemination by donor. *Journal of Psychosomatic Obstetrics and Gynaecology, 13,* 267–275.

Leiblum, S. R., Kemmann, E., & Lane, M. (1987). The psychological concomitants of in vitro fertilization. *Journal of Psychosomatic Obstetrics and Gynaecology, 6,* 165–178.

Leiblum, S. R., Kemmann, E., & Taska, L. (1990). Attitudes toward multiple births and pregnancy concerns in infertile and noninfertile women. *Journal of Psychosomatic Obstetrics and Gynaecology, 11,* 197–210.

Leiblum, S. R., Palmer, M. G., & Spector, I. P. (1995). Non-traditional mothers: Single heterosexual/lesbian women and lesbian couples electing motherhood via donor insemination. *Journal of Psychosomatic Obstetrics and Gynaecology, 16,* 11–20.

Leiblum, S. R., & Williams, E. (1993). Screening in or out of the new reproductive options: Who decides and why. *Journal of Psychosomatic Obstetrics and Gynaecology, 14,* 37–44.

Neumann, P., Winstein, M., & Gharib, S. (1994). The cost of a successful delivery with in vitro fertilization. *New England Journal of Medicine, 331,* 239–243.

Reiss, R. (1996). Children. *Resolve of New Jersey Newsletter, 17*(1), 6.

Robertson, J. A. (1995). Ethical and legal issues in human embryo donation. *Fertility and Sterility, 64*(5), 885–894.

Robertson, J. A. (1996). Legal troublespots in assisted reproduction. *Fertility and Sterility, 65*(1), 11–12.

Sauer, M., Paulson, R., & Lobo, R. (1995). Pregnancy in women 50 or more years of age: Outcomes of 22 consecutively established pregnancies from oocyte donation. *Fertility and Sterility, 64*(1), 111–115.

Shushan, A., Eisenberg, V., & Schenker, J. (1995). *Fertility and Sterility, 64*(3), 459–469.

Smith, K., & Buyalos, R. (1996). The profound impact of patient age on pregnancy outcome after early detection of fetal cardiac activity. *Fertility and Sterility, 65*(1), 35–40.

Wagner, M., & Stephenson, P. (1993). Infertility and in vitro fertilization: Is the tail wagging the dog? In P. Stephenson & M. Wagner (Eds.), *Tough choices: In vitro fertilization and the reproductive technologies* (pp. 1–22). Philadelphia: Temple University Press.

Wright, L. (1996, January 15). Silent sperm. *The New Yorker,* 42–55.

Wylie, K. (1993). Psychological morbidity in unexplained morbidity. *Sexual and Marital Therapy, 8*(1), 27–35.

CHAPTER 2

Infertility Diagnosis and Assisted Reproductive Options: A Primer

PATRICIA M. McSHANE

As women defer childbearing into their later reproductive years, they are more likely to experience infertility. In spite of the newer therapeutic approaches, infertility diagnosis and treatment may still be a protracted and difficult process for couples. This chapter will summarize the basic infertility workup and the approach to therapy.

DIAGNOSIS

The medical definition of infertility is one year of unprotected intercourse without conception. In most cases, an infertility investigation is not undertaken until a couple has tried to conceive for one year, since 85% of couples will be successful during the first year. However, earlier diagnosis or therapy may be indicated if there is a pertinent medical history or symptoms such as menstrual irregularities, tubal infections, or radiation/chemotherapy in either partner. Because of the profound impact of age on fecundability (ability to conceive and bear a child), infertility diagnostic testing is usually begun after six months of attempting conception when the woman is over age 35. Although it is presumed to take longer to become pregnant at that stage of reproductive life, the delay in making a diagnosis and instituting therapy may have more profound consequences.

Most couples are not aware that the average chance of conceiving in a month is only about 15%. Much of this inefficiency is apparently due to failure of the fertilized oocyte to implant and continue development. The few studies that have addressed human reproductive wastage have shown both preimplantation and postimplantation embryonic loss. Genetic analysis of IVF (in vitro fertilization) embryos has demonstrated that many embryos have chromosomal abnormalities, which certainly could account for substantial reproductive inefficiency (Munne, Alikani, Tomkin, Grifo, & Cohen, 1995). Maternal age increases the rate of embryonic chromosomal abnormalities, paralleling the rise in miscarriage and chromosomal abnormalities of the newborns of older women. Miscarriage (spontaneous abortion) occurs in approximately 15% of documented pregnancies; it is the most obvious, but probably not the most frequent, form of embryonic wastage in women of normal fertility.

A careful history regarding the outcome of any previous pregnancies, timing and frequency of sexual intercourse, genital tract infections, DES exposure, menstrual pattern, and so on, will often reveal major issues that will direct the subsequent investigation. It is essential to have the cooperation of both partners in diagnosis and treatment, since it is rarely the case that only one partner needs to be committed for the outcome to be successful.

The initial infertility evaluation includes investigation of semen quality, ovulatory function, sperm/cervical mucus interaction and tubal/uterine anatomy. Approximately three quarters of all couples will have a diagnosis at the conclusion of the basic investigation. The remainder may need more invasive tests such as laparoscopy to obtain a definitive diagnosis. Perhaps 5% to 10% will have unexplained infertility.

Semen Quality

Normal men produce an average of 50 million sperm daily, but the number of sperm present on a single semen analysis may vary substantially. Sperm count depends on time from last ejaculation, seasonal variations, and possibly major or minor perturbations in testicular function. Most semen analyses from normal men will fall into the normal range, but occasionally, specimens may fall below "normal." Although the ranges of normal for the semen parameters have been established, the ranges are not absolutely predictive of fertility. Some normal fertile males will have specimens in the subfertile range, while other men with semen quality that is apparently normal may have fertilization failure on attempted in vitro fertilization. The fertility of the female partner may account for some of these apparent contradictions, as infertility is always a phenomenon of a couple, not a single individual, the obvious exception being donor insemination.

At least a quarter of infertility is due principally to poor semen quality, while milder forms of sperm deficiency may be a contributing factor in another 15% to 25%. Sperm numbers (count), motility (percentage of sperm which are moving), rate of forward progression, and percentage of normal forms should be determined on at least two occasions because of the variability in some individuals. Specialized tests such as sperm antibodies or hormonal testing may be indicated in certain instances. In most cases, the semen analysis alone will suffice to exclude the diagnosis of male factor infertility. A careful history seeking toxic exposures (including cigarette smoking and alcohol intake) (Vine, Margolin, Morrison, & Hulka, 1994), genital infections, and medications known to affect sperm quality, will sometimes point to the cause of deficient semen quality.

If any deficiencies are noted in the basic analysis, the male partner should be examined by a urologist (Skakkebaek, Giwercman, & deKretser, 1994). Most male infertility or subfertility is idiopathic (unexplained), but it is important to rule out treatable conditions such as hormone deficiency or varicocele. Complete absence of sperm in the ejaculate is termed azoospermia, and is usually due to testicular failure, obstruction, or pituitary/hypothalamic deficiency. This observation has important diagnostic and therapeutic ramifications.

Hormonal deficiency is relatively uncommon, and is generally diagnosed when a boy fails to undergo normal puberty. The condition is readily treatable with regular injections of the missing hormone; the diagnosis should be sought if there are any signs or symptoms. If sperm are absent, but there is no indication of a hypothalamic or pituitary hormone deficiency, surgical exploration of the scrotum and/or testicular biopsy may be recommended to rule out obstruction, a potentially treatable disorder. Obstruction may be the result of genital tract infection; cystic fibrosis also may cause obstruction, but many cases have no obvious etiology. Of course, voluntary sterilization and failed sterilization reversal would fall into this category as well.

Most often, deficient sperm quality is due to a testicular problem, rather than a hypothalamic/pituitary defect or obstruction. The most severe form of greatly reduced or absent sperm production, primary testicular failure, is often congenital. Cancer chemotherapy or radiation may lead to secondary ("acquired") testicular failure. If a man is found to have complete testicular failure resulting in azoospermia (absence of sperm on several semen analyses), there is no proven therapy, although recent attempts to obtain immature sperm forms from the testicle surgically may ultimately prove successful (Nagy et al., 1995). Microinjection of testicular sperm into the oocyte would be required, however, since testicular sperm are incapable of motility and fertilization.

If the man has sperm present, but in reduced number or with subnormal motility, varicocele should be ruled out. A varicocele, or dilated venous system in the left, right, or both hemiscrotums, is a common finding in fertile men, usually asymptomatic (World Health Organization, 1992). Whether varicocele causes infertility, and whether surgical ligation may improve semen parameters, has been controversial. Varicocele has been associated with progressive deterioration in sperm quality (Chehval & Purcell, 1992). Whether treatment is indicated in the presence of infertility with normal semen parameters is still unproven.

Masturbation is the preferred method of semen collection in most instances. Although higher semen parameters may be found in specimens collected from sterile condoms following sexual intercourse, this is impractical in most instances. Most men have no difficulty providing a sperm sample by masturbation, although the lay infertility literature is replete with harrowing tales about the experience! Sometimes, this is due to poor facilities or insensitivity on the part of the staff.

For some men, there are strong cultural or religious taboos against masturbation, which may not be apparent to the medical personnel and may interfere with the diagnosis and treatment of infertility. For others, the pressure to "perform on demand" may prove difficult, especially with protracted infertility treatment. This is particularly true for performance of the postcoital test (discussed later in this chapter) but may also be a barrier to obtaining a semen analysis for initial diagnosis. Anecdotally, it may prove a stress in the relationship. Often, the women will seek to protect her partner from the pressure of having semen testing or providing specimens for insemination. She may recognize that her partner is unwilling to participate beyond a certain point.

I have been impressed by the willingness of the female partner and the physicians, both male and female, to "protect" the infertile male's ego. On occasion, the female patient insists that she also has an infertility problem, even when the condition seems inconsequential compared with her husband's/partner's. It seems as though the women, and occasionally the medical personnel, confuse fertility with other aspects of masculinity. This unfortunate attitude has resulted in situations in which a women may have several surgeries before her partner has a semen analysis. More recently, there appears to be more recognition of the high incidence of male infertility, and of combined male and female infertility; however, this is not accepted in all cultures. Clinicians treating infertility need to be aware of the cultural context and the potential impact on the relationship of semen testing.

Determination of Ovulation

The presence of fairly regular (21–35 days) cyclic menses is a reflection of repetitive ripening and properly timed release of an oocyte (egg) from the ovary. Ovulation is an absolute requirement for natural fertility, whether occurring spontaneously, or induced with medications. Ovulation is a very consistent process marked by a series of hormone fluctuations, including estrogen, LH (luteinizing hormone), and progesterone. The growth and eventual rupture of the follicle (fluid-filled sac containing the oocyte) can be observed on serial ultrasound scans of the ovary; the endometrial lining of the uterus, where the embryo will ultimately implant, undergoes a series of changes in response to the hormonal levels that can be observed noninvasively by ultrasound or by physical sampling of the tissue (endometrial biopsy).

Many couples are aware that they can determine the approximate date of ovulation with home testing or urine for LH (luteinizing hormone) (Luciano et al., 1990) and of basal body temperature (BBT). Women often perform either or both of these tests for months prior to seeking medical advice and may continue to do so during prolonged infertility treatment. While many couples express frustration at the daily ritual of temperature taking, and grow to resent it, others find that it becomes part of a daily routine and they continue to do so even when advised that it is no longer necessary. For many, the results are uninterpretable for various reasons, often difficulty reading the thermometer.

The basal body temperature is a bioassay of the presence of progesterone, which has a slight hyperthermic effect on brain thermoregulatory centers. If the

BBT charts consistently show one-half to one degree Fahrenheit temperature elevation for 10 to 14 days preceding the menses, this is strong presumptive evidence of ovulation. However, the test has no predictive value to determine the fertile time of a woman's cycle in an individual month. In a woman with quite consistent cycles, it may be possible to predict a window of several days of fertility. This may be helpful or reassuring to the couple. However, therapeutic decisions should be based on more objective forms of ovulation monitoring, such as determination of the serum progesterone level. Therefore, I seldom suggest that couples perform the BBT testing for more than a cycle or two, although it is occasionally informative.

Home urine ovulation detection kits have become readily available, although they are quite expensive ($30 to $60 for one month's testing). For most women, the tests are readily interpretable, which means that it is possible to distinguish the color change on the test stick occurring just prior to ovulation. The kits have been shown to be about 85% accurate, although occasionally ovulation by ultrasound criteria antedates the urine LH surge, or may not be seen for as long as two days later. Sources of inaccuracy are the different characteristics of the LH surge in different individuals, the presence of high baseline LH levels in some women, and the delay that occurs between the serum peak and the urine peak. Urine concentration also varies between different urine samples, although this can be controlled somewhat with intentional manipulation of fluid intake and voiding intervals.

The principal utility of home urine LH testing is to time midcycle procedures, such as the postcoital tests or inseminations. As a primary test for the presence of ovulation, the kits are somewhat expensive, time consuming, and ambiguous compared with the serum progesterone level.

The serum progesterone level is a relatively inexpensive and highly accurate test of ovulation. Relying on a discriminatory progesterone level of 10 ng/ml will also exclude the diagnosis of luteal phase deficiency (LPD) in almost all cases. LPD is a condition of developmental lag in the endometrial lining of the uterus in the luteal phase of the ovarian cycle (Li & Cooke, 1991). If the ovarian follicle containing the mature oocyte is inadequately developed or unable to make sufficient progesterone once the follicle becomes the corpus luteum, luteal phase deficiency may result. Without an adequate serum concentration of progesterone, the endometrium cannot mature properly. This in turn may lead to failure of the embryo to implant, or to recurrent miscarriage.

Sampling the endometrial cavity of the uterus through the cervix by means of a metal or plastic sampling device has long been the mainstay of ovulation testing, and still has a role. The most accurate way to make the diagnosis of LPD is to evaluate a properly timed endometrial sample. The biopsy is also valuable in diagnosing irregular vaginal bleeding, and excluding malignancy or premalignant conditions, especially in perimenopausal or menopausal women.

The endometrial biopsy may be experienced as a very painful procedure, although most women report mild to moderate discomfort, which may be lessened by pretreatment with mild analgesics such as ibuprofen. In some instances, the procedure is technically difficult because of cervical stenosis (tightness) or extreme angulation of the uterus on the cervix. Use of local anesthetics should be tried if the procedure is difficult and the patient is experiencing more than mild pain.

Ultrasound, while noninvasive, is expensive and must be performed on several occasions at midcycle to get an accurate picture of the adequacy of ovulation. Its role is mainly to monitor cycles in which a medication is used to induce ovulation (Ritchie, 1985). Transvaginal ultrasound is usually painless, but women experiencing pain with vaginal penetration may experience less discomfort if allowed to place the probe into the vagina themselves.

Sperm/Cervical Mucus Interaction

Another anatomic site reflecting the hormonal changes of the normal ovulatory cycle is the uterine cervix. Just prior to ovulation, the mucus within the cervical canal, ordinarily scant and tacky, becomes clear and copious, the consistency of egg white. With special microscopy, channels that facilitate travel of the sperm into the uterus can be appreciated. For days after sexual intercourse, the cervical crypts function as a sperm reservoir, slowly releasing sperm into the upper reproductive tract for possible fertilization of the oocyte in the fallopian tube. Some women have abnormalities in the cervix resulting from DES exposure (diethylstilbestrol) or as a result of procedures such as cone biopsy. These may result in reduced cervical mucus.

The postcoital (PK) test is a simple and inexpensive way of determining whether intravaginal ejaculation is occurring, whether adequate cervical mucus is present, and whether sperm are able to move freely within the mucus, at least initially. Simple in concept, the PK test is remarkably frustrating in practice. The most common cause of poor results on the PK test is timing in the menstrual cycle. If the test is performed too far in advance of ovulation, or following ovulation, the cervical mucus is thick and inhospitable. Given the difficulty predicting ovulation, this is a major source of frustration for couples and medical personnel. Variability within the cervical canal may be another source of spurious poor results. If adequate mucus is not withdrawn, the area with the highest sperm concentration may be missed.

Another common cause of poor postcoital test results is poor semen quality. In most cases, the PK test results will not influence the course of therapy, but rarely will offer some additional insight in this situation, especially if the semen quality is variable. Antisperm antibodies in the male or female partner may be present, impeding the entry of sperm into the mucus or reducing their viability.

The reproducibility and predictive value of the PK test have been questioned (Glatstein et al., 1995), but most practitioners still believe that it has a role; this is because couples with poor PK tests results but reasonable sperm quality appear to have a higher pregnancy rate with intrauterine inseminations. For this reason, the test has been retained in the basic investigation.

From the couple's perspective, the PK test may be a source of significant stress and performance anxiety, especially if very rigid parameters are set as to the timing of coitus. Although more sperm will be present if the mucus is examined two hours after intercourse, intervals of 10 hours or even more are generally adequate to make sure that at least some motile sperm are present. It is easier for most couples to come in for the test after having sexual relations the previous night, rather than having intercourse early on the morning of the test.

Tubal/Peritoneal Factor

Obstruction or damage to the fallopian tubes and the surrounding structures of the pelvic peritoneum is responsible for approximately 25% of infertility (American Fertility Society, 1993b). The majority of cases are apparently due to sexually transmitted diseases, the most common of which is chlamydia infection, although pelvic surgery and endometriosis are also important. In the past several decades, the causal relationship between the microorganism chlamydia and tubal factor infertility, as well as ectopic pregnancy, has been recognized (Jones, Ardery, Hui, & Cleary, 1982). Often asymptomatic in both men and women, the organism may cause infection of the cervix and then ascend into the fallopian tubes. Partial or complete destruction of the delicate tubal lining tissue may occur; in some cases, major damage to one or both tubes may occur with obstruction, adhesion (scar tissue) formation around the tubes and ovaries, and/or chronic pelvic pain. The degree of infertility and the success of any reparative surgery is proportional to the degree of damage to the tubes and pelvis. If the tubes are both obstructed or there are major pelvic adhesions, the woman is essentially infertile without therapy.

A history of clinical tubal infections (pelvic inflammatory disease) with or without positive cultures for a causative organism is an important piece of historical data which should prompt an early investigation of tubal/peritoneal status. Likewise a history of pelvic surgery, commonly for an ovarian cyst, should raise the index of suspicion of postoperative adhesions. Luckily, cesarean section does not seem to increase the risk of pelvic adhesion formation.

Endometriosis is a common gynecologic disorder which may be present with ovarian cyst formation, pelvic pain, or infertility (Olive & Schwartz, 1993). It is also a common finding in otherwise normal asymptomatic women. Endometriosis consists of the presence of glands from the endometrium (uterine lining) outside their normal position, typically on the ovary, or on the pelvic peritoneum in the area of the bladder, rectum, and/or fallopian tubes. In more severe cases, this glandular tissue apparently causes a major inflammatory reaction with resulting pelvic adhesions and even destruction of normal ovarian tissue through cyst (endometrioma) formation. In many cases, though, only a few implants of endometriosis are found. Whether infertility is associated with minor grades of endometriosis is somewhat controversial. Research findings suggest that endometriosis is associated with an alteration of the chemical environment of the pelvis. Sperm motility, tubal motility, and implantation of the embryo are thought to be affected.

Aside from the patient's history, the two most significant indicators of possible tubal/peritoneal factor infertility are hysterosalpingogram (HSG) and laparoscopy. HSG is a radiologic screening test utilizing dye passed transcervically to determine the shape of the uterine cavity and the patency of the tubes. It is widely used early in the infertility investigation, especially if no other causes of infertility have been uncovered or if there is a high degree of suspicion of tubal disease on the basis of history. With careful attention to premedication of the woman for uterine cramps and with gentle technique, the procedure will most often be perceived as mildly painful. Sadly, not all physicians appreciate that the procedure may be very uncomfortable unless preprocedure medication and local anesthesia are used. For this reason, many patients state that the HSG is a procedure they would never undergo a second time.

Laparoscopy is a surgical procedure conducted under general anesthesia. Through a small "belly button" incision, carbon dioxide gas is placed into the abdomen. The gas creates a space for the safe initial placement of the laparoscope and other instruments to visualize and manipulate pelvic and abdominal structures. One or more incisions of five to ten millimeters length are made in the lower abdomen. The procedure may take only a few minutes if no pathology is found, or up to several hours if correction of abnormalities is undertaken. After a short recovery period, the women returns home and ordinarily experiences moderate discomfort and disability for up to a week.

Laparoscopy has revolutionized gynecologic surgery in the past several decades. Many gynecologic procedures that would have required major abdominal surgery (laparotomy) can now be performed through the laparoscope with a great reduction in postoperative recovery time and equally good or even superior clinical results (American Fertility Society, 1993b). The cost savings are often not dramatic because of the increased cost of the necessary instrumentation, however. Laparoscopic surgery is not a panacea, though, because much of the infertility due to tubal disease is due to damage to the internal or microscopic anatomy of the tube. Correction of tubal obstruction or removal of peritubal/periovarian adhesions will not necessarily improve the microscopic damage done to the tube during the initial infectious process.

Traditionally, no infertility workup was considered complete until the woman underwent a laparoscopy unless the degree of ovulatory or sperm deficiency was adequate to explain continued infertility. Recently, the role of laparoscopy has been questioned in low-risk female patients, especially in those with no evidence of prior chlamydial infection by serum testing. Often no pathology or only minor findings are encountered. Although the risk of bowel injury, vascular injury, or anesthesia complications is low, the amount of minor morbidity such as nausea and pain is fairly high. The procedure is also costly.

Uterine Factor

The HSG is a valuable tool for diagnosing uterine factor infertility, as well as tubal obstruction. Alternatively, a hysteroscopy (transcervical procedure to look into the uterus) may be performed in an office setting, or under general anesthesia at the time of laparoscopy.

Often overlooked, uterine factor may be an important cause of infertility. A woman may have congenital defects in the shape of the uterine cavity, leading to a reduced chance of implantation of the embryos or increased chance of miscarriage. Alternatively, problems such as polyps or fibroids may develop during a woman's reproductive life, sometimes without symptoms. It is important to take a careful history to rule out such risk factors as prenatal exposure to diethylstilbestrol (DES), which is associated with various uterine and tubal structural abnormalities (Barnes et al., 1980; Kaufman et al., 1984). A history of a dilatation and curettage (D&C) is also important, especially in the setting of a miscarriage or postpartum hemorrhage, as this may cause intrauterine adhesions.

TREATMENT

Ovulation and Hormonal Disorders

Among the various infertility diagnoses, ovulatory disturbance carries the best prognosis because is usually is treatable with fairly simple therapy (American College of Obstetrics and Gynecology, 1994). Although some types of ovulation dysfunction are relatively simple to correct, others such as polycystic ovarian syndrome may be quite resistant. After testing and correction of any abnormality in the prolactin or thyroid function, the first-line therapy is usually clomiphene citrate (Clomid; Serophene). Taken orally for five days early in the menstrual cycle, clomiphene citrate corrects most minor ovulatory disturbances and luteal phase defect. The medication is moderately expensive, but very inexpensive compared with most fertility therapies. It is possible to conduct clomiphene therapy with very little monitoring, but it is best to repeat the postcoital test to make sure that the antiestrogenic effect of clomiphene has not led to inhospitable, thick cervical mucus. If that is the case, intrauterine insemination should be performed. Some women will also have development of an ovulatory follicle, but delay in the LH surge. Optimally, ultrasound and/or LH monitoring by blood or serum testing will be reassuring.

Simple in its application, clomiphene may be poorly tolerated because of side effects. Mood disturbances such as anxiety, depression, and irritability are common. Exacerbation of menstrual-related symptoms such as pain with ovulation and premenstrual breast and abdominal symptoms are also frequent. An important consideration is the risk of multiple birth, occurring in approximately 10% of clomiphene citrate induced pregnancies, almost exclusively twins. Although welcomed by many couples as "two for the price of one," multiple pregnancy is high risk because of the increased likelihood of prematurity and the attendant infant morbidity and mortality. Birth defects are more common in multiple gestation as well. Most multiple births with fertility therapy occur in women under the age of 38 years, especially those younger than 34 years.

Women with more profound ovulation disorders or those who do not conceive on clomiphene therapy after four to six ovulatory cycles are candidates for gonadotropin therapy. The original gonadotropin available was Pergonal, which is a mixture of LH and FSH (follicle stimulating hormone) extracted from the urine of postmenopausal women. More recently, other preparations have become available, including some that are highly purified or bioengineered, rather than a human product. These include Metrodin (urinary FSH), Humegon (FSH and LH) and others that are available outside the United States. These preparations are virtually identical in clinical usage, with a slight preference for one or another preparation in selected circumstances.

In many ways, gonadotropins are more physiological than clomiphene, since they are natural hormones virtually identical to those that the body normally secretes to control ovarian function. In fact, side effects are usually less bothersome than with clomiphene citrate. However, the therapy has many other disadvantages, including the need for daily injections, close monitoring with pelvic ultrasound and blood hormone levels, and high cost, averaging $1,000 per month for medication alone.

Pregnancy rates per cycle range from 10% to 25% depending on the age and diagnosis of the woman. The presence of male factor will lead to substantially lower per cycle pregnancy rates. These rates are roughly double those seen with clomiphene citrate. However, the rate of multiple birth is approximately 25% because it is usually not possible to induce the formation of only one follicle. In some cases, so many follicles form that the cycle must be canceled because of risk of high order (greater than two) multiple birth or ovarian hyperstimulation syndrome.

Ovarian hyperstimulation is a potentially life-threatening complication of gonadotropin therapy. Following ovulation, the follicles refill with fluid and eventually form multiple corpora lutea producing progesterone. In approximately 1% of cycles, the number of such cysts is excessive and the total ovarian size may exceed 10 cm. in diameter. Associated fluid shifts occur, with severe metabolic disturbances in some cases. With modern management, the mortality rate is extremely low, but hospitalization of a week or more may be required, especially in the setting of pregnancy.

Several studies have suggested that ovulatory agents may increase somewhat the risk of ovarian cancer later in life. Ovarian cancer occurs in about 1% of American women, usually in the fifth decade or beyond. It is the most serious gynecologic malignancy. Childbearing and the use of oral contraceptives afford about 50% reduction in the baseline risk of the disease. Family history of ovarian cancer and a personal history of breast cancer are important risk factors. Whether infertility itself, ovulation disorders, or the use of the fertility drugs was responsible for the increase in ovarian cancer, observed in a

paper by Whittemore, is unclear. Whittemore, Itnyre, and Harris (1992) ana-
lyzed a number of previously published studies in an attempt to determine
whether exposure to fertility drugs resulted in increased risk of ovarian cancer.
Women who never bore children had an increased risk of ovarian cancer; however, the conclusions have been criticized on a number of methodological bases,
particularly that the type or amount of fertility medications was not documented
and that patients with cancer are more likely than healthy individuals to remember having taken medications in the past. Prospective studies are under-
way to elucidate these important questions, but the answers will not be known
for years, perhaps decades. Women who have taken these drugs without achieving a pregnancy are understandably concerned; they should be regarded as possibly at increased risk of ovarian cancer. Unfortunately, the available screening
tests are limited to physical examination, pelvic ultrasound, and several blood
studies. Each test has serious limitations and it is unlikely that population-based
screening will be advisable with the current technology.

An alternative approach to ovulation induction for clomiphene-resistant patients is GnRH (gonadotropin-releasing hormone) (Filicori et al., 1991). GnRH
is the hypothalamic hormone that controls pituitary secretion of FSH and LH.
It is secreted every 60 to 90 minutes during the phase of follicle development.
When given by intravenous infusion, development of a single ovarian follicle
can be achieved in almost all anovulatory women with virtually no risk of twins
or hyperstimulation. The main disadvantage of the treatment is the route of administration, which necessitates wearing an infusion pump for several weeks
during the cycle. Some monitoring of ovarian function is usually necessary.
Pregnancy rates are comparable to those of gonadotropin therapy.

Luteal phase defect is usually approached with simple therapy such as
clomiphene or progesterone vaginally or intramuscularly. In refractory situations, gonadotropin therapy may be required. The success rate of therapy is quite
high if not associated with any other infertility problems such as male factor or
tubal disorders.

When thyroid, adrenal, or prolactin abnormalities are present, correction
should be undertaken; in some cases, the associated ovulatory disorder may be
corrected without need for further treatment. Often, however, there will be a
need for adjunctive therapy. Medications given for thyroid and adrenal disorders and high prolactin levels are usually well tolerated. However, a significant
percentage of women taking bromocriptine (Parlodel) for hyperprolactinemia
will experience minor bothersome side effects such as nausea, nasal stuffiness,
or low blood pressure with sudden changes in position. Clinicians may need to
adjust the dose and route of administration in many women.

Tubal/Peritoneal Factor

The approach to peritoneal factor infertility is usually surgical, although severe
degrees of tubal disease or endometriosis are often better treated with in vitro

fertilization (IVF). Success with surgical therapy is dependent on the degree of tubal damage and pelvic adhesions. The shift from major abdominal surgery (laparotomy) to laparoscopy has greatly reduced the morbidity for patients without compromising the results. Recovery from laparoscopy generally requires about a week out of work, although patients are only admitted to the hospital for less than a day. This compares to five to seven days in the hospital and at least a month out of work for laparotomy. Although the morbidity and lost work time is less with laparoscopy than with laparotomy, pregnancy rates are nevertheless disappointing in the first two years after surgery. Average pregnancy rates range from 20% to a maximum of 50%, depending on the degree of initial tubal and pelvic damage. One difficulty with surgical therapy by either route is the high rate of recurrence of pelvic adhesions and/or tubal occlusion following surgery. Even if the pelvis appears normal, internal tubal anatomy may not be normal and therefore, tubal function is compromised. Current diagnostic techniques do not allow determination of internal tubal architecture prior to surgery, although newer fiberoptic technologies may allow this in the future. This would enable women with poor prognosis to avoid surgery altogether and utilize IVF instead.

There has been a decided shift away from tubal surgery and toward IVF as the pregnancy rates from IVF have increased. Nevertheless, diagnostic and therapeutic laparoscopy still has a role, especially when insurance reimbursement for IVF is lacking. Another advantage of the surgical approach is that a woman may experience several pregnancies following one surgery and the rate of multiple birth is very low unless adjunctive fertility medications are employed.

IVF is often utilized for initial therapy when a combination of tubal and male factor makes success unlikely with infertility surgery, or when the woman is older and has intrinsically reduced fertility.

Uterine Factor

The approach to uterine factor infertility is usually surgical, attempting to normalize the uterine cavity by incising a septum, removing intracavitary fibroids, or cutting intrauterine adhesions. Previously performed by laparotomy, most uterine defects are now approached transcervically with operative hysteroscopy; this reduces morbidity in a fashion similar to laparoscopy. With DES uterine anomalies, the surgical approach is rarely successful. Although early pregnancy may result in many DES-exposed patients following conventional infertility treatment, the rate of miscarriage, tubal pregnancy, and other obstetrical complications limits the rate of successful live birth.

When ovarian function is normal but uterine factor cannot be corrected, use of a gestational carrier for the couple's embryos is a possibility where it is not limited by state law. IVF technology is used to produce one or more embryos, which are then placed into the uterus of the carrier.

Male Factor

A comprehensive andrology examination will reveal any treatable causes of reduced semen quality, such as obstruction, infection, varicocele, or hormone deficiency. The majority of male factor infertility has no apparent cause, however, and no effective treatment. Occult hormonal deficiency may be approached through the use of clomiphene citrate, which exerts a stimulatory effect on the testicle somewhat analogous to that on the ovary. Other nonspecific medications have been tried for male factor infertility; none have proven successful.

When there is no treatable etiology, the approach to therapy is empiric. Intrauterine insemination (IUI) of the female partner at the time of ovulation with washed sperm that have been concentrated and freed of bacteria and contaminating cells is performed. This procedure is thought to be efficacious for male factor (American Fertility Society, 1991), although the per cycle pregnancy rates increase only by a modest percentage. The expected fecundability per month with male factor depends on the degree of impairment, but may be only 2% or 3% per month. IUI may increase this to 5% per month, higher if the degree of impairment is not so severe.

If the female partner has any ovulatory dysfunction or is over 38 years of age, clomiphene citrate or gonadotropins with IUI are often utilized. If a course of inseminations with the woman's natural cycle is not successful, superovulation (use of fertility drugs to increase the number of follicles in a woman with normal ovulation) and IUI may be tried with some success unless there is a severe male factor. For severe male factor, no therapy except IVF demonstrably increases pregnancy rates over the low background rate expected.

IUI is usually a simple procedure, although inconvenient in many cases because of the difficulty predicting ovulation. Usually virtually painless, there may be pain if introduction of the catheter is difficult because of cervical tightness or angulation. Other women experience uterine cramps after the procedure, regardless of apparent ease of insertion. As noted previously, production of a semen specimen for washing is at best an inconvenience and at worst an impossibility for the male.

If four to six cycles of intrauterine insemination do not prove successful, then IVF should be considered as both a diagnostic and therapeutic procedure. Often, low rates or absence of fertilization of oocytes are noted, indicating a very low likelihood of success with continued IUIs. Also, the per cycle pregnancy rate of IVF is considerably higher than that of IUI with or without superovulation. GIFT may be tried, but GIFT success rates are diminished greatly if there is any significant degree of male factor.

Sperm/Cervical Mucus Interaction

Occasionally, there is a treatable etiology of poor sperm cervical mucus interaction such as cervical mucus infection or poor ovulatory function. More often, there is no known etiology and no specific treatment. In this case, four to six cycles of IUI may be tried with an approach similar to the one for male factor. Generally the treatment begins with natural cycle IUI and if unsuccessful progresses to superovulation IUI. Pregnancy rates are somewhat higher than with timed intercourse alone.

Unexplained Infertility

Having completed a diagnostic workup without a definitive diagnosis is a frustrating situation for an infertile couple, although the prognosis is better than with most other disorders. In our technological era, couples may find it difficult to believe that we cannot establish a diagnosis. Still, there are many therapeutic options. The success of empiric therapy with superovulation and IUI would lead one to believe that occult ovulatory or male factor infertility may be the root of the problem in many instances. However, many couples with unexplained infertility of short duration (less than two years) have spontaneous pregnancies. Another way of looking at the increase in pregnancy rate observed with superovulation IUI is compressing several months of ovulatory experience into one calendar month.

Many couples are not successful with superovulation IUI and turn to assisted reproductive technology (ART). Occasionally, some unexpected diagnostic information will result, such as low fertilization rate or poor embryo quality. Most often though, the cause of the infertility remains indeterminate, even when the couple successfully bear a child.

ASSISTED REPRODUCTIVE TECHNOLOGY

Initially utilized as a last resort following failure of conventional infertility treatments, assisted reproductive technologies (ARTs) are being employed as a first-line therapy more frequently as success rates have risen and the limits of conventional therapy have been recognized. Nonetheless, these instances are still uncommon. Most couples still come to the ARTs after long-term therapy with a variety of other approaches, often depleted of financial and emotional reserves.

In Vitro Fertilization

In vitro fertilization (IVF), which means fertilization "under glass," was historically the first ART and is still the most commonly used. The indications include the gamut of fertility problems. Initially developed to circumvent tubal factor infertility uncorrectable by surgery, the power of IVF in addressing male factor and unexplained infertility was quickly recognized. In most clinics' series, tubal factor is the most common diagnosis; however, patients with other diagnoses constitute more than half of all procedures.

The basic technique of IVF is retrieval of one or more oocytes from the woman, insemination with prepared sperm under laboratory conditions, and replacement of the resulting embryos into the uterus. Currently, there are many variations including natural cycle, stimulated cycle, microinjection of sperm into the oocyte, and hatching of the embryo. The approach most commonly employed uses a precise sequence of fertility drugs, with monitoring of the ovarian response by blood estrogen levels and/or ultrasound on multiple occasions. When oocyte readiness is confirmed, an injection of hCG is used to mimic the LH surge; oocyte retrieval is carried out approximately 36 hours later.

Oocyte retrieval is a minor surgical procedure performed in either an office or ambulatory surgery facility. Anesthesia or analgesics by injection are given. With transvaginal ultrasound imaging, ovarian follicles can be accessed readily in almost all cases. With fertility drug stimulation, an average of 10 oocytes is obtained, with some women having scores of oocytes, and some only a few. With normal semen parameters, approximately 60% to 70% of oocytes are expected to fertilize. The majority of fertilized oocytes will cleave (divide), forming embryos. Typically three or four embryos are then transferred into the uterus, by means of a simple procedure analogous to an IUI. If available, more embryos may be transferred to older women to compensate for their lower pregnancy rate per embryo and lower risk of multiple birth.

If more embryos are available than the number desired for transfer, cryopreservation (freezing) may be performed. If cryopreserved embryos are available, superovulation with fertility drugs and oocyte retrieval are not required to try to conceive in a subsequent cycle; the woman may undergo monitoring of her natural cycle for replacement of the thawed embryos. If the fresh embryo transfer cycle results in a birth, transfer of thawed cryopreserved embryos can be tried to achieve a second pregnancy from the same batch of embryos.

Pregnancy rates with this technology depend heavily on the age of the female partner, and to a lesser extent, on the semen parameters (Tan et al., 1992; Duncan, Glew, Wang, Flaherty, & Matthews, 1993). Approximately 1 in 10 of the embryos transferred into the uterus will be noted to have formed a gestational sac in the uterus by ultrasound several weeks later, indicating pregnancy. The rate per embryo for younger women may be dramatically higher, leading to recommendations to transfer three or fewer embryos in an effort to avoid multiple gestations (Callahan et al., 1994). Women over age 40 are typically noted to have 2% or 3% implantation per embryo, most likely on the basis of genetic abnormalities. The number of oocytes is also likely to be lower, and the incidence of poor response leading to cycle cancellation is also higher with increasing age.

Reduced semen parameters traditionally limited the fertilization rates, often resulting in no embryos being available for transfer, but effective approaches to male factor have now narrowed this gap considerably (Nagy et al., 1995). The most dramatic of these developments is ICSI (intracytoplasmic sperm injection). This procedure enables men with as few as several dozen sperm, or immotile sperm, to fertilize their partner's oocytes with a high degree of efficiency.

ICSI involves penetration of the zona pellucida (the outer coat or shell of the oocyte) with delicate microinstruments to inject a solitary sperm into the cytoplasm. Fertilization rates approximating those of conventional IVF with normal semen parameters are achieved in successful ICSI programs. Implantation efficiency of transferred ICSI embryos appear to equal that of conventionally inseminated embryos. Thus, pregnancy rates should be similar to those of conventional IVF. Indeed, the more successful programs have started using ICSI instead of conventional insemination for all couples. One limitation of this practice is that occasionally an oocyte may be destroyed by the manipulation. Also, the number of babies born to date with this technology is still limited, although the rate of birth defects does not appear to be increased.

The question of the genetics of male factor infertility remains highly speculative and somewhat troubling. In the case of obvious diagnoses such as varicocele, the cause of reduced semen quality is thought not to be genetic. In other cases, the problem appears to be defective testicular sperm production. Whether this is secondary to a transmissible genetic defect is not known; these men have been unable to reproduce prior to microinsemination technologies such as ICSI. The molecular basis of sperm defects will likely be better understood in the near future, so we may get information before the male offspring of these pregnancies reach the age of fertility.

Assisted hatching of embryos is another micromanipulation technique which is being utilized widely (Schoolcraft, Schlenker, Gee, Jones, & Jones, 1994). Through this technique, the zona pellucida of the embryo is breached chemically, mechanically, or by other means such as with laser energy, thus allowing escape of the embryo at the time of implantation. Many embryos appear to have abnormally thick zonas; others seem to have hardening of the normally formed zona pellucida during the culture of the embryos in the laboratory. Embryo hatching seems to be particularly valuable in older women or those with multiple cycles without implantation of normal appearing embryos.

The Society of Assisted Reproductive Technology (SART), a committee of the American Society for Reproductive Medicine, reports annually on ART programs in North America (Society for Assisted Reproductive Technology, 1995). The latest report gives the 1993 results from across programs: 31,900 IVF cycles were performed, 31,419 with medication stimulation; the average live-birth rate for women under age 40 years was 18.8% per stimulation cycle; women over age 40 years had 6.7% live-births per attempted stimulation. Approximately 1.5% of cycles were performed without fertility medications. Sixteen were successful, for 4.5% live-births per attempted procedure. Of the 6,672 cryopreservation thaw cycles, 791 live-births resulted, for a rate of 11.9% deliveries per thaw.

The multiple birth rate for stimulated cycle IVF was 34%. The rate of birth defects in these younger women was 2.3%. Cycles with male factor as defined by the World Health Organization (WHO) standards had slightly lower delivery rates per initiated cycle than those with no significant male factor.

It is difficult to determine whether the pregnancy rate on repeated IVF cycles stays constant, and how many cycles should be undertaken by a couple with reasonable parameters during a cycle, but without accomplishing a pregnancy. The largest published series suggests a slight decline over successive cycles (Tan et al., 1992), but there are insufficient data to conclude how many cycles should be the maximum. In practice, few couples try IVF more than three or four times, often for financial reasons. In states with mandated insurance coverage, however, the utilization rate per couple is not dramatically higher, suggesting that noneconomic factors are also relevant. The number of couples able to try IVF initially appears to be higher where coverage is available, though. Most couples describe IVF as an emotional roller coaster ride, exacerbated no doubt by the tendency of the medications to cause irritability and anxiety in a significant minority of women.

Gamete Intrafallopian Transfer

With gamete intrafallopian transfer (GIFT), oocytes and sperm are placed into a normal fallopian tube, mimicking the natural situation at the time of fertilization. Usually, controlled hyperstimulation is used. Oocyte retrieval and laparoscopy for placement of the oocytes and sperm into the tube are performed under general anesthesia. Rarely, the planned GIFT procedure will be technically impossible or inadvisable due to pelvic anatomy or pathology. Occasionally, the sperm parameters will be lower than anticipated, and the procedure may be converted to an IVF procedure in either case to utilize the oocytes that have been stimulated.

GIFT requires less laboratory sophistication than IVF, and the pregnancy rates are higher in general. However, the couples eligible for GIFT are not comparable to those for IVF, since at least one normal tube and reasonable normal semen parameters are necessary to undertake GIFT (Nelson et al., 1993). The few research series randomizing eligible couples to receive either GIFT or IVF have not shown a difference in pregnancy rates. Since laparoscopy is required, a greater degree of postoperative morbidity is expected, as well as a higher rate of complications. Therefore, many successful ART facilities perform few GIFT procedures.

One role for GIFT is in conjunction with a diagnostic and/or therapeutic laparoscopy, although scheduling may be difficult for both the medical team and the patient. Excellent pregnancy rates have been reported.

Programs performing GIFT should have IVF capability in the event that "excess" oocytes are obtained (American Fertility Society, 1988). Guidelines for the number of oocytes to transfer into the fallopian tubes are comparable to those for the number of IVF embryos; this depends on the age and history of the patient. In most cases, there will be oocytes remaining. These are inseminated unless the couple has ethical/religious objections to IVF or cryopreservation. These embryos may then be used in the future without need for medication stimulation or oocyte retrieval.

MEDICAL ASPECTS OF THIRD PARTY REPRODUCTION

Donor Sperm

Many couples faced with male factor infertility have traditionally chosen donor insemination as a means of family building, although others will not find this alternative acceptable. More and more, ART therapy is allowing these couples to try to conceive with the male partner's sperm, although the financial and emotional drain can be severe, and sometimes the treatments are not successful no matter how committed the couple may be. It is likely therefore, that donor insemination will remain a viable choice for many.

Since the advent of the HIV epidemic, and with the understanding that semen is the major vector of HIV transmission (Araneta et al., 1995), frozen quarantined sperm has been used in place of fresh sperm. This results in a loss of sperm motility and decreased efficiency in therapy. Reported pregnancy rates per insemination cycle with otherwise healthy women approach 10% to 15% if IUI is used (Edvinsson, Forssman, Milsom, & Nordfors, 1990). Women failing to become pregnant after a course of therapy with natural cycle become candidates for the traditional infertility diagnostic tests and treatment, including ART in some instances.

Donor Oocyte

Using oocytes donated by another individual has enabled thousands of women to become pregnant who never previously had the opportunity. It has also challenged the foundations of our beliefs regarding motherhood and opened up many disturbing ethical dilemmas, including the possibility of pregnancy in women in their 50s and 60s (Sauer, Paulson, & Lobo, 1992). Initially, the technique was reserved for women who had undergone premature menopause, either naturally or medically. As IVF was practiced in a number of ovulatory women in their later reproductive years, the existence of "perimenopause" further evolved— that portion of a woman's reproductive life in which she is still menstruating regularly, but is subfertile. With the success of donor oocyte treatment, it became clear that many women with low response to ovarian hyperstimulation, high FSH levels, or over 40 years of age can benefit.

Ideally, the oocyte donor should be under age 36 years, although some programs will extend the age cutoff, especially for known donors. She undergoes extensive screening and counseling (American Fertility Society, 1993a). Medically identical to the regimen that infertile women undergo, the stimulation regimen is carried out. A transvaginal oocyte retrieval is performed and the donor relinquishes her oocytes at that point. The male partner of the recipient couple provides semen; resulting embryos are transferred into the uterus of the recipient, who needs hormone replacement therapy to prepare the endometrium for implantation. Excess embryos, if any, can be cryopreserved for later transfer, without need for further involvement of the donor. Pregnancy rates are excellent because of the young age and normal gynecological history of the donor in most instances. Compared with ovulatory women in their 40s undergoing IVF or GIFT, the success rates is severalfold higher since the embryos are much more likely to implant.

Gestational Carrier

Women who do not have a uterus, or those with major uterine anatomic defect but normal ovarian function, may become genetic mothers through the process of oocyte retrieval and insemination, with transfer of embryos to the normal uterus of a hormonally synchronized recipient. The process is quite similar to that of oocyte donation, but the gestating mother (who is not the genetic mother) relinquishes the offspring to the genetic mother in this case. Much more limited in its application than donor oocyte, the process is similarly quite successful. Of course, the emotional and legal issues involved in allowing a women to carry to term a pregnancy for another couple are much more substantial than for donor oocyte, and more fraught with legal difficulty (American Fertility Society, 1994).

Traditional surrogacy, which is insemination of a women with semen of the male partner of an infertile couple, with the intent to gestate a pregnancy and relinquish the infant to the couple, is medically straightforward and low tech. However, because the genetic and gestating mother are the same, the situation is more prone to disputes; both traditional surrogacy and gestational carrier are illegal in some countries, and in some states in the United States.

REFERENCES

American College of Obstetrics and Gynecology. (1994). Technical bulletin. Managing the anovulatory state: Medical induction of ovulation, (1–7).

American Fertility Society. (1988). Minimal standards for Gamete intrafallopian transfer (GIFT). *Fertility and Sterility, 50,* 20.

American Fertility Society. (1991). Guideline for practice. Intrauterine insemination. 1–6.

American Fertility Society. (1993a). Guidelines for oocyte donation. *Fertility and Sterility, 59,* 5S–9S.

American Fertility Society. (1993b). Tubal Disease. Guideline for practice. 1–8.

American Fertility Society. (1994). Ethical considerations of assisted reproductive technologies. Surrogate gestational mothers: Women who gestate a genetically unrelated embryo. *Fertility and Sterility, 62,* 67S–70S.

Araneta, M. R. G., Mascola, L., Eller, A., O'Neil, L., Ginsberg, M., Bursaw, M., Marik, J., Friedman, S., Sims, C., Rekart, M., & Collie, F. (1995). HIV transmission through donor artificial insemination. *New England Journal of Medicine, 273,* 854–858.

Barnes, A. B., Colton, T., Gundersten, J., Noller, K., Tilley, B., Strama, T., Townsend, D., Hatab, P., & O'Brien, P. (1980). Fertility and outcome of pregnancy in women exposed in utero to diethylstilbestrol. *New England Journal of Medicine, 302,* 609–613.

Callahan, T., Hall, J. E., Ettner, S., Christiansen, C., Greene, M., & Crowley, W. F. (1994). The economic impact of multiple-gestation pregnancies and the contribution of assisted reproduction techniques to their incidence. *New England Journal of Medicine, 331,* 244–249.

Chehval, M. J., & Purcell, M. H. (1992). Deterioration of sperm parameters over time in men with untreated varicocele: Evidence of progressive testicular damage. *Fertility and Sterility, 57,* 174–177.

Duncan, W. W., Glew, M. J., Wang, X. J., Flaherty, S. P., & Matthews, C. D. (1993). Prediction of in vitro fertilization rates from semen variables. *Fertility and Sterility, 59,* 1233–1238.

Edvinsson, A., Forssman, L., Milsom, I., & Nordfors, G. (1990). Factors in the infertile couple influencing the success of artificial insemination with donor semen. *Fertility and Sterility, 53,* 81–87.

Filicori, M., Flamigni, C., Meriggiola, M. C., Cognigni, G., Valdiserri, A., Ferrari, P., & Campaniello, E. (1991). Ovulation induction with pulsatile gonadotropin-releasing hormone: Technical modalities and clinical perspectives. *Fertility and Sterility, 56,* 1–13.

Glatstein, I. Z., Best, C. L., Palumbo, A., Sleeper, L. A., Friedman, A. J., & Hornstein, M. D. (1995). The reproducibility of the postcoital test: A prospective study. *Obstetrics and Gynecology, 85,* 396–400.

Gompel, A., & Mauvais-Jarvis, P. (1988). Induction of ovulation with pulsatile GnRH in hypothalamic amenorrhoea. *Human Reproduction, 3,* 473–477.

Hurry, D. J., Charles, D., & Larsen, B. (1984). Effects of postcesarean section febrile morbidity on subsequent fertility. *Obstetrics and Gynecology, 64,* 256–260.

Jansen, R. P. S. (1995). Elusive fertility: Fecundability and assisted conception in perspective. *Fertility and Sterility, 64,* 252–254.

Jones, H. W., Jr., & Toner, J. P. (1993). The infertile couple. *The New England Journal of Medicine, 329,* 1710–1715.

Jones, R. B., Ardery, B. R., Hui, S. L., & Cleary, R. E. (1982). Correlation between serum antichlamydial antibodies and tubal factor as a cause of infertility. *Fertility and Sterility, 38,* 553–558.

Kaufman, R. H., Adam, E., Gray, M., Hilton, J., Irwin, J., Jefferies, J. A., & Noller, K. (1984). Upper genital tract abnormalities and pregnancy outcome in diethylstilbestrol-exposed progeny. *Obstetrics and Gynecology, 148,* 973–984.

Li, T. C., & Cooke, I. D. (1991). Evaluation of the luteal phase. *Human Reproduction, 6,* 484–499.

Luciano, A. A., Peluso, J., Koch, E. I., Maier, D., Kuslis, S., & Davison, E. (1990). Temporal relationship and reliability of the clinical, hormonal, and ultrasonographic indices of ovulation in infertile women. *Obstetrics and Gynecology, 75,* 412–416.

Munne, S., Alikani, M., Tomkin, G., Grifo, J., & Cohen, J. (1995). Embryo morphology, developmental rates, and maternal age are correlates with chromosome abnormalities. *Fertility and Sterility, 64,* 382–391.

Nagy, Z., Liu, J., Cecile, J., Silber, S., Devroey, P., & Steirteghem, A. V. (1995). Using ejaculated, fresh, and frozen-thawed epididymal and testicular spermatozoa gives rise to comparable results after intracytoplasmic sperm injection. *Fertility and Sterility, 63,* 808–815.

Nelson, J. R., Corson, S. L., Batzer, F. R., Gocial, B., Huppert, L., Go, K. J., & Maislin, G. (1993). Predicting success of gamete intrafallopian transfer. *Fertility and Sterility, 60,* 116–122.

Olive, D. L., & Schwartz, L. B. (1993). Endometriosis. *New England Journal of Medicine, 328,* 1759–1769.

Ritchie, W. G. M. (1985). Ultrasound in the evaluation of normal and induced ovulation. *Fertility and Sterility, 43,* 167–180.

Sauer, M. V., Paulson, R., & Lobo, R. A. (1992). Reversing the natural decline in human fertility. An extended clinical trial of oocyte donation to women of advanced reproductive age. *Journal of the American Medical Association, 268,* 1275–1279.

Schoolcraft, W. B., Schlenker, T., Gee, M., Jones, G. S., & Jones, H. W. (1994). Assisted hatching in the treatment of poor prognosis in vitro fertilization candidates. Efficacy of assisted hatching in poor prognosis IVF candidates. *Fertility and Sterility, 62,* 551–554.

Skakkebaek, N. E., Giwercman, A., & deKretser, D. (1994). Pathogenesis and management of male infertility. *The Lancet, 343,* 1473–1478.

Society for Assisted Reproductive Technology, American Society for Reproductive Medicine. (1995). *Fertility and Sterility, 64,* 13–20.

Soliman, S., Collins, J., Daya, S., & Jarrell, J. (1993). A randomized trial of in vitro fertilization versus conventional treatment for infertility. *Fertility and Sterility, 59,* 1239–1244.

Tan, S. L., Royston, P., Campbell, S., Jacobs, H. S., Betts, J., Mason, B., & Edwards, R. G. (1992). Cumulative conception and livebirth rates after in-vitro fertilisation. *The Lancet, 339,* 1390–1394.

Vine, M. F., Margolin, B. H., Morrison, H. I., & Hulka, B. S. (1994). Cigarette smoking and sperm density: A meta-analysis. *Fertility and Sterility, 61,* 35–42.

Whittemore, A. S., Itnyre, J., & Harris, R. (1992). Characteristics relating to ovarian cancer risk: Collaborative analysis of 12 U.S. case-control studies. Invasive epithelial ovarian cancers in white women. *American Journal of Epidemiology, 136,* 1184–1203.

World Health Organization. (1992). The influence of varicocele on parameters of fertility in a large group of men presenting to infertility clinics. *Fertility and Sterility, 57,* 1289–1293.

CHAPTER 3

Ethical Issues Associated with the New Reproductive Technologies

SUSAN COOPER

The birth of Louise Brown in 1978 heralded a new era in the field of reproductive medicine. The ability to fertilize ova in vitro paved the way for reproductive technologies that were previously unimaginable. Couples who were considered "hopelessly infertile" less than 20 years ago, can now give birth to their genetic offspring. Infertile men who have few sperm, making penetration of an egg impossible, are now able to have biological offspring; couples who are carriers for certain genetic diseases are now able to know if their potential offspring—at the four-cell embryo stage—carries the defective gene, and if so, they can discard that embryo for genetically normal ones. Because the process of in vitro fertilization allows for the separation of genetic, gestational, and social parenting, women who have gone through menopause, either early or late, are now able to gestate and birth children, and women who have had their uteruses removed are able to rear their genetic children. These are a few of the wonders that have been brought about by the reproductive revolution.

In the minds of all the infertile couples who are now parents of "miracle" children, and the practitioners who witness these miracles on a daily basis, these technologies are a blessing. To other people—those who would turn back the clock—they are a curse; a threat to basic family values. No matter what side of the fence one sits on, however, the new reproductive technologies pose ethical dilemmas of an increasingly complex and perplexing magnitude. Furthermore, each of the new technologies raises an additional, perhaps overriding, ethical question: Just because we can do something, should we do it? And as the technology becomes even more advanced, this latter question will become increasingly crucial.

These complex ethical issues have prompted discussion and debate among a wide range of professionals. Although traditionally, medical ethics is a field that has been entered from either the legal or philosophical side (those who have backgrounds in either law or philosophy), more recently mental health specialists have entered the medical ethics ring because many ethical questions raise psychological issues. This is especially true in the field of reproductive medicine where the perspectives of law, ethics, and psychology frequently intersect. This chapter provides an overview of the ethical issues in assisted reproductive technology today, from the viewpoint of a psychologist.

PRINCIPLES OF MEDICAL ETHICS

Ethicists are concerned with the physical and emotional health of human beings—with their ability to lead happy, fulfilling, and productive lives. To achieve these ends, three philosophical principles are frequently used as guidelines for decision making in the area of medical ethics: autonomy, beneficence, and justice.

The first principle, *autonomy,* places value on the human being, recognizing that humans have special status: they are more than property. Autonomy encompasses the notion that humans should be allowed to make their own decisions, providing those decisions do not infringe on the rights of other people. Autonomy, in relation to medical ethics, also refers to the individual's right to receive accurate information about his or her medical condition, to be informed about treatment possibilities, and to decide which treatment options to accept or reject.

Beneficence is probably the most touted principle in medical ethics. It refers to the concept of doing good (performing acts of kindness to other people). Beneficence includes an obligation to refrain from harming another; an obligation to actively remove or prevent harm to another person; and a responsibility to actively promote good. A problem frequently facing medical caregivers is that of balancing the potential risks of treatment with its benefits. Sometimes to refrain from doing harm (beneficence), caregivers may compromise a patient's autonomy by refusing to provide a treatment. In these situations, medical caregivers are often accused of being paternalistic.

The principle of *justice* refers to the distribution of burdens and benefits. The operating assumption is that everyone should be treated fairly and receive what he or she needs and deserves. Thus denying people that to which they are entitled or can legitimately claim is seen as an injustice. The concept of "distributive justice" refers to an equitable distribution of political, economic, and social burdens and benefits. Distributive justice presumes that goods or services designed to assist a certain category of people ought to be available to everyone in that category (Beauchamp & Walters, 1982).

The notion of helping infertile couples become parents through available technology can be seen as an ethical goal that in spirit supports the preceding three principles. It supports an individual or couple's right to autonomy—to receive accurate information about treatment options and to make choices based on that information. It supports the concept of doing good by helping people achieve an intensely sought-after goal and by creating a new life (a concept generally viewed in society as positive). Furthermore, treatment of infertility supports our notion of justice in that those who are in need of and deserving of resources are able to receive them.

Although these three principles are frequently used as guidelines in the practice of medicine, they do not always illuminate the road to ethical decision making. A closer look at the underlying ethical issues that lie at the heart of many treatments and alternative treatments frequently reveals there is no simple point of view. Although helping infertile couples have families is an ethically sound goal that most people would support, specific instances may very well indicate the opposite to be true. Conflicts may also arise when one's rational beliefs conflict with one's religious or moral beliefs, or when legal precedent impedes a decision that might otherwise be based on the principles of autonomy, beneficence, or justice. All too frequently, moral judgments are based on faulty assumptions, and once the facts are garnered—often a difficult if not impossible task—the ethically sound decision will be more clear.[1]

Many of the ethical issues in the new reproductive technologies are dependent on facts that are not easily subject to verification; certainly not in the short run. Making ethically sound decisions therefore is a complicated process that involves sorting through rights and duties, or moral beliefs and rational beliefs, facts and assumptions, while using the principles of autonomy, beneficence, and justice as guidance. Many of the ethical issues discussed in this chapter overlap, and many of the broad issues encompass narrower issues of utmost importance. Some ethical issues refer to situations in which both husband's and wife's gametes will be used to create a child. Other ethical questions involve third parties such as ovum or sperm donors, surrogates, and gestational carriers. Although this chapter does not presume to be inclusive of all the ethical issues inherent in assisted reproductive technology (ART), it will explore some of the most salient issues that perplex medical personnel, mental health professionals, lawmakers, and ethicists, on an almost daily basis.

THE RIGHTS OF INDIVIDUALS TO REPRODUCE VERSUS THE RIGHTS AND BEST INTEREST OF THE UNBORN OFFSPRING

Those who work in the infertility field are painfully aware that when it comes to fertility, life is unfair. Stories in the media about infertile couples going to great lengths to produce biological offspring are juxtaposed with articles about parents who abuse, neglect, abandon, even murder their children. The U.S. Constitution gives people the right to procreate—coitally. The question is whether the Constitution also gives individuals the right to produce noncoitally if that is their only route to parenthood.

---

[1]The author is indebted to Natalie Bluestone, PhD for her comments regarding ethical issues in ART centers.

John Robertson, professor of law at the University of Texas at Austin, argues convincingly that infertile couples have the right to procreative liberty. He contends that having children satisfies a basic biological, social, and psychological drive for many people and that "noncoital reproduction should thus be constitutionally protected to the same extent as is coital reproduction, with the state having the burden of showing severe harm if the practice is unrestricted" (Robertson, 1994, p. 39).

Although the law gives people the right to reproduce, it does not, however, give people the right to parent the children they produce if they are deemed unfit in a court of law. When it comes to adoption, many states have outlawed private adoptions and require that couples seeking to adopt children pass a homestudy conducted by a licensed social worker before they are allowed to become parents. Other states that allow private adoptions require a visit from a professional appointed by the court before the adoption becomes legal. In these instances, the state is acting in their best interests of the children who are yet to be placed in their new families. Although it is extremely rare for an adoption to "fall through" because a couple was deemed unfit, it does happen occasionally. The purpose of the law is to protect children from harm and the duty of the state is therefore to advocate for their best interest.

Although gatekeeping has long been sanctioned in the field of adoption, it is unclear whether clinicians in the field of reproductive medicine should also act in that capacity. In fact, some mental health practitioners do consider themselves gatekeepers, mandated to act in the best interest of the potential child. They believe it is their responsibility to make recommendations about whether an individual or couple should receive medical treatment based on psychological fitness. Other mental health practitioners intentionally avoid becoming gatekeepers, citing that no one monitors the reproductive lives of fertile couples—and many of them are unfit parents. They feel their job is to offer education, support, and advice about available treatments and about alternatives to biogenetic children, but believe they should not pass judgment on who is fit to become a parent. Still others take a middle-of-the-road view, offering guidance, information about the psychological and social aspects of the various options, and assistance with decision making. These middle-of-the-road clinicians tend to exclude from treatment only those couples in extreme situations.

No matter what position a practitioner takes vis-à-vis gatekeeping, there are always some cases that are greatly troubling—perhaps instances where one or both parents have serious mental or physical disabilities—causing clinicians to feel reluctant at best about bringing children into the world under such circumstances. The following cases are examples of situations that were disturbing to the medical team of an IVF program, and which necessitated a great deal of discussion before decisions were made regarding treatment.

Case Example

A 50-year-old childless attorney who had gone through 10 years of infertility treatment requested ovum donation. She was engaged to a 55-year-old man who had three grown children from a prior marriage. They came together for the initial consultation, during which time the psychologist learned that their relationship had broken up on several occasions. The woman had refused to have any contact with him during those times, but each time she eventually returned to the relationship. At the time of the ovum donation consultation, she stated that she considered the relationship permanent.

This case raises other ethical issues involving the use of donor gametes which we will discuss later in this chapter. However, it is a good example of a situation in which the physicians and psychologists involved had grave concerns about bringing a child into this family situation. The age of the parents was a primary consideration since no one wanted to bring a child into the world whose parents would likely be ill, infirm, or deceased, before the child was an adult. Furthermore, the psychologist who interviewed the woman characterized her as highly manipulative and emotionally unstable. For years, she had been relentless in her pursuit of a biogenetic child, and when this became impossible, she turned to ovum donation. She was extremely defensive and at times seemed volatile. Her fiance was ambivalent about having another child, and very worried that she would end the relationship at any time. He agreed to have a child with her because he knew that she would leave him otherwise. The patient was aware of her fiance's feelings. The medical team, after much deliberation, decided to refuse treatment to her, in part due to her age, but primarily due to their fears about the quality of parenting the offspring would receive. However, when her attorney sent a letter to the medical director threatening a lawsuit, the clinic relented.

Case Example

A couple conceived and successfully carried a child through IVF and had five remaining embryos cryopreserved. Shortly after childbirth the woman learned she had ovarian cancer. Her reproductive organs were surgically removed and she was given chemotherapy treatments. Her prognosis was fair to poor. They found a gestational carrier and asked the clinic to transfer the embryos to her. The woman stated that if she was going to die, it would be easier to do so knowing that she has two children in the world.

This second case involves a different but equally troubling situation in which the best interests of the unborn child are seen to conflict with the wishes of the couple. The medical team, that had on occasion helped couples become parents via a gestational carrier, was very reluctant to bring a child into the world whose mother would most likely die before it was old enough to remember her. They believed that it would not be in a child's best interest to be deliberately brought into the world having a mother who most likely has a terminal illness. However, since the clinic treated single women, some team members felt they could not justify refusing treatment on the grounds that a child ought not to be born to a single parent. On the other hand, several members argued that the experience of losing a parent to whom one has become attached, and watching her die, is far more tragic than being born to one healthy parent. Fortunately, the couple themselves decided against the process, and the team never had to make a final decision.

Case Example

A 42-year-old woman married to a 50-year-old man present at an IVF clinic. They are requesting donor sperm. The man, who has two grown children from another marriage is fertile. He has practically no relationship with his children. He was very clear during the initial consultation that he has no desire to become a parent again. His current wife moved out when he told her that he was not willing to have more children. During the separation the husband realized that his wife was important to him and that he would rather be married to her and have a child in the house, than to be apart from her. They came up with a "creative" solution: they would use donor sperm and that way the husband would not be the child's biological father. The husband and wife intended to sign an agreement stating that he would not be the child's legal father, and that in the event of his wife's death, he would not assume custody of the child.

In these circumstances the medical team felt extremely uneasy about agreeing to donor insemination. When pressed, the man acknowledged that he hoped once the child was born he would be happy about its existence but he could not predict with any certainty that his feelings would change. The team felt particularly troubled about helping to bring a child into the world with a "father" who did not want him or her, whose resentment toward the child was bound to characterize their relationship. If the woman had come to the clinic as a single woman, however, she would have been treated with donor insemination. The potential harm that might be caused to the child, however, was weighed against the woman's strong desire to parent, and although the practitioners involved felt very uncomfortable about treating this couple, they eventually did because they did not feel they had an adequate reason for refusing treatment. It was predicted that the marriage probably would not last and that the woman would probably be a "good enough" single mother.

Each of these cases illustrates the conflict that can occur when two moral principles collide: in this case autonomy and beneficence. In each of the three cases there were practitioners who convincingly argued that to refuse treatment would be a violation of the patient's autonomy—specifically the right to procreative liberty. Others argued convincingly that treating the person would involve inflicting harm on another person—a person who is not yet born, or, as in two of the cases, conceived.

THE RIGHT TO INFORMATION REGARDING ONE'S GENETIC ORIGINS

The history of gamete donation began in the late 1800s. William Pancoast, who performed the first insemination of donor sperm claims to have done it secretly;

thus began a tradition that has continued for almost a century. Anonymity has occurred along with secrecy in donor insemination, and secrecy has often been equated with privacy—a right that many legal scholars claim is guaranteed by the Fourteenth Amendment. Secrecy, however, is different from privacy, and it has only been in the past 10 to 20 years that anyone (primarily mental health professionals and ethicists) has questioned whether this concept must be built into the practice of donor insemination.

The Right to Procreate with Unknown Gametes

Although procreation with known third parties is becoming increasingly more common, especially among couples opting for ovum donation, the vast majority of couples involved in gamete donation use anonymous sperm or eggs. This practice raises an ethical question: *Is it morally acceptable to bring a child into the world with an unknown genetic parent?* This question has been historically overlooked, perhaps because until recently, nurture, rather than nature, has been thought to play the primary role in human development. Genetics was thought to be relatively unimportant in determining who a person would ultimately become. Thus if nature was not very relevant, one could argue that it did not matter where one's genes came from, and it could be concluded that it is morally acceptable to bring a child into the world with an unknown genetic parent.

The past 10 or 15 years have deepened our understanding of the role of genetics. Although scientists have not finished mapping the human genome, more and more information about biological destiny is unfolding on an almost daily basis. We now understand that genetics plays a very large role in determining one's physical and mental health as well as personality. And although no one knows exactly what the nature/nurture equation is, human nature is being weighted much more heavily on the side of nature than was previously assumed. Thus the ethics of bringing a child into the world with unknown genetic origins is more questionable if one recognizes the importance of genetics in determining who the child ultimately becomes.

This ethical question brings up the "best interest" question that we have previously considered—is it in the best interest of a child to be brought into the world with an unknown genetic parent(s)? Currently, both our legal and social policy say that it is ethical—that opting for donor gametes is exercising one's procreative liberty (autonomy) and is doing good (beneficence) by bringing a life into the world. However, there are professionals who disagree and feel strongly that children should not be intentionally created with unknown parental origins. Elias and Annas, a physician-geneticist and attorney-ethicist respectively, (1986) discuss both sides of this issue. They argue:

> [Donor insemination] places the private contractual agreement among the participants regarding parental rights and responsibilities above the "best interest of the child," and . . . raises a series of societal issues that remain unresolved. . . . Assuming that deciding about parenthood by contract is socially accepted as currently practiced, we ignore the relevance of legitimacy, lineage,

and individual identity tied up in kinship, and thus bypass fundamental questions about the definition of fatherhood and its role in the life of the child.

The authors also point out that since issues regarding legitimacy are no longer important social considerations in this country, and hereditary titles are not bestowed by lineage, questions about genetic parenthood may be irrelevant. However, the extent to which individual identity is connected to information regarding one's genetic origins, remains unclear, probably because it varies from individual to individual. Those who argue against the practice of anonymous gamete donation believe that it is an individual's right to know about his or her genetic heritage, which includes access to one's medical history (one's biological family's medical history). They believe that to develop a positive, secure sense of identity and avoid genealogical bewilderment (a sense of confusion about who one is or to whom one belongs), a child needs to know who his or her genetic parents are.

Many in the field assume a middle-of-the-road position. Believing that genetics plays an important role in the formation of a person, and that knowledge of one's genetic origins helps in identity formation, some physicians, mental health clinicians, lawyers, and ethicists recommend that nonidentifying information about the donor be made available to couples and to their offspring. Robertson (1994) writes:

> Since most children who are told of their collaborative birth will desire knowledge of the missing parent, at the very least nonidentifying information about the donor or surrogate should be collected so that parents can provide as much information as possible. . . . Because *nonidentifying* information about donors will be immensely important to offspring, physicians who perform sperm, egg, or embryo donation should collect this information and provide it to the couple so that they may later inform the child.

In many such situations, the nonidentifying information may be enough to satisfy the offspring's curiosity about him or herself. In other situations, the offspring may wish to meet the donor, in which case there may be a clash between two ethical principles: the donor's right to privacy and the offspring's medical or psychological need to know the donor.

The Right to Know the Truth about One's Genetic Origins

Knowing the truth about one's genetic origins is different from having knowledge of one's genetic parents. As long as the practice of anonymous sperm donation continues in this country—and it is quite prevalent—and the laws surrounding it do not change, neither donor offspring nor their parents will have access to the donor. Depending on the sperm bank used, offspring will have little, or perhaps extensive nonidentifying information about the donor. Given the current climate, the question of whether donor offspring have a *right* to the truth about their conception—even though identifying information is lacking—is one that plagues clinicians and ethicists in the field of reproductive technology.

Research indicates (Klock, 1993) that most couples who form their families via anonymous sperm donation do not plan to tell their children how they were conceived. In seven studies that addressed this question, the percentage of couples who stated they do not plan to tell their children ranged from 61% to 86%. The most common reason stated for not telling the child was that it would unnecessarily complicate his or her life (Klock & Maier, 1991). Another reason has to do with fears that relatives might not accept the child if they knew the truth. Some ethnic groups have strong proscriptions against the use of donor gametes, and relatives who are not linked by blood are accorded a lesser status. Still another common reason for not telling the truth to offspring is that society stigmatizes donor offspring, much as it stigmatizes adoptees. A further reason commonly given by couples opting for secrecy is that if their child cannot have access to the donor, telling the truth would only contribute to greater frustration and confusion about identity. Finally, couples worry that their child may reject his or her father, should the truth be revealed.

Much has been written in recent years, primarily by family therapists and donor offspring, about the possible unfortunate consequences of keeping a family secret and the accompanying sense of shame that surrounds it (Baran & Pannor, 1989; Mahlstedt & Greenfeld, 1989; Noble, 1987). Mahlstedt and Greenfeld, although recognizing that certain situations, based on cultural or religious traditions, may necessitate secrecy, offer compelling arguments for being open with donor offspring:

> There is a growing body of research documenting the negative effects of family secrets and their unique power in the family. Since there is no psychological theory which supports secrecy in any situation, secrecy about one's beginnings is particularly difficult to justify, as it places a lie at the center of the most basic of relationships—the one between parent and child.

Baran and Pannor (1989) whose research about donor insemination spanned six years and involved 171 subjects including donor offspring, donor couples, sperm donors, single women, and lesbians, relate chilling stories in their book—stories about children who learned they were donor offspring after a parent had died or while sitting on a parent's deathbed because he or she did not want to carry the secret to the grave. Other anecdotes involve divorce or family arguments in which the secret "accidentally" spilled out. In almost all these situations, the parents had every intention of keeping donor insemination a secret, yet the truth was revealed in unfortunate circumstances.

Many offspring interviewed described feelings of confusion, anger, and a sense of betrayal for not having been told the truth all along. For many, learning the truth was a great relief; it explained why they felt there was something different about them or why they felt out of place in their family. The consensus of most of the donor offspring was that it is not the fact of donor insemination to which they objected, rather it was the climate of secrecy in which it was carried out.

Being truthful about a child's donor origins allows family members to be close to one another without having to create emotional barriers. Keeping a secret means that there is likely to be some distance between those who hold the secret and those who are not supposed to know it. The barrier may serve as an unconscious protection from inadvertent revelation. If the secret is learned after many years, particularly if it is learned under adverse circumstances, it may seriously jeopardize the bond of trust, so necessary for healthy parent-child relationships. George Annas (1980), an attorney/ethicist who has written extensively about the new reproductive technologies states:

> It seems to me a similar argument can be made for consistently lying to the child—i.e. that it is a violation of parental-child confidence. There is evidence that AID [artificial insemination by donor] children do learn the truth . . . If AID is seen as a loving act for the child's benefit, there seems no reason to taint the procedure with a lie that could prove extremely destructive to the child.

Being truthful means that donor offspring will not have to lie inadvertently to physicians when revealing their medical history. And, should a medical emergency arise in which locating the donor could mean life or death, the offspring would not have to deal with the emotional trauma—on top of the medical trauma—that would undoubtedly surface. It is also possible that the offspring's father will develop a serious medical condition as he ages, and the offspring will worry about whether he or she inherits a genetic predisposition for the illness—a problem the child could not possibly have inherited, at least from the person *believed* to be the biological father.

Although whether an individual has a right to know the truth about his or her genetic origins is an ethical issue, the preceding arguments show that it is a psychological and emotional issue as well. Once again, the principles of autonomy and beneficence may clash if the parents' desire for privacy about this issue interferes with a child's best interest—the right to know.

The Right to Privacy as a Gamete Donor

Currently, only one sperm bank in the United States offers sperm from donors who agree to be identified. These identity-release donors sign an agreement allowing offspring to contact them when they reach the age of 18 years. The vast majority of couples who form their families through donor insemination, however, use sperm from an anonymous donor. And although known ovum donation seems to be much more common than known sperm donation, the majority of couples seeking ovum donation also do so anonymously.

Physicians have hypothesized that if donors were required to make their identity known, there would be few, if any donors available. However, this has not been the case in Australia and Sweden, where laws have been passed mandating registries for gamete donors. At this time in the United States, the law protects the privacy of the donor, and in the minds of many who have a stake in this issue, in doing so it overlooks what might be considered the off-spring's best interest. Thus once again ethical principles collide: The right of the couple to procreate in the manner they choose, may in fact, cause future psychological harm to their child.

Another ethical dilemma is raised when one considers that the donor is likely to have children of his or her own; consequently, these children (assuming the gamete donation resulted in a successful pregnancy) will have genetic half-siblings whom they presumably will never know. In many instances, a child, particularly an only child, might want to know about their existence. One might argue too that the donor's mate also has a right to know whether her spouse has genetic offspring and her children have genetic half-siblings. These ethical dilemmas can plague practitioners who have to make decisions about treating infertile people.

Case Example

A 39-year-old single woman presents for IVF treatment. She brings a known donor with her to the initial consultation. The patient and the potential donor have been friends for a few years. The man is married and has two children. He does not plan to tell his wife that he intends to donate sperm for his friend.

Although the potential donor and the patient claimed that they were good friends and did not have a romantic or sexual relationship, the medical team felt uncomfortable about the intentional planned deception. Furthermore, the donor had very young children and they both lived in the same community. The couple were told that they could carry through with their plans only if they were willing to bring in the donor's wife for a consultation and if she agreed to the procedure. One might argue in this situation that since anonymous donors do not have to sign an agreement that they will reveal the donation to a spouse or child, known donors should also have this same right to anonymity.

LIBERATION VERSUS EXPLOITATION OF WOMEN FOR REPRODUCTIVE PURPOSES

The new reproductive technologies have raised ethical controversies previously unforeseen and unimagined in medicine. Although countless couples view these technologies—and the children they have produced—as nothing short of mirac-ulous, there are others who believe that they are a curse on families, and es-pecially on women. Those who view them as a curse include both political and religious conservatives and those who call themselves radical feminists. Con-servatives argue that procreation should occur through coital reproduction, that third-party assistance is an affront to traditional family values, and that the creation of life should be in God's hands. Radical feminists have different reasons for their negative viewpoint. They argue that in vitro fertilization dehumanizes women, that it was developed not to help infertile couples, but to give male physicians more control over women's bodies and to further their technological experiments. Elaine Baruch (1988) writes:

> It is a common belief among feminists now that the new technology with its in vitro fertilization and embryo transfer was designed less to help the infertile than to appease men's envy of women's reproductive power. . . . It is no small surprise to find that on the issue of reproductive technology, some radical feminists sound more like the women of the New Right than anyone else. They too fear men's intrusion into motherhood, the *sanctum sanctorum.*

Elizabeth Bartholet, an attorney, adoptive mother, and author of *Family Bonds* (1993), is a strong critic of the new reproductive technologies. She believes that IVF programs intentionally mislead desperate infertile couples who believe that the only meaningful resolution to infertility is to produce a biogenetic child. She believes also that something is inherently wrong with a society that causes people to place a greater value on families that are created from genetic ties, rather than on those that are built on emotional attachments. She argues that proper counseling can steer infertile couples away from technological means of reproduction to adoption.

Both Baruch and Bartholet believe that assisted reproductive technology demeans and exploits women, taking advantage of them at a time when they are most vulnerable. Many other people, including some who regard themselves as feminists, believe that these technologies actually liberate women by offering them more choices and giving women greater control over their bodies. They believe that women (and of course couples) should be able to choose whether, when, and how to have children. Thus assisted reproductive technology (ART) is empowering in that it offers women more choices and likewise more parenting possibilities.

Medical Risks and Side Effects of ART

One of the criticisms of ART is that unless a woman is undergoing a natural IVF cycle (her ovaries are not being stimulated by medication), she is subjecting her body to numerous unpleasant and potentially dangerous side effects. Until recently, there was no evidence that any fertility drugs were linked to long-term problems. However, a study published by Whittemore (1992) pooled data from three studies and reported that infertile women who used fertility drugs and did not become pregnant had between a 3- and 27-fold increased chance of developing ovarian cancer. An even more recent study (Rossing, 1994) also linked the fertility drug clomid, to a higher risk of developing ovarian cancer. Although many researchers and physicians in the field have been quick to point out the methodological flaws in this research, until further studies are performed, the conclusions cannot be assumed to be correct or incorrect.

At this point, in the absence of definitive data, each woman (couple) must decide for herself what potential risks she is willing to undertake. Certainly, no woman wants to think that the "cure" she is taking for her childlessness might result in a life-threatening problem. Ethicists often make difficult decisions by weighing the lesser of two evils. Since the long-term side effects of fertility drugs are not really known, physicians continue to support the use of them as a means of overcoming the socially and emotionally devastating condition of childlessness. Furthermore, it can be argued that even a greatly increased risk of a disease does not mean that one will develop it. However, this ethical question becomes even more complicated when applied to ovum donors. Since the long-term medical risks of hormonal therapy for women are unknown, and there is a slight possibility of short-term medical complications, many physicians question whether young, healthy, fertile, women who volunteer to be donors should be subjected to these risks. In addition, those women who have not completed their families, are assuming some degree of risk to their future fertility by undergoing an IVF cycle.

Financial Compensation for Gamete Donors and Surrogates

Financial compensation to third parties (gamete donors and surrogates) raises an array of ethical dilemmas. Currently, federal law bans baby selling and this law is extended to include payments to surrogates and gestational carriers. Many couples and agencies have been able to circumvent this law, however, by claiming that they are not paying for a child—rather they are paying the woman for the time, effort, and personal risk she undergoes to produce the child. Critics of paid surrogacy argue though, that whatever the payment is stated to represent, the fact is that full payment is usually conditional upon placement of the child. Critics also argue that surrogacy in any form is tantamount to exploitation—that wealthy couples will find poor women in need of money to "breed" children for them. Many are additionally concerned that surrogacy will also lead to the commodification of children, a result no one wants to see.

Women who serve as surrogates or gestational carriers are usually paid between $10,000 and $15,000 for their efforts. Those who argue against surrogacy say the dollar amount can easily entice poor women, who would never consider surrogacy were it not for financial need, to enter into such agreements. On the other hand, these same critics can point to the number of hours involved in pregnancy, the physical risk the woman undergoes, the pain and inconvenience of pregnancy and childbirth, and claim that the compensation is insultingly low!

Payment to gamete donors is a somewhat different issue. Although a few countries have banned payment to gamete donors, current federal and state laws make the buying or selling of organs illegal, but not the sale of gametes (Robertson, 1994). Sperm donors generally receive in the vicinity of $40 to $50 per sample; ovum donors, due to the increased time, effort, and physical risk involved are usually compensated between $1,000 and $3,000, depending on the program; $1,500 appears to be the mode.

Again, depending on one's perspective, the fee (particularly in the case of ovum donors) may be considered sufficiently high, such that women, who would never consider volunteering, may feel financial pressure to become donors. Others argue, as they do about surrogacy, that when the time, risk, effort, and physical pain are added up, the compensation is negligible. Supporters of paid gamete donation argue that donors therefore must have other, more altruistic, motivations. And although research on the motivations of donors is sparse, in fact Ken Daniels (1987) found that 91% of the sperm donors in his study indicated that the desire to help infertile couples was the main reason—or a reason—for being a donor; 59% indicated it was the only reason.

Social and Emotional Risks of Traditional and Gestational Surrogacy

Pregnancy and childbirth always involve medical risk to the woman. Although medicine has come a long way from the days in which it was not uncommon for a woman to die in childbirth, harm to the mother—including mortality—is always a possibility. In addition to possible medical risks to surrogates or gestational carriers, there are emotional and social risks involved in bearing/gestating a baby for another couple. Although most situations involving traditional surrogates or gestational carriers go smoothly (Cooper & Glazer, 1994), there have been some situations that have ended in disasters.

Case Example

A 24-year-old woman who had given birth two weeks previously, sought counseling. She had agreed to be a surrogate for her sister and brother-in-law who had gone through many years of infertility treatment. The baby was conceived with her brother-in-law's sperm and the surrogate's egg. The clinic that performed the inseminations told the commissioning couple that they thought counseling would be a good idea for everyone involved. The couple said they did not feel they needed counseling, and the clinic agreed to proceed without it. During the eighth week of pregnancy, the surrogate had some spotting, threatening a possible miscarriage. Although the pregnancy continued normally, the surrogate became aware that she was becoming emotionally attached to the fetus, and would have a very difficult time giving up the baby. Because of her family loyalties, and because she had given her word and would not break her promise, she knew she had no option other than to go through with her plan. Two weeks after the birth (five days after she had relinquished custody of the baby) she could not imagine how she would be able to stay connected to her family.

Although the physicians involved in the preceding situation would probably feel very badly if they knew the outcome of their treatment, they would most likely argue that each party involved was exercising the right to procreative liberty, and it is not the role of the physician to question that right. Others would argue that the surrogate was exploited by her sister and brother-in-law, as evidenced by their refusal to seek counseling, and that the physicians were remiss in their role not to have insisted on it. In this case, what was clear was that harm had been done—albeit unintentionally—to the surrogate.

Critics of contractual surrogacy arrangements argue that it is unreasonable to expect a woman to know how she will feel about placing a child prior to its conception or birth. Just as women who have made adoption plans for their unborn children may change their minds after giving birth, surrogates too, may desire to keep the child they have conceived and gestated. Michelle Harrison (1991), a psychiatrist, has spoken out frequently about surrogacy. She argues:

> The last time in the history of the United States that human beings were bred for transfer of ownership was during slavery. Slave women bore babies, some of whom were fathered by the slave owners themselves. Not since slavery have we attempted to institutionalize the forced removal of infants from their mothers— except in cases of abuse or clear lack of fitness.

Surrogacy, however, does not involve forced removal of infants from their mothers, and many who support surrogacy as a viable way for infertile couples to create families, including the American College of Obstetricians and Gynecologists, agree that certain measures must be taken to protect the surrogate's reproductive liberty both during and after pregnancy. This liberty includes the decision to retain custody of the infant.

Gestational care, often referred to as gestational surrogacy, in which a woman/carrier gestates a child conceived with the egg and sperm of another couple, is a very different situation. However, many ethicists writing about surrogacy fail to make a distinction between gestational and traditional surrogacy. They feel that genetic ties are not nearly as important as gestational ties when determining issues of maternity. George Annas (1991), professor of health law at Boston University School of Medicine writes:

> The woman who gives birth to the child should irrebuttably be considered the child's mother. She could agree to give the child up for adoption, but only after its birth, and in accordance with the state's adoption laws.

Others involved in the practice of gestational care believe that if the child is not genetically related to the carrier, the child is irrebuttably the offspring of the genetic (and intended) parents. In the case of *Johnson v. Calvert* (1993) the California Supreme Court reached similar conclusions. Anna Johnson, a gestational surrogate, sued for custody of the child she had carried for the Calverts. The judge, in awarding custody to the genetic parents, focused not only on the issue of genetics, but also on intent, stating that the original intentions of all parties should prevail.

Social and Emotional Risks of Gamete Donation

The recruitment of men and women for the purpose of sperm or egg donation, is another practice that has been viewed by some people as exploitive. Although there is general agreement that donating sperm does not involve a medical risk for men, there is some disagreement about whether it involves potential long-term emotional or social risks that sperm banks do not readily discuss with prospective donors (Cooper & Glazer, 1994). On the other hand, clinics offering ovum donation tend to have psychological screening of the donor built into the process. In a recent survey of 82 ovum donation programs (Braverman, 1993), it was reported that 78.4% required psychological screening of donors. However, the extent to which psychological screening of a donor involves a discussion of potential long-term consequences, probably varies significantly from program to program.

Experiences involving gamete donors may not appear to be as exploitive as surrogacy arrangements, but situations involving coercion, especially in known gamete donation do occur. A parent may put pressure (either subtle or overt) on a "resistant" daughter to donate to an infertile (probably older) sister. In other situations, the sister herself, desperate to have a child, may pressure her younger sibling to donate. Family ties are such that even women who generally feel strong enough to say no under ordinary circumstances, may fear emotional repercussions within the family system. Although gamete donation among relatives (especially sisters) is a common practice, and one that works well for many families, it is not an alternative for everyone, due to the relational complications it entails. In a sister-to-sister donation, for example, an offspring's social aunt will also be the child's genetic mother. Another reason why known ovum donation may be problematic, is that many people view their gametes as their potential children and cannot imagine watching them be raised by someone else—even a close relative.

A particularly controversial form of ovum donation, and one that almost all mental health clinicians in IVF programs scorn,[2] is daughter-to-mother donation. This situation may arise when the mother is in a second or third marriage. Although women with adult daughters may view them as ideal donors due to their youth and genetic bond, and the daughters may be willing to donate, clinicians have strong reservations about this practice. Due to the nature of the parent-child relationship, in which children may always feel in some way indebted to their parents, ovum donation would be viewed as inherently coercive, and therefore exploitive of that relationship.

Anonymous gamete donation may have fewer relational complications than known ovum donation. However, prospective anonymous donors must be asked to think very carefully about the nature of gametes, and what it might mean to them in the future to realize that they have genetic offspring in the world they will never know. To not raise these questions—and several others as well—might be considered tantamount to exploitation, for donors cannot truly give informed consent unless they fully understand to what they are consenting.

---

[2]An informal survey of approximately 80 mental health professionals attending the American Society for Reproductive Medicine's Psychological Special Interest Group's 1994 Postgraduate course (representing IVF programs nationwide) indicated that only three programs have/would ever consider it.

In these instances, as well as in others discussed in this section, the ethical principles of autonomy and beneficence may be in conflict. A potential surrogate, carrier, or gamete donor may argue that she is merely exercising her right to choose (autonomy) when she applies to an IVF clinic. The physician or psychologist who evaluates her, however, may feel that her decision is primarily based on either financial compensation or external pressure—and that she is being subtly (or perhaps overtly) pressured to undergo physical and emotional risk to satisfy a couple's desire to become parents. The clinician may refuse to accept the woman if her choice to donate is viewed as one that may cause her harm in the future, violating the principle of beneficence.

THE MORAL STATUS OF EMBRYOS

The development of in vitro fertilization (IVF) revolutionized human reproduction by making it possible for conception to occur outside the female body. Thus for the first time ever, human begins (conceived via IVF) spent their first 48 to 72 hours as embryos in a petri dish. [These embryos are often referred to as preembryos because their cells are undifferentiated prior to implantation, which occurs between six and nine days after conception.] The existence of these embryos, and the ramifications of their existence, which include questions about cryopreservation, disposal, experimentation, and ownership, raise even more fundamental questions about what the moral (and legal) status of an embryo is.

There are essentially three viewpoints about the moral status of an embryo. On the one hand, is the viewpoint of the Catholic Church, which regards an embryo as a human being. According to the Church, life exists on a continuum, beginning at fertilization and ending upon the death of that human being. The Church believes that because an embryo has the potential to become a human being it should be treated as such. According to the *Instruction on Respect for Human Life in Its Origin and on the Dignity of Procreation* (Rutzinger & Bovone, 1987), a document that has served as the basis for the beliefs of the Catholic Church regarding the status of embryos:

> . . . the fruit of human generation, from the first moment of its existence, that is to say from the moment the zygote has formed, demands the unconditional respect that is morally due to the human being in his bodily and spiritual totality. The human being is to be respected and treated as a person from the moment of conception; and therefore from that same moment his rights as a person must be recognized, among which in the first place is the inviolable right of every innocent human being to life.

On the other hand, the opposite point of view from that of the Catholic Church is that embryos are like property and those people who "own" them are free to make decisions affecting them. In other words, there should be no limits imposed on the use of embryos, and those individuals or couples who created them may take any action they see fit regarding their disposition.

The third point of view, and the one that is most widely held among those who have a stake in this issue, is somewhere in the middle. Embryos are neither human beings nor property, but because they have the potential to become a person under certain conditions, they should be treated with respect and dignity. The Warnock Committee, which was convened in London and consisted of physicians, lawyers, researchers, social workers, and theologians, published a report (Warnock, 1984) affirming that embryos have special status due to their human potential, but that they do not have the moral status of a living person. The report makes over 60 recommendations, which are frequently used as guidelines the world over for setting standards regarding the new reproductive technologies, including the use of human embryos in research.

The Disposition of Unwanted Embryos

To maximize a couple's chances of a pregnancy, IVF clinics stimulate a woman's ovaries via injection of a powerful drug in an attempt to produce a large cohort of eggs. The more eggs obtained, the more likely the couple is to have several good embryos to transfer. Most reputable clinics restrict the number of embryos they will transfer: usually between three and six (depending on the age of the woman) because they wish to maximize the chances of pregnancy while minimizing the chances of multiple birth. Excess embryos may then be cryopreserved for use in another cycle, should the woman fail to become pregnant. If pregnancy and a successful birth result, the couple may wish to have another child at a later time. Occasionally, a couple does not want their frozen embryos, most likely because they feel their family is complete, or because other circumstances have intervened. They must then make a decision regarding the disposition of their cryopreserved embryos.

Because embryos do not have legal rights, most clinics have provisions regarding the disposition of unwanted embryos that allow for donation to another couple or for discard. Three states, however, (Illinois, Louisiana, and Minnesota) have statutes that might arguably ban the intentional destruction of embryos (Robertson, 1994). Other states allow research to be performed on embryos under certain conditions, and couples who do not wish to have their embryos transferred to themselves, or donated to another couple, may opt to donate their embryos to research in lieu of discarding them.

There have been occasional disputes among couples, usually in situations involving divorce, regarding disposition of their jointly created embryos. Because of their competing interests, these disputes have found their way into the courtroom, the most well known of which is the case of *Davis v. Davis* (1992).

The Davises, a divorcing couple, had been through six unsuccessful IVF cycles and had seven cryopreserved embryos at the time they filed for divorce. Mary Sue Davis wanted to have the embryos transferred into her uterus. She claimed that they were living and that she, as the mother, had a right to have them implanted. Junior Lewis Davis, no longer wished to become a father and sought to prevent the clinic from implanting them in Ms. Davis or in any other woman.

The lower court argued that the embryos were equivalent to human beings whose best interest was to be implanted, and thus it ruled in favor of Ms. Davis. Mr. Davis, however, appealed this decision and the Tennessee appellate court agreed with his argument that he should not be forced to become a father against his will. Later, the Tennessee Supreme Court affirmed this decision declaring that the burden to Mr. Davis of unwanted reproduction would be greater than the burden to Ms. Davis if the decision were otherwise. (At that point Ms. Davis had decided she wanted to donate the embryos to another couple.) The court expressed the opinion that even if she had wanted to transfer the embryos to herself, unless she had no other means of having a child, her interest in procreating with the embryos should not outweigh her husband's interest in not procreating (*Davis v. Davis,* 1992).

It is easy to see that differing viewpoints on the moral status of an embryo formed the basis for the differing legal opinions dictated by the court. If an embryo is seen as equivalent to a human being and therefore has an interest in being given life, the legal ruling would always be in favor of the parent who wishes to give it life. However, if an embryo is not accorded the moral status of a human being, then, at least according to the Tennessee Supreme Court, the decision about whose wishes would prevail should be in favor of the person who would feel the greatest burden if the ruling were otherwise.

Preimplantation Genetics

Questions involving the moral status of an embryo bring up additional questions regarding what is acceptable to do to an embryo and when it is acceptable (if at all) to do it. The Catholic viewpoint, as one might surmise, is that because an embryo is essentially equivalent to a human life, it must not be subjected to experimentation or tampering of any sort. The Warnock Committee, on the other hand, recognizing the value of research in improving quality of life, came up with over 60 recommendations, many of which pertain to the use of embryos in research. The greater good, namely the outcome of future research, was thought to be a justification for experimentation on embryos.

Preimplantation genetics, the process of examining the genetic material of an early embryo before it is transferred into the uterus—usually at the four-cell stage—is a recent development in advanced reproductive technology. It involves highly technical manipulation on early embryos and is available to couples who are carriers of a genetic disease and do not wish to pass it on to their offspring. Preimplantation genetics involves removing one cell from a four-cell embryo and examining its chromosomal makeup to see if the embryo in question is a carrier of the defective gene. If it is, the embryo is discarded, and only nondefective embryos are transferred into the woman's uterus.

Those who do not view an embryo as a person tend to be enthusiastic supporters of preimplantation genetics as it prevents children from being born with a terrible disease or handicap. However, the implications for this technology have given rise to new ethical dilemmas—far more perplexing than many of the current ones—that will soon become commonplace challenges among clinicians working in this field. Although scientists have not yet mapped the entire human genome, it will probably not be too long before they can do so. Soon they will be able to determine physical, intellectual, and perhaps emotional and social characteristics in a potential person (an embryo). At this point in time, there are some genetic markers that can be detected indicating the presence or absence of certain diseases. Gender can easily be determined. Thus, in the not too distant future it will be possible for parents to select some of their offspring's characteristics. And although many people would support the use of preimplantation genetic selection for couples who are carriers of a disease such as cystic fibrosis, many will not support this technology for couples who wish to have a child of a particular sex—or in the future, a child with blue eyes, or musical talent, or who will be tall.

Preimplantation genetics, like many other technologies, raises the question of whether, because something can be done, it should be done. Many who believe in the concept of procreative liberty believe it should include not only the right to reproduce a child, but also the right to "select" the child one wants to reproduce. Others who may also believe in the rights of individuals to reproduce, may see inherent dangers in society if couples are allowed to choose the characteristics of their offspring. The question is where to draw the line—if anywhere—on the slippery slope of preselection/preimplantation genetic technology.

Posthumous Reproduction

The technology of cryopreservation has made it possible for children to be born to one or two deceased parents. Even prior to IVF, it was possible to freeze sperm—in many instances from men who were about to be treated for cancer and who would most likely be rendered sterile after the treatment. In some of these cases, men have died and wives have chosen to be inseminated to bear their husband's offspring. And although it is currently not possible to freeze ova (eggs), the ability to cryopreserve embryos has made it possible to bring children to life whose mother is deceased.

There may be instances in which either a husband or wife has died, they have joint cryopreserved embryos, and the remaining spouse desires to have his or her offspring. If the man has died, the woman might want the embryos transferred into her body; when it is the wife who has died, the husband may wish to find a gestational carrier for them. In other, more far-reaching scenarios, if both genetic parents have died, the inheritors of their estate (which may include their frozen embryos) might wish to find a gestational carrier to bring the embryos to life.

Decisions regarding embryo disposition are instances when religious and rational beliefs can collide, bringing fundamental ethical principles again into conflict. If an embryo is regarded as a human being then the state has an interest in preserving its potential life, and the autonomy of the genetic parents may therefore be compromised. In other circumstances, practitioners may feel that bringing an embryo to life (without one or both genetic parents) would be to intentionally inflict psychological harm on a potential person. These situations will probably be few and far between, but they may occur from time to time, underscoring the need for prior written agreements between spouses regarding the disposition of their embryos should death or divorce come between them.

ACCESS TO MEDICAL TREATMENT FOR INFERTILITY

Access to medical treatment for infertility seems to be one of the injustices in the field of reproductive medicine. Some people, due to their financial situation, insurance coverage, geographic location, or personal attributes have far easier access to treatment than do many others who would also benefit from it. Access to treatment is a complicated issue because healthcare dollars are not endless, and frequently practitioners are called on to make determinations about who should be a beneficiary when supplies are limited. A question that is frequently posed in such situations is whether there should be equal access to treatment when all diagnoses and prognoses are not equal. The field of medicine has traditionally built in systems for prioritizing patients in certain circumstances. For example, not everyone who needs an organ transplant will receive one: Age, prognosis, lack of availability, and financial constraints are limiting factors. Access to medical treatment for infertility, however, may be even more unequal than access to other kinds of medical treatment.

Financial Access

Infertility is not seen as a medical condition by most health insurance companies. Consequently, treatment for infertility is not a reimbursable expense for most people. Treatment for infertility has been likened to cosmetic surgery and seen as frivolous. Infertile women have been seen by many clinicians (medical as well as mental health) as having a psychological problem linked to unconscious hostility toward the feminine role, or to a hatred of men. Presently, in large part due to efforts by RESOLVE Inc., a national organization providing support, medical information, education, counseling, and advocacy to infertile couples, 10 states have mandates requiring private insurance companies to either offer or cover infertility treatment. Unfortunately, the rest of the country—most of it—does not have coverage, and even those states with mandated benefits do not provide coverage to those who are insured through public programs (e.g., Medicaid). Since most infertility treatment is very expensive, in particular the new reproductive technologies, in states that do not have mandated coverage, only the financially comfortable can afford it.

  This unequal access to treatment appears to violate the principle of justice, as not all infertile people are being treated equally, and many of those in need are not getting the help that is available to them. Efforts to revamp the healthcare system during the Clinton administration have proven disastrous, and the hopes of many infertile couples have been dashed. With cost as the bottom line, and with the proliferation of managed care in this country, those states without insurance mandates will probably be hard pressed in the future to pass the necessary legislation providing everyone—at least those with health insurance—equal access to treatment.

Even when insurance coverage is available to a couple, the question is raised as to whether *any* couple should be able to avail themselves of *any* treatment. For example, the odds of delivering a baby from an IVF procedure decrease with the age of the women, and after age 40 the success rates for a "take home baby" are very low—about 5% per cycle. After age 45, the success rates are close to zero. Other diagnoses may also lead to equally poor prognoses. Since healthcare dollars are not unlimited, and the cost of an IVF cycle is approximately $6,000 to $9,000, a question is raised about whether it is reasonable to expect insurance companies to cover a treatment that has such a slim chance of working.

Access Based on Personal Criteria

There are people who have the ability to pay for treatment for infertility, but who are denied it based on medical, social, or moral reasons. These reasons may be considered discriminatory, and may someday be tested in a court of law. Until legal precedent is established, however, physicians are forced to make decisions about treatment according to their ethical perspectives.

Single Women

Until recently, many in vitro fertilization programs in this country refused to treat single women; some still refuse. Although physicians have always had the discretion to deny treatment if they had moral objections, refusing to treat single women may be a violation of antidiscrimination statutes. The following case is an example of a situation that was problematic for the medical team at an infertility clinic. The patient's single status made the situation even more disturbing.

Case Example

A 43-year-old single woman presented at a clinic requesting donor insemination. She had a history of manic-depressive illness that necessitated three hospitalizations; the last one was two years ago. Her illness has appeared to be in control since then. She has a steady, well-paying job. Her psychopharmacologist suggested she find other outlets for her nurturing instincts. Her psychotherapist has taken a neutral stand.

This case also raises the question, which we have previously addressed, about whether or not the practitioner should also be a gatekeeper. In this situation, the medical team was willing to play that role and they ultimately did decide against treating the woman. However, if she had been married to an emotionally stable man, the decision probably would have been otherwise. In making the final decision, many factors were considered: It was determined that she had few supports in her life to whom she could turn if she became ill; because of her history, it could be presumed that she would experience other episodes of depression or mania leading to hospitalization; because of her single status the offspring would not have the benefit of having another more stable parent. Furthermore, she was at increased risk for psychiatric illness during pregnancy or, more likely during her postpartum. No one on the medical team felt that a child should be deliberately conceived under such circumstances, and they could not, in good conscience, offer her treatment. The patient was disappointed to learn of the decision, yet she understood why it had been made and was able to accept it.

Lesbian Couples

Many clinics refuse to treat lesbian couples; others open their doors, providing that there is a documented infertility problem, and still others will treat the couple even if all they require is donor sperm.

Case Example

A lesbian couple recently applied to a well-known IVF program requesting that one of them go through stimulation and egg retrieval, that the eggs be inseminated with the sperm of her partner's brother, and that the resulting embryos be transferred into the partner. Although presumably either woman was capable of conception via artificial insemination, each wanted to have a biological stake in the offspring—one through providing her genetic material and the other through her gestational connection.

The medical team discussed the request and ultimately decided against treating the couple because neither had a "legitimate" infertility problem. Another local program, however, granted their request. This situation also raises a related question about access: Should insurance companies pay for treatment (in states that have mandated coverage) if a couple is not technically infertile? In this situation, the couple has what might be called "gender-related infertility"—neither has a Y chromosome, and their goal of producing a child who is biologically a product of the two of them is not possible without medical intervention.

Age

The issue of age is a fairly new ethical dilemma for those in the field of reproductive medicine, due to the recent proliferation of ovum donation programs. Prior to ovum donation, a woman had to end treatment when she became menopausal or perimenopausal; that is, all tests indicated that her egg quality was not sufficient for conception. Because ovum donation is now available, age is no longer a barrier to pregnancy. The question facing medical ethicists, as well as those who treat infertile couples, is whether, and if so, when, is a woman too old to bear and raise a child?

There are practitioners who claim that their responsibility is not to make judgments about how old women should or should not be when they give birth, but rather to help infertile couples have children if and when they desire them. Consequently, there are many physicians who report having helped women in their late 50s and early 60s bear children. Other clinics and physicians, believing that it is not in the best interest of a child to be born to older parents, have taken a stand and set age limits for treatment eligibility. In a recent survey of 82 IVF programs that offered ovum donation, 22 reported they had no upper age limits (Braverman et al., 1993). This issue is one in which legal and ethical considerations intersect; although it has not yet been tested in a court of law, some attorneys believe age may be protected under antidiscrimination statutes.

Treating HIV-Positive Couples

This is currently a controversial topic in reproductive medical centers, many of which require HIV testing prior to treatment. Many clinics have refused to treat HIV couples because they believe it is unethical to bring a child into the world who is likely to have a fatal disease and who will experience the loss of a parent. On the other hand, some argue that it is more unethical to deny these patients treatments if they are making an informed choice, especially if the odds are in favor of having a healthy (HIV negative) child. Clinics may also be concerned about the welfare of their staff—in particular those who handle blood and semen products—and do not want to expose them to possible HIV infection.

Recent data has appeared that may soon make this issue moot. Studies indicate that if a particular sperm washing protocol is performed on the semen of HIV-positive men, the risk of passing on the virus to the fetus is practically eliminated—providing the mother tests negative for HIV (Semprini, 1993). Research also indicates that perinatal transmission of the virus in women who test positive for HIV can be greatly reduced if certain treatment regimens are followed (Mofenson & Balsley, 1994). Furthermore if clinical staff members handling bodily fluid exercise universal precautions, the risk of contracting HIV through their job is virtually nonexistent. As this evidence becomes empirically validated, clinics may have to rethink their policy regarding treatment of HIV-positive couples.

One might convincingly argue that to refuse treatment to people based on age, sexual orientation, health, or marital status is a violation of the principles of autonomy and justice—that the new reproductive technologies are available to people who need them, and that those in need are entitled to them and are exercising their right to personal autonomy and procreative liberty. On the other hand, practitioners can argue that treating such couples puts their offspring at risk and is a violation of the basic tenet: to do no harm. The ethical issues involved in treating older women, single women, lesbian couples, and people with human immunodeficiency virus also interface with the law in that they may pertain to antidiscrimination statutes. If the law is tested at the level of the Supreme Court, clinics may not be allowed in the future to refuse treatment to these categories of patients. Thus lawmakers whose job is to uphold the

Constitution by protecting an individual's fundamental right to life, liberty, and the pursuit of happiness may sometimes find themselves clashing with the viewpoints of those working in the field of reproductive medicine.

CONCLUSION

The principles of autonomy, beneficence, and justice—ethical principles that have been employed frequently in the field of medical ethics—have been explored in relation to the new reproductive technologies. This chapter has covered many of the prominent questions, issues, and dilemmas debated frequently by practitioners of these technologies, yet it has not, by any means, been an exhaustive survey. Five broad issues have been identified: the rights of individuals to reproduce versus the rights/best interest of offspring; the right to information regarding one's genetic origins; liberation versus exploitation of women for reproductive purposes; the moral status of embryos; and access to treatment. And, as we have seen, each of these broad issues gives rise to additional, often more complex ones.

The process of ethical decision making is indeed complicated in the field of reproductive technology. What might be good for one person, or one group of people, may not be good for someone else who associates closely with that person or who may be born as a result. What is good for an individual or couple may not be what is good for society in the long run. What is morally acceptable to one person may be unacceptable to another. Furthermore, the principles of autonomy, beneficence, and justice do not always exist in harmony with one another, and in making ethically sound decisions, one or more of these principles may have to be compromised.

Despite the desire of some to turn back the clock, it continues to tick. Each year the world of high technological treatment brings new advances—each more astounding than the last. And each step up the high-tech ladder puts practitioners on an even more slippery slope, in which the stakes are significantly higher than they were in 1978, prior to the birth of Louise Brown. Today, the possibilities facing infertile couples are numerous; yet there are drawbacks. Treatment can become prolonged, expensive, and invasive, and couples can easily become overwhelmed by the social, psychological, legal, and—as this chapter has demonstrated—the ethical implications of these new technologies.

REFERENCES

Annas, G. (1980). Beyond the best interests of the sperm donor. *Family Law Quarterly, 14,* 1–13.

Annas, G. (1991). Determining the fate of gestational mothers. *Women's Health Institute Journal, 1,* 158–160.

Baran, A., & Pannor, R. (1989). *Lethal secrets.* New York: Warner Books.

Bartholet, E. (1993). *Family bonds.* Boston: Houghton Mifflin.

Baruch, E. (1988). A womb of his own. In *Embryos, ethics, and human rights* (pp. 135–139). New York: Haworth Medical Press.

Beauchamp, T. L., & Walters, L. (1982). *Contemporary issues in bioethics.* Belmont, CA: Wadsworth.

Braverman, A. M. (1993). Ovum donor task force of the psychological special interests group of the American Fertility Society. Survey results on the current practice of ovum donation. *Fertility and Sterility, 59,* 1216–1220.

Cooper, S., & Glazer, E. (1994). *Beyond infertility: The New paths to parenthood.* New York: Lexington Books.

Daniels, K. (1987). Semen donors in New Zealand: Their characteristics and attitudes. *Clinical Reproductive Fertility, 56,* 177–190.

Davis v. Davis, 842 S.W. 2d 588, Tennessee Supreme Court, 1/28/92.

Elias, S., & Annas, G. (1986). Social policy considerations in noncoital reproduction. *Journal of the American Medical Society, 255,* 62–68.

Harrison, M. (1991). Financial incentives for surrogacy. *Women's Health Institute Journal, 1,* 145–147.

Johnson v. Calvert, 851 P. 2d 776 (1993) Daily Appellate Report (California Supreme Court.

Klock, S. (1993). Psychological aspects of donor insemination. In D. Greenfeld (Ed.), *Infertility and reproductive clinics of North America* (pp. 455–470). W. B. Sanders Co., Philadelphia, PA.

Klock, S., & Maier, D. (1991). Psychological factors related to donor insemination. *Fertility and Sterility, 56,* 484–495.

Mahlstedt, P., & Greenfeld, D. (1989). Assisted reproductive technology with donor gametes: The need for patient preparation. *Fertility and Sterility, 52,* 908–914.

Mofenson, L., & Balsley, J. (1994). Recommendations of the U.S. Public Health Service task force on the use of zidovudine to reduce perinatal transmission of human immunodeficiency virus. *Morbidity and Mortality Weekly Report, 43,* 1–20.

Noble, E. (1987). Having your baby by donor ensemination. Boston: Houghton Mifflin.

Robertson, J. A. (1994). *Children of choice: Freedom and the new reproductive technologies.* Princeton, NJ: Princeton University Press.

Rossing, M. A., Daling, J., Weiss, N., Moore, D., Self, S. (1994). Ovarian tumors in a cohort of infertile women. *New England Journal of Medicine, 331,* 771–776.

Rutzinger, J. C., & Bovone, J. (1987). Instruction on respect for human life in its origin and on the dignity of procreation. Vatican: *Congregation for the Doctrine of the Faith.*

Semprini, A. (1993). Insemination of HIV-negative women with processed semen of HIV-positive partners. *The Lancet, 341,* 1343.

Warnock, M. (1984). The Warnock report on human fertilization and embryology. London: Her Majesty's Secretary Office.

Whittemore, A. S., Itnyre, J., & Harris, R. (1992). Collaborative analysis of twelve U.S. case-control studies. *American Journal of Epidemiology, 136,* 1184–1203.

CHAPTER 4

Stress and Infertility in Women

ALICE D. DOMAR

HISTORICAL BACKGROUND AND LITERATURE REVIEW

Stress and infertility have been linked since biblical times, when it was written that a woman's emotions could lead to a barren state. This assumption was only challenged in the latter part of this century, when a series of studies failed to document a psychological basis for infertility in women. Indeed, the pendulum swung far in the direction of the medical model in the 1980s, with leading infertility textbooks describing an organic cause for 95% of infertility, with the remaining 5% attributed to "unexplained" or as yet undiagnosed infertility. Thus, until approximately five years ago, the medical community focused on organic causes and highly technological treatments for overcoming infertility, and stress was acknowledged as *the result* of and not a potential cause of fertility difficulties.

The concept of infertility as a significant stressor is well supported. In a recent study of 338 infertile women and 39 matched fertile controls, the prevalence and predictability of depression were assessed (Domar, Broome, Zuttermeister, Seibel, & Friedman, 1992). The infertile women had significantly higher depression scores than the control subjects and also had twice the prevalence of depressive symptoms. Infertile women are not only significantly more depressed than their fertile counterparts, their depression and anxiety levels are equivalent to women with heart disease, cancer, or HIV-positive status (Domar, Zuttermeister, & Friedman, 1993). Multiple studies on women with infertility have demonstrated significantly higher levels of anxiety and depression than in fertile women. The prevalence of depressive symptoms is worrisome, with research indicating that up to 11% of infertile women meet the criteria for a current major depressive episode. Women undergoing high-tech treatment may be even more at risk. In one study of in vitro fertilization (IVF) patients, depression as measured by the Beck Depression Inventory was noted in 34% of the women prior to starting a cycle and in 64% after completing an unsuccessful cycle (Garner, Arnold, & Gray, 1984). Infertile women usually report that infertility is the worst crisis of their lives, worse even than divorce or the loss of a parent (Mahlstedt, MacDuff, & Bernstein, 1987).

With the explosion of highly technological treatment for overcoming infertility, such as in vitro fertilization (IVF), gamete intrafallopian transfer (GIFT), and other modifications of so-called test-tube treatments, infertile couples are faced with numerous treatment choices, many carrying high financial prices and low chances of success. Recent highly publicized reports of a possible link between infertility medications and ovarian cancer have served to only burden these couples more. Many infertile women now have nightmares of finally giving birth to their "miracle baby," only to die from the side effects of the medications used to make that miracle possible.

Infertile women report stress from numerous sources including the treatment itself, effects on the marital relationship, the financial impact of treatment, acute jealousy when friends, family members, or coworkers conceive, interference with job/career plans, and lack of support from loved ones. Infertility treatment can create distress both from physical and psychological factors. Many treatments involve close monitoring by vaginal ultrasound and blood work, often assessed in the early morning on a daily basis, for up to two weeks per cycle. Infertility medications can lead to physical symptoms such as fatigue, nausea, bloating, headaches, and hot flashes, and psychological symptoms such as irritability, depression, and anxiety. The marital relationship is affected by numerous factors, including scheduled intercourse, conflicting opinions on the course of treatment, and different reactions to the infertility itself. The financial impact can be profound on infertile individuals living in any of the 40 states in the United States without mandated infertility insurance coverage. Pergonal, one of the more frequently prescribed medications, can cost $2,000 per treatment cycle. IVF costs anywhere from $7,000 to $12,000 per cycle. Despite the high cost of treatment, many infertile women report that one of the most difficult aspects of infertility is dealing with their emotions of jealousy and envy when learning of the pregnancies of others. Since most infertile women are in their late 20s, 30s, or early 40s, most are surrounded by evidence of others' fertility. In addition, the impact of infertility on job or career plans can be profound. Since many treatment cycles require daily morning monitoring, women are often late to work. Most infertile women avoid travel during the time of ovulation to ensure ready access to their husband. Many infertile women turn down promotions or new job opportunities, preferring to stay with a less attractive job but one with more flexibility to pursue treatment. Finally, many infertile women report inadequate support from family and friends. Despite good intentions, telling an infertile woman to "just relax," or "just don't think about it so much," places the responsibility of nonconception on the woman. It suggests that she is too tense or uptight, and may be construed as a case of "blaming the victim."

Since it is intolerable for many infertile women to be in close proximity to pregnant women or infants, they tend to avoid social and family gatherings, resulting in further isolation. In addition to these tangible stressors, infertile women often blame themselves for their infertility, feeling guilty for early sexual activity, prior abortions, or poor health habits. Thus, infertility can adversely affect a woman's physical and mental health, marriage, job, financial situation, and social and family networks.

The fact that infertility creates a significant amount of distress, however, does not necessarily mean that the relationship is unidirectional. It is quite possible that infertility causes stress and that stress may contribute to infertility.

Several studies indicate stress may play at least a contributory role in infertility in women. High levels of distress can lead to tubal spasm, irregular ovulation, and/or hormonal abnormalities. In a study of women undergoing donor sperm insemination (Demyttenaere, Nijs, Steeno, & Koninckx, 1988), women completed the Spielberger State Trait Anxiety Inventory prior to starting the insemination process. Those with higher levels of general trait anxiety prior to undergoing inseminations took significantly longer to conceive and were also significantly more likely to miscarry than those with lower levels of anxiety. Recent research supports a connection between psychosocial distress and ovarian dysfunction (Wasser, Sewall, & Soules, 1993). In this prospective study on women at the beginning of their infertility diagnostic workup, certain aspects of psychosocial stress, including lack of social support, conflict with her father, and inadequate support from her best friend, were significantly related to hormonally based infertility, such as luteal phase defect.

Other prospective research has documented conceptions in infertile women after demonstrating spontaneous decreases in infertility-related anxiety (Rodriguez, Bermudez, Ponce de Leon, & Castro, 1983). In addition, depression may have an adverse impact on fertility in women. In a study of 330 women who completed a battery of psychological questionnaires as they were preparing to start an IVF cycle (Thiering, Beaurepaire, Jones, Saunders, & Tennant, 1993), there was a significant association between depression and conception among the women who had previously experienced an unsuccessful IVF cycle. There was a 29% conception rate in the women who were not depressed prior to commencing treatment, compared to a 13% conception rate in the women who did report significant depressive symptoms prior to their IVF cycle.

If we hypothesize that stress may contribute to infertility, then it may be hypothesized that stress reduction will improve conception rates. Five studies, including one drug study, have supported this hypothesis.

In a randomized prospective study, Rodriguez et al. (1983) assigned 14 women with unexplained infertility to either an experimental or control group. Subjects in the experimental group received 16 individual sessions of relaxation training, cognitive restructuring, and self-instructional management over an eight-week period. Control subjects received no training. Within the two-month study period, four of the seven experimental subjects conceived while none of the control subjects conceived. In a nonrandomized study, 14 of 63 women scheduled to undergo an IVF cycle accepted an invitation to receive relaxation training over two sessions (Farrar, Holbert, & Drabman, 1990). Sessions included information on what to expect during an IVF treatment cycle, focused breathing techniques to reduce pain, how to cope with pain and anxiety, and instruction in deep muscle relaxation. The women who chose to attend the sessions were significantly more likely to conceive on their first IVF attempt and were also more likely to continue trying if the first attempt failed, resulting in significantly more subsequent pregnancies than women who decided not to attend the sessions.

One drug intervention study supports the role of anxiety reduction in increasing conception rates in infertile women (Sharma & Sharma, 1992). The efficacy of a mild anxiolytic was assessed in 452 women with unexplained infertility. Three hundred ten women took 5 mg thioridazine one hour after their evening meal from days 8 to 18 of their menstrual cycles. The 142 control subjects took a placebo (lactobacillus) at identical times. Patients were followed for the one-year study period. Ninety-four (30.2%) of the experimental subjects conceived compared with 22 (15.42%) of the control subjects, a statistically significant difference. There were no significant differences between the two groups in the rate of miscarriage, fetal malformations, or perinatal mortality.

The final two studies were based on my own work, a clinical behavioral medicine treatment program for infertile women, The Behavioral Medicine Program for Infertility. This group program is based on the Rodriguez et al. model, and was started in 1987 at the New England Deaconess Hospital in Boston. The 10-session program includes instruction in numerous relaxation techniques that elicit the relaxation response, including progressive muscle relaxation, meditation, imagery, yoga, body scan, diaphragmatic breathing, and autogenic training. The program also includes multiple stress-management strategies including learning cognitive restructuring, challenging automatic negative thought patterns, learning or relearning how to be good to oneself, learning how to express emotions through journaling and assertiveness training, and using humor to reduce stress. There is also nutritional and exercise counseling as related to infertility (Domar, Seibel, & Benson, 1990; Domar, Zuttermeister, Seibel, & Benson, 1992). The 110 subjects included in the two studies attended the program from 1987 to 1989 and all participants had documented infertility, with an average duration of over three years.

Participants demonstrated significant preprogram to postprogram reductions in anxiety, depression, anger, and fatigue. Participants also monitored physical symptoms such as insomnia, headaches, and premenstrual symptoms and reported significant reductions in these symptoms by the end of the program. In addition, an average of 34 percent of the participants conceived within six months of completing the program. Of the population who underwent IVF treatment during or immediately following completion of the program, 37% conceived on that cycle, approximately twice the national rate.

Since the clinical program was started in 1987, there have been 30 groups with an average of 15 patients per group. There has been a consistent average conception rate of 35% to 40% during this time. All patients complete the Beck Depression Inventory and the Revised Symptom Checklist 90 both prior to beginning and again after completing the program. All groups demonstrate significant reductions on both scales.

These psychological and conception rate data are based on a nonrandomized, self-selected population, which precludes concluding that stress reduction definitively increases conception and decreases psychological symptoms. However, if one includes the previously mentioned studies, there is a distinct, consistent trend toward conception in women offered stress management and relaxation training. Spontaneous reductions in psychological symptoms in women currently undergoing infertility treatment are rare. In fact, symptoms usually increase with duration of treatment, so that it is likely that the psychological improvement is indeed related to the interventions employed.

There is a paucity of research on psychological interventions for infertile women. Support groups are routinely offered throughout the United States, but there are no published data to date on their efficacy. The application of relaxation training and stress management with infertile women shows early promise in psychological symptom reduction, and an indication of improved conception rates. Since there are no known adverse side effects to this approach, it is logical to continue the investigations on conception rates while simultaneously applying this clinical approach for psychological symptom relief.

THE BEHAVIORAL MEDICINE PROGRAM FOR INFERTILITY

The Behavioral Medicine infertility program is a clinical 10-session weekly evening group program offered to women at any phase of infertility. All patients in the program must have documented infertility (unprotected intercourse for at least one year for those under 35 and for at least six months for those over 35), be under the care of a physician, and must still be pursuing conception. Single women, women with secondary infertility (those with a biological child), women who have adopted but are still pursuing treatment, women who have no problem conceiving but have experienced multiple miscarriages, and women who are attempting conception through either egg or sperm donation are all accepted into the program, based on research that supports the notion that infertility is infertility, no matter what the circumstance (Domar, Broome, Zuttermeister, Seibel, & Friedman, 1992). Approximately half of the participants are involved in the advanced reproductive technologies.

All prospective patients meet with the group leader for a 45- to 50-minute individual assessment appointment. The patient's medical, mental health, social, and health habit history are reviewed. Scores on the Beck Depression Inventory and the Revised Symptom Checklist are assessed to determine if excessive levels of depressive or anxiety symptoms are present. If a patient has the symptoms of a severe clinical depression, alternative or adjunctive therapies are explored with the patient, since cognitive-behavior therapy is not the treatment of choice for severe depression. On many occasions, if it is a borderline situation, the group leader gets an agreement from the patient that if her depressive symptoms do not improve significantly within four weeks of starting the program, she will agree to seek out psychotherapy and/or a psychopharmacological consult.

The middle third of the appointment is spent discussing the patient's goals and expectations. The goal of the program is to assist patients in reducing their level of psychological distress. If the patient's only stated goal is pregnancy, this is thoroughly discussed, since it has not yet been proven that attendance in such a program does indeed increase the chance of conception. Since the current data from the program indicate that 60% of the participants will not get pregnant, it is important for patients to understand the psychological improvement goals as being extremely worthy themselves.

During the last third of the session, the group leader presents information on the peer counselor and buddy systems, describes each session, and provides the opportunity for questions.

Each group includes two peer counselors who attend all sessions. The peer counselors are infertile women who are graduates of a previous group, have mastered the cognitive-behavioral skills, and are of the personality type that they wish to reach out and help others. The peer counselors provide experiential examples throughout the program and in general, serve as role models of infertile women who have used their new skills to "get their lives back."

The buddy system involves each participant being assigned their "buddy" during the first session. Buddies are normally assigned based on geographic proximity of their home, but if there are two people with the same situation (e.g., both having experienced a late pregnancy loss), they are assigned to each other. Buddies are expected to share at least one telephone call each week. When a participant misses a class due to medical procedures, work conflicts, or vacation, her buddy takes notes for her and collects any handouts for her. In addition, since each session begins at 5:30 P.M. and most participants come directly from their workplace, each week a buddy pair is responsible for bringing in a snack for the entire group. The snack is served at the beginning of each session and often becomes very elaborate. By the eighth session, it is not unusual to have flowers, tablecloths, and multiple courses!

Each participant completes a weekly diary card in which she notes how often she elicited the relaxation response, how often she did "mini" breath-focused exercises, any changes in nutrition and exercise habits, and any infertility-related results within the past week. She also notes the frequency, intensity, and any improvement in her symptoms. All participants monitor infertility distress as their primary symptoms and most participants also monitor any other symptoms that they experience, such as insomnia, back, neck, or abdominal pain, depressive symptoms, and PMS.

All participants are charged a materials fee that provides them with a copy of the published patient workbook used in the Division of Behavioral Medicine, *The Wellness Book* (Fireside Press, 1993), a relaxation response audiotape for daily use, and a yoga audiotape, in which the exercises match the figure drawings in *The Wellness Book*. The daily relaxation audiotape contains narrative instruction in breath focus, body scan, and meditation on Side A, and mental imagery of walking to a mountain stream on Side B.

All participants are encouraged to elicit the relaxation response at least once per day for 20 minutes, either by listening to one of their two tapes or by eliciting the relaxation response on their own through an alternative technique learned during the program or known previously. Each week, participants learn a new way to elicit the relaxation response; by the end of the program participants know how to do body scan, breath focus, diaphragmatic breathing, meditation, mindfulness, imagery, yoga, autogenic training, progressive muscle relaxation, and exercise. Patients are also encouraged to elicit the relaxation response during periods of increased stress and/or during medical procedures, since previous research has demonstrated that when patients elicit the relaxation response during invasive medical procedures, there are significant reductions in anxiety, pain, and medication use (Mandle et al., 1990).

The 10 sessions are outlined in Table 4.1. With the exception of Sessions 1, 4, 7, and 10, all sessions begin with a 30-minute optional sharing/support time, followed by a 20-minute relaxation response exercise. Participants then pair up to discuss their progress while the group leader and peer counselors go into a different room to review each patient's diary card. The group leader returns with the peer counselors and anonymously discusses any problems or accomplishments noted in the diaries. There is then a brief lecture on the topic of the week, followed by a paired or small group exercise on that theme. A general group discussion of the exercise follows, and each group ends with a "mini" relaxation exercise.

Session 1, which includes the husbands/partners, is mostly lecture and a general introduction to the program. Session 4 is a 4½ hour session, which includes 90 minutes of yoga, dinner together as a group, and lectures on nutrition and exercise. Session 7 includes the husbands/partners once again; for the first 90 minutes the men have their own meeting with a male therapist to discuss how they are doing while the women discuss emotional expression. The final hour is spent together, listening to the experiences of two prior participants who adopted. Session 9 is the all-day Sunday session, again with husbands/partners.

Case Example

Presenting Problem and Client Description

Rachel (all identifying information has been changed for confidentiality purposes), a 36-year-old substitute junior high school teacher, was seen following a referral by her husband Mark. He had heard about a group treatment program for infertile women from a friend and called the program director. During this preliminary conversation, he reported that he and his wife Rachel had been trying to conceive for three years, and that he could no longer emotionally handle Rachel's distress. He stated that she cried on a daily basis, was disinterested in any of the activities they had previously enjoyed including skiing and bicycling,

TABLE 4.1 Sessions of the Behavioral Medicine Program for Infertility

Session	Topics
1	Introduction to the physiology of the fight or flight response Introduction to the physiology of the relaxation response Program format, goals Participant introductions Relaxation exercise Questions/answers
2	Physiology of diaphragmatic breathing "Mini" relaxation exercises
3	How to be good to yourself How to prioritize one's life to include oneself
4	Yoga Nutrition Exercise Mindfulness
5	Introduction to cognitive restructuring
6	Cognitive restructuring continued Challenging automatic negative thoughts
7	Safe expression of emotions through journaling
8	The impact of infertility on emotional expression Healthy ways to cope with and express anger
9	Yoga How to reduce stress through humor (video) Potluck lunch Mindful walk to feed ducks Couples' paired listening exercise
10	Summary of program Time for participants to discuss and plan meeting on their own Assertiveness training Goodbyes

and refused to attend any social activity if she knew that an infant or a pregnant woman would be present. He reported that for the first two years of conception attempts, Rachel was willing to make love only at midcycle, during ovulation, but since they had attempted more invasive treatment, she was less focused on midcycle intercourse. She had not initiated intercourse in more than a year but was receptive if he initiated it. Mark felt that he had lost the woman he had married and was agreeable to trying anything to help Rachel feel better. He denied that he was significantly affected by the infertility himself. He had been amenable to adoption for the past year, but Rachel refused to discuss it.

Mark was advised to tell Rachel that he had spoken to the program director and that if she was interested in learning stress management and relaxation skills, she should call. She called less than 30 minutes later. She tearfully reported that the infertility was "making her crazy" and "ruining her life." It was agreed that she would be seen for an evaluation.

During the evaluation appointment, Rachel cried frequently, especially when describing the quality of her life. She reported that she and Mark had enjoyed the first two years of their marriage together, had had very satisfying careers, and an excellent sexual relationship. After two years, they stopped using birth control with the anticipation of starting their family. Neither expected a problem, since both were in excellent health and both had fertile siblings. After 15 months, Rachel consulted her gynecologist who did some preliminary tests on both Rachel and Mark. All the tests were normal. Rachel took the medication clomiphene for six months, without success. After a total of two years of trying, Rachel was referred to an infertility specialist who similarly could not determine a physical cause for their fertility problem. Rachel completed three cycles of Pergonal, a daily injected medication, with intrauterine inseminations at ovulation. When these cycles also were unsuccessful, Rachel and Mark completed three cycles of in vitro fertilization. Although Rachel produced multiple normal eggs that fertilized each cycle, conception did not occur. It was at this point that she recognized that she was completely distraught.

Rachel reported that she was "obsessed" with the infertility and that it was adversely impacting many aspects of her life. She had left her job as a college administrator and started substitute teaching because of the demands of the treatment; she avoided friends who were pregnant or had children; she would not let herself exercise or drink alcohol in order to enhance her chances of becoming pregnant; she felt diminished sexual desire; she talked frequently about the infertility with Mark; and she flew into a rage when family members suggested that if she stopped thinking about the infertility, she would conceive. She had attended the first two sessions of an infertility support group but had dropped out when she could not tolerate hearing the infertility histories of the other members. She had been advised by the support group leader to seek out individual psychotherapy, but she said she was not interested in counseling.

Rachel described an unremarkable childhood. She had an older brother who was married with three children, and her parents were alive and in good health. When Rachel first became sexually active at the age of 19, she immediately obtained a diaphragm for birth control and remembers the nurse warning her about the problems of unplanned pregnancy. This warning affected her; she alluded to it several times during the evaluation. She interpreted the warning as a confirmation of her excellent fertility, and thereafter was extremely careful about birth control.

Although Rachel had only one sibling, she had many first cousins and remembered enjoying caring for the younger cousins as she was growing up. The fact that most of these younger cousins were now parents themselves was a source of pain to her. In fact, she reported that all pregnancy announcements were unbearable; she tended to stay home for several days after each one, crying, and refused to attend baby showers or christenings. The only exception to this was the christening for a niece who was her godchild.

Rachel presented as an attractive, well-educated, articulate woman. She could talk about her infertility history calmly but cried when talking about the quality of her current life. Her score on the Beck Depression Inventory was 19, which is in the severe depression range. Her scores on the Symptom Checklist, where the scores are given as T scores with a mean of 50 and a standard deviation of 10, were also high (Table 4.2). Her scores on three of the nine subscales were more than three standard deviations above the mean, with a general severity score of nearly three standard deviations above normal.

She reported that her husband was not "consumed" by the infertility as she was and that they were beginning to argue about it. He wanted to move on to adoption and was reluctant to continue medical treatment. Furthermore, he did not want to listen to her talking about it all the time.

The pros and cons of a group treatment program versus individual treatment were discussed with her. Despite her departure from the support group, she very much wanted to attend our group program, stating that a friend had attended the program and had recommended it highly. In addition, she had seen clips about the group program on the local news and thought that the women on TV looked as if they were having fun together. She reported that in the support group, the other members had spoken of how difficult their infertility was to handle. Rachel felt that she knew how difficult infertility was and did not like hearing it from others, whereas she anticipated learning specific coping skills in the behavioral treatment group. She stated that she wished to become less angry and sad, to learn how to calm herself when distressed, and most of all, to experience relief from the emotional pain. Her written goals for the program were "peace of mind," "feeling better inside," and "to feel whole again."

Case Formulation

Although it was unusual for a patient's husband to make the first contact, in many ways Rachel was a relatively typical infertility patient who presents for treatment. She was experiencing marital strain, career stalling, isolation from family

TABLE 4.2   Rachel's Symptom Checklist 90-Revised Scores*

SCL-90R Dimension	Preprogram	Postprogram
Somatization	68	42
Obsessive Compulsive	81	64
Interpersonal Sensitivity	81	58
Depression	75	56
Anxiety	72	59
Hostility	79	49
Phobic Anxiety	61	54
Paranoid Ideation	72	49
Psychoticism	81	57
General Severity Index	79	56

*Given as T scores with a mean for a nonpsychiatric female sample of 50 and a SD of 10.

and friends, and a strong need for relief. Like many patients who present to our Behavioral Medicine Program for Infertility, she apparently had "hit bottom."

Although Rachel was characteristic of other infertile women in the program in terms of age, duration of infertility, and stage of treatment, her level of distress was somewhat higher than normal. The average Beck Depression Inventory score for patients entering the program is 13.5, which is in the low moderate range, compared to Rachel's score of 19, which places her in the severe range. Her Symptom Checklist scores were also higher than the group norms.

With women like Rachel, we usually consider a number of options. Option 1 is to allow her into the group, monitoring her distress level and impact on the rest of the group closely. Option 2 is to allow her into the group conditionally; she may attend the group but only if she agrees to also attend individual psychotherapy with a therapist experienced with infertility patients. Option 3 is to postpone entry into the group until she has experienced some relief from individual therapy.

Rachel appeared highly motivated to attend the group program and reported that she had no interest in individual psychotherapy. She was very specific about her desire to learn specific coping techniques in a group setting so she could observe the experiences of other patients. We agreed that she would be allowed into the group program with the stipulation that the plan would be reassessed four weeks later. If her level of distress was disruptive to the group, or if she did not notice a significant improvement in her mood, then she would agree to individual treatment. It was possible that she might be asked to leave the group if other participants found her level of distress to be problematic for them.

Course of Treatment

Rachel was accepted into the 10-week behavioral treatment program and her husband accompanied her to the first session. At the first session, when it was her turn to introduce herself, she told the group that infertility was ruining her life and she was desperate for relief. At this session, she learned about the physiology of stress, the physiology of the relaxation response, and general mechanics of the program. All participants are taught to elicit the relaxation response, the physiological changes that accompany any of a number of relaxation techniques. When one elicits the relaxation response, heart rate, blood pressure, and rate of breathing decrease for the duration of the relaxation session. Participants learn a new relaxation response exercise each week.

As stated earlier, each participant is assigned a buddy, another participant who lives closest to her, with the expectation that buddies will speak by telephone weekly and provide a snack for the whole group for one session. Since Rachel's group had an odd number of participants, one of the buddy pairs was instead a triplet group. Rachel was assigned to the triplet group, to decrease the potential impact her high level of distress might have on only one buddy.

Each participant completes a daily diary reporting on their practice of new skills, exercise, and nutrition habits, and general progress. They also note which symptoms they wish to monitor. Rachel chose infertility distress, teeth clenching, and abdominal pain.

By the second session, as noted in her diary, Rachel had started her fourth IVF cycle and reported side effects from the infertility medications. She practiced the relaxation response on five of the previous seven days. During this second session, she learned about diaphragmatic breathing and how to do "mini" relaxation exercises. At the third session, Rachel reported increased infertility distress due to the current IVF cycle, elicited the relaxation response four out of seven days, and did "minis" on a daily basis. She learned about taking time for herself during the day, and kept a "time pie" of her daily activities to monitor how she spent her free time.

The fourth session is a half-day session, dedicated to yoga, exercise, and nutritional counseling. In her diary, she reported that she was having a difficult time keeping her anxiety under control during the IVF cycle, had only elicited the relaxation response twice, but had noted decreased abdominal pain. She also noted improvements in her eating habits. At the fifth session, Rachel noted in her diary that the IVF cycle was going well, that she was eating three well-balanced meals per day and nutritional snacks, and had elicited the relaxation response five times during the week. However, her teeth clenching was worse.

During the fifth and sixth sessions, cognitive restructuring was introduced, a method developed to identify and alter negative thought patterns. Rachel told the group that her most recurrent negative thought was "this is all my fault." When questioned by the group leader and the other participants, she recollected that in her efforts to use birth control most effectively as a college student after the "fertility warning" from the nurse, she had used whole tubes of spermicide in her diaphragm. She was convinced that the spermicide overdose had somehow damaged her cervix, causing her infertility. It was explained to her that it was highly unlikely that spermicide would damage her cervix, and even if it had, the inseminations and IVF treatments completely bypassed her cervix, so that it was impossible that her birth control behavior was the cause of the infertility. She then started to cry, saying that if the infertility wasn't her fault, then who could she blame for her misery? She reported that there had to be a reason for her infertility. Several group members went up to Rachel, hugged her, and told her that they too were constantly seeking a reason for the infertility but that sometimes things are just bad luck or fate. When Rachel was asked to restructure her negative thought from "this is my fault," she came up with "I didn't cause the infertility and I am doing everything I possibly can to try to get pregnant."

At the sixth session, Rachel told the group that her IVF cycle was unsuccessful. She reported feeling "numb," rather than the uncontrolled anxiety she had experienced after previous unsuccessful IVF cycles. On her diary card, her infertility distress was unchanged, the teeth clenching was worse, but the abdominal pain was improved. She had elicited the relaxation response eight times the previous week but had slacked off on the "mini" relaxations and nutritional improvements. This session was devoted to a continuation of participants taking turns doing cognitive restructuring in small groups. Rachel was very supportive to others in her group, sharing how extremely effective the exercise had been for her.

By the seventh session, Rachel reported in her diary that she was feeling calmer about her infertility and was considering adoption. She told the group that she had suddenly realized that her child did not have to be her flesh and blood to make her a mother. This session was devoted to emotional expression, using Pennebaker's work on the healing power of writing down one's thoughts and feelings (Pennebaker, Kiecolt-Glaser, & Glaser, 1988). Rachel wrote for 20 minutes and reported feeling relieved by the end of the exercise. She was markedly less anxious during this session, and other participants commented on her obvious improvement.

The eighth session was the all-day Sunday session with the husbands. The day was spent doing 90 minutes of yoga, viewing a videotape on how to reduce stress using humor, a mindful walk along the river behind the hospital feeding ducks, paired listening exercises with their spouse, and a potluck lunch. Rachel laughed throughout the day and was openly affectionate with Mark, holding his hand during the video and hugging him after the walk. In her diary, she reported having infertility decisions to make but no increase in distress. At the ninth session, she reported that she had loved the Sunday session. She felt that it had been the best day she had had with Mark in years. She had made an appointment to get a second opinion from another infertility specialist and was continuing to work on cognitive restructuring, which she was finding very helpful in decreasing her distress.

At the tenth and final session, Rachel reported both in her diary and to the group that she was feeling much better. She was experiencing less infertility-related distress, and fewer physical symptoms. She also told the group that she had chosen an adoption agency and had requested an application. She thanked the group for helping her turn her life around, and stated that she felt again like the person she had been prior to the infertility.

Outcome and Prognosis

During her individual discharge assessment appointment with the group leader, Rachel was cheerful and appreciative. She was scheduled to undergo her fifth IVF cycle at a different hospital but had also nearly completed the adoption application. She reported that when the new IVF center had to postpone a test, she was surprisingly calm and rational. Rachel proudly reported that Mark had been amazed at this new calmness, and could not believe how much she had improved in such a short time. Rachel also commented that her mother and other family members had remarked at how happy she was.

When Rachel's test scores from the intake assessment were shown to her, and compared with the current scores (Table 4.2), she showed no surprise at the significant improvement. She said that she knew that she had become psychologically healthy again. Her Beck Depression Inventory score went from a score of 19 preprogram to a current score of 6, well within the normal range. In fact, the average fertile woman's score is 5 (Domar, Broome, Zuttermeister, Seibel, & Friedman, 1992). Rachel also demonstrated an excellent improvement in health habits.

Rachel reported decreased infertility distress, abdominal pain, and teeth clenching by the end of the program. When questioned, she attributed most of her improvement to the use of relaxation and cognitive restructuring.

Two months after the program ended, Rachel underwent her fifth IVF cycle. She reported that she remained calm and felt in control during the treatment, and continued to practice her new coping skills. Two weeks later, she had a

positive pregnancy test and the pregnancy is progressing normally. She attributed the pregnancy to two things: her improved emotional state achieved from
participation in the treatment program, as well as a slightly different treatment
protocol at the new IVF center. There is no way to determine if either of these
changes were directly responsible for the pregnancy, or if instead Rachel finally
got lucky.

Although Rachel is happy and enjoying her pregnancy, even reveling in her
morning sickness, she is now experiencing what many infertile women report
upon conceiving. She is becoming increasingly aware of other stressors in her
life that she ignored during the crisis of infertility, such as financial worries, her
parents' advancing ages, and the career she had abandoned due to infertility.
She has been encouraged to use her behavioral skills to help with these life stressors, and in fact reported that she feels more confident now in her ability to
weather difficult situations.

Rachel worked hard to learn methods and skills that she could use to help
herself feel better. She learned that it is permissible to feel anger, she learned
how to laugh at difficult situations, and she learned how to take care of herself.
As motherhood approaches and with it new stressors and challenges, Rachel has
been able to use her newly recognized strengths to buffer the difficult times.
She learned that she can survive a crisis, which will serve her well in the future.

CONCLUSION

The case example shows the application of a behavioral medicine approach for
individuals with a physical problem that causes psychological distress. Since it
is well documented that infertility causes significant psychological distress,
and because it is suspected that such distress may then contribute to the infertility problem itself, a chicken-and-egg kind of situation is produced. Relaxation training and stress management can break the vicious cycle in some
patients where stress may be contributing to the infertility. For other patients
who have a completely organic cause for their infertility but who are suffering
psychologically from the process, a treatment approach such as the one described in this chapter can relieve them of much of their distress. Thus, since
there is no way at the current time to predict who will conceive following behavioral treatment, but because virtually all patients who attend such a program experience psychological relief, it makes sense to offer such a treatment
approach to all infertility patients. At the very least, participants will feel better, a worthy goal on its own.

Although Rachel was highly emotional during the first several sessions,
which had the potential of alienating or frightening other participants, her obvious pain served to facilitate group bonding. They came together to help her
feel better. In addition, a number of other members of the group actually reported that listening to her early on in the program actually made them feel better about how they were handling their infertility! They reported that their
husbands and friends had made them feel that they were overreacting to the in-

fertility, but Rachel's obvious extreme level of distress made them feel that they were in fact coping pretty well.

Although Rachel and the group itself did very well, it might be advisable to have several individual sessions with such a distressed patient prior to enrolling in the group program. It is often a safer situation for the group as a whole to treat truly acute distress prior to allowing a member into the group. The group leader could have seen Rachel on an individual basis to teach her relaxation skills. When Rachel was feeling calmer and more in control, she could join the next group. It was lucky that Rachel brought the group together, rather than scaring them off. A similar patient might alienate the whole group, causing members to drop out.

I am currently directing in a five-year NIMH-funded study to establish if it is possible to prevent depression in infertile women. Three hundred women who have been attempting conception for one to two years are being randomized to participate in a behavioral medicine group, a support group, or routine care. Subjects are being followed until they conceive or until they reach four years of infertility. The goals of this project are to determine whether it is possible to prevent the development of depression in infertile women; which intervention is the most effective at preventing depression and treating anxiety, low self-esteem, and marital difficulties; and whether either intervention leads to increased conception rates.

The Behavioral Medicine Program for Infertility is an excellent treatment for emotional distress in infertile women. It is not known whether women who participate in this program have a greater chance of conceiving. I hope the answer will be forthcoming at the completion of the five-year study in 1999. In the meantime, relieving intense emotional pain is enough.

REFERENCES

Demyttenaere, K., Nijs, P., Steeno, O., & Koninckx, P. (1988). Anxiety and conception rates in donor insemination. *Journal of Psychosomatic Obstetrics and Gynecology,* 8, 175–181.

Domar, A., Broome, A., Zuttermeister, P., Seibel, M., & Friedman, R. (1992). The prevalence and predictability of depression in infertile women. *Fertility and Sterility,* 58, 1158–1163.

Domar, A., Seibel, M., & Benson, H. (1990). The Mind/Body Program for Infertility: A new treatment program for women with infertility. *Fertility and Sterility,* 53, 246–249.

Domar, A., Zuttermeister, P., & Friedman, R. (1993). The psychological impact of infertility: A comparison with patients with other medical conditions. *Journal of Psychosomatic Obstetrics and Gynecology,* 14, 45–52.

Domar, A., Zuttermeister, P., Seibel, M., & Benson, H. (1992). Psychological improvement in infertile women following behavioral treatment: A replication. *Fertility and Sterility,* 58, 144–147.

Farrar, D., Holbert, L., & Drabman, R. (1990, July). Can behavioral-based preparation counseling increase pregnancy after in vitro fertilization? Paper presented at the meeting of In Vitro Fertilization Psychologists, Melbourne, Australia.

Garner, C., Arnold, E., & Gray, H. (1984). The psychological impact of in vitro fertilization. *Fertility and Sterility, 41* (abstr. suppl), 28.

Mahlstedt, P., MacDuff, S., & Bernstein, J. (1987). Emotional factors and the in vitro fertilization and embryo transfer process. *Journal of In Vitro Fertilization and Embryo Transfer, 4,* 232.

Mandle, C., Domar, A., Harrington, D., Leserman, J., Friedman, R., & Benson, H. (1990). The use of the relaxation response in alleviating pain and anxiety in patients undergoing femoral arteriograms. *Radiology, 174,* 737.

Pennebaker, J., Kiecolt-Glaser, J., & Glaser, R. (1988). Disclosure of traumas and immune function: Health implications for psychotherapy. *Journal of Consulting and Clinical Psychology, 56,* 239–245.

Rodriguez, B., Bermudez, L., Ponce de Leon, E., & Castro, L. (1983, December). The relationship between infertility and anxiety: Some preliminary findings. Paper presented at the Second World Congress of Behavior Therapy, Washington, DC.

Sharma, J., & Sharma, S. (1992). Role of thioridazine in unexplained infertility. *International Journal of Obstetrics and Gynecology, 37,* 37.

Thiering, P., Beaurepaire, J., Jones, M., Saunders, D., & Tennant, C. (1993). Mood state as a predictor of treatment outcome after in vitro fertilization/embryo transfer technology (IVF/ET). *Journal of Psychosomatic Research, 37,* 481.

Wasser, S., Sewall, G., & Soules, M. (1993). Psychosocial stress as a cause of infertility. *Fertility and Sterility, 59,* 685–689.

CHAPTER 5

The Course of Infertility: Immediate and Long-Term Reactions

SANDRA R. LEIBLUM and DOROTHY A. GREENFELD

> All my life I dreamed of having babies. I cannot imagine a life that does not include them.

> We were so careful, we wanted to wait until the time was right. What a waste!

> We come from such big families, this makes no sense. Nothing like this has ever happened to us before.

Infertility is not uncommon—one in six couples will be affected (Aral & Cates, 1983; Mosher, 1987; Mosher & Pratt, 1991)—but it is almost always *unexpected.* And though reports of infertility are frequently featured in the news, the experience for most couples is still one of isolation and desolation, a sense of being infertile in a fertile and child-centered world. Gradually coming to terms with the reality of the problem is usually a painfully distressing process that affects some more than others, and changes over time, but it is this distress that often prompts the infertile client or couple to seek psychotherapy.

Most people take their fertility for granted. Couples entering infertility treatment typically have scrupulously guarded against an unplanned pregnancy in order to wait until the "time was right" to begin their families (Leiblum, 1987). Often their initial confidence in their ability to procreate is so great that, when there is a problem, denial and disbelief are their first responses. Denial is the usual beginning of what is commonly referred to as a "life crisis" for infertile couples (Batterman, 1985; Covington, 1988; Menning, 1980). Denial may be followed by an acute phase of anxiety and uncertainty and, as infertility treatment extends over time, may become chronic (Berg & Wilson, 1991) and culminate in feelings of loss, depression, and grief (Mahlstedt, 1985; Menning, 1980).

Although clinically significant psychopathology in this population is rare (Downey et al., 1989; Freeman et al., 1987; Morrow, Thoreson, & Penney, 1995), infertility is undeniably psychologically stressful (Downey et al., 1989; Freeman et al., 1987; Mahlstedt, MacDuff, & Bernstein, 1987), and the stress may vary over time (Berg & Wilson, 1990). Recent advances in medical technology have given infertile couples hope, but the promise of medical treatment of infertility is not without emotional and psychological costs. It is now generally acknowledged that not only is the experience of infertility distressful, but also the rigors of its accompanying medical workup and treatment (Berger, 1980; Daniluk, 1988; Takefman, Brender, Boiven, & Tulandi, 1990).

The combination of infertility and its arduous treatment can have a long-lasting and deleterious impact on marital, sexual, social and familial relationships (Daniluk, 1988; Leiblum, 1994; see also Leiblum, Chapter 8, this volume). How do these changes manifest themselves? Is there a common pattern to these reactions for individuals and couples when confronted with infertility? Can there be an ultimate resolution, or do infertile women and men struggle with this "insult" indefinitely? What can the psychotherapist do to help? This chapter will describe the typical course of dealing with infertility, examining both immediate and long-term psychological responses of individuals and couples affected with this problem. Gender differences between women and men receiving the diagnosis of infertility will be explored in greater depth in Chapter 6 by Daniluk. The role of the psychotherapist working with the infertile couple will be discussed along with an extended case illustration and suggestions for both brief and long-term psychotherapeutic interventions.

IS INFERTILITY ASSOCIATED WITH PSYCHIATRIC DISORDER?

Historically, women were considered responsible for infertility—either directly, through anatomic or endocrinologic defects or indirectly—through unconscious fear, anger, and repression. Indeed, the psychiatric and gynecologic literature during the 25-year period from 1945 to the early 1970s nearly uniformly supports the hypothesis that psychological state—particularly in women—plays an important role in causing infertility (Benedek, 1952; Bos & Cleghorn, 1958; Deutsch, 1944; Fischer, 1953; Kroger & Freed, 1950).

The psychogenically sterile female, although consciously wanting a baby, was thought subconsciously to reject pregnancy, childbirth, and motherhood (Deutsch, 1944; Kroger & Freed, 1950). In addition to rejecting motherhood, she was believed to be involved in a "hostile mother identification"—anger and rejection of her own mother (Benedek, 1952; Deutsch, 1944; Rubenstein, 1951). Early psychoanalytic authors suggested that infertility also often signaled a conflict between motherhood and career for some women (Sandler, 1961).

In the late 1960s and early 1970s, studies began to appear that questioned such simplistic ideas about psychological causes of infertility by comparing matched groups of fertile and infertile women and finding no significant differences in their psychological makeup (Mai, Munday, & Rump, 1972; Noyes & Chapnick, 1964; Seward, Wagner, Heinrich, Block, & Myerhoff, 1965). In addition, clinical reports indicated that there are certain predictable and apparently normal emotional responses to infertility and its treatment; that couples experiencing infertility need emotional support; and that there is an important role for mental health professionals in the infertility service for psychological assessment, supportive counseling, and education of infertile couples (Berger, 1977; Menning, 1975, 1976, 1979, 1980). Attention has focused more recently on supporting infertile individuals and minimizing the destructive emotional consequences of infertility.

THE SIGNIFICANCE OF PROCREATION

The importance of procreation to most couples is widely acknowledged. It is an important part of adult development and identity to be *capable* of reproduction, even if ultimately couples decide they do not want to become parents. Most women need to feel reassured about the "proper" functioning of their reproductive selves, that they are not "defective" or deficient since their view of themselves as women is traditionally associated with their potential procreative role as mothers. Many men, too, need to be capable of successful penetration and impregnation in order to feel secure in both their masculinity and sexuality. These needs and concerns are distinct from, though obviously related to, the wish to have and raise children (Rosenthal, 1993). Infertile couples are confronted with issues and questions that couples from the so-called fertile community may never have faced or even considered. Questions such as "How important is it to have children? Can we lead full, productive lives without them? Can we love an adopted child?" are discussed and thoughtfully, even obsessively, considered.

Some infertile patients will become pregnant shortly after ending treatment. Others will eventually conceive only after months or even years of physically rigorous, financially costly, and psychologically challenging treatment in infertility centers. A third group will never become pregnant. Whether a couple conceives after brief treatment, whether the process to achieve pregnancy is prolonged and complex, or whether conception never occurs, the evaluations and interventions associated with infertility are typically frustrating and stressful. Although individuals differ in their reactions to the stress of infertility, most acknowledge that it is a major life crisis, a stressor akin in severity to divorce and death (Mahlstedt, 1985). Domar, Broome, Zuttermeister, and Friedman (1992) reported that the anxiety and depression scores of infertile women are similar to those associated with other serious medical conditions (e.g., chronic pain, cancer, hypertension, and cardiac disease).

INITIAL REACTIONS TO AN INFERTILITY DIAGNOSIS

One client describes this unexpected predicament with dismay and some bitterness:

> We thought we were doing everything right. We waited until we both had grad-
> uated from school, both had excellent careers, we even bought a home. We
> wasted so much time. . . . I can't believe this is happening to us. I guess it's such
> a stupid thing to say, now that I know more about it, but my husband and I both
> come from big, fertile families. In fact, when I was a child the standing joke
> between my mother and her sisters was that they need only look at their hus-
> bands and they got pregnant! It seems like such a sick joke now. . . .

An ongoing issue for infertile individuals is the pressure of time. Therapists hear a great deal from their infertile clients about how much time they feel they have wasted using birth control, protecting themselves from getting pregnant, even time spent making the critical decision about whether or not to have children. Envy and resentment toward those around them for their seemingly eas-ily conceived pregnancies turns into guilt and self-recrimination for feeling such ungenerous thoughts toward friends and family. Anger and resentment is sometimes turned on the medical treatment team and their apparent failure to appreciate this time pressure:

> All those months I wasted with my gynecologist who kept telling me nothing
> was wrong, that "these things take time." And, then, one year went by in which
> nothing was done. I've lost a whole year! *I'm almost 35 and I feel that time is*
> *running out!*

Women who are over 40 are particularly plagued by feelings of having "wasted" precious years in career pursuits while ignoring the "ticking" of their biological clocks. Now, they are intolerant about any delays in the initiation of active treatment interventions. As long as some "procedure" is shortly antici-pated or is actually occurring, they are reassured that a pregnancy is possible. When forced to wait several months or an indefinite period of time for yet an-other in vitro fertilization (IVF) cycle or for an ovum donor, their anxiety about the loss of time increases.

It is not only the pressure of time that is so frustrating for infertile women, but the sense that they have little or no control over their lives. Some infertile women are successful professionals who have delayed childbearing until achieving career success. Their secret to success has been their devotion to their work and their ability to stay with a task until it is accomplished. When confronted with infertility, they attempt to use these skills in the medical arena. They become well informed about the proposed medical procedures, consult with a variety of specialists and select the program that appears to have the highest take-home baby rate. They monitor all aspects of their treat-ment and follow instructions diligently. When, despite their best efforts, they are impotent in effecting a successful pregnancy, they feel overwhelmed not only by disappointment but by a profound sense of helplessness.

A Typical Scenario

A common scenario for couples who receive a diagnosis of infertility is the following: Contraception is discontinued and conception attempts begin in earnest as ovulation is charted and intercourse scheduled. But, menses occurs each month. Worries that "something is wrong" lead to gynecologic consultations. Couples are told "not to worry, just relax." However, when a year of unprotected intercourse without conception occurs, infertility workups begin. Low-tech procedures are started: use of fertility drugs like Clomid or Pergonal to regulate ovulation and increase the number of oocytes produced, intrauterine inseminations to increase the likelihood of connection between sperm and egg. When six or more months pass without conception, high-tech procedures may be recommended such as in vitro fertilization (IVF) or ovum donation.

After agonizing over whether to undertake these procedures, the couple may decide to go ahead. Each new procedure is anticipated optimistically, only to be followed by frustration and dejection (Leiblum, Kemmann, & Lane, 1987). And, then the process of intervention-disappointment-evaluation-intervention begins anew. Many describe this process as an emotional roller coaster, with its cycles of positive anticipation and crashing disappointment. Others say it is like having a chronic medical condition that requires monitoring and active intervention.

The Stress of Infertility

Infertility is unquestionably stressful. In a study of 200 IVF couples, Freeman, Boxer, Rickels, Tureck, and Mastroianni (1985) reported that 48% of the women and 15% of the men described infertility as the worst experience of their lives; in a study of 63 infertile women and 37 infertile men, Mahlstedt, MacDuff, and Bernstein (1987) reported that subjects felt frustrated, hopeless, and depressed; and Downey et al. (1989) reported that in a study of 59 infertile women, 76% felt that infertility had serious psychological consequences for them.

In addition to the emotional distress and financial sacrifices of infertility treatment, individuals may confront ethical and moral dilemmas that are associated with some of the newer reproductive alternatives (e.g., is selective reduction of implanted embryos justifiable; should unused embryos be destroyed or donated to other infertile couples? etc.). Cooper, in Chapter 3, addresses the myriad ethical quandaries associated with the new reproductive options. It is not unusual for couples undergoing some of the newer assisted reproductive techniques to experience some conflict with their personal or parental moral and religious values or beliefs.

Reactions to Secondary Infertility

Secondary infertility refers to the inability to conceive or carry a pregnancy to term despite having previously been successful in giving birth. Although women display much the same reactions to secondary infertility as to primary infertility, their friends and family are often less sympathetic to their plight, making the experience of infertility more poignant.

One patient explained that having a child meant that her whole world was shaped by her commitment to parenthood—most of her social relationships revolved around those who had children and children were ever-present. She could not protect herself from feelings of grief over her thwarted parenthood wishes by avoiding children's shops or birthday parties: They were an integral aspect of her life as a mother.

In a group of six women dealing with secondary infertility, a variety of explanations were offered as to why the experience was so painful and isolating. One woman said that having only one child was a "tease"; she had devoted herself to motherhood with the expectation that this would be her primary role for many years and now she felt cheated. Another said she felt angry at her husband who minimized her distress, saying that he had been willing to do everything possible to have one child, but now, it simply was not worth the effort and expense to attempt another conception. Another woman said that she was worried about the child she *did* have. She felt she would be overly invested in an only child and become too protective because of her anxiety at the thought of losing that child.

The reactions to being unable to have a second child are complex and involve the woman's feelings about herself, her child, her partner, and even her extended family, all of which must be considered when counseling is undertaken. Mental health professionals can be extremely helpful in challenging some of the self-defeating and/or erroneous beliefs that women hold and in supporting their efforts to cope with current realities (Leiblum, 1996).

CHANGING REACTIONS TO INFERTILITY OVER TIME

While the initial reaction to the diagnosis of infertility is often intense and characterized by anxiety during the evaluation stages and depression during failed treatment cycles, the intensity of reactions appear to change over time.

Boiven, Takefman, Tulandi, and Brender (1995) studied the reactions of three groups of women with varying amounts of treatment failure: a "no failure" group consisting of infertile women who had not become pregnant but had not started formal medical infertility treatment, a "moderate failure group," women who had been unsuccessful with conventional treatments such as ovulation induction and donor insemination and had failed an average of 4.4 cycles per year of treatment, and a "high failure" group, women who had been unsuccessful with conventional and more aggressive treatment and were contemplating undertaking IVF as their final treatment effort.

These investigators reported that women who had experienced moderate treatment failure experienced the most personal and marital distress—more than the women who had experienced the most treatment failure. The authors suggest that cumulative treatment failure, like a definitive diagnosis of sterility rather than a diagnosis of unexplained infertility, may result in women's eventual acceptance that conception will not occur. Once they accept this reality, personal feelings of distress may diminish. They no longer experience cognitive dissonance, that is, the belief that they will eventually become pregnant if they just "work at it."

The authors suggest that the model that best explains reactions to infertility over time is curvilinear in which women who experience a moderate amount of treatment failure feel the worst. Moreover, it appears to be the number of treatment failures per se rather than the duration of treatment overall that determines the emotional response to treatment.

Berg and Wilson (1990) studied 104 couples over a three-year period: When they first entered treatment, in the second year of treatment, and again in the third year. During the first year, in the acute phase, people were upset, anxious, and angry. During the second year, these feelings leveled off. As treatment became prolonged and extended to a third year, patients became depressed. Other studies have confirmed these changes in the psychological response to infertility over time (Daniluk, 1988; Domar, Zuttermeister, Seibel, & Benson, 1992; Edelmann, Humphrey, & Owens, 1994).

Whether they are just beginning treatment and confronting their infertility or deeply involved in the process, the experience of loss and grief are common and repetitive. Mahlstedt (1985) described eight common losses often associated with the long-term experience of infertility:

1. Loss of a (potential) relationship.
2. Loss of health.
3. Loss of status or prestige.
4. Loss of self-esteem.
5. Loss of self-confidence.
6. Loss of security.
7. Loss of a fantasy or hope of fulfilling an important fantasy.
8. Loss of something or someone of great symbolic value.

Any one or any combination of these losses may result in feelings of depression.

PSYCHOTHERAPY IN THE EARLY STAGES OF INFERTILITY

The therapeutic process with infertile individuals and couples often consists of brief treatment involving basic reassurance and counseling to guide couples through the typical emotional responses to unanticipated infertility. Indeed, Daniluk (1988) suggests that since the time of the initial medical interview diagnosing infertility is often perceived by individuals as the most stressful time, the provision of psychological services at that time may be most beneficial. Such counseling can assist couples in dealing with their anxiety, exploring the upcoming medical evaluations and their physical and emotional concomitants, anticipating the impact that infertility evaluation(s) may place on their marital and sexual relationship, and discussing how to avoid some of the more obvious sources of distress, such as engaging in self-recrimination or regret.

Much of the initial counseling involves a "normalization" of the emotional reactions to the diagnosis of infertility. Often, though, therapy moves to a consideration of deeper underlying issues that go well beyond the presenting symptoms. In either case, it is helpful if the therapist has an accurate and thoughtful grasp of the psychological issues of infertility—its etiology, medical treatment, and psychological impact.

Case Example

Bill, a 45-year-old business executive, appeared for counseling only because his wife threatened divorce if he remained as irritable, despondent and sexually avoidant as he had been for the past several years.

Upon initial presentation, he was expansive and arrogant, boasting of his professional success and only alluding to his humiliation about being unable to impregnate his wife. He admitted that his adopted son and stepdaughter did not fulfill his dream of having a biological child, but that "it was no big deal."

It was only over several sessions that he became less defensive and the following story emerged. As the oldest son of a hard-driving, competitive Italian immigrant, he was raised to believe that "you have to be twice as good to get half as far." At college, he did indeed, excel. Socially, he was less confident but sexually active in a promiscuous way. After accidentally getting a woman pregnant at age 19, he avoided intravaginal ejaculation. Eventually, he married a divorced mother because she was "sexy, smart, and ambitious." He continued to practice coitus interruptus as birth control until he decided he wanted a child. His wife who was in her late 30s was agreeable. To his chagrin, he discovered that not only could he not ejaculate in his wife's vagina, but semen analysis revealed his sperm to be deficient both in form and volume. The feelings of humiliation and shame about being unable to impregnate his wife were extreme and intense. He blamed himself totally for their conception difficulties (although there was a female factor involved as well) and obsessively compared himself unfavorably with his wife's former lovers. Although he and his wife eventually adopted, he remained devastated and depressed by his infertility. His sexual relationship with his wife deteriorated. Marital conflict escalated. Finally, after his wife threatened divorce, he agreed to a psychological consultation.

In this case, the crisis of infertility and its accompanying feelings of humiliation triggered a major depressive reaction in a psychologically vulnerable individual. While the feelings of shame and "defectiveness" in this case were extreme, the initial diagnosis and the aftermath of prolonged, invasive, and often, embarrassing infertility evaluations and procedures can lead to profound feelings of inadequacy and despair in individuals with fragile self-esteem. In such cases, infertility counseling can lead to longer-term psychotherapy.

UNEXPLAINED INFERTILITY

The diagnosis of unexplained infertility appears to be the most difficult diagnosis to accept (Wylie, 1993). Without a known cause identifying the reason for the failure to conceive, it is difficult to abandon the thought that each new cycle may result in a pregnancy. In fact, natural pregnancies do occur in these cases. Wylie (1993) suggests that 72% of this population conceive within two years, although these statistics differ across studies. In an early extensive, retrospective study of pregnancies in medically treated and untreated couples, Collins, Wrinon, Janes, and Wilson (1983) reported that 44% of women with ovulatory difficulties conceived without treatment, 60% of women with endometriosis and tubal defects or partners with seminal deficiencies conceived without treatment and 96% of women with cervical factors or "idiopathic" (e.g., unexplained) infertility. In all, 266 of 1,143 infertile couples (23%) had apparently treatment-independent pregnancies.

While recognizing that couples with unexplained infertility may eventually conceive—with or without treatment—it is also important for therapists to recognize that unexplained infertility is especially upsetting for most couples. Acknowledging that the uncertainty involved makes directive action difficult may be helpful to some couples, as well as advising them to develop some time frame as to when they might want to consider more certain paths to parenthood.

The following example describes the therapy with an infertile couple where the wife is diagnosed with "unexplained infertility." Initially, the couple was seen for brief treatment focused on their concern that they were psychologically responsible for their infertility and that they were making themselves "crazy." After they achieved some symptomatic relief, they decided to remain in treatment and explore some of the significant underlying issues in their relationship which were exposed and exacerbated by the infertility.

Case Example

Ann E, a 34-year-old systems analyst called the therapist with the following plea, "I am not the sort of person who goes into therapy. I've always worked hard and gotten what I want. I take pride in not asking for help but lately, I feel as though I'm starting to lose my mind—and my husband."

The E's are an attractive couple who have been married for five years. Ann is the oldest of three daughters born to a middle-class Catholic couple. She describes her parents as intelligent but not well educated and herself as the "family success." Her most ardent supporter, her father, encouraged her to pursue an education, but died while she was in college. She states that she maintains a close relationship with her mother and sisters. However, she worries about her sisters who dropped out of school and have not followed in her educational footsteps.

Her husband Phil is a 36-year-old attorney who is the youngest of two children raised in an upper-middle-class Protestant family. His parents and older sister live on the opposite side of the country and he has little contact with them.

Ann and Phil met in college, where each excelled academically. Ann describes their relationship as one in which there was always a clear plan. "Even in college, we talked about our future, and we were committed. We would go our separate ways during graduate school since we would be living in different states, but once we graduated, we would get fabulous jobs in the same city, move in together, and plan our wedding—and that's what we did."

Once they were married, they agreed on a 5-year "plan": save money, buy a house, and start a family. Things did not go as they had anticipated. After two years of trying to conceive, they were forced to admit that they couldn't make this part of their plan happen by simply working harder at it.

An articulate couple, the E's self-composure vanished as they told their story. Ann became tearful when she explained how the monthly treatment cycle was affecting her:

ANN: I feel like my whole life has been taken up with trying to get pregnant. The first half of the month I get my hopes up and the second half I feel such despair about getting my period.

Phil, though initially gregarious, sat silently through the session, passing tissues to his wife and patting her shoulder when she started crying.

THERAPIST: How has this affected you, Phil?
PHIL: I can't deny it. I am really disappointed when she gets her period. But it doesn't get to me the way it does to her. I'm really worried about Ann. She never just settles down and relaxes, never gets away from the pressure to solve this problem.
THERAPIST: Ann, on the phone, you told me that you were afraid that you were losing your husband. What did you mean?
ANN: Things seem to be breaking down between us. He's impatient with me—thinks I'm a wimp. We end up fighting and I think he's starting to care less. I don't know any more if he wants kids or is beginning to think the whole thing isn't worth it.
PHIL: You know I want to have children. I just don't like what this is doing to you. You just aren't there for me. And, frankly, our sex life stinks.

It is obvious that the E's are demoralized and frightened by their current situation. They are also bewildered that their typical pattern of handling stress—defining a problem and actively seeking a solution—so effective until now, has failed to produce results. Though they were and are devoted to each other, they are worried that their alliance is cracking down under the stress of repeated failures.

At this point, the therapist offered reassurance that Ann was not "going crazy," that her distress was characteristic of women struggling with this problem, and that Phil's apparent emotional withdrawal was, in fact, his way of dealing with his own feelings of loss and disappointment. Three additional sessions were agreed on for the upcoming month.

Most couples find it reassuring if the therapist suggests a limited number of meetings, particularly since the couple is concerned about how "pathological" one or both of them appear. During the initial consultation, the clinician can reassure couples that they are not severely disturbed (if this is, in fact, true!), that their emotional responses to infertility fall within the normal range, and that the therapist is familiar with both the medical and psychological aspects of the process and can serve as a guide to help them cope with their feelings and with the decisions they face.

When Ann and Phil entered the therapist's office on their third visit, it was immediately apparent that they were distressed. Ann appeared to be fighting back tears and Phil shifted around in his chair and sighed before speaking.

PHIL:	Just when it seemed that things were looking up; we get some news and Ann acts like someone died, for God's sake!
	(Ann begins to cry.)
THERAPIST:	What happened?
PHIL:	Ann's sister Patty, the one who recently got married—to a jerk, I might add—is pregnant. And Ann has come undone about it.
THERAPIST:	How do you feel about the news, Phil?
PHIL:	It's ridiculous. They don't have a penny and the kid will be just as messed up as they are.
THERAPIST:	So, you're angry.
PHIL:	Well, okay, I'm upset. Especially when I find out that Patty went out of her way to tell us it was an accident.
THERAPIST:	I guess it feels pretty unfair.
ANN:	I feel so terrible. I hate my sister and then I hate myself for feeling that way. I couldn't even offer congratulations. I handed the phone to Phil.
THERAPIST:	It must feel pretty unfair to both of you. You've worked so hard to prepare to have a baby.
ANN:	Of course, my mother is just thrilled. When I cried and told her that I had wanted to give her the first grandchild, she told me that I was being my usual self-centered self.

The news that one's friends or family members have achieved a pregnancy can be extremely upsetting for couples. They may wish to be happy for others but find it impossible in practice. They feel guilty about their intense feelings of envy and resentment, and the conflict is even greater when the news comes from a younger sibling. There is often an "unwritten rule" that older sisters are supposed to have the first children. The grief and disappointment they feel for themselves, as well as their feeling of failure to provide a longed-for grand-child may exacerbate their feelings of indignation and outrage when they discover someone close has "beat them to it."

Infertile women often have difficulty discussing their infertility with their mothers. Their fertile mothers almost by definition cannot fully comprehend their daughter's dilemma. Often, mothers inadvertently make insensitive comments suggesting that their daughters are causing their infertility by their failure to "just relax and let it happen" or by being "too neurotic."

During the next session, Ann and Phil began where they had left off—with Ann's anger at her sister for getting pregnant and at her mother for being unsupportive of her.

PHIL:	I wish Ann could just stay away from her family.
ANN:	You mean like you do, Phil? I wouldn't want to have a cold, distant relationship with my family like you have with yours.
PHIL:	It's just that when you're around them you seem more upset. Your sisters take advantage of you and your mother protects them.
ANN:	(crying). If my father were here . . . (Phil puts arm around Ann).
THERAPIST:	How do you imagine things would be different if your father were here?
ANN:	My father always knew the right thing to say. He always knew how to make me feel better.
THERAPIST:	You miss him very much.
ANN:	(crying harder now). Our baby was supposed to be named after him.

The therapist observed how much Phil reached out to Ann during this exchange and how isolated he felt. Ann clearly was caught up in unresolved grief for her father, and her relationships with her mother and sisters were conflicted and difficult.

Further exploration revealed the depth of Ann's sense of loss following her father's death and her feeling of obligation to "take care of" her sisters and mother. The identified "family success," Ann was both resented and relied on at a time when she herself was grieving, vulnerable, and needy. Ann had struggled to gain distance from her mother and sisters and had succeeded during the years she and Phil were pursuing their careers. Feeling more secure in her emancipation during the recent past, she had "become closer" to her family, only to find that they could not relinquish old patterns and grievances when she was in a crisis.

The therapist and the couple met for several additional sessions. Some of their work together was focused on Ann's need to grieve for her father and for her infertility. As therapy progressed, Ann began to see that the pain of her infertility was a catalyst for reawakening the loss she felt at the death of her father and the unmet needs and problems she associated with her mother. At the same time, the therapy dealt with Phil's feelings of being excluded and how he excluded himself as well when things became too painful, which left Ann feeling more isolated and abandoned.

The therapist helped Ann and Phil reestablish a sense of control in their lives by employing the tactic that had always worked for them in the past: organization and planning. At the therapist's urging, they met with their infertility specialist to determine a definite treatment plan. They were prepared with a list of questions and a notebook. Once they developed a specific plan, they felt a greater sense of control over their treatment and what they would do if they did not achieve a pregnancy within one year.

Two years later, the therapist received a letter reporting that Ann and Phil had decided to terminate infertility treatment a year earlier. They were now the proud parents of a baby girl adopted from China.

Obviously, the resolution of the struggle with infertility may take a variety of forms and differs from couple to couple. For Ann and Phil, brief therapy was effective in circumventing potential marital and sexual problems. Their style of working together and their commitment to each other facilitated the therapeutic process.

ADAPTATION TO PROLONGED INFERTILITY

While most couples arrive at some sort of accommodation to their infertility, clinically one sees some women who simply are unable to "give up" biological attempts to conceive, despite the cost to them and their families. These are the women who continue to pursue infertility treatment despite the advice of their physicians and the distress of their husbands. In these cases, preexisting psychopathology is often present and long-term psychotherapy is called for.

Case Example

Mrs. L, a mother of two children, was referred for psychological counseling by her physician, following 13 cycles of unsuccessful medical treatment, including 8 cycles of IVF.

A religious Catholic woman from an Eastern European country, she told the therapist that she had undergone a tubal ligation when she discovered she was pregnant with her third child. Her husband had insisted she have both an abortion and a tubal ligation because he felt they could afford no more children. Although she felt coerced by her husband, she reluctantly agreed when being seen for her abortion. As soon as she awakened from the anesthesia, she was overcome with feelings of remorse and regret. She berated her husband and subsequently became obsessed with obtaining surgery to restore her fertility. Although the surgery was performed, she was unsuccessful in becoming pregnant.

She then pursued infertility treatment, demanding trial after trial of IVF. After 8 cycles, it became increasingly clear that she was not going to conceive; further her obsessive pursuit of pregnancy was again destroying her family life. It was at this time that she was refused further medical treatment, pending psychological counseling.

Therapy centered on helping her ventilate feelings of grief and guilt about her abortion. She was helped to forgive herself for what she believed was a wicked and sinful decision. In a number of family sessions she was confronted by her husband and children who told her how much they missed their "old mother" and needed her involvement in ongoing family life. They impressed on her that they felt unloved and uncherished by virtue of her obsession with conceiving. Eventually, after months of therapy, both individual and family, she was able to acknowledge that her obsessive pursuit of pregnancy was both fruitless and harmful.

It was clear that this woman's perseveration with becoming pregnant was a symbolic attempt to undo her abortion and resolve her ambivalence about both wanting and not wanting more children. She was a severely obsessive and compulsive person, with chronic dysthmic tendencies. Treatment, while extended, ultimately was helpful in restoring marital and family functioning.

THE COPING REACTIONS OF INFERTILE PATIENTS

Couples engage in a variety of strategies for dealing with their infertility. Some work better than others. The coping strategies employed appear to influence the kind and degree of stress experienced by the infertile individual. In a recent study, Morrow, Thoreson, and Penney (1995) assessed the severity of psychological distress in a large sample of infertile men and women by administering the Global Severity Index subscale of the Symptom Checklist-90 and a Ways of Coping questionnaire, which assessed the type of coping strategies employed. The results confirmed that for 10% of the women and 15% of the men, clinically significant distress ratings were reported (e.g., 2 standard deviations above the mean). More revelant, though, was the finding that of the three ways of dealing with stress—self-blame and avoidance, informational/emotional support seeking, and cognitive restructuring—the use of self-blame and avoidance was most highly correlated with psychological distress.

In another study of 30 infertile women, six primary coping responses were observed clinically (Davis & Dearman, 1991): distancing from reminders of infertility, instituting measures for regaining control, engaging in actions to increase their self-esteem in other realms, searching for the hidden meaning in infertility, giving in to feelings, and sharing the burden with others. Typically, more women than men tend to seek the advice, support, and reassurance of others, particularly other infertile women which is why the organization RE-SOLVE[1] is helpful for so many couples.

The research literature suggests that either professionally led or self-help infertility support groups are helpful in reducing anxiety and depression as well as increasing well-being for the infertile men and women who attend them (Domar, Zuttermeister, Seibel, & Benson, 1992).

The best coping strategies involve active, problem-focused planning, networking, and information seeking, while self- or partner-blaming and avoidance/denial are counter-productive and ultimately, destructive.

TREATMENT IMPLICATIONS AND SUGGESTIONS

Psychological counseling with infertile couples appears to be particularly helpful at two distinct stages of treatment, at the time of initial diagnosis (Daniluk, 1988) and after a moderate number of unsuccessful conception attempts (Boiven, Takefman, Tulandi, & Brender, 1995). Initially, therapists can normalize the reactions that men and women may be having to the diagnosis of infertility and help couples better understand the treatment options available along with the range of emotional, financial, physical and psychological costs associated with them.

After many trials of unsuccessful medical intervention, couples and individuals may begin to display signs of increased inter- and intrapersonal distress. Husbands may be ready to terminate treatment sooner than their wives (Blenner, 1990), and this issue may become a source of couple conflict. Deciding on how much additional time and money to be spent on medical treatment is another source of conflict, as well as agreeing on which infertility option(s) are to be pursued. Counseling can be focused on developing skills in negotiation and communication as well as exploring and resolving the sexual issues that often accompany long-term infertility treatment (see Chapter 7 for a fuller discussion on counseling couples and Chapter 8 for a discussion of the marital and sexual concomitants of infertility).

Rosenberg and Epstein (1993) have suggested that couples can help themselves successfully cope with infertility by utilizing a variety of strategies, including relaxation and imagery techniques. They provide nine "pointers" for helping individuals achieve a pregnancy; their recommendations are useful for infertility counselors as well[2]:

---

[1]RESOLVE is a self-help, nonprofit, charitable organization. It offers referrals, support, and counseling to people affected by infertility as well as information and assistance to professionals in the field of infertility.

[2]Rosenberg and Epstein's pointers have been revised slightly in this rendition but the reader may be interested in consulting their book *Getting Pregnant When You Thought You Couldn't* (New York: Warner Books, 1993).

1. *Educate yourself about infertility.* This is a solid recommendation for both patients and clinicians. One needs to be familiar with the nature and side effects of diagnostic tests, procedures, and medications used in infertility treatment.

2. *Identify your feelings.* Be familiar with the typical reactions to infertility and normalize them for patients.

3. *Engage in cognitive assessment and challenge unrealistic cognitions.* Dispute patients' irrational beliefs about their infertility (e.g., "I'm being punished for having an affair three years ago"). Help couples develop accurate and adaptive ways of looking at their infertility.

4. *Encourage couples to work together.* Remind patients that infertility is a couple, rather than an individual, problem, irrespective of who bears the initial diagnosis. Encourage them to acknowledge their common pain.

5. *Organize your social life.* Rosenberg and Epstein (1993) encourage patients to give themselves permission to avoid stressful family or social occasions. This can be very helpful advice for individuals who feel great pressure to do what is expected of them, despite their private feelings of resentment or sadness. Patients find that learning to be kind to themselves and respecting their internal wishes can be liberating.

6. *Be active consumers.* Patients need to be informed and active consumers of their medical treatment and not passive recipients. They can complain, confront, and challenge as well as question their healthcare providers.

7. *Be organized.* Remind patients to keep medical records and be certain about the tests and procedures they have undergone. This will increase their credibility with physicians and provide them with a measure of control over their treatment.

8. *Have a plan.* Rosenberg and Epstein (1993) recommend that couples decide on a six-month plan that identifies how much money they are willing to spend on treatment, how long they want to remain in treatment, how much physical and emotional trauma they can withstand, etc. After six months, their plan can be reassessed to see if it agrees with current realities.

9. *Don't give up.* Rosenberg and Epstein (1993) recommend that couples do not give up on their quest to become pregnant since one out of two infertile couples will eventually be successful in having a baby and since reproductive technology is ever-evolving. While it is important to maintain a stance of cautious and realistic optimism, it is equally as important to confront the emotional, physical, and psychological costs of pursuing a goal that may appear (and indeed, may be) elusive and unrealistic. This is where the clinician must be informed about the realistic probability of success, given the client's situation and fantasized probability of success. Infertile couples tend to overinflate their likelihood of achieving a successful pregnancy (Zoeten, Tymstra, & Alberda, 1987; Leiblum et al.,

1987; Collins, Freeman, Boxer, & Tureck, 1992) and may need assistance in considering the costs versus the benefits of putting their life on hold.

CONCLUSION

It is obvious that individuals vary considerably in their reactions to both the initial diagnosis of infertility and to the experience of prolonged infertility. Consider these three different responses to a question concerning "final thoughts" about infertility:

"I feel inadequate and a failure as a woman and am slowly (and with the hope of adoption), trying to rebuild my self-esteem and my overall life."

Written by a 34 year old woman following 8 years of infertility treatment.

" 'Bad' things happen in everyone's life. I feel that infertility was one of the 'bad' things that happened in my life. It was difficult to get over this, but I have many 'good' things in my life and I try to focus on all of these things. And I am grateful for what I do have."

Written by a 48 year old woman following 9 years of infertility treatment.

"Since my final surgery . . . , I have spent most of my time raising my son (biological, age 12) and my *adopted identical twin girls* (now 5). But even though our twins filled a very big hole, I still feel some kind of loss when I see a woman expecting or a new baby. That feeling of having something taken away from me will never leave and is just something I had to learn to live with and accept."

Written by a 42 year old woman following 4½ years of infertility treatment.

Finally, some women are convinced that they will be very different kinds of parents as a result of their struggle with infertility. As one woman wrote (after 7 years of unsuccessful treatment):

In addition to "testing" our endurance as a "committed couple for life," we know that we will be different parents than if I had become pregnant on our honeymoon. We know that we will be more grateful, more attentive to our child, and especially more aware of what is and what is *not* important in life. A baby doesn't bring happiness; you must be happy, secure, and comfortable with yourself and together to bring happiness to a family. We look forward to becoming parents this year—through adoption—and we feel a renewed sense of hope and understanding.

From these comments, it is obvious that individuals have different emotional, spiritual, and psychological resources for coping with prolonged infertility. While some women are able to express optimism and a belief in the possibility of a fulfilled and fulfilling life with—or without—children, others continue to feel defective and deficient, even after becoming adoptive parents. Since women and their partners differ so dramatically, treatment must be individually tailored. Ideally, however, some form of counseling should be offered to all couples, both upon the initial diagnosis of infertility and after years of unsuccessful medical intervention.

While few couples emerge completely unscathed from the frustrations and repeated disappointments that accompany infertility treatment, psychological counseling at critical times can help prevent the development of damaged relationships. For many couples, the experience of infertility, while undoubtedly stressful, ultimately leads to a greater sense of gratitude and fulfillment when parenthood—by whatever means—is finally achieved.

REFERENCES

Aral, S. O., & Cates, W. (1983). The increasing concern with infertility. Why now? *Journal of the American Medical Association, 250,* 2327–2331.

Batterman, R. (1985). Comprehensive approach to treating infertility. *Health and Social Work, 10,* 46–54.

Benedek, T. (1952). Infertility as a psychosomatic defense. *Fertility and Sterility, 3,* 527–535.

Berg, B. J., & Wilson, J. F. (1990). Psychiatric morbidity in the infertile population: A reconceptualization. *Fertility and Sterility, 53,* 654–661.

Berg, B. J., & Wilson, J. F. (1991). Psychological functioning across stages of treatment for infertility. *Journal of Behavioral Medicine, 14*(1), 11–26.

Berger, D. M. (1977). The role of the psychiatrist in a reproductive biology clinic. *Fertility and Sterility, 28,* 141–145.

Berger, D. M. (1980). Infertility: A psychiatrist's perspective. *Canadian Journal of Psychiatry, 25,* 553–559.

Blenner, J. (1990). Passage through infertility treatment: A stage theory. *IMAGE: Journal of Nursing Scholarship, 22,* 153–158.

Boiven, J., Takefman, J., Tulandi, T., & Brender, W. (1995). Reactions to infertility based on extent of treatment failure. *Fertility and Sterility, 63*(4), 801–807.

Bos, C., & Cleghorn, R. A. (1958). Psychogenic sterility. *Fertility and Sterility, 9,* 84–95.

Collins, A., Freeman, E., Boxer, A., & Tureck, R. (1992). Perceptions of infertility and treatment stress in females as compared with males entering in vitro fertilization treatment. *Fertility and Sterility, 57*(2), 350–356.

Collins, J., Wrinon, W., Janes, L., & Wilson, E. (1983). Treatment—independent pregnancy among infertile couples. *New England Journal of Medicine, 309*(20), 1201–1206.

Connolly, K. J., Edelmann, R. J., Cooke, I. D., & Robson, J. (1992). The impact of infertility on psychological functioning. *Journal of Psychosomatic Research, 36,* 459–468.

Covington, S. N. (1987). Psychosocial evaluation of the infertile couples: Implications for social work practice. *Journal of Social Work and Human Sexuality, 6,* 21–36.

Daniluk, J. C. (1988). Infertility: Intrapersonal and interpersonal impact. *Fertility and Sterility, 49*(6), 982–990.

Davis, D., & Dearman, C. (1991). Coping strategies of infertile women. *Journal of Obstetric, Gynecologic & Neonatal Nursing, 20,* 221–228.

Deutsch, H. (1944). *The psychology of women.* New York: Grune & Stratton.

Domar, A. O., Broome, A., Zuttermeister, P. C., Seibel, M., & Friedman, R. (1992). The prevalence and predictability of depression in infertile women. *Fertility and Sterility, 58,* 1158–1163.

Domar, A., Zuttermeister, P., Seibel, M., & Benson, H. (1992). Psychological improvement in infertile women after behavioral treatment: A replication. *Fertility and Sterility, 58,* 144–147.

Downey, J., & McKinney, M. (1992). The psychiatric status of women presenting for infertility evaluation. *American Journal of Orthopsychiatry, 62,* 196–205.

Downey, J., Yingling, S., McKinney, M., Husami, N., Jewelewicz, R., & Maidman, J. (1989). Mood disorders, psychiatric symptoms, and distress in women presenting for infertility evaluation. *Fertility and Sterility, 52,* 425–432.

Edelmann, R. J., Humphrey, M., & Owens, D. J. (1994). The meaning of parenthood and couples' reactions to male infertility. *British Journal of Medical Psychology, 67*(3), 291–299.

Fischer, I. C. (1953). Psychogenic aspects of sterility. *Fertility and Sterility, 4,* 466–471.

Freeman, E. W., Boxer, A. S., Rickels, K., Tureck, R., & Mastroianni, L. (1985). Psychological evaluation and support in a program of in vitro. *Fertility and Sterility, 43*(1), 48–53.

Freeman, E. W., Rickels, K., Tausig, J., Boxer, A., Mastroianni, L., & Tureck, R. W. (1987). Emotional psychosocial factors in follow-up of women after IVF-ET treatment. *Acta Obstetrica et Gynocologica Scandanavia, 66,* 517–521.

Glazer, E. S. (1990). *The long-awaited stork.* New York: Lexington Books, Maxwell Macmillan International.

Harrison, R. F., OMoore, M., & OMoore, R. (1986). The management of stress in infertility. In L. Dennerstein & J. Fraser (Eds.), *Hormones and behavior* (pp. 25–40). Amsterdam, The Netherlands: Elsevier/North Holland.

Kroger, W. S., & Freed, S. C. (1950). Psychosomatic aspects of sterility. *American Journal of Obstetrics and Gynecology, 59,* 867–874.

Leiblum, S. R. (1987). Infertility. In E. Blechman & K. Brownell (Eds.), *Behavioral medicine for women* (pp. 116–125). New York: Pergamon Press.

Leiblum, S. R. (1994). The impact of infertility on marital and sexual satisfaction. *Annual Review of Sex Research, 4,* 99–120.

Leiblum, S. R. (1996). Love, sex and infertility: The impact of infertility on the couple. *In Session, 2,* 29–40.

Leiblum, S. R., Kemmann, E., & Lane, M. K. (1987). The psychological concomitants of in vitro fertilization. *Journal of Psychosomatic Obstetrics and Gynaecology, 6,* 165–178.

Mahlstedt, P. P. (1985). The psychological component of infertility. *Fertility and Sterility, 43,* 335–346.

Mahlstedt, P. P., MacDuff, S., & Bernstein, J. (1987). Emotional factors and the in vitro fertilization and embryo transfer process. *Journal of In Vitro Fertilization and Embryo Transfer, 4,* 232–236.

Mai, F. M., Munday, R. N., & Rump, E. E. (1972). Psychiatric interview comparisons between infertile and fertile couples. *Psychosomatic Medicine, 12*(1), 46–59.

Mai, F. M., & Rump, E. E. (1972). Are infertile men and women neurotic? *Australian Journal of Psychology, 24*(1), 83–86.

Mazure, C. M., & Greenfeld, D. A. (1989). Psychological studies of in vitro fertilization/embryo transfer participants. *Journal of In Vitro Fertilization and Embryo Transfer, 6,* 242–249.

Menning, B. E. (1975). The infertile couple: A plea for advocacy. *Child Welfare, 54,* 545–560.

Menning, B. E. (1976). Resolve: A support group for infertile couples. *American Journal of Nursing, 76,* 258–259.

Menning, B. E. (1979). Counseling infertile couples. *Contemporary Ob/Gyn, 13,* 101–108.

Menning, B. E. (1980). The emotional needs of infertile couples. *Fertility and Sterility, 34,* 313–319.

Morrow, K., Thoreson, R., & Penney, L. (1995). Predictors of psychological distress among infertility clinic patients. *Journal of Consulting and Clinical Psychology, 63*(1), 163–167.

Mosher, W. D. (1987). Infertility: Why business is booming. *American Demographics, 9,* 42–43.

Mosher, W. D., & Pratt, W. F. (1991). Fecundity and infertility in the United States. Incidence and trends. *Fertility and Sterility, 56,* 192–193.

Newton, C., Hearn, M., & Yuzpe, A. (1990). Psychological assessment and follow up after in vitro fertilization: Assessing the impact of failure. *Fertility and Sterility, 54,* 879–886.

Noyes, R. W., & Chapnick, E. M. (1964). Literature on psychology and infertility. *Fertility and Sterility, 15*(5), 543–548.

Rosenberg, H., & Epstein, Y. (1993). *Getting pregnant when you thought you couldn't: The interactive guide that helps you up the odds.* New York: Warner Books.

Rosenthal, M. (1993). Psychiatric aspects of infertility. In D. A. Greenfeld (Ed.), *Infertility and reproductive medicine clinics of North America* (pp. 471–482). Philadelphia: W. B. Saunders.

Rubenstein, B. B. (1951). An emotional factor in infertility. *Fertility and Sterility, 2,* 80–86.

Sandler, B. (1961). Infertility of emotional origin. *Journal of Obstetrics & Gynaecology of the British Empire, 68,* 809–815.

Seward, G. H., Wagner, P. S., Heinrich, J. F., Block, S. K., & Myerhoff, H. L. (1965). The question of psychophysiologic infertility: Some negative answers. *Psychosomatic Medicine, 27,* 533–545.

Shapiro, C. H. (1986). Is pregnancy after infertility a dubious joy? *Social Casework: Journal of Contemporary Social Work, 67,* 306–313.

Takefman, J. E., Brender, W., Boiven, J., & Tulandi, T. (1990). Sexual and emotional adjustment of couples undergoing infertility investigation and the effectiveness of preparatory information. *Journal of Psychosomatic Obstetrics & Gynaecology, 11,* 275–290.

Wylie, K. (1993). Psychological morbidity in unexplained infertility. *Sexual and Marital Therapy, 8*(1), 27–35.

Zoeten, J., Tymstra, T., & Alberda, A. (1987). The waiting list for IVF: The motivations and expectations of women waiting for IVF treatment. *Human Reproduction, 2,* 623–626.

CHAPTER 6

Gender and Infertility

JUDITH C. DANILUK

> and the Lord said, go ye forth, be fruitful and multiply and replenish
> the earth
> —Genesis 1:27, 28

Many infertile couples with whom I have worked over the past 15 years suggest that infertility, and the often long and protracted pursuit of medical solutions, is one of the most challenging and difficult experiences they have been faced with, both personally, and in their marriages. In the words of one infertile client:

> Infertility challenges everything. . . . Your beliefs about yourself, about what's important, about marriage, about what is fair and just, about God. Being infertile makes you question the purpose of marriage and of life . . . nothing is left unaffected by this experience . . . it changes you, subtly but profoundly . . . I think that the biggest thing that we've had to work through as a couple and me as a person is just learning to live with it . . . because it changes everything . . . being infertile changes everything.

Helping couples to find ways to "live with it," to cope with the numerous strains and stresses of this difficult life event and emerge from the experience with their self-esteem and their marriages intact, is an important contribution that helping professionals can make to the approximately 3.5 million couples in the United States who experience infertility (Ulbrich, Coyle, & Llabre, 1990) and spend years pursuing solutions to their inability to produce a child.

With relatively high rates of infertility throughout the world, most mental health practitioners will have infertile men and women in their caseloads. To be effective in helping infertile couples negotiate what is commonly referred to as an unanticipated life crisis (e.g., Mahlstedt, 1985; Menning, 1982), however, it is necessary to understand the psychosocial sequelae of infertility. It is also important to be aware of the differences in the ways in which men and women respond to being infertile, and cope with the medical investigations and interventions that characterize the treatment of impaired fertility. According to many researchers, men and women differ in their response to infertility, in terms of their level of psychosocial distress, and in how they experience this distress across the various stages of medical intervention (e.g., Abbey, Andrews, & Halman, 1991; Berg, Wilson, & Weingartner, 1991; Greil, 1991; Newton & Houle, 1993; Ulbrich et al., 1990; Wright, Allard, Lecours, & Sabourin, 1989). If this is so, mental health practitioners need to take these differences into consideration when working with infertile individuals and couples.

In this chapter, I discuss common responses to the experience of infertility with particular attention to the apparent differences in responses of men and women. I examine possible reasons for these gender differences as a backdrop to addressing how mental health practitioners can help both men and women cope with the intrapersonal and interpersonal toll exacted by the pursuit of medical solutions to their infertility, and assist couples in constructing meaningful and satisfying lives and relationships, irrespective of treatment outcome.

FACTORS AFFECTING RESPONSES TO INFERTILITY

A substantial body of research, clinical, and anecdotal literature supports the contention that infertility exacts a heavy toll on couples. Being unable to bear a child and, in particular, undergoing the invasive and time-consuming medical investigation and treatment of infertility have been reported to have far-reaching negative consequences, in terms of sexual functioning and satisfaction, marital communication and adjustment, impaired interpersonal relationships, and emotional and psychological distress. Infertile men and women have been found to consistently demonstrate elevated levels of psychosocial distress compared with their fertile counterparts (e.g., Andrews, Abbey, & Halman, 1991; Berg & Wilson, 1991; Daniluk, 1988; Koropatnick, Daniluk, & Pattinson, 1993; McEwan, Costello, & Taylor, 1987; Wright et al., 1989; Wright et al., 1991). Couples undergoing treatment for infertility commonly report feelings of anger, betrayal, powerlessness, isolation, depression, hostility, and diminished self-esteem, as well as difficulties in their intimate relationships (Abbey et al., 1991; Link & Darling, 1986; Ulbrich et al., 1990). Being infertile has been found to profoundly challenge individuals' basic assumptions regarding justice, fairness, and the meaning of life (Daniluk, 1991; Greil, 1991; Mahlstedt, 1985; Menning, 1982). Some men and women experience infertility as an assault on their masculinity or femininity (Daniluk, 1991; Berg et al., 1991; Menning, 1982). Many report acute feelings of loss and grief in being unable to fulfill their hopes and dreams for producing a child that is the product of the love they share for each other (Daniluk, 1996; Mahlstedt, 1985; Menning, 1982).

Factors that appear to be associated with a more negative response to infertility include being the partner with the identified source of the fertility problem (Abbey et al., 1991; Daniluk, 1988; Mason, 1993; McEwan et al., 1987; Nachtigall, Becker, & Wozny, 1992); advanced age and duration of infertility

(Berg & Wilson, 1991; Daniluk, 1988; Koropatnick et al., 1993; McEwan et al., 1987; van Balen & Trimbos-Kemper, 1994); receipt of an ambiguous diagnosis such as unexplained infertility (Abbey et al., 1991; Berg et al., 1991; Daniluk, 1988, 1991; Koropatnick et al., 1993; Link & Darling, 1986; Mahlstedt, 1985; McEwan et al., 1987; Sandelowski, 1987; Ulbrich et al., 1990); and gender (e.g., Abbey et al., 1991; Adler & Boxley, 1985; Andrews et al., 1991; Daniluk, 1988; Greil, Leitko, & Porter, 1988; Link & Darling, 1986; McEwan et al., 1987; McGrade & Tolor, 1981; Newton & Houle, 1993; Ulbrich et al., 1990; Wright et al., 1989, 1991).

GENDER DIFFERENCES IN RESPONSE TO INFERTILITY

Women's Responses

Researchers who have examined sex differences in response to infertility have reported that women experience considerably greater psychosocial distress, more somatic difficulties, lower self-esteem, higher levels of depression, and greater interpersonal sensitivity related to their infertility (e.g., Abbey et al., 1991; Berg & Wilson, 1991; Greil et al., 1988; Koropatnick et al., 1993; Link & Darling, 1986; Ulbrich et al., 1990). In a review of 30 controlled research protocols Wright et al. (1989) found convincing evidence to support the assumption that "women tend to be more distressed by the whole experience of infertility and its modern medical management" (p. 137) than men.

When fertility problems occur, women appear to attribute the cause of the infertility to their own biological failure, or to past behaviors or perceived transgressions such as relinquishing a child for adoption, having an abortion, or having an extramarital affair (Berg et al., 1991; Daniluk, 1991; Greil, 1991; Mahlstedt, 1985). This self-attribution of responsibility appears to be evident, even when the couple receive an exclusively male factor diagnosis (Mason, 1993; Webb & Daniluk, in press). Women report a decrease in sexual satisfaction with prolonged infertility treatment, and perceive their inability to conceive as a direct assault on their self-image and self-esteem, and on their sense of themselves as complete and competent women (Berg et al., 1991; Greil, 1991; Lalos, Lalos, Jacobsson, & Von Schoultz, 1986; McGrade & Tolor, 1981). They appear to be more sensitive to fertility-related stimuli (e.g., pregnant women, babies, etc.) (Berg et al., 1991; Daniluk, 1991), and are more distressed by the comments of others regarding their childless status (Mahlstedt, 1985; Menning, 1982). These sentiments are powerfully expressed in the words of one infertile woman with whom I worked:

> Every week I seem to hear about someone else who's pregnant, and each time I hear someone is pregnant I feel like I've died inside . . . no one will ever understand this, but it's like every time they give life, in my mind it's like giving death.

Infertile women also appear to be more committed to the goal of having children, and to the pursuit of medical options to achieve this goal (Greil, 1991; Ulbrich et al., 1990; Wright et al., 1991).

Several factors have been identified as differentiating between those women who report more severe levels of psychosocial distress in response to infertility and those whose lives and self-structures seem less threatened by this experience. Greater distress is reported by those women who have poor self-esteem (Koropatnick et al., 1993; Lalos et al., 1986; Link & Darling, 1986), and by those who are primarily invested in the motherhood role in terms of their identity and self-image (Berg et al., 1991; Greil et al., 1988). Women report more marital and sexual distress the longer they are involved in medical investigations and treatment (Berg & Wilson, 1991; Koropatnick et al., 1993; Lalos et al., 1986; Ulbrich et al., 1990; van Balen & Trimbos-Kemper, 1994), with distress being particularly acute for those whose diagnostic status remains ambiguous (Daniluk, 1988; McEwan et al., 1987; Sandelowski, 1987). Poorer adaptation has also been reported for women who experience their fertility outcome as being out of their control (Stanton, Tennen, Affleck, & Mendola, 1991). Gender role orientation has been implicated in the responses of women to infertility, although the precise role of this variable in enhancing or moderating distress remains to be determined (Adler & Boxley, 1985; Berg et al., 1991; Koropatnick et al., 1993). Finally, women who are less socially isolated demonstrate higher levels of life satisfaction and more adaptive coping in response to the stresses of infertility (Abbey et al., 1991; Greil, 1991; Lalos et al., 1986; Mahlstedt, 1985; Wright et al., 1989).

The picture for infertile women, however, is not as bleak as it might appear. While women report more overt distress in response to their inability to produce a child, they tend to employ more problem-focused coping strategies and escape-coping when dealing with infertility than their husbands, strategies that have proven to be quite adaptive in effectively managing chronic and long-term stressors (Abbey et al., 1991; Stanton et al., 1991). Infertile women appear to more actively seek information and solutions to the couples' fertility problems than their male counterparts, potentially serving as a buffer against feelings of powerlessness and uncertainty (Abbey et al., 1991; Stanton et al., 1991). Women also appear better able to identify and access sources of emotional support outside their marital relationships (Greil, 1991; Lalos et al., 1986; Wright et al., 1989, 1991). This would suggest that while being faced with the inability to reproduce is a difficult and often distressing life experience, women have important resources that may help them cope with, and adapt to, the stress, pain, and loss associated with being infertile.

Men's Responses to Infertility

From an anecdotal perspective, infertile women are often quoted as lamenting that their partners appear to be less sensitive to, and less distressed by, the couple's childlessness (Greil, 1991; Mahlstedt, 1985; Menning, 1979). Although few studies have been conducted with the specific intent of examining men's responses to infertility, a review of the literature would tend to support the contention that men do not appear to respond as negatively to infertility as their partners do. Men not only report less overt distress in response to their experience of being infertile (e.g., Abbey et al., 1991; Berg et al., 1991; Daniluk, 1988; Draye, Woods, & Mitchell, 1988; Newton & Houle, 1993; Ulbrich et al., 1990; Wright et al., 1989), but also appear to adapt with considerably greater ease to failed treatment and the prospect of permanent biological childlessness (Greil, 1981; Mahlstedt, 1985; Ulbrich et al., 1990). In terms of coping, infertile men appear to engage in denial, distancing, or avoidance (Abbey et al., 1991; Stanton et al., 1991; Wright et al., 1991), strategies that may exacerbate marital tensions and prolong the pursuit of alternate solutions to the couple's childlessness. Infertile men also appear to remain considerably more isolated in this area of their lives, emphasizing privacy relative to the couple's fertility struggles and turning to their partners as their primary source of communication and emotional support (Collins, Freeman, Boxer, & Tureck, 1992). However, communication between partners in infertile marriages about these issues is often quite strained, as couples appear to adopt gender-specific ways of dealing with the pain and stress wrought by infertility. This is exemplified in the words of one infertile man:

> If my wife was sobbing at night on one side of the bed, I would just turn over and not be any sort of comfort . . . I couldn't really listen to her . . . to what she was communicating and the feelings and emptiness . . . the feelings of being alone, of feeling hurt . . . my reaction was to be very silent, withdrawing, not wanting to talk about it because I couldn't fix it.

The one factor that appears to be associated with a more negative male response to infertility is the receipt of a male factor diagnosis. Men in infertile marriages characteristically assume that their wives are the source of the couple's fertility problem, and are often quite disbelieving when a shared or male-factor etiology is diagnosed (Abbey et al., 1991; Mahlstedt, 1985; Webb & Daniluk, in press). The few studies that have been conducted with the specific intent of examining men's responses to infertility suggest that receipt of the news that they are unable to produce a child is as distressing an experience for a man as it is for many infertile women (Berger, 1980; Feuer, 1983; Kedem, Mikulincer, Nathanson, & Bartoov, 1990; MacNab, 1986; Nachtigall et al., 1992).

In interviews with 16 couples experiencing male factor infertility, Berger (1980) reported a 63% rate of temporary impotence lasting one to three months following diagnosis. Elevated levels of depression and social isolation, as well as lowered self-esteem and decreased marital satisfaction were also reported in Feuer's (1983) investigation of the psychological impact of infertility on the lives of men, with greatest distress being evident for the men diagnosed as oligospermic, perhaps due to the uncertainty associated with this diagnosis. The results of MacNab's (1986) study of 30 men in infertile marriages concur with those of Feuer in identifying infertility as a major life stressor for these men; with the stress of infertility being further compounded by prolonged investigations and treatment and by an uncertain diagnosis. In research by Kedem et al. (1990), 107 men who only *suspected* they were infertile reported lower self-esteem than 30 fertile men.

Mason (1993) reported strong, negative reactions on the part of the 22 men she interviewed who had been diagnosed with male factor infertility. In in-depth interviews these men reflected on the difficult and painful process of learning to cope with the fact that they would never have their own biological children; these feelings included guilt and shame, anger, isolation, loss, and a sense of personal failure. In in-depth interviews with 23 men who received a male factor diagnosis, Nachtigall et al. (1992) also found considerable evidence that these men exhibited a "more negative emotional response to infertility than men without a male factor with respect of feelings of stigma, loss, and self-esteem" (p. 116). According to these authors, regardless of whether *both* partners were identified as contributing to the couple's infertility problem or not, men diagnosed with a male factor problem "tended to respond as did women," attributing derogatory terms to themselves such as "dud" or "loser." Words like "failure," "useless," "garbage," and "defective" appear to be fairly common labels that infertile men apply to themselves (Webb & Daniluk, in press), suggesting that infertility may indeed be a difficult and distressing life event for some infertile men. In explaining the communication difficulties between he and his partner, one infertile client said:

> I did not want to seriously examine *my* feelings because I did not want to face the feelings of pain, sorrow, disappointment and inadequacy . . . and I did not want to hear my wife's feelings of pain and anger about *my* infertility . . . a lot of it was not having the ability or the honesty to know what I was feeling.

WHY DO MEN AND WOMEN RESPOND DIFFERENTLY?

The inability to produce a child and the invasive and sometimes humiliating procedures that women and men are required to undergo in the investigation and treatment of infertility are bound to present a significant challenge to the psychological and emotional resourcefulness and well-being of infertile women and men. So why then do the research results examining responses to infertility continue to support the hypothesis that infertility is a more difficult experience for women? There may be several reasons for these apparent gender differences, including methodological considerations, the gender-specific focus of the medical workup and treatments, and the social context within which infertile men and women have been raised and must negotiate the experience of being unable to produce a child.

Methodological Considerations

In their reviews and critiques of the research literature on the psychosocial consequences of infertility, Wright et al. (1989, 1991), and Newton and Houle (1993) suggest that much of the research on which the assumptions of gender differences are made, is based on small, homogeneous samples of white, middle class, married couples who voluntarily agreed to participate in the research. Potentially significant differences in men's and women's experiences of infertility based on their ethnicity, class, marital status, or sexual orientation have not been addressed to date in this literature, limiting the generalizability of these findings. It is also important to note that men are characteristically underrepresented in much of this research, a fact that has implications for the generalizability of many of these findings.

Also, questions have been raised regarding the cross-sectional nature of much of this research, and the absence of diagnostic information prior to the onset of infertility, making it difficult to ascertain the actual impact of infertility-related stress and to differentiate between the degree to which gender differences reflect different reactions to being infertile or to the stresses involved in infertility treatment (Wright et al., 1989, 1991). Questions have been raised regarding the use of standardized measures that may be more sensitive to the ways in which women characteristically express psychosocial distress (Abbey et al., 1991; Berg et al., 1991), and about the possible tendency of men to underreport emotional distress and respond in a more socially desirable manner (Greil, 1991). Given masculine gender role socialization in our culture, the distress experienced by the infertile man may not be manifested in ways that are characteristically expected and measured in studies examining psychosocial responses to infertility.

Finally, in most of the research comparing the responses of infertile men and women, the source of couples' infertility was not included as a variable in the analysis, despite considerable evidence to suggest that the partner who perceives being responsible for the couple's problem may experience greater psychosocial distress in response to the infertility (e.g., Daniluk, 1988; McEwan et al., 1987). These methodological considerations suggest that results of studies supporting differences in the ways in which men and women respond to being infertile should be interpreted with considerable caution.

Medical Context

In attempting to interpret the available literature on gender differences in response to infertility, it is also important to consider that much of this research was undertaken while couples were undergoing medical investigations and treatment for infertility—investigations that are both physically and psychologically invasive—exposing even the most intimate and private aspects of couples' lives together to the scrutiny of strangers. Despite the rather even distribution in the causes of infertility (35% female, 35% male, 20% combined, and 10% unexplained—Mosher, 1988), until recently, the medical profession's knowledge of women's reproductive biology has been considerably more advanced than that of men's (Daniluk & Fluker, 1995). As a result, other than requests for blood work and semen samples from male partners, men have been relatively peripheral players in the medical infertility drama. Rather, it is the woman who most frequently is the primary focus of these medical investigations and treatment efforts (Daniluk & Fluker, 1995; Greil, 1991; Salzer, 1991). Infertile women endure most of the technological investigations and treatments for the *couple's* impaired fertility (e.g., numerous genital examinations, blood tests, basal body temperature charting, laparoscopy, hysteroscopy, tubal reparative surgery, ovulation induction, endometrial biopsy, in vitro fertilization, donor or husband inseminations, etc.), a fact that has significant implications for both the experience and expression of distress. As one client stated, "When you are an infertile woman you have to give your body over totally to the control of strangers." What researchers may actually be reporting then, are gender differences in response to the medically invasive investigations and treatment of infertility, rather than to the experience of being infertile.

It is also important to note that infertility treatments characteristically include the use of fairly powerful hormonal medications such as clomiphene citrate, human menopausal gonadotropins, and GnRH analogs, which for some women may be associated with psychological reactions ranging from minor mood swings and depressive symptoms, to full-blown psychotic reactions (for a review of the literature related to the emotional and psychological side effects of these reproductive medications, see Daniluk & Fluker, 1995). None of the studies that have reported gender differences in response to infertility have considered the role of these reproductive medications or procedures in heightening or exacerbating the psychosocial sensitivity or responsiveness of infertile women. It is impossible to say with any certainty then, how much of the emotional lability and expressivity of infertile women is a consequence of the medications commonly prescribed in the treatment of infertility.

Also, as pointed out by Greil (1991), irrespective of the source of a couple's infertility problem, it is the woman who fails to become pregnant and who must live with the monthly reminders of her failure that play themselves out within her body. Given that medical treatment has traditionally been based on the conceptualization of infertility as a disease, the cure for which is a viable pregnancy (Martin, 1987), menstruation comes to symbolize this disease, a monthly reminder of the infertile woman's failure to conceive. Like reproduction itself, the failure of men to reproduce is less apparent, as long as they are able to adequately perform sexually. This too may be significant in understanding the differences in the tangible experience of failure between women and men in infertile marriages.

With the current advancements in reproductive technology (e.g., bilateral epididymal sperm aspiration, micromanipulation of gametes), infertile men may have to assume a more active role in some of these treatment regimens and, as such, may experience more overt distress in response to these investigations.

At present, however, with the focus of medical testing and intervention being primarily on the female partner, clinicians need to interpret the findings regarding gender differences with caution, being cognizant of the importance of assisting infertile women in coping with the often painful and invasive medical procedures that they are required to endure in their pursuit of a pregnancy.

Social Context

Finally, and some might argue most significantly, it is important for mental health practitioners to situate their understanding of gender differences in response to being unable to reproduce within the social context in which men and women experience infertility. It is possible that these apparent gender differences may "reflect general gender differences in the ways in which men and women have been socialized to cope with negative affect" (Abbey et al., 1991, p. 298). In fact, the findings of several researchers and clinicians (Abbey et al., 1991; Berg et al., 1991; Daniluk, 1991; Mahlstedt, 1985) confirm that men and women tend to adopt gender-specific roles in responding to and coping with their infertility. These differences may well result in the erroneous perception that because men are less demonstrative about their distress, they are not as bothered by their inability to produce a child. In interpreting apparent differences in response to infertility clinicians must remember:

> Gender roles, from which gender differences emerge, are the social expression of gender identity, reflecting the social and cultural context of individual's lives, not simply their personal psychology. Differences between women's and men's response to infertility can be attributed to different perceptions of the procreative role specified for one's gender. (Nachtigall et al., 1992, p. 118)

While parenting is strongly supported as an important developmental milestone in the lives of adult men and women, gender role socialization prescribes motherhood as *the* defining role for women in our culture (Chodorow, 1978; Rich, 1977). Not surprisingly, both intentionally and involuntarily childless women experience and perceive greater pressures to assume a motherhood role, and more negative sanctions in response to their childlessness (e.g., being considered selfish, unfulfilled, etc.) (Ireland, 1993). Alternately, fatherhood is generally considered to be an important but secondary role in the lives of men, with career and economic accomplishments being the primary symbol of men's success (Kaufman, 1993). Men without children report less social pressure to parent, and fewer negative social sanctions as a result of their childless status (Veevers, 1980).

The social worlds of infertile men and women are also differentially affected by the experience of infertility. Many infertile men with whom I have worked report that their friendships with other men undergo relatively few changes when these men add the role of father to their lives. As one male client recently stated:

It's funny, but even though my closest buddy became a dad this year, things really haven't changed much. We still play hockey every Friday night and get together for a beer or coffee after work a few times a week. We might make jokes now about how when he gets home he's handed a squawking baby with dirty diapers while his wife, who really needs a break heads for the mall, but overall things aren't really different.

For many women, however, their close friendships with other women are dramatically altered when these women become mothers, and caretaking, domestic, and sometimes occupational responsibilities consume the space that was once reserved for their friendships. Unlike her male counterpart then, it would appear that the infertile woman pays an additional price for her infertility. She must cope with the many losses associated with being unable to produce a child, as well as dealing with the pain of being excluded from the lives of other significant women in her life who have made the transition into the world of motherhood.

A strong social link exists between femininity, motherhood, and value for women in North American culture (Chodorow, 1978; Ireland, 1993; Rich, 1977). It should not be surprising, therefore, that involuntarily childless women feel stigmatized by their inability to produce a child, and experience a sense of failure when their efforts to fulfill their purported "biological destiny" are frustrated (Wright et al., 1991). As stated by Nachtigall et al. (1992), "Any failure to fulfill the motherhood role negatively affects a woman's perception of herself because the failure to biologically reproduce represents a failure to meet gender role expectations" (p. 119). While more role options are becoming available for women, motherhood is still the primary defining role for women in our society. As such, social context must be taken into consideration when making assumptions about the differing motives and responses of infertile men and women, and when working with women who feel compelled to pursue medical interventions that appear to have a low probability of success.

IMPLICATIONS FOR CLINICAL PRACTICE— HOW CAN WE HELP?

In light of the literature reviewed in this chapter, what are the implications of these purported gender differences when working with infertile men and women? First, it is important that clinicians *not assume* that men and women will respond differently or stereotypically to being infertile, or that their responses mean that they are not equally invested in having a child. Many researchers and clinicians agree that the experience of infertility and the pursuit of treatment has a "major psychological impact on both men and women" (Collins et al., 1992). Both infertile men and women score higher on measures of psychosocial distress than their fertile counterparts, suggesting that the experience of infertility challenges the psychosocial competencies of most individuals irrespective of their sex (Andrews et al., 1991; Daniluk, 1988; Koropatnick et al.,

1993; McEwan et al., 1987; Wright et al., 1989, 1991). Psychological intervention needs to focus on *both* members of the infertile couple, with attention being paid to selecting interventions that are sensitive to the particular needs and social and medical realities of infertile women and men (Berg et al., 1991; Greil, 1991; Mahlstedt, 1985; Menning, 1982; Newton & Houle, 1993).

Clinicians need to be aware of how women and men manifest infertility-related distress and to be alert to both situational and contextual factors that might exacerbate the distress of a particular member of the infertile couple (e.g., cultural values, economic resources, being identified as the partner with the fertility impairment, being the primary focus on medical interventions), as well as being cognizant of intrapersonal characteristics that might put a person at greater risk for experiencing acute distress (e.g., low self-esteem, strong needs for control). It is important to be sensitive to problematic gender-stereotypic communication patterns that develop in some infertile marriages as couples attempt to negotiate the trials and tribulations of infertility treatments (Abbey et al., 1991; Mahlstedt, 1985), patterns that may lead to misinterpretation and miscommunication. Also, any interventions aimed at alleviating the distress of infertile women need to take into consideration the potential synergistic effects of the reproductive medications that are routinely used in the treatment of infertility, most of which are prescribed to the female member of the couple (Daniluk & Fluker, 1995).

The experience of infertility and the pursuit of treatment may involve literally years of a couple's life together, with the needs of couples differing based on whether they are undergoing initial medical investigations, are involved in treatment, or are attempting to deal with the consequences of successful or failed treatment. A discussion of the salient counseling issues at each of these stages follows, with a focus on possible differences in the needs of men and women at each of these stages. The goals of intervention at all stages in this process are to assist couples in coping with the considerable stressors associated with infertility; to facilitate informed and satisfying decision making regarding the available treatment interventions and parenting options; and to help couples construct satisfying lives and marriages irrespective of the outcome of treatment.

Initial Medical Investigations

Couples are considered to be infertile after one year of regular, unprotected intercourse, with medical investigations usually being initiated after the couples have been coping with their inability to conceive for an average of one or two years. Research indicates that most frequently women initiate the process of seeking medical solutions to the couple's inability to conceive or carry a viable pregnancy to term, a role that they generally persist in throughout treatment (Abbey et al., 1991; Newton & Houle, 1993). From the beginning then, the female partner is set up as the primary player in the infertility drama, a fact that is reflected in the tendency of most medical facilities to keep medical records and appointments in the woman's name, rather than in the name of the couple—implying that the male partner's role in procreation is secondary at best. As such, it is important from the outset that mental health counselors encourage clients to view infertility as the "couple's problem," to reinforce a necessary solidarity and alliance between the couple prior to being faced with a diagnosis and various treatment options, and to reduce the tendency to place blame or instill feelings of guilt if one partner is identified as being the source of the couple's fertility impairment.

Men should be encouraged to become actively involved in the pursuit of solutions to the couple's fertility concerns at each stage in the process, attending medical appointments together and accessing resources and discussing information on infertility and the various treatment and parenting options (Wright et al., 1991). This includes being informed about, and present for the often uncomfortable, humiliating, and invasive procedures (e.g., endometrial biopsy, laparoscopy, etc.) that are required of their wives in the investigation and treatment of infertility, and of ways that they may help them cope with these procedures. Couples should be encouraged to keep the lines of communication open between them, to be reasonable in their expectations of each other, and to be tolerant of differences in coping styles (Daniluk, 1991; Mahlstedt, 1985). It is particularly important that couples not make assumptions about the other's thoughts, feelings, or motivations regarding parenting and the pursuit of various treatment options, and that mechanisms be set in place early in this process to set workable boundaries around the couple's communications about their infertility (Greil, 1991). An emphasis on shared responsibility and commitment to pursuing medical solutions appears to serve as an important buffer to feelings of depression, marital unhappiness, and sexual dissatisfaction, particularly for infertile wives (Link & Darling, 1986).

While research indicates that couples are frequently quite anxious about what might be required of them during the initial medical investigations (Berg & Wilson, 1991; Daniluk, 1988), their fears are usually balanced with optimism and hope, believing that the source of their problem will be identified and a medical solution will be forthcoming. Without dashing these hopes, clinicians can help prepare couples for some of the personal and relationship strains characteristically experienced during the medical investigations, can normalize their fears and concerns, and can help couples develop strategies for coping with feelings of powerless and the loss of control that is often experienced during the medical process (Daniluk, 1991). It is also important to prepare couples for possible differences in their responses to the experience of being infertile, and to contextualize these differences, not as an indication of individual psychopathology, but as understandable responses to societal expectations and lifelong gender-role socialization, and to the pain and losses involved in being unable to produce a child (Berg et al., 1991; Daniluk, 1991; Greil, 1991; Nachtigall et al., 1992).

At this stage in the process then, support and information are particularly important. Clinicians can help couples become informed consumers of medical services (medications, procedures, etc.) and can support them in their efforts to find ways of ensuring that their needs are met and their rights are respected within a medical system that is often experienced as foreign and intimidating. Strategies such as relaxation techniques, self-hypnosis, and visualizations are useful aids for coping with the unpleasant and sometimes painful investigative procedures. Also, couples may need assistance in dealing with the disclosure of information regarding their past sexual and reproductive histories, particularly in cases where this information has not been previously shared within the couple's relationship.

Diagnosis and Treatment

The analogy most frequently used by couples to refer to this stage in the infertility process is an emotional "roller coaster" (Daniluk, 1991; Mahlstedt, 1985; Menning, 1982). After what for most couples has been years of attempting to produce a child, receipt of a definitive diagnosis, if one is forthcoming, is initially met with relief by the couple ("We finally have an answer"), and considerable emotional upheaval by the partner who is identified as being the source of the couple's problem (Daniluk, 1988; McEwan et al., 1987; Nachtigall et al., 1992). Research suggests that, consistent with societal perceptions that infertility is a woman's problem, most infertile men and women assume that the couples' infertility problem will be attributed to female factor abnormalities (Berg et al., 1991; Menning, 1982; Newton & Houle, 1993). As stated by one client who was shocked at the receipt of a male factor diagnosis:

> I just assumed that it obviously wasn't my problem, it had to be her's. . . . Infertility is not a male problem, it's a female problem. The woman can't have the baby. Not the man, it's the woman . . . the woman is the one who needs to be tested, not the man.

News of a male factor problem, then, is usually met with considerable disbelief on the part of both partners, with both wives and husbands often continuing to assume that there must be something wrong with her as well (Greil, 1991; Mason, 1993; Nachtigall et al., 1992; Webb & Daniluk, in press). The immediate response to a male factor diagnosis is for many men to use denial as a coping mechanism, or to retreat into other activities as a way to avoid dealing with the grief and loss, and feelings of profound inadequacy at being unable to father a child (Mason, 1993; Nachtigall et al., 1992; Stanton et al., 1991; Webb & Daniluk, in press). While denial can be an adaptive short-term response to infertility, long-term it can become quite problematic, preventing the couple from making important treatment decisions and acting on other available parenting options. When denial is employed as a long-term coping response, clinicians may need to focus on helping the infertile man break through this denial, and work through his pain so that he can begin to come to terms with some of the implications and losses associated with being infertile. In reflecting on the depth of this loss, one male client said:

> It was more grief than I had with the loss of my grandfather. It was just grief—physical, emotional grief, that I had lost—this gift, this ability—fertility—the idea that I would never see, never have a child, a biological child that would have some of my characteristics.

Another client described his sense of inadequacy in the following way:

> A man should be able to have children . . . to give his wife children. So because I couldn't I wasn't a real man . . . simple, straightforward . . . that's why I felt an attack on my maleness . . . it all comes down to one word—inadequate.

Since the expression of emotion is not consistent with male gender role socialization, and the lack of their partners' ability to share their feelings about being infertile is a primary complaint of many infertile wives (Mahlstedt, 1985; Menning, 1982; Wright et al., 1991), clinicians may need to be creative in this regard. Some individual counseling sessions with the male partner can be helpful, and men can be encouraged to communicate their feelings to their partner in writing if they are uncomfortable doing so verbally. For example, one infertile client reflected on the letter he wrote to his wife, trying to express to her his feelings:

> With a lump in my throat I wrote that I felt unmanly, inadequate, and powerless when I compared myself to other men who have children . . . I also explained that I felt inadequate sometimes when my performance as a sexual partner was not perfect . . . and I told her I'd give her freedom to find a more worthy, manly husband who could give her the children she wanted and deserved.

Women who are diagnosed with a fertility problem tend to respond with shame, guilt, and self-blame (Daniluk, 1996; Lalos et al., 1986; Mahlstedt, 1985), and exhibit an increased vulnerability to psychological distress (Stanton et al., 1991). They frequently initiate a life review process, searching their pasts for perceived transgressions that may help them make sense of their inability to produce a child. Unlike their partners, they readily assume the blame for the couple's problem, and are often anxious to initiate treatment solutions. Perceived or expressed reluctance on the part of their partners to immediately pursue treatment often exacerbates the distress and isolation experienced by infertile women, who are usually very cognizant of the biological time limits placed on their fertility (Mahlstedt, 1985; Salzer, 1991). One client reflected on her response to her husband's apparent reluctance to pursue in vitro fertilization:

> I wanted so desperately to have my own biological child . . . at any cost, and when he didn't seem interested in doing IVF, I went crazy . . . he used to say, "well I married you for you, I didn't marry you for having children, we didn't get married to procreate, we married because we loved each other" . . . I didn't want to hear that he didn't feel the same way I did. I felt quite alone. Even though he was very understanding, I knew he didn't feel the way I felt so when he tried to be understanding, I would just get more angry. There was a lot of anger and

denial . . . that really took it's toll on our marriage . . . it took a long time to work through.

Helping men understand the urgency experienced by their partners to continue pursuing solutions, is an important part of assisting couples at this stage in the treatment process.

Clinicians need to help women clients work through their feelings of loss, guilt, and shame associated with being infertile and to separate the biological reality of their fertility status from the concept of punishment. This is often highly emotional work, but given the ease with which many women engage in this type of exploration and the expression of feelings, the work can usually be undertaken with both members of the couple present. Whether the diagnosis is male factor, female factor, or combined, to make treatment and parenting decisions that both members of the couple can live with, it is important that the needs of both partners are given voice in counseling (Anton, 1992; Daniluk, 1991; Menning, 1982; Salzer, 1991).

Often the most difficult situation for the couple to cope with is the receipt of an ambiguous or uncertain diagnosis (commonly referred to as "unexplained" or *"normal"* infertility). Research results consistently report the enhanced difficulties experienced by the approximately 10% of couples whose fertility problems cannot be medically explained (e.g., Koropatnick et al., 1993; McEwan et al., 1987; Nachtigall et al., 1992). Specifically in reference to the experiences of infertile women, Sandelowski (1987) discusses the notion of "hope born out of ambiguity" (p. 71), and the tendency for couples, and women in particular, to become "stuck" in the process of coming to terms with their infertility when they are uncertain of what treatment options they should realistically pursue given that everything appears to be *normal.* These couples in particular often find it very difficult to "'quit' and move on with their lives." When working with couples who receive an equivocal diagnosis, clinicians need to help them find ways to cope with the ambiguity and uncertainty, and live with not knowing why biological parenthood is being denied to them. Not unlike trying to make sense of an accidental death, this often requires both existential and spiritual exploration, in terms of reconciling the reality of their loss and learning to live with the unknown.

Whatever the source of their difficulties, the receipt of a medical diagnosis is usually followed by a cycle of fears, hopes, and disappointments as couples are faced with deciding between a host of often expensive, controversial, and time-consuming treatment options, each of which is accompanied by a set of statistically generated "success rates," the interpretation of which would prove challenging to even the most well-trained researcher. Depending on the diagnosis, the list of treatment options may include the use of synthetic hormones to induce ovulation or diminish endometrial tissue; hours of microsurgery to repair damaged or blocked tubes; insemination with the husband's sperm or donor semen; in vitro fertilization with the wife's eggs and the husband's sperm, with donor eggs and the husband's sperm, with the wife's eggs and donor sperm, or with donor eggs fertilized with donor sperm. In some states, surrogacy is also an option, with an embryo from one or both members of the couple, or with a donor embryo. Couples often progress from one treatment regime to another, facing numerous decision points throughout the process until they are either successful in achieving a live birth, until they decide that they can no longer afford to continue pursuing treatment (emotionally or financially), or until treatment options run out.

Pursuing infertility treatment is often extremely protracted, sometimes consuming literally years of the couple's life together. Several of the treatments are also quite expensive, taxing the financial resources of many couples, and prohibiting the pursuit of certain options for others. Mental health counselors can assist infertile couples during this stage in the process by helping them to make informed treatment decisions based on their unique needs and values and in consideration of their personal circumstances and resources (Daniluk, 1991; Mahlstedt, 1985). Couples require validation of their feelings and support for their choices, even when these choices appear to have a relatively remote probability of success. They may require assistance in coming to agreement about the most appropriate course of action. While women, both outside and within their relationships, tend to access social support (Berg et al., 1991; McEwan et al., 1987), infertile men may need help seeking additional sources of support rather than placing the entire burden on their wives to help them cope with the considerable stresses associated with treatment (Abbey et al., 1991).

Posttreatment

Infertile clients often need help in assuming control over their treatment choices and setting limits on the extent of treatment they are willing to endure. The research is mixed in terms of the relationship between duration of treatment and level of adaptation. Some researchers have reported a relationship between duration of treatment and poorer psychosocial adaptation (e.g., Berg & Wilson, 1991; Link & Darling, 1986), while others have identified an interaction between time in treatment and variables such as diagnostic status, gender role orientation, self-esteem, coping styles, social support, marital quality, and financial and employment status (e.g., Adler & Boxley, 1985; Koropatnick et al., 1993; Link & Darling, 1986; McEwan et al., 1987; Ulbrich et al., 1990; van Balen & Trimbos-Kemper, 1994). What is apparent, however, is that for most couples the pursuit of infertility treatment takes up a considerable amount of space in their lives, resulting in other significant life decisions being kept "on hold" while the couple's future parental status remains uncertain (Daniluk, 1991; Mahlstedt, 1985; Menning, 1982; Salzer, 1991). As such, infertile couples may require assistance in extricating themselves from the medical system when they no longer have the emotional, financial, or personal resources to continue pursuing medical solutions to their infertility.

Couples often find it difficult to determine when "enough is enough," when it is time to abandon treatment and relinquish the hope of having their own biological child. In terms of gender differences, the literature suggests that infertile women in particular appear to have greater difficulty than their partners in making a decision to abandon treatment and in accepting the possibility of remaining childless (Mahlstedt, 1985; Menning, 1982; Newton & Houle, 1993; Sandelowski, 1987). Perhaps because parenting is only one of the legitimate adult roles that define success for men, they appear to negotiate the transition to biological childlessness with greater ease (Ulbrich et al., 1990). Infertile women, however, must deal with the relative absence of other socially sanctioned role options (Ireland, 1993), and with monthly reminders of their "failure" to do what most other women appear capable of doing with relative ease, making it more difficult to accept and resolve their infertility. In fact, in a recent study (Lieblum, Kemmann, & Lane, 1987), 93% of infertile women in an IVF program, who claimed to have resolved their infertility, indicated a willingness to participate in any new treatment options that might become available in the future, underscoring their difficulty in reconciling themselves to their biologically childless status. Women often need help in overcoming their feelings of failure, in abdicating their sense of responsibility for pursuing *all* available treatment options, and in finding ways to reconcile themselves to their biological childlessness (Berg et al., 1991; Greil, 1991; Nachtigall et al., 1992; Newton, Hearn, Yuzpe, & Houle, 1992). Clinicians can help the infertile woman redefine success, from the achievement of a pregnancy, to the creation of a meaningful life structure separate from her status as a biological parent.

A poignant example of this difficulty in letting go is apparent in the story of a client who came face to face with the extent of her desperation in pursuing infertility treatments and was forced to confront the futility of her efforts to conceive a child:

> Following several years of investigations, my physician informed me that extensive surgery would provide my only hope of conceiving a child. My immediate response was "book it." "But don't you want to know what it involves," said the physician, to which I responded "book it." "But don't you even want to know the probability of success or the risks," said he. I implored him, "Please, just book it." At that moment, I realized that had the physician told me women with one leg had a better chance of conceiving a child, I would have unhesitatingly offered to have my leg cut off. I knew then that it was time to quit . . . that it wasn't making sense anymore.

While dramatic, this anecdote underscores the level of anguish and desperation experienced by many infertile women as they attempt to make "informed decisions" about the continued pursuit of medical intervention. Men, too, may find it difficult to terminate treatment, particularly if their partners are highly invested in continuing to pursue options, or if they are the sole cause of the couple's infertility. As one male client said:

> How could I possibly tell her I wouldn't participate in any more treatment or in trying to adopt. After all, it was my fault that we were going through all this . . .

it was *my* fault that I wasn't able to fulfill my role and give her a baby. Whatever she wanted, it had to be okay with me, even if what she wanted was a different partner who could give her a baby.

Mental health practitioners may need to assist couples in examining their respective motivations for continuing treatment, and in exploring alternative parenting options that may be available to them, including the possibility of remaining child-free.

Whether couples have selected to reject further treatment, whether medicine no longer has treatment options to offer them, or whether they are finally successful in achieving a pregnancy, it is important for clinicians to be aware that the experience of infertility does not end when treatment ends. Rather, while couples often experience tremendous relief that their bodies and lives will no longer be invaded by medications, probes, and practitioners, the end of treatment also brings them face to face with the reality of their infertility (Daniluk, 1991, 1996).

Couples who are successful in making the transition to parenthood usually feel blessed in their good fortune and grateful to those whose knowledge and skill and caring have helped them achieve this precious "gift of life." However, following years of coping with infertility couples may still require assistance in coping with the stress of bringing a pregnancy to term and effectively parenting the child (or children in the case of multiple births) that they have invested so much time and energy in creating. Should they decide to increase their family size at some point in the future, they may need assistance and support as they are again faced with the reality of their infertility and contemplate the prospect of putting themselves through another stressful and potentially expensive medical process that may or may not result in a subsequent pregnancy.

More frequently counselors are faced with helping the 50% of couples who have not been successful in achieving a pregnancy through medical intervention. These couples require assistance in coping with feelings of anger and frustration at having had this important life experience denied to them, and having been failed by a system into whose care they had put their lives and their trust. As one infertile client reiterated:

You go through all that grief and aggravation and all the medication . . . and you give your body over totally to the control of total strangers . . . and when it doesn't work, you're left with nothing.

With the end of treatment, couples often need help in coping with intense feelings of grief associated with the loss of the son or daughter that they will never know, the loss of a meaningful life role, the loss of genetic continuity, and the loss of their lives together as they had been envisioned. For the woman whose socialization and biology serve as constant reminders of her fertility status, infertility may be experienced as a loss of the self. In the words of one infertile client:

There is something about childlessness that goes to the very core of your being ... it's almost like it's the only thing that we can do that's really so unique to ourselves ... when we cannot do that it really goes very deep ... nothing else can be compared.

Facilitating the expression and resolution of this grief is an important part of helping infertile couples come to terms with their infertility. According to Menning (1979), "failure—or, more accurately, inability—to grieve is the single most common presenting problem" (p. 104) for infertile couples. In the words of one client:

Who do you invite to this funeral where there's no body? There hasn't ever been a body, let alone having one present there. We talked about it and never have been able to come to a resolution as to how we would mark the passage, the loss of this child that we could never have.

One way of helping men and women express their grief is to ask both members of the couple to write letters to their unborn child. The letters, which partners can later be asked to share with each other, serve as a powerful vehicle for expressing clients' pain and grief at having never had a chance to know and experience this child as part of their lives (see Daniluk, 1991). Couples can also be encouraged to create rituals that help them say goodbye to their hopes and dreams of producing a child together. Affective and expressive techniques such as rituals are particularly useful in helping couples bring some closure to this part of their lives (Anton, 1992). For example, one couple with whom I worked recently, completed a ritual during which they put the names on two helium balloons, of the son and daughter they had hoped to conceive, and in a private location that had personal significance for them, they released the balloons into the air and together read the poem "Burial" (author unknown). Another couple returned to the beach where they first made plans to have children together, and there in the sand they buried their hopes for the child that they would never produce.

It is also important for clinicians to help infertile men and women find a way to incorporate their infertility into their self-structures; into their identities. For both men and women, infertility is an assault on their self-esteem, on their sense of masculinity and femininity, and on their identities (Abbey et al., 1991; Berg et al., 1991; Koropatnick et al., 1993; Mason, 1993; Nachtigall et al., 1992). As long as couples pursue treatment, there is always a possibility that their tenancy in the land of the infertile will only be temporary. As Greil (1991) states, until hope is abandoned, the infertile person perceives him- herself as "not yet pregnant." When treatment ends and couples are faced with the permanence of their infertility however, they often need help in beginning the process of more fully incorporating their infertility into their lives and self-structures and consolidating a new sense of themselves as biologically childless, individually, and as a couple. As stated by one infertile client: "It's like a part of yourself that you

have to redefine. Because for me it's always been a part of my self-concept . . .
that I'm going to be a mum someday." A client diagnosed with male factor infertility stated:

> If I'd had a good self-image, a good hold on what it meant to be masculine, what
> it meant to be male, I think infertility would have affected me a lot less. Be-
> cause maleness doesn't come from having kids . . . or having the ability to give
> a woman a baby . . . it's something else.

Part of this process then, involves helping infertile men and women to separate
their concept of masculinity and femininity from their ability to procreate, as
well as helping them identify and value other meaningful role options and other
personal strengths. Clinicians can also assist by reinforcing the couple's respective strengths and resourcefulness in having survived a very difficult and
painful life experience.

Infertile women may also need assistance in coping with the loss of significant relationships with other women who once were an important part of their
social worlds but who have now made the transition to biological motherhood—
a world denied to the infertile woman. Clinicians can help women redefine and
renegotiate these important relationships, as well as helping them to reinvest
their time and energy in relationships with other women for whom mothering
is not a central component of their lives.

Finally, when couples have developed a long-term life plan that includes a
large part of their lives focused on raising children, the inability to achieve this
goal often leaves them at a loss in terms of what the future might look like.
The prospect of permanent childlessness frequently leaves couples questioning
their commitments to a home, to their careers, and to their plans for the future.
To be able to move forward, couples first need assistance in working through
and reconciling the past, in terms of the years spent attempting to conceive
and the time and quality of life lost to them while engaged in the pursuit of
medical and nonmedical solutions to their infertility. Subsequently, it is important for clinicians to help infertile couples look toward the future and set
new goals, based on a reassessment of the importance of parenting in their lives
and on the viability of parenting and nonparenting options. It is important to
help couples find ways to make sense of their infertility and to reconstruct a
meaningful life vision that will bring them fulfillment even though it does not
include biological children (see Daniluk, 1991; Greil, 1991; Mahlstedt, 1985;
Salzer, 1991).

CONCLUSION

The extent of emotional upheaval for both women and men caused by their inability to produce a child and the prolonged pursuit of medical treatment should
not be underestimated. Not all individuals experience infertility as a "crisis"

(Menning, 1979); however, infertility represents a difficult, painful, and challenging life experience for many individuals and couples. While the research suggests that infertility is a more distressing experience for women, and that women have greater difficulty in reconciling themselves to being biologically childless, clinicians must base their understanding of gender differences in response to infertility in light of the medical and social context within which the infertile couple must negotiate their experience of infertility. It is important for counselors to be aware of the differing needs of men and women as they seek solutions to their infertility, and of the factors that serve to exacerbate the distress of *both* members of the infertile couple. Finally, clinicians need to approach their work with infertile couples with the understanding that while infertility can challenge all aspects of an individual's and couple's life together, it can also have beneficial effects, in terms of increased levels of trust, intimacy, and communication, and a renewed and deeper commitment to the relationship (Daniluk, 1988; Greil, 1991; Stanton et al., 1991; Webb & Daniluk, in press). It seems appropriate to close with the words of one infertile man:

> I could never have imagined that an area that had kept us so distant from each other, infertility, and in such pain, could make us feel so close. . . . Infertility has tested us. It has taken us to the edge of despair and has brought us to new understanding and depths; new tightness together as a couple . . . I wouldn't wish this experience on anyone, but in some ways, its made us so much stronger . . . when you come out the other end, whether you have been blessed with a child or not, you're different because of having gone through this . . . you're not the same, and neither is your partner or your marriage. If your marriage can survive infertility, it can survive anything!

REFERENCES

Abbey, A., Andrews, F. M., & Halman, L. J. (1991). Gender's role in responses to infertility. *Psychology of Women Quarterly, 15*, 295–316.

Adler, J. D., & Boxley, R. L. (1985). The psychological reactions to infertility: Sex roles and coping styles. *Sex Roles, 12*, 271–279.

Andrews, F. M., Abbey, A., & Halman, L. J. (1991). Stress from infertility, marriage factors, and subjective well-being of wives and husbands. *Journal of Health and Social Behavior, 32*, 238–263.

Anton, L. H. (1992). *Never to be a mother: A guide for all women who didn't—or couldn't—have children.* New York: HarperCollins.

Berg, B. J., & Wilson, J. F. (1991). Psychological functioning across stages of treatment for infertility. *Journal of Behavioral Medicine, 14*, 11–26.

Berg, B. J., Wilson, J. F., & Weingartner, P. J. (1991). Psychological sequelae of infertility treatment: The role of gender and sex-role identification. *Social Sciences and Medicine, 33*, 1071–1080.

Berger, M. D. (1980). Impotence following discovery of azoospermia. *Fertility and Sterility, 34*, 154–156.

Chodorow, N. (1978). *The reproduction of mothering: Psychoanalysis and the sociology of gender.* Berkeley: University of California Press.

Collins, A., Freeman, E. W., Boxer, A. S., & Tureck, R. (1992). Perceptions of infertility and treatment stress in females as compared with males entering in vitro fertilization treatment. *Fertility and Sterility, 57,* 350–356.

Daniluk, J. C. (1988). Infertility: Intrapersonal and interpersonal impact. *Fertility and Sterility, 49,* 982–990.

Daniluk, J. C. (1991). Strategies for counseling infertile couples. *Journal of Counseling & Development, 69,* 317–320.

Daniluk, J. C. (1996). When treatment fails: The transition to biological childlessness for infertile women. *Women & Therapy.*

Daniluk, J. C., & Fluker, M. (1995). Fertility drugs and the reproductive imperative: Assisting the infertile woman. *Women & Therapy, 16,* 31–47.

Draye, M. A., Woods, N. F., & Mitchell, E. (1988). Coping with infertility in couples: Gender differences. *Health Care for Women International, 9,* 163–175.

Feuer, G. S. (1983). The psychological impact of infertility on the lives of men. (Doctoral dissertation, University of Pennsylvania, 1993.) *Dissertation Abstracts International, 44,* 706A–707A.

Greil, A. L. (1991). *Not yet pregnant: Infertile couples in contemporary America.* London: Rutgers University Press.

Greil, A. L., Leitko, T. A., & Porter, K. L. (1988). Infertility: His and hers. *Gender & Society, 2,* 172–199.

Ireland, M. S. (1993). *Reconceiving women: Separating motherhood from female identity.* New York: Guilford Press.

Kaufman, M. (1993). *Cracking the armour: Power and pain in the lives of men.* Toronto, Ontario, Canada: Penguin Books.

Kedem, P., Mikulincer, M., Nathanson, Y., & Bartoov, B. (1990). Psychological aspects of male infertility. *British Journal of Medical Psychology, 63,* 73–80.

Koropatnick, S., Daniluk, J., & Pattinson, H. A. (1993). Infertility: A non-even transition. *Fertility and Sterility, 59,* 163–171.

Lalos, A., Lalos, O., Jacobsson, L., & Von Schoultz, B. (1986). Depression, guilt and isolation among infertile women and their partners. *Journal of Psychosomatic Obstetrics and Gynecology, 5,* 197–206.

Lieblum, S. R., Kemmann, E., & Lane, M. K. (1987). The psychological concomitants of in vitro fertilization. *Journal of Psychosomatic Obstetrics and Gynecology, 6,* 165–178.

Link, P. W., & Darling, C. A. (1986). Couples undergoing treatment for infertility: Dimensions of life satisfaction. *Journal of Sex & Marital Therapy, 12,* 46–59.

MacNab, R. T. (1986). Infertility and men: A study of change and adaptive choices in the lives of involuntarily childless men. (Doctoral dissertation, The Fielding Institute, 1984.) *Dissertation Abstracts International, 47,* 774A.

Mahlstedt, P. P. (1985). The psychological component of infertility. *Fertility and Sterility, 43,* 335–346.

Martin, E. (1987). *The woman in the body: A cultural analysis of reproduction.* Boston, MA: Beacon Press.

Mason, M. C. (1993). *Male infertility—Men talking*. London: Routledge.

McEwan, K. L., Costello, C. G., & Taylor, P. J. (1987). Adjustment to infertility. *Journal of Abnormal Psychology, 96,* 108–116.

McGrade, J. J., & Tolor, A. (1981). The reaction to infertility and the infertility investigation: A comparison of the responses of men and women. *Infertility, 4,* 7–27.

Menning, B. E. (1979). Counseling infertile couples. *Contemporary Obstetrics and Gynecology, 13,* 101–108.

Menning, B. E. (1982). The emotional needs of infertile couples. *Fertility and Sterility, 34,* 313–319.

Mosher, W. D. (1988). Fecundity and infertility in the United States. *American Journal of Public Health, 78,* 181–182.

Nachtigall, R. D., Becker, G., & Wozny, M. (1992). The effects of gender-specific diagnosis on men's and women's response to infertility. *Fertility and Sterility, 57,* 113–121.

Newton, C. R., Hearn, M. T., Yuzpe, A. A., & Houle, M. (1992). Motives for parenthood and response to failed in vitro fertilization: Implications for counseling. *Journal of Assisted Reproduction and Genetics, 9,* 24–31.

Newton, C., & Houle, M. (1993). Gender differences in psychological response to infertility treatment. *The Canadian Journal of Human Sexuality, 2,* 129–139.

Rich, A. (1977). *Of woman born: Motherhood as experience and institution*. New York: Basic Books.

Salzer, L. P. (1991). *Surviving infertility: A compassionate guide through the emotional crisis of infertility* (2nd ed.). New York: HarperPerrennial.

Sandelowski, M. (1987). The color gray: Ambiguity and infertility. *IMAGE: Journal of Nursing Scholarship, 19,* 70–74.

Stanton, A. L., Tennen, H., Affleck, G., & Mendola, R. (1991). Cognitive appraisal and adjustment to infertility. *Women & Health, 17,* 1–15.

Ulbrich, P. M., Coyle, A. T., & Llabre, M. M. (1990). Involuntary childlessness and marital adjustment: His and hers. *Journal of Sex & Marital Therapy, 16,* 147–158.

van Balen, F., & Trimbos-Kemper, T. C. M. (1994). Factors influencing the well-being of long-term infertile couples. *Journal of Psychosomatic Obstetrics and Gynecology, 15,* 157–164.

Veevers, J. (1980). *Childless by choice*. Toronto, Ontario, Canada: Butterworth.

Webb, R., & Daniluk, J. C. (in press). The end of the line: Infertile men and the experience of biological childlessness. *masculinities.*

Wright, J. W., Allard, M., Lecours, A., & Sabourin, S. (1989). Psychosocial distress and infertility: A review of controlled research. *International Journal of Fertility, 34,* 126–142.

Wright, J., Duchesne, C., Sabourin, S., Bissonette, F., Benoit, J., & Girard, Y. (1991). Psychosocial distress and infertility: Men and women respond differently. *Fertility and Sterility, 55,* 100–108.

PART TWO

Clinical Considerations and Treatment

CHAPTER 7

He Does, She Doesn't; She Does, He Doesn't: Couple Conflicts about Infertility

YAKOV M. EPSTEIN and HELANE S. ROSENBERG

This chapter deals with disagreements and conflicts that couples experience as they cope with infertility. We define a conflict as a set of opposing preferences. An example of infertility-related opposing preferences is one partner wanting to spend money on infertility treatment and another wanting to spend money on adoption. Research studies have reported that infertility conflicts are common and that negative reactions such as anger, hostility, isolation, blaming and feeling blamed, feeling unsupported, feeling misunderstood, feeling that one's spouse is not equally committed to having children, and worrying about a possible breakup of the relationship, are consequences of these conflicts (Mahlstedt, 1985; Mazor, 1984; Spencer, 1987; West, 1983; Woollette, 1985). Despite these negative responses, other research finds that couples facing infertility exhibit normal levels of marital satisfaction (Wright et al., 1991; Callan & Hennessey, 1989). Some studies even report increased closeness, love, and partner support (Fleming & Burry, 1988; Honea-Fleming, 1986). To understand how couples handle infertility-related disagreements and to become familiar with the conditions under which those disagreements can adversely affect a marriage, it is necessary to discuss some aspects of conflict and its resolution (Deutsch, 1973; Pruitt & Rubin, 1986).

Attitudes, emotions, cognitions, and fantasies are variables that influence the course and outcome of a conflict. A great disparity in important attitudes can contribute to conflicts that are difficult to resolve. For example, we have seen couples in conflict over attitudes concerning the acceptability of selective reduction of fetuses. Dissimilar cognitions may involve a pessimistic partner who believes "Things will never change—I'll never get pregnant" and an optimistic one who believes, "What we've suffered are just temporary setbacks."

The personality characteristics of the parties can also heighten or reduce marital strain. We will examine how certain personality pairings can increase tensions between infertile spouses. We will also examine how differences in ways of explaining setbacks to oneself, what Martin Seligman calls "explanatory style" (Seligman, 1990) can create problems for couples. Finally, we will focus on how gender differences in dealing with infertility can contribute to conflict.

Another important factor is the motivation of each party to resolve the conflict. We will discuss male-female differences in motivation noting that some studies have found women to be more highly motivated to have children than men are (Greil, 1991; Ulbrich, Coyle, & Llabre, 1990). Differences in life circumstances, such as when one partner has children from a previous marriage and the other has never been married or had children, can be another motivational factor. In our work with infertility patients, we have noticed that often the partner who has children is less motivated to participate in expensive and emotionally draining infertility treatments. A final motivational variable is the resources available to the parties. Resource scarcity makes conflict harder to resolve productively. Two important resources are the availability of money and the quality of insurance coverage.

The content of issues and the way they are framed are other important factors. Much of this chapter will be devoted to an exploration of the important issues that become the arena for infertility related conflicts. How these issues are formulated is very important (Fisher, 1964; Fisher & Ury, 1983). Roger Fisher (1964), an expert in negotiations, has discussed the importance of *issue control.* How a husband and wife define the issues will determine whether they will be magnified or minimized. It is much easier to resolve issues that are confined to a specific point in time and to a specific action and its specific consequence, than to deal with principles or rights. It may be much easier, for example, for spouses to settle a conflict phrased as "Shall we or shall we not spend $15,000 on treatment" than to deal with "Are you or are you not a stingy person who never wants to spend any money on things that are important to me."

The nature of interested audiences to the conflict should also be considered. Conflicts that are known by others or conflicts that take place in front of an audience are more difficult to resolve than conflicts enacted privately. Family and friends can become important audiences who comment on the couple's childlessness (Mahlstedt, 1985; Menning, 1982). The tensions between spouses may be enacted in front of these interested audiences. A mother or father or an in-law may express strong opinions about whether the couple should pursue treatment or "let nature take its course." These audiences can egg on one of the participants who may need to take a more rigid posture to please this audience.

Throughout this chapter, we will present cases of infertile couples who experienced tension in their relationship. Where possible, we will refer to the preceding variables to help clarify the source of the tension. We will describe our interventions to help these couples manage their conflicts productively.

GENDER DIFFERENCES IN DEALING
WITH INFERTILITY

The topic of gender differences in response to infertility is treated in great detail by Daniluk in Chapter 6 of this book. In this chapter, we will focus on how these gender differences may contribute to infertility-related marital conflict. Greil (1991) points out that American society has a "motherhood mandate" but does not have a similar "fatherhood mandate." This differential societal expectation may trigger more feelings of distress in women than in men. In her review of research, Daniluk (Chapter 6) cites studies indicating that compared with men, women experience more psychosocial distress, lower self-esteem, and more depression. Greil (1991) notes that women view infertility as a devastating experience, whereas men view it as a "bad break." Women locate the cause of their infertility in themselves—either in terms of some biological deficit or as a result of some past misdeed (Daniluk, 1991). Many women view infertility as pervading their entire existence, whereas it is a much more circumscribed experience for men (Greil, 1991). This difference in views and experiences can lead to differing motivations to seek medical treatment for the fertility problem (Greil, 1991; Ulbrich et al., 1990; Wright et al., 1991). We hypothesize that this difference in motivation may contribute to some of the conflicts we have witnessed in therapy.

Research has shown that generally speaking, women are much more willing to disclose to others information about upsetting personal matters (Cozby, 1973; Davidson & Duberman, 1982; Peplau & Gordon, 1985). Consequently, women may be more likely than men to talk about their infertility concerns with their friends and colleagues. One can mistakenly assume that because men talk and focus less on infertility, they are less upset about it. Daniluk (Chapter 6) cautions clinicians to avoid assuming that the outward male response to infertility means that men are less invested than women in having a child. The different ways that men and women respond to infertility may, in fact, be a reflection of gender-related differences in coping with *any* upsetting situation.

Indeed, research has found that women are emotional specialists, seeking to talk and vent about what's bothering them and men are instrumental specialists bent on "fixing" a problem (Allen & Haccoun, 1976; Rubin, 1983). Thus, although a man may be upset about infertility, he may not choose to talk about it. His wife may mistakenly attribute his unwillingness to talk about it as a sign of disinterest rather than as a style of coping. Her misattribution may fuel conflict.

DIFFERENCES IN EXPLANATORY STYLE

Infertility is an upsetting and stressful experience. Faced with infertility, some people let nature take its course believing that "what will be will be." Others consult a gynecologist, follow her advice about monitoring temperature and timing intercourse, and then if they don't get pregnant, give up and become depressed. At the other extreme are couples who constantly undertake new medical procedures, repeat cycles of the most advanced treatments, and persist until they become pregnant. What accounts for the differences between those people who give up easily and those who never give up?

Seligman's (1990) research on explanatory style may shed light on this question. To paraphrase Seligman, an infertile man who has been diagnosed with a male factor problem and who is likely to give up easily will say to himself, "My wife's infertility is because of *me.* She'll never get pregnant. Infertility is ruining my whole life." In contrast, a woman who has a very different explanatory style to make sense of her infertility is likely to think, "The treatments we've been doing so far haven't been the right ones. Maybe next month we'll do something different. Maybe next month is the month I'll get pregnant. Anyway, there's much more to my life than infertility. I have a good job and a loving husband."

Each of these explanations consists of three elements: *permanence, pervasiveness,* and *personalization.* If one member of a couple views infertility as a permanent condition and the other sees it as transitory, they may experience tension. If one person focuses on personal responsibility for the failures and the other looks to external forces, they may have difficulty commiserating. Finally, where one sees infertility as a circumscribed aspect of life and the other sees it as pervading every facet of existence they may feel that they don't share a common problem. One of those partners can be viewed as an optimist and the other as a pessimist. The optimist will want to hang in, find creative solutions, keep trying new approaches, and look for ways to finance treatment even in the face of dwindling finances. The pessimist will become depressed and will want to give up.

Case Example

Nina and Patrick exemplified very different explanatory styles. Nina displayed two of the three characteristics associated with pessimism. She took personal responsibility for her infertility and she considered her situation to be permanently hopeless. When we first met her, Nina told us, "Even before I met my husband I always knew that I'd never get pregnant. I didn't have any medical information to tell me so, but I felt it in my gut ever since I was a teenager. Now I see that I'm right. I'm not pregnant and I'll never get pregnant." On the other hand, Nina did not consider her infertility to pervade her entire life. She liked her work and felt that she had a good marriage. Patrick, on the other hand, was an optimist. He told us that "Nina will get pregnant. I'm sure of it. Maybe her eggs aren't good. But we can use an egg donor. Then we'll have good eggs and Nina will get pregnant. It's just a matter of time." Although Nina and Patrick had a good marriage, they fought about whether to undertake an egg donor procedure. Nina thought it was futile but Patrick really wanted a baby and believed that using an egg donor would solve the problem.

We have focused on differences in explanatory style as an example of a personality disposition that can fuel infertility conflict. Couple mismatches in other personality dispositions can also contribute to conflict. Some important ones that should be considered include internal versus external locus of control (Rotter, 1966), assertiveness (Alberti & Emmons, 1990), and depression (Beck, 1967).

Rotter (1966) described personality differences in perceived locus of control over reinforcements. Individuals described as *externals* attribute control over their outcomes to sources outside of themselves: fate, luck, or the vagaries of nature. In contrast, those individuals described as *internals* believe that their actions strongly influence their outcomes. Miller Campbell, Dunkel-Schetter, and Peplau (1991) constructed a scale to measure behavioral and cognitive control over infertility. They asked women to rate how much behavioral and cognitive control they believed they could exert over the likelihood that they would get pregnant, over the negative feelings they experienced about their infertility, and over the medical treatment they received. Miller Campbell et al. found that the more control women perceived they had over various aspects of their infertility, the less depressed they were.

Individuals may also differ in the degree to which they behave assertively. Assertiveness involves expressing one's thoughts and feelings directly and honestly and doing so in a manner that respects the rights of others. Assertiveness is distinguished from aggressiveness which is characterized by violating the rights of others in an attempt to gain one's own objectives. Goldfried and Davison (1976) suggest that people may be unassertive for a variety of reasons including: not knowing what to say, not knowing how to behave, fearing that assertive behavior will lead to a very negative response, or believing that it is not "proper" to behave assertively.

Case Example

Susan was a very assertive individual. Her father had died when she was 14, and she learned that if she wanted something to happen she had to behave assertively. Her husband Michael was more passive and less assertive. Susan behaved assertively with her doctors, much to the consternation of her husband. In one instance, Susan was scheduled for a hysteroscopy. The procedure was scheduled for 10 A.M. Susan was instructed not to eat or drink anything after midnight on the evening preceding the hysteroscopy. When Susan arrived for the procedure she discovered that there was a delay. By 2 P.M. that procedure had not yet taken place. Susan had a blood sugar deficiency and was feeling faint and nauseous from the lack of food and water. She demanded to speak with a doctor and to be given food and something to drink, stating that if she didn't get it she would leave. Michael was mortified by Susan's "rebellion" and tried to apologize for her unseemly behavior. But Susan persisted, and the doctors acceded to her demands and conducted the procedure shortly afterward.

CONFLICT OVER ISSUES RELATED TO INFERTILITY

What follows is a discussion of issues related to infertility that often cause conflict in a relationship. Money, the logistics of the procedure, the perceived ambiguity of the treatment, managing social life, and the decision to continue treatment are typically problematic issues for couples. Often, they are the primary presenting problems when couples seek psychological treatment for infertility-related problems in their marriage.

Money Issue

Conflict over money can take many different forms. We have categorized money conflicts into three common prototypes: spend for treatment versus save, spend for treatment A versus spend for treatment B, and spend for treatment versus spend for adoption.

Spend versus Save

One common pattern involves one partner who wants to spend on treatment and the other who wants to save for some of life's pleasures such as a house, a major vacation, or other valued large purchases. We have encountered the spend versus save dilemma most often in couples who are contemplating egg donation, particularly in those couples where one partner has children from a previous marriage and the other has none.

Case Example

Sean had grown children from his first marriage. Colleen had never been married and never been pregnant. After they had completed an unsuccessful IVF cycle, they were told that Colleen was perimenopausal. The doctors suggested egg donation. The couple agreed to spend $14,000 of their savings on an egg donor cycle, which unfortunately was unsuccessful. When the couple came to us for counseling, Colleen reported that she was eager to try again but Sean was unwilling to spend his nest egg on another cycle. He said "I've got grown kids. I really don't want any more. I went along with your request to do IVF and we spent a fortune and didn't get pregnant. Then you were told that your eggs are no good and we were advised to do egg donation. I went along with that and it failed. I'm unwilling to commit any more money to another cycle. I'm 55 years old. I've always dreamed of having a boat. I've saved my money and I only have enough left to buy that boat. If we do egg donation again, I'll lose my chance to get the boat, at least while I'm young enough to enjoy sailing. I'm unwilling to do that."

With our help, Colleen was able to tell Sean that "I don't feel like much of a woman. All my life I wanted to have a baby—to feel a baby kicking inside me. I waited a long time to get married, until I found the right man—you. I wanted to get married at least in part so I could have a family. I want to have a baby. You've raised kids. I'm not part of their lives. You've had that chance. I never did." The difference in life circumstances between Sean and Colleen was an important contributor to the conflict. In therapy, we helped Colleen appreciate why Sean was reluctant to keep trying. Likewise, by helping Colleen share her private world of hopes, wishes, and frustrations, Sean came to appreciate how very important it was to Colleen to have the opportunity to experience a pregnancy.

Spend versus Spend

In contrast to the previous pattern, other mates are each willing to spend on treatment but disagree on how to allocate funds for treatment.

Case Example

Kim and Phil had completed three unsuccessful IVF cycles. Phil had a severe male factor problem and the doctors suspected that there was also a problem with the quality of Kim's eggs. They had $25,000 left in the lifetime cap that their insurance would cover for infertility treatment. Kim wanted to spend a little at a time and undergo treatment consisting of Pergonal injections and intrauterine inseminations with donor sperm. She wanted to have as many trials as possible, to spend as little as possible on each trial, and to use her own eggs. She believed that her insurance would cover all of the expenses of six cycles. She knew that after six cycles her insurance would be depleted. If after six cycles she had not become pregnant, she wanted to reassess her options. Phil, on the other hand, wanted to go for broke and spend their money on one IVF cycle using both donor sperm and donor eggs; he wanted the highest possibility of achieving a pregnancy. His rationale was that insurance would pay for all of the medical procedures of this expensive, high-odds procedure, but only if they undertook this treatment first, before they had depleted their lifetime insurance cap. If this treatment failed, he believed that they could afford to adopt.

On the surface it appeared that Kim and Phil were fighting over a money issue. A closer examination, however, revealed a large web of intertwined issues that needed to be addressed and resolved. Underlying the conflict were personality and situational issues. Kim was a low risk taker whereas Phil was a high risk taker. Kim was conventional whereas Phil was nonconventional. Additionally, Kim was much closer to and involved with her family than Phil was with his. As we talked with the couple about the financial issues, we learned that time, disclosure, and fairness were also an aspect of the conflict. The real stumbling block was the equity issue. Phil felt that it was unjust that Kim could contribute genetically to their offspring and he could not. Therefore, he advocated for a double donor procedure wherein neither spouse would be linked genetically to the baby. If that failed, he wanted to try adoption where, again, neither party would have a genetic tie to the baby. As we talked about this issue, Phil was able to discuss other areas of the marriage that he considered unfair. He verbalized his dissatisfaction with his current job which he kept primarily for the medical insurance benefit it provided. One of the conflict resolution principles that we employed was the concept that an issue stated as a matter of principle is very difficult to resolve. It must be reframed specifically. Kim and Phil would make no progress so long as they argued over justice in the abstract. Instead, they needed to problemsolve about whether to use one or two sets of donated gametes. Before they could do this, Phil needed to express his frustration with his feelings of injustice and

Kim needed to validate and acknowledge these feelings. Having done so, they were able to examine and resolve the other issues.

Spend for Treatment versus Spend for Adoption

The final type of financial conflict is one where one partner wants to spend on treatment and the other wants to adopt.

Case Example

Mona and Saul had no insurance coverage. They both had good, but not high-paying jobs. They had saved $30,000 and had spent $15,000 of it on one unsuccessful IVF cycle. Mona wanted to spend the remaining $15,000 on another IVF cycle because she desperately wanted to experience a pregnancy. Saul wanted to become a parent and felt that the odds were better for successfully adopting than for achieving a pregnancy through IVF. He therefore wanted to spend the remaining $15,000 on adoption.

Many of these financial conflicts are irreconcilable. Given limited available resources, only one option may be financed. What is most important is to prevent these conflicts from becoming so destructive that they threaten the viability of a marriage. We helped this couple by assisting them in communicating openly with one another. We had each partner state why he or she believed that their preferred option was important and reasonable. We enabled the partners to feel validated and understood. Saul, for example, came to realize how important it was for Mona to feel a baby kicking inside her. At the same time, Mona became more cognizant of Saul's strong desire to parent. Mona and Saul were able to cry together during the session and express their love for each other. The calm resulting from these affirmations of love and understanding paved the way for a more rational examination of the probability of attaining a successful outcome. Eventually Mona agreed that the couple had a better chance of becoming parents by pursuing adoption. Though sad about giving up her dream of experiencing a pregnancy, she was able to appreciate the positive aspects of adopting.

Nitty-Gritty Issues

The extent to which infertility diagnosis and treatment impinge on one's daily life is often overwhelming. Couples seeking counseling often report that each aspect of the treatment, viewed independently, would not be devastating, but the combined procedures month after month cause conflict. Clients complain most often about giving and receiving injections, and the numerous daily life hassles involved with complying with the requirements of the procedure.

Injections

Some individuals undergoing fertility procedures have commented on how unusual and anxiety arousing they find the requirement that laypersons, rather than medical staff, give injections of fertility drugs (Rosenberg & Epstein, 1995). We have seen three types of problems connected to this requirement. First we have seen "needle-phobic" husbands. When a couple describes this problem to us in therapy, our response is "your job is not to cure his phobia, but to find someone to give you injections." A related problem is the husband who is "all thumbs." We advise couples experiencing this problem to try additional practice sessions first, and if that fails, find someone else to give injections. It's important for individuals to realize their limitations. There is no need for a husband to experience lowered self-esteem in connection with a skill he neither expected to have nor ever wanted to acquire. The most important thing is to adopt a problem-solving stance. If a man can't adequately give injections, find someone who can and move on.

We generally see the needle-phobic and the clumsy husbands *before* they have to do the procedure. In contrast, couples with an overconfident husband generally come to see us after the husband has experienced a problem giving injections. The overconfident husband presents an air of bravado to his wife. Typically he says, "No problem—I've got this completely under control." Then, late at night when it's time to give the injection, he panics and does not know what to do. Often, the clinic is closed and there is nobody with whom to consult. When we see such couples, we help the husband explain to the wife what happened. We encourage the wife to forgive her husband. We also ask the wife to take some responsibility for learning how injections should be given so that she can coach her husband the next time. Further, we encourage the couple to schedule a refresher teaching session with the clinic so that the husband is more confident the next time.

Hassles

Richard Lazarus and his colleagues (Lazarus, DeLongis, Folkman, & Gruen, 1985) have written about the way in which daily hassles can contribute to the experience of stress. Many of the requirements associated with participation in infertility treatment can be appraised as daily hassles that are elements of stress and consequently fuel couple conflict. Examples of daily hassles are taking morning basal body temperature, using a home ovulation predictor kit, driving to the clinic each morning for blood work, and waiting for phone calls prescribing the amount of medication to take. None of these are major catastrophic events, but cumulatively they can lead to considerable stress.

Case Example

Rona and Leroy came to us in conflict. They seemed to fight about everything. They had previously succeeded in having a baby by donor insemination. That attempt had required only one treatment cycle. Now they had been trying to conceive for two years. Leroy had had it with treatment. He complained about the never-ending hassles. In our sessions, Leroy was able to express his frustration and how it was preventing him from enjoying the time he had available to spend with his two-year-old. Rona acknowledged that she, too, felt deprived of the opportunity to enjoy her baby and admitted that her focus on getting pregnant was so all-consuming that it was contributing to the conflict. Eventually, the couple agreed that they were unwilling to pay this price for treatment and agreed to pursue a foreign adoption. Today, they are enjoying the time they are able to spend with their two children.

Improving communication is the most useful intervention for dealing with procedural hassles. Typically, neither partner is aware of the inner world of their partner. They don't appreciate why their partner's position seems so important to him or her. Often they adopt a communication style that heightens conflict. Virginia Satir (1972) has described some of the dysfunctional communication styles as "blamer," "placater," "distracter," and "computer." Satir describes the *blamer* as "a faultfinder, a dictator, a boss who acts superior and seems to be saying 'if it weren't for you, everything would be all right'" (p. 86). She describes the *placater* as one who "talks in an ingratiating way, trying to please, apologizing, and never disagreeing, no matter what" (p. 85). The *distracter* is a person who tries to interject irrelevant comments in an effort to move the topic of conversation away from uncomfortable topics. Finally, the *computer* is a person who displays no emotion and focuses only on what is reasonable or rational. None of these styles allows the partners to validate one another's concerns. We teach our clients to actively listen to one another and to clearly state their own position so that it is understood by their partner. We emphasize that neither partner must agree with their spouse's position; rather, they must accord *legitimacy* to their partner's concerns. Once they are able to do this, they can often find compromise alternatives or they can agree to disagree in an atmosphere that preserves the love between them and emphasizes their common bond and common struggle.

Conflicts Related to "Life on Hold"

Many infertility-related conflicts can be ascribed to putting life on hold (Rosenberg & Epstein, 1993); it is a hallmark of infertility treatment. Such treatment is demanding and creates a great deal of ambiguity (Sandelowski, 1986, 1987), which affects many important life decisions. Buying a home, changing jobs, and even making vacation plans are affected. Couples do not want to buy a new house because they do not know whether they should relocate in a neighborhood with lots of young children or in a community with singles and childless couples. Couples are often unwilling to make job changes because a new job may mean a change in insurance coverage, which may not include infertility treatment, or if it includes such treatment, may rule out individuals with a preexisting condition. Consequently, one or both partners may remain in a position below their capabilities or one in which they are unhappy.

Case Example

Many times couples share the view that their life is on hold, but that this situation is tolerable for a while longer. Conflicts arise when one member of the couple is no longer able to tolerate this condition. Jane and Stanley came to us after their last fight about "that room." Jane and Stanley had bought a house about five years earlier, when they began infertility treatment. Jane designated one of the rooms as "the nursery" and refused to furnish or decorate it in any way. During each of the treatment cycles, Jane would sit in the room and pray for the cycle to be successful. Each time it failed, she would sit in the room alone and cry. When Stanley watched Jane torment herself, he vowed that they would do something to change "that room." During the last cycle, which ended in a miscarriage, Stanley watched Jane sleep in the room and not emerge for hours on end. He offered to turn the room into Jane's studio, to make floor to ceiling shelves to store all Jane's books, to do anything that would help Jane get past believing that the procedure would never succeed.

In many ways, this story, which is not uncommon, is reminiscent of the room that Beth Jarrett refused to change after her son Buck was killed in a boating accident in the movie *Ordinary People.* In the same way that the mother of a son who died wants to preserve his memory, the mother of a child that never was is unwilling to take any steps that will distort the image of "that room" as she envisions it in the near future.

In therapy sessions, we were able to help Jane recognize the symbolic importance of the room. We helped her understand that sometimes the need to preserve a symbol was incompatible with a practical need. Having acquired that understanding, Jane, nonetheless took an adamant position that "practicality be damned—I want to hold on to my dream."

So long as Jane and Stanley continue in medical treatment, we believe that it makes sense to allow Jane to hold on to her dream by preserving "that room" in its present state. However, should some emergency arise, such as a need to house Stanley's aging mother in their home, we would help the couple focus on the choice between preserving a dream and putting Stanley's mother out on the streets. If there was no such emergency and Jane and Stanley decide, after many failed attempts that they will live child-free, and if Stanley wanted to turn the room into a studio, we would encourage Jane to consider that request or to develop an alternate proposal for using the room. To adamantly hold on to a dream when she has stopped taking steps to make it happen is to plunge into unreality, which we do not consider psychologically healthy.

Conflicts Related to the Decision to End Treatment

When a couple has invested time, money, and psychological energy in a treatment cycle that does not result in a pregnancy, the disappointment can be overwhelming. But having invested all these resources, couples are often eager to try another cycle hoping that this time they will succeed. At some point in time, after repeated unsuccessful cycles, they need to consider the possibility of ending treatment. At this juncture, couples often experience a conflict: One member wants to try another cycle and the other wants to stop. In our experience, the pressure to continue more often comes from the wife and the impetus to stop comes from the husband.

Case Example

Mindy and Stefan, a couple coping with repeated miscarriages, exemplified this pattern of conflict (Rosenberg & Epstein, 1993). Mindy and Stefan were both in their late thirties. We saw them shortly after Mindy's second miscarriage. Stefan was demoralized and wanted to quit. Mindy wanted to try another cycle of IVF.

To help Mindy and Stefan we used a negotiation activity (Rosenberg & Epstein, 1993). We begin by explaining to our clients that the goal of negotiation is to understand how your partner's desires are reasonable for him or her even if you have a different set of wishes and desires. We point out that people mistakenly believe that if your spouse does not value your wishes, he does not value you as a person. An important aspect of the negotiation activity is to learn why your partner's wishes make sense to her or him. Each partner has to try to ask himself or herself "Do I really understand why he or she feels this way?"

The discussion in our consulting room, as reported in Rosenberg and Epstein (1993) began with an air of great tension. This couple, who had been through so much infertility treatment together and had comforted and supported one another for years, were now furious with each other. Each regarded the other as "stubborn and irrational." We spent a great deal of time coaching them in ways of actively listening and leveling with one another. Active listening means trying to understand the inner world of one's partner by questioning and sharing reactions to statements. Leveling means sharing one's inner world with their partner. Listening and leveling are reciprocal processes. Active listening encourages leveling which in turn fosters more listening. Despite this coaching, they repeatedly fell back upon former habits of assuming they knew what their partner was thinking and feeling. Their dialogue was merely a recitation of what each wanted, and neither party paying much attention to what their partner was saying:

MINDY: I want to try again.

STEFAN: Enough is enough. We tried so many times. We had two pregnancies and two miscarriages. I'd say that's giving it a reasonable shot.

MINDY: I just want to try one more time. I think it'll work next time.

STEFAN: And then if that does not work, you'll want to try again. How long will it go on?

MINDY: Why are you being so unreasonable? You used to be so supportive.

At this stage in the dialogue, all that was being communicated was desperation and accusations. After much work, they were finally able to have the following productive dialogue:

STEFAN: Let me tell you what I'm feeling. I'm so frustrated. I feel like we've done everything in our power. We've spent tons of money. We've devoted four years to this quest. We're getting older. We still have time and money to adopt. Two years from now, we might be too old and too poor to adopt. Let's get on with it.

MINDY: Your points are valid. I know it seems like we've been doing this forever. And I appreciate all the support you've given me. I love you for what you've done. But I need one more chance.

STEFAN: Why is having one more chance so important to you?

MINDY: Because I feel like a failure, and I need one more time before I can allow myself to give up the idea that I can be a biological mother. It's hard to explain, I know, but one more try will make all the difference in how I see myself.

STEFAN: Well, I can't say I understand your reasons, but I'm willing to accept what you say. The thing that's worrying me, though, is that if we try and you miscarry again, you'll come back with the same statement again that, "I need just one more time." Then we're right back on the merry-go-round.

MINDY: But there's one difference. We still have one more IVF attempt that insurance will cover. Please, let's just try that one last time, and if it does not work, we'll quit.

Now they were making some progress. They understood one another, but they still were unable to resolve their differences. As a result of their discussion, however, they understood the issues that were dividing them.

Once the parties communicate their positions and the reasons underlying them, each spouse reiterates his or her understanding of the partner's position and attempts to convince the partner that the partner's position is reasonable even if it differs from their own position. Having communicated this mutual understanding, the next phase of the negotiation involves brainstorming to generate a list of possible solutions to the problem. Following this phase, the partners try to design a proposal to remedy the disagreement. The proposal involves compromise and trade-offs.

We helped Mindy and Stefan develop an agreement they could both live with. With our assistance, Mindy and Stefan wrote an agreement that they signed and dated. The agreement said: "We agree to try one more IVF attempt. We are hopeful that it will succeed and that a resulting pregnancy will go to term. However, should we fail to conceive, or get pregnant and have a miscarriage, we agree that we will end our efforts to have our own biological child. Instead, we will begin to explore adoption as a way to have a family."

Trouble Dealing with Social Situations

Although social support can be a helpful buffer against stressful situations (Cohen & Wills, 1985), couples dealing with infertility often withdraw from social situations. Consequently, rather than gaining helpful supporters, they may alienate friends and suffer alone. If husband and wife are able to be united and offer support to one another, they can usually weather the stresses of infertility. Research has demonstrated that in couples facing infertility, women provide more esteem and affirmation support to their husbands than men provide to their wives (Abbey, Andrews, & Halman, 1991). A problem arises, however, when one member of the couple wants to participate in social situations and the other does not. In our experience, it is usually the man who wants to participate and the woman who wants to withdraw.

It's useful to classify social situations into three categories: business related, family, and milestone. Business-related situations are those social obligations that relate directly to one's job. An example of a business-related situation is the dinner party with colleagues. Here the individual believes that failure to attend will negatively impact career ladder considerations. A family social situation includes those celebrations such as Christmas or Thanksgiving or Passover when many family members are present. Failure to attend is an ambiguous cue that can be interpreted in many ways, usually unfavorably. Milestones refer to events such as high school reunions, weddings, or Bar Mitzvahs that highlight the passage of time. They accentuate the progress of others compared with the couple's marching in place.

Trouble Dealing with Business Social Situations

Because many couples prefer to keep their infertility a secret from others, the people participating in social gatherings are often unaware that a couple is facing infertility. Because they are unaware, they often ask embarrassing questions (Miall, 1985).

Case Example

Ted, a young member of a prominent law firm was invited to a dinner party with some partners and their wives. Ted's wife Marie was reluctant to attend. "They'll all whip out pictures of their children. I know they're going to ask me when we're planning to start our family. I'm afraid I'll cry and embarrass you," she said in the therapy session we had with this couple. Ted told Marie how important it was for them to attend this function. "The partners are going to judge me by how we hold up in these social situations. If we do not show up, I'm sure they'll pass me over for a partnership." Marie agreed with Ted that it was important to attend but felt incapable of doing so. We helped the couple to develop a nonverbal communication signaling system to make an exit if things were getting too difficult for Marie. She would open her purse and take out her compact and that would be the signal for Ted to make his apologies and for them to leave. We helped the couple rehearse their lines so that they had their stories straight.

Trouble Dealing with Family Social Situations

Almost every couple complains of difficulties dealing with family social situations. Usually the problem arises when the function involves a pregnant woman, or a gathering involving many young children. Family social situations provide an audience to the conflict, which can exacerbate the problem. They can heighten tensions by expressing opinions about whether the couple should or should not pursue treatment. They can pressure the couple by asking them "So when will you guys have a baby?"

Conflict arises when one member of the couple wishes to attend family social functions and the other does not. The one who wants to attend these functions says things like "Life should be as normal as possible despite treatment," needs support provided by the family, does not want to feel ostracized and isolated, and often does not want to risk the alienation of family members. The other spouse counters by saying such things as "seeing the family together, particularly with babies and young children is too difficult for me," reports being too depressed to handle the situation, and finds dealing with the remarks of family members particularly debilitating.

Paradoxically, this area of disagreement can serve as a useful bargaining chip for other areas of negotiation that the couple must face. Walton and McKersie (1965) have discussed integrative agreement strategies that can allow couples to successfully negotiate a mutually satisfactory outcome. Pruitt and Rubin (1986) discuss two specific integrative agreement strategies that we have used to help infertile couples negotiate. One strategy, *nonspecific compensation,* allows one spouse to get what she wants on a specific issue while the other is compensated by getting a concession on an unrelated issue. For example, in the case of Sean and Colleen described earlier, Colleen wanted to undertake a second infertility treatment cycle and Sean wanted to stop. Sean was also upset with Colleen because he wanted to attend family get-togethers, whereas Colleen, upset by the babies present and inevitable talk about children, refused to attend these gatherings. In their bargaining sessions in therapy, Sean agreed to doing a treatment cycle in return for having Colleen agree to attend his family's gatherings.

A second integrative agreement strategy is *cost cutting.* This strategy involves giving one spouse what he or she desires but reducing the costs that the partner incurs in making that happen. We used cost cutting with Mel and Eileen. Eileen wanted to proceed rapidly with treatment and do as many cycles as possible in the coming year. Mel was reluctant to undergo any treatment. Using a cost-cutting strategy, Eileen agreed that she would try one more cycle and if that failed, would have no more than one additional cycle for the remainder of the year rather than initiating a treatment each month. Seeing that Eileen was willing to compromise and realizing that her proposal reduced his medical expenses, Mel agreed to comply with Eileen's wishes.

Another way in which couples who are reluctant to attend family functions can be helped is to provide them with "Ready Retorts," a way to prepare for difficult remarks (Rosenberg & Epstein, 1993). We ask couples to imagine the family gathering and the difficult statements they are likely to hear. Together, husband and wife create retorts to these statements, rehearse them, and use them when they are confronted by these comments. For example, Gloria and Norm expected Norm's cousin to say "so when are you guys going to have a kid?" at the upcoming Passover Seder. Gloria wanted to be somewhat provocative so she and Norm decided on a "saucy" response and rehearsed it in advance. Sure enough the cousin asked the expected question and armed in advance, Gloria responded, "Maybe nine months from this morning!"

Milestone-Induced "Agoraphobia"

Events that do not seem to be particularly fertility related can prove to be equally or even more devastating than baby-related events. Occasions such as Bar Mitzvahs, first communions, high school graduations, or sweet sixteens are public occasions marking milestones in children's lives. To an infertile woman, and to a lesser extent to an infertile man, these growth and development milestones seem particularly out of reach and make her feel out of phase with everyone around her.

One woman told us how she was unable to look out of the window on the first day of each school year. Watching the mothers and fathers taking their children to wait on the corner for the school bus reminded her, "I will never ever walk to the school bus holding my child's hand. I can't bear it and won't look at it."

A second category of milestone-related events are those that specifically mark the passage of time. High school reunions and anniversaries are prominent examples. Susan told us that "Right after my second miscarriage I was supposed to attend my 20th high school reunion. I couldn't go. I felt old and barren and couldn't face the girls I went to high school with. Some of them were even grandmothers."

Situations such as these can induce couple conflict when one spouse wants to attend and the other does not. Some therapists recommend that women overcome their reluctance to attend (Reading, 1991). Writing in a chapter on psychological interventions for infertility Reading (p. 191) states:

> Avoiding a baby shower may generalize to avoiding contact with friends who attend it and to places where children or pregnant women are likely to be seen. Such avoidant behaviors can limit sources of pleasure, distraction, and social support, thereby increasing vulnerability to depression. Such a pattern needs to be recognized early and treated by graded exposure to distress provoking situations, combined with coping statements to overcome self-defeating thoughts about the situation. (Reading, 1991, p. 191)

Our position is somewhat different. We believe that first and foremost, the woman needs to understand why these situations are difficult for her. Second, she needs to be able to tell her spouse, her friends, and her family, why she cannot attend these situations. She also needs to be able to differentiate between those situations in which staying away has no major consequences and those in which avoidance can jeopardize important relationships. In the former, she can give herself permission to stay away knowing that when her circumstances change, she will eagerly attend. In the latter, however, she needs to "bite the bullet" and attend.

CONCLUSION

We have discussed some factors that can play a role in conflicts experienced by couples dealing with infertility. We noted that research studies have found that infertile couples engaged in infertility treatment are as satisfied with their marriages as couples who have children. Indeed, Callan and Hennessey (1989) report that infertile couples who are in treatment are as happy and experience marital satisfaction equal to couples with children and couples who have decided that they do not ever want to have children. These findings, however, may be the result of methodological problems in the research studies.

Couples who are the subjects in these investigations are those couples who have chosen to engage in treatment for their infertility. This population is self-selected and may represent a skewed distribution with respect to marital satisfaction. As Callan and Hennessey (1989) state, "IVF can be an emotionally demanding procedure for many couples, and as a result of a selection effect, only couples in close relationships may persist in this procedure" (p. 110). This speculation is consistent with our clinical impressions of the couples we have worked with. Surely there must be many infertile couples who do not enter treatment but instead opt to let nature take its course. Given the low odds of conception that these couples face, there is a strong possibility that their marriage may become more troubled with each month in which conception does not occur.

In our experience, we have only seen couples who are engaged in treatment but have not become pregnant, or who have stopped treatment and have decided to adopt. We have not worked with couples, whom we shall call *involuntarily childless-nontreatment couples,* who have failed to become pregnant through treatment and have chosen not to adopt or to continue treatment. We distinguish between involuntarily childless-nontreatment couples, and those who have considered their options, grieved about their inability to have children, and decided to live child-free. The latter group has probably resolved their dilemma and can move on with their life. But the former probably has not. Nobody knows how many couples fall into this category or what the fate of their marriage may be.

It's almost inevitable that couples dealing with infertility will experience conflicts. In this chapter, we have listed some of the nitty-gritty issues such as how to allocate scarce financial resources, concerns about giving and receiving injections, uncertainty about where to live or whether to change jobs, issues that are the central focus of infertile couples' day-to-day existence. These conflicts are not necessarily or typically symptomatic of a troubled marriage. But they must be resolved for the couple to move ahead.

There are a number of ways that clinicians can help couples cope with these inevitable conflicts (Rosenberg & Epstein, 1993). First, they can encourage the couple to *work as a cooperative team.* Using interventions to improve marital communication, they can help husbands and wives to support each other in their common struggle. Research has shown that cooperatively structured groups function effectively when members become specialists, each doing a task that the other cannot perform (Deutsch, 1973). So as a cooperative team, a husband may become the task specialist and his wife may become the emotional specialist. Like Daniluk (Chapter 6), we urge that husbands become active participants in treatment, accompanying their wives to medical visits and questioning physicians.

Second, clinicians can encourage a couple to *educate themselves about infertility,* learning the important medical terminology and treatment options available to them. By becoming educated, the couple can feel a greater sense of control and perhaps feel less depressed.

Having become educated about infertility, a couple is better equipped to *become active partners in their medical treatment.* The clinician can help them learn assertive behavior skills that are needed to take an active role in treatment. Finally, clinicians can help couples *learn to manage their social life.* The clinician can help the couple explore how they deal with upsetting social situations. They can provide opportunities for couples to role-play problem situations and to rehearse effective coping responses. The clinician can help them learn to respond to insensitive comments, avoid pressure exerted by family members, and deal with participation in upsetting social situations.

A clinician can help resolve marital conflict about infertility by using traditional marital therapy techniques coupled with a unique knowledge about and appreciation of the special set of issues that infertile couples must face.

REFERENCES

Abbey, A., Andrews, F. M., & Halman, L. J. (1991). The importance of social relationships for infertile couples' well-being. In A. L. Stanton & C. Dunkel-Schetter (Eds.), *Infertility: Perspectives from stress and coping research* (pp. 61–86). New York: Plenum Press.

Alberti, R., & Emmons, M. (1990). *Your perfect right: A guide to assertive living.* San Luis Obispo, CA: Impact Books.

Allen, J. G., & Haccoun, D. M. (1976). Sex differences in emotionality: A multidimensional approach. *Human Relations, 29,* 711–720.

Beck, A. T. (1967). *Depression: Causes and treatment.* Philadelphia: University of Pennsylvania Press.

Callan, V. J., & Hennessey, J. F. (1989). Psychological adjustment to infertility: A unique comparison of two groups of infertile women, mothers, and women childless by choice. *Journal of Reproductive and Infant Psychology, 7,* 105–112.

Cohen, S., & Wills, T. A. (1985). Stress, social support, and the buffering hypothesis. *Psychological Bulletin, 98,* 310–357.

Cozby, P. C. (1973). Self disclosure: A literature review. *Psychological Bulletin, 79,* 73–91.

Daniluk, J. (1991). Strategies for counseling infertile couples. *Journal of Counseling and Development, 69,* 317–320.

Davidson, J., & Duberman, L. (1982). Same-sex friendships: A gender comparison of dyads. *Sex Roles, 8,* 809–822.

DeLongis, A., Coyne, J. C., Dakof, G., Folkman, S., & Lazarus, R. S. (1982). Relationship of daily hassles, uplifts, and major life events to health status. *Health Psychology, 1,* 119–136.

Deutsch, M. (1973). *The resolution of conflict.* New Haven, CT: Yale University Press.

Fisher, R. (1964). Fractionating conflict. In R. Fisher (Ed.), *International conflict and behavioral science: The Craigville papers* (pp. 91–109). New York: Basic Books.

Fisher, R., & Ury, W. (1983). *Getting to yes.* New York: Penguin Books.

Fleming, J., & Burry, K. (1988). Coping with infertility. In D. Valentine (Ed.), *Infertility and adoption: A guide for social work practice* (pp. 37–41). New York: Haworth.

Goldfried, M. R., & Davison, G. C. (1976). *Clinical behavior therapy.* New York: Holt, Rinehart and Winston.

Greil, A. L. (1991). *Not yet pregnant.* New Brunswick, New Jersey: Rutgers University Press.

Honea-Fleming, P. (1986). Psychosocial components in obstetric/gynecologic conditions with a special consideration of infertility. *Alabama Journal of Medical Sciences, 23,* 27–30.

Lazarus, R. S., DeLongis, A., Folkman, S., & Gruen, R. (1985). Stress and adaptational outcomes: The problem of confounded measures. *American Psychologist, 40,* 770–779.

Mahlstedt, P. P. (1985). The psychological component of infertility. *Fertility and Sterility, 43,* 335–346.

Mazor, M. D. (1984). Emotional reactions to infertility. In M. D. Mazor & H. F. Simons (Eds.), *Infertility: Medical, emotional, and social considerations* (pp. 23–35). New York: Human Sciences Press.

Menning, B. E. (1982). The emotional needs of infertile couples. *Fertility and Sterility, 34,* 313–319.

Miall, C. E. (1985). Perceptions of informal sanctioning and the stigma of involuntary childlessness. *Deviant Behavior, 6,* 383–403.

Miall, C. E. (1987). The stigma of adoptive parent status: Perceptions of community attitudes toward adoption and the experience of informal social sanctioning. *Family Relations, 36,* 34–39.

Miller Campbell, S., Dunkel-Schetter, C., & Peplau, L. A. (1991). Perceived control and adjustment to infertility among women undergoing in vitro fertilization. In A. L. Stanton & C. Dunkel-Schetter (Eds.), *Infertility: Perspectives from stress and coping research* (pp. 133–156). New York: Plenum Press.

Peplau, L., & Gordon, S. (1985). Women and men in love: Sex differences in close relationships. In V. O'Leary, R. Unger, & B. Wallston (Eds.), *Women, gender, and social psychology* (pp. 257–291). Hillsdale, NJ: Erlbaum.

Pruitt, D. G., & Rubin, J. Z. (1986). *Social conflict: Escalation, stalemate, and settlement.* New York: Random House.

Reading, A. (1991). Psychological interventions and infertility. In A. L. Stanton & C. Dunkel-Schetter (Eds.), *Infertility: Perspectives from stress and coping research* (pp. 183–196). New York: Plenum Press.

Rosenberg, H., & Epstein, Y. (1993). *Getting pregnant when you thought you couldn't.* New York: Warner Books.

Rosenberg, H., & Epstein, Y. (1995). Follow-up study of anonymous ovum donors. *Human Reproduction, 10,* 2741–2747.

Rotter, J. B. (1966). Generalized expectancies for internal versus external control of reinforcement. *Psychological Monographs, 80* (Whole No. 609).

Rubin, L. B. (1983). *Intimate strangers: Men and women together.* New York: Harper & Row.

Sandelowski, M. (1986). Women's experiences of infertility. *IMAGE: Journal of Nursing Scholarship, 19,* 270–274.

Sandelowski, M. (1987). The color gray: Ambiguity and infertility. *IMAGE: Journal of Nursing Scholarship, 19*(4), 140–144.

Satir, V. (1972). *Peoplemaking.* Palo Alto, CA: Science and Behavior Books.

Seligman, M. (1990). *Learned optimism.* New York: Pocket Books.

Spencer, L. (1987). Male infertility: Psychological correlates. *Postgraduate Medicine, 81,* 223–228.

Ulbrich, P. M., Coyle, A. T., & Llabre, M. M. (1990). Involuntary childlessness and marital adjustment: His and hers. *Journal of Sex and Marital Therapy, 16,* 147–158.

Walton, R., & McKersie, R. B. (1965). *A behavioral theory of labor negotiations: An analysis of a social interaction system.* New York: McGraw-Hill.

West, S. (1983). Infertility-couples in crisis. *The Australian Nurses Journal, 13,* 40–41.

Woollette, A. (1985). Childlessness: Strategies for coping with infertility. *International Journal of Behavioral Development, 8,* 473–482.

Wright, J. W., Duchesne, C., Sabourin, S., Bissonnette, F., Benoit, J., & Girard, Y. (1991). Psychological distress and infertility: Men and women respond differently. *Fertility and Sterility, 55,* 100–108.

CHAPTER 8

Love, Sex, and Infertility: The Impact of Infertility on Couples

SANDRA R. LEIBLUM

For approximately 10% to 15% of couples of reproductive age, fertility cannot be taken for granted (Blank, 1985; Daniluk, 1988). Approximately one in six couples will have unanticipated difficulty conceiving and/or carrying a pregnancy to term (U.S. Center for Health Statistics, 1985). The determination of an exact diagnosis identifying the cause(s) of infertility and the search for successful treatment is usually emotionally, financially, and psychologically consuming. The monthly cycle of anticipation and expectation followed by frustration and disappointment is stressful. The psychological impact on both the individual and the couple can be considerable.

In some respects, infertility is similar to other chronic medical disorders, such as multiple sclerosis or coronary heart disease, that diminish or dampen a sense of well-being. Feelings of depression, inadequacy, anxiety, and low self-esteem are common concomitants of infertility and although not life-threatening in any way, infertility challenges a sense of bodily integrity, self-concept, emotional stability, future plans, and the fulfillment of social roles (Daniluk, 1988; Leiblum, 1987). However, unlike other medical stressors, infertility is often associated with feelings of shame and guilt, which add to its burden. Moreover, infertility typically occurs in the context of a couple relationship and, consequently, both partners are usually profoundly affected—either directly or indirectly—by the diagnosis, treatment, and interventions associated with the infertility experience.

The chronic yet unpredictable nature of infertility creates special problems. Couples are often told stories of women who "miraculously" conceived after years of unsuccessfully trying or couples who become pregnant without medical intervention after adopting.[1] There are no clear guidelines as to when to abandon efforts to conceive. Even if they eventually decide to accept a life

---

[1] The research on natural conception after adoption indicates that *there is no greater probability of becoming pregnant after adoption than before* but these are the particular stories that people tend to marvel at.

without biological children, it is difficult to avoid reminders of their former reproductive quest. Even women who have declared themselves "finished" with pregnancy attempts privately acknowledge that the fantasy of discovering that they are pregnant occurs sporadically and poignantly.

Moreover, couples must deal with societal expectations regarding the importance of having children and the implications associated with childlessness. Worldwide statistics suggest that only 5% of married couples elect to remain voluntarily childless (Daniluk, 1988). The achievement of parenthood is seen as a near-universal expectation and a major life goal for many women and men. As Daniluk (1988) points out, parenthood is regarded by many as essential for personal fulfillment, social acceptance, achievement of adult status, religious membership, sexual identity, and psychological adjustment. It is no wonder, then, that for many couples involuntary childlessness becomes a uniquely painful stressor that can and often does impact on marital satisfaction in many ways.

GENDER DIFFERENCES IN REACTIONS TO INFERTILITY

There are differences in how men and women react to the diagnosis of infertility, as Daniluk discusses in Chapter 6. Overall, it appears that when the diagnosis of infertility is either unspecified or due to female factors, women display more stress, anxiety, depression, and grief over the inability to conceive than do men (Beaurepaire, Jones, Thiering, Saunders, & Tennant, 1994; Leiblum, 1994; Nachtigall, Becker, & Wozny, 1992; Platt & Leiblum, 1995; van Balen & Trimbos-Kemper, 1993; Wright et al., 1991). Often, women feel insufficiently supported and misunderstood by their spouse. The pain of infertility is exacerbated by the pain of isolation.

Although infertility is indisputably stressful, the underlying reasons for the stress associated with infertility appear to differ for men and women (Andrews, Abbey, & Halman, 1992). For men, it appears that the dynamics and feelings associated with infertility are quite similar to the dynamics of stress reactions associated with other life problems, such as financial or vocational problems. For women, however, fertility problems appear to constitute a unique stressor in that there are stronger and more deleterious effects on sexual self-esteem, sexual dissatisfaction, and a sense of self-efficacy. Further, women are more likely than men to regard childlessness as a personal failure since historically, conception and pregnancy was regarded as the sole responsibility of women and the major expectation and accomplishment of her gender role.

EFFECT OF INFERTILITY ON RELATIONSHIPS

Infertility does not always have a negative impact on marital satisfaction and adjustment. Some studies suggest that coping with the crisis of infertility results in increased couple commitment and closeness while other studies suggest the reverse. For example, Ravel, Slade, Buck, and Lieberman (1987) found that more than half of the women in a sample of 47 couples undergoing infertility investigation reported having experienced some marital problems after the diagnosis of infertility. These authors also reported a significant reduction in such problems after the initiation of infertility treatment. On the other hand, Benazon, Wright, and Sabourin (1992) found that marital distress increased as treatment investigations were undertaken and even greater levels of marital distress were observed in couples who had undergone extensive infertility treatment and did not conceive.

In a study by Cook, Parsons, Mason, and Golombok (1989), of the 71% of women who were undergoing either in vitro fertilization or artificial insemination using donor sperm, similar percentages of women reported positive as reported negative effects on their relationship. Those reporting positive effects said such things as "It's been like a grief that we've shared" and "We've always been close but this seems to have brought us closer." Negative reports centered on the fact that infertility became a preoccupation and obsession for one of the partners, resulting in feelings of estrangement and isolation.

Several explanations have been offered for the conflicting research findings about the impact of infertility on marital satisfaction. In his attempt to reconcile a similar inconsistency regarding the absence of general maladjustment in infertile samples with the clinical observation that infertility is extremely stressful, Reading (1993) suggests that the methodologies used in many research studies may mask the subtle issues under study. He hypothesizes that infertility adversely stresses couples who are already in conflicted relationships but has a neutral or even positive impact on couples who are in solid relationships. Further, he notes that the measures typically used in assessing marital adjustment and satisfaction are insufficiently sensitive to detect dissatisfaction or that couples deny problems for fear of being disqualified from treatment. During "official clinic evaluations," couples may feel obligated to deny or minimize problems although they may be perfectly willing to acknowledge them in the privacy of a therapist's office. Finally, the stage at which assessments are made may influence research findings. Couples tend to report few problems at the start of infertility treatment when optimism is high, but then, after months or years of unsuccessful reproductive attempts, acknowledge that the multiple stresses of dealing with infertility has eroded marital satisfaction.

While changes in the content and nature of marital (and sexual, as we shall be discussing) interactions necessarily undergo changes as couples ponder the innumerable decisions and frustrations of infertility treatment, it is not known whether changes in marital interaction and satisfaction continue after the "infertility crisis" is resolved—either by the arrival of an infant or by decision to forgo active parenting. When couples are successful in conceiving or adopting, do marital relations return to pretreatment levels of satisfaction? Do they worsen? What about couples who decide to live without children after years of unsuccessful infertility treatment. Do they enjoy a more satisfying relationship than couples who become parents after coping with infertility? The answers to these questions are, as yet, unknown.

Irrespective of the research literature, clinicians are usually aware of the multiple ways in which infertility can stress a couple's relationship. While not all infertile couples seek or require counseling, short-term focused therapy can be extremely beneficial in helping avert the potentially negative impact of unsuccessful procreative attempts on relationship dynamics.

The remainder of this chapter will review the ways in which infertility may create difficulties for both the individual and couple. Suggestions for obviating or reducing couple conflict will be offered.

FEELINGS OF BLAME AND GUILT ASSOCIATED WITH INFERTILITY

For many individuals, feelings of self-blame and guilt accompany the diagnosis of infertility. Both women and men may express the belief that infertility is a punishment for sexual indiscretions or past behavioral infractions. For example, late in the assessment of a couple who sought sex therapy, the husband admitted that, although he knew it was not realistic, he believed that his wife's failure to conceive as well as his current problems with achieving and maintaining erections were due to his having committed a major "sin" 25 years earlier. As a young army private, he had been cajoled into accompanying his buddies on a visit to a German prostitute. Despite misgivings, he engaged in sexual relations with this woman. Years later, when he and his wife were unable to conceive, he developed the theory that God was punishing him for his lack of religious observance and sexual misbehavior. Now, at age 63, he still clung to the unspoken belief that his sexual escapade was the cause of his erectile and fertility problems.[2]

For some individuals, feelings of shame, self-blame, and guilt may be so great that the individual diagnosed with infertility feels unworthy of his partner's love and commitment. Some couples urge their mates to seek other relationships or believe that their marriage should be dissolved.

On the other hand, the fertile partner may feel angry, antagonistic, or resentful toward an infertile partner and these feelings may be expressed either directly, by way of furious accusation, or indirectly, by emotional or physical withdrawal.

For example, it is not uncommon among ambitious professional couples that conception attempts are postponed until some substantial measure of career success is achieved. Then, when infertility is later diagnosed, the spouse who has been more eager to start a family feels indignant and resentful. "If you hadn't

[2] In this case, a ritual was suggested in which the patient was required to go to synagogue, confess his past sexual indiscretions and beg God for forgiveness. The opportunity to clear his conscience resulted in improved sexual functioning.

insisted on finishing medical school [or passing the bar, or buying a house, or whatever], we would not be having these problems now!" is the accusation.

Case Example

The C's, an attractive, professional couple, were in their early 40s when they were first seen for couple counseling.

They were clearly angry with each other. When entering the office, they selected seats at a distance and barely glanced at the other. With little prodding, Mrs. C. blurted out that she was furious. She blamed her husband for her current inability to conceive, shouting "If you had agreed to having a baby 13 years ago, I wouldn't need donor eggs now!"

It appeared that when she had wanted to get pregnant, her husband had stalled, declaring, "I'm not ready to become a father, yet." When he was ready to begin conception attempts, his wife had just entered graduate school and she decided that the timing was bad. Her refusal to attempt conception was also an expression of her resentment that her husband was "calling the shots." Pregnancy attempts were indefinitely postponed although both partners declared themselves "willing" to accept a pregnancy if "it happened." After six years had gone by without conception, Mr. C. insisted his wife go for an infertility workup. It was discovered that she was perimenopausal and would need to use donor eggs in order to conceive. Not surprisingly, she was unenthusiastic about the prospect of becoming pregnant at the age of 43 with donated ovum. In reality, she was still locked into an intense power and control battle with her husband.

While the ferocity of the anger between this couple was a central feature of their relationship, struggles over the timetable for beginning pregnancy attempts are not atypical. When couples arrive for counseling, there is often long-standing bitterness between them because when one partner was ready to get pregnant, the other obfuscated or balked. Delays or postponements in abandoning contraception and waiting for the "perfect time" to conceive and deliver are often an obvious subterfuge for internal conflicts about becoming a parent or an expression of other underlying individual or relationship conflicts.

While the underlying conflicts about becoming parents must be explored if they exist, it is fruitless to spend too much time on "Monday morning quarterbacking." However, allowing people to verbalize regrets and resentments in the privacy and safety of the therapist's office can sometimes prevent the expression of hostile accusations at home. Couples can usually be helped to accept that while infertility is unjust and grievous, it is not a blameworthy diagnosis. No one chooses infertility. Normalizing feelings of outrage and injustice is reassuring.

OVERT AND COVERT COERCION TO COMPLY WITH INFERTILITY TREATMENT

Two partners rarely share the same motivation or commitment to having a biological child but when pregnancy occurs effortlessly, partners usually share a sense of celebration and joy. When conception does not readily or "naturally" occur, differences in motivation for becoming parents are more obvious. In these cases, it is not unusual that the partner who is more invested in having a baby to place considerable pressure—either overtly or covertly—on the less enthusiastic partner. This may take the form of insisting on continuing infertility treatment when the probability of success is remote or participating in infertility treatment(s) that may be unacceptable to one's spouse. For instance, in a recent case, when a wife learned that her husband was azoospermic, she insisted he agree to the use of donor insemination. The husband was not given any opportunity to grieve the unexpected and devastating loss of his fertility. Psychologically, he could not and would not consent to the use of an anonymous sperm donor. The wife threatened divorce if he did not agree to artificial insemination. Acrimonious exchanges followed and the couple sought "crisis" marital counseling.

Different degrees of motivation for becoming a parent need not pose a serious problem if both partners are invested in achieving a pregnancy. However, when one partner already has a biological child (or children) from a previous marriage or is more ambivalent generally, tension develops. The partner, usually, though not always a woman, who yearns for a baby feels angry and alienated. She may become overtly insistent or covertly manipulative in securing her partner's cooperation in infertility treatments or adoption applications. Sometimes this has unexpected results. In a recent case, for example, the husband who had two biological children from his former marriage reluctantly agreed to participate in his wife's infertility treatment. He knew that her age and possession of a single ovary significantly reduced the likelihood of conception and he secretly counted on the fact that she would miscarry if a pregnancy occurred. When, after two miscarriages, she successfully gave birth to a baby boy, he announced he was leaving the marriage because he did not want to be a father again.

Conflicts arise, too, about which parenthood option to pursue, given various considerations. One partner may want to pursue adoption as a certain way of achieving parenthood, whereas the other is insistent about wanting a biological child. Alternatively, one partner may only acquiesce to the use of a "known" sperm or ovum donor in order to keep the genetic "match" as close as possible, while the other partner anticipates "family complications" if a close relative donates and prefers the privacy of anonymous donors. The number of decisions associated with infertility treatment may require sophisticated negotiation and communication skills, which not all couples possess. Poor communication and/or inflexibility can create considerable relationship distress.

Lesbian couples are not immune from these problems. Pressure to actively support or passively acquiesce to pregnancy attempts for one or the other partner can be intense. In recent years, increasing numbers of lesbian couples have elected to become parents, through donor insemination (Golombok & Rust, 1986; Leiblum, Palmer, & Spector, 1995; Pakizegi, 1990). It is not uncommon for one or the other woman to feel conflicted about or unwilling to accept the financial and emotional responsibilities of parenthood yet the pressure to support a partner who longs to become pregnant is great. Sometimes, lesbian partners in a committed relationship experience conflict over "who goes first" when they both want to have a biological child.

Case Example

Although Gina and Patricia had been together for only eight months, they felt deeply committed to each other. Shortly after moving in together, Gina announced that she wanted to quit her job and have a baby. She was 37 and felt that "time was running out." Now that she felt emotionally secure, she wanted to begin donor inseminations immediately. Patricia had been unaware of the strength of Gina's desire for motherhood. She was surprised by the intensity of Gina's insistence on having a child, and worried about the financial impositions this would entail. Moreover, she was not at all certain about her inclination or ability to be a "mother." She had never enjoyed spending time with children and had no "biological urge" to conceive herself. Nevertheless, after declaring her commitment to Gina, she felt she had no option other than to support her. Privately, she felt resentful and coerced.

FINANCIAL CONFLICTS

Infertility treatment is expensive. The price of a complete IVF cycle can run anywhere from $8,000 to $12,000 per cycle and even the cost of ovulation-induction medication, such as Pergonal, is considerable, costing about $2,000 per treatment cycle. Most insurance companies do not cover all of these expenses and therefore, for most couples, financial resources are taxed. Conflicts can and do arise over how much money to allocate for medical treatments, particularly those with a low likelihood of success. Sometimes couples disagree on whether to spend their hard-won savings on private or international adoption—which typically results in the eventual arrival of a child within 12 to 14 months—or whether to pursue medical interventions that might or might not result in the more desired option of a biological pregnancy. Disagreements over when (and whether) to stop infertility treatment is a difficult and emotionally laden issue, as discussed by Braverman in Chapter 11.

EMPATHIC FAILURE

For the woman or man who longs for a biological child, the repeated disappointment of infertility interventions and/or miscarriage, can be devastating. When infertility treatment has been ongoing for years or even decades, the feelings of despair, anger, and hopelessness can be profound. When one partner seems to be "taking too long" to recover from an unsuccessful reproductive attempt, it is not unusual for the other partner to become impatient and irritated.

"Why doesn't she (he) get over this already? It's been three months?" or "What about me and our relationship? Doesn't she value what we have together?" At the same time, the grief-stricken partner feels isolated and misunderstood.

Cases involving secondary infertility are especially likely to lead to empathic failure between partners. Typically, husbands resign themselves more readily to having only one child than do their wives who sometimes cannot abandon the thought of having a "complete family."

Case Example

Susan was 39 years old and the mother of a daughter when she requested individual therapy. She had been obsessed with having a second child for three years and viewed herself as a personal and professional failure by virtue of her lack of reproductive success. As a child specialist, she felt "fraudelent" posing as an expert when she was the mother of an only child. Further, she really believed that two children were necessary to constitute a family. Her obsessive pursuit of infertility treatments alienated her husband who felt that "enough was enough." He wanted to spend no more money or devote any more time listening to Susan's expressions of despair and anger over her inability to conceive. He felt that since she was already the mother of a healthy child, she "should be grateful." Susan felt misunderstood and angry at what she considered his insensitivity and lack of empathy. Marital and sexual tensions were escalating.

CONFLICTS RELATED TO PRIVACY VERSUS DISCLOSURE

Individuals have very different ideas about what kinds of information should be shared with others and what should be kept private. Typically, one partner seeks support and reassurance from others while the other views infertility as a "private matter." In a recent case, it was the husband who wanted to share with his brother all the details of the infertility experience—the tests his wife was undergoing, his concerns about achieving a pregnancy, the toll it was taking on his sexual life, et cetera. His wife was furious that he spoke to his brother even once about their current situation. She viewed his conversation(s) as a betrayal of her privacy and as an expression of lack of loyalty.

The issue of what, whom, and when to tell others about their life was an ongoing source of conflict for this couple and significantly reduced their sense of trust and connectedness with each other. Their infertility compounded an existing relationship "sore spot."

MARITAL CONSTRICTION

Relationships flourish when couples share joy as well as disappointment and grief. While the stress of infertility can, indeed, bring couples closer together by improving communication, increasing sensitivity, and fostering commitment, years of enduring the frustrations and disappointment of infertility treatment can sap relationship vitality. Life may seem bleak and pleasureless.

Couples need encouragement and permission to take "vacations" from medical interventions and ovulation scrutiny. They must be reminded that relationships need tending and that neglect may result not only in the loss of a biological child, but also in the loss of a partner.

Case Example

In this case, the therapist's strong recommendation that a couple take a much needed vacation from infertility treatment had fortuitously happy results.

Theresa and Sam had spent more than a decade trying to conceive. Sam had a daughter from his first marriage but he was committed to becoming a parent with Theresa, his second wife. Theresa, the owner of a successful travel agency, had delayed pregnancy attempts until her mid-30's, feeling that she wanted to "see the world" before she settled down. Despite months of infertility evaluations and years of unsuccessful treatment, a definitive diagnosis of her infertility had not emerged. At times, she conceived and then suffered a miscarriage or an ectopic pregnancy. During her last in vitro fertilization, she unknowingly became pregnant with twins. One fetus was lost because it became lodged in her fallopian tubes. A second fetus was identified weeks later, but diagnosed as being hydrocephalic. Although her physician strongly recommended a therapeutic abortion, Theresa anguished over the decision to abort. She was raised as a Catholic and felt it would be "murder." Sam, who was Jewish, sided with the doctor and urged Theresa to undergo an abortion. Although she eventually acquiesced, she was severely depressed for months afterward. Finally, distressed by the emotional and sexual withdrawal of his wife, Sam initiated the request for couples' therapy.

Theresa and Sam were seen together for several months. Supportive counseling was provided with an opportunity to grieve over their current and past losses. After some time, it became apparent that Theresa would benefit from the support of her family who lived in Italy. They were encouraged to go for a visit. Upon arriving home, she was warmly embraced. Her demonstrative extended family provided loving and solicitous care for both Theresa and Sam. Their visit culminated in a recommitment of their marital vows before the entire village.

When they returned to the United States, they discovered that Theresa was pregnant! For months, she could not believe that a viable pregnancy existed and that it had happened without medical intervention. Nevertheless, nine months later (after an anxiety-ridden pregnancy in which Theresa had to spend several months in bed), she delivered a healthy baby boy.

A note of caution must be extended here since too often, when doctors glibly tell couples to "relax and let it happen," they are perceived as insensitive and ignorant. Women who are obsessed with becoming pregnant cannot readily "relax" and this advice suggests that they are somehow responsible for "causing" their infertility. Nevertheless, as Domar discusses in Chapter 4, stress reduction techniques can sometimes be effective in enhancing the likelihood of conception, and in this case, the vacation to Italy appears to have served as a most effective "treatment."

In the case of Theresa and Sam, the focus on infertility had robbed the couple of any joy in their relationship. The never-ending cycles of hope and despair had resulted in emotional exhaustion of both partners. Moreover, the estrangement that followed Theresa's abortion had aggravated the strain in their marriage. The vacation helped revitalize their relationship, which was generally good. Although they were apprehensive about going to Italy, the actual experience of leaving the country and being enveloped in the love and support of family and friends had a positive effect on their relationship and perhaps, indirectly, on achieving a viable pregnancy.

THE POSITIVE EFFECT OF INFERTILITY ON MARITAL RELATIONS

Although the emphasis in the preceding pages has been on the ways in which marital satisfaction can be diminished by a preoccupation with infertility issues and decisions, as indicated earlier the research literature also provides instances of marital relationships being strengthened or unchanged (Leiblum, Kemmann, & Lane, 1987; Schover, Collins, & Richards, 1992; Ulbrich et al., 1990; Wright et al., 1991).

In one study of couples undergoing in vitro fertilization, respondents reported better than average marital satisfaction both before and after treatment (Leiblum et al., 1987). When asked specifically how infertility had affected their marriage, about half the wives and husband reported improved marital communication, sensitivity to partner's feelings, and a sense of closeness. More than 25% of the wives reported that the infertility problem had increased their sense of marital intimacy and marital satisfaction. More than one quarter of the husbands reported that the infertility difficulty had enhanced their ability to solve disagreements and increased their sense of marital commitment. Most typically, the majority of husbands and wives reported no change in their marital relations as a result of infertility.

Case Example

Ben and Betty, an outgoing, professional couple in their late 30s, had experienced four miscarriages in the six years they had been married. A thorough diagnostic evaluation eventually revealed that Betty's eggs were the problem—while Betty could probably conceive again, the likelihood of pregnancy loss was extremely high. Both Ben and Betty were devastated by this news, but soon rallied and began exploring reproductive options. They read about and considered reproductive alternatives in depth. Ben became protective of Betty and began looking out for her physical well-being and psychological comfort in a way he had not previously displayed. He expressed great sympathy for the testing and miscarriages that Betty endured and repeatedly declared that her health and survival were more important than any "genetic" offspring. He assured her of his willingness to pursue either adoption or ovum donation with equal dedication and comfort. For her part,

Betty was surprised and gratified by Ben's expressions of love and concern. She said that although they had married out of a sense of mutual respect and values rather than out of passion, "which ends," their sense of closeness, communication, and commitment had never been greater. Both felt that the trials wrought by infertility had enhanced their relationship.

THE IMPACT OF INFERTILITY ON SEXUAL RELATIONS

While it may seem obvious that the infertility workup and the extended nature of infertility treatment might have a deleterious impact on sexual satisfaction and function, the research evidence is somewhat contradictory. Most investigations do not focus on sexual adjustment explicitly and often, only one or two questions about sexual functioning are included in infertility research studies, seemingly as an afterthought to a more general focus on psychological adjustment. It is not altogether surprising that while many studies find evidence of sexual disruption, others do not (Daniluk, 1988; Fagan, Schmidt, Rock, 1986; Freeman, Boxer, Rickels, Tureck, & Mastroianni, 1985; Freeman, Garcia, & Rickels, 1983; Leiblum et al., 1987; Platt & Leiblum, 1994).

Nevertheless, there are many ways in which the sexual relationship changes during the years of infertility evaluation and treatment. For example, the sexual "script" (Gagnon, Rosen, & Leiblum, 1982) may be significantly altered. Time devoted to sensual foreplay may be abbreviated as well as efforts to increase arousal. While male ejaculation is clearly necessary for conception, female orgasm is not and therefore, efforts devoted to stimulating female orgasm are sometimes abandoned. Indeed, the woman herself is often less interested in arousal and orgasm than in her having her husband ejaculate at the right time of the month.

When expensive (and sometimes uncomfortable) ovulation induction injections have been used, the pressure to have sexual intercourse during the "fertile" days is considerable. There can be no "headaches" or "sexual disinterest" if two thousand dollars of medication have been taken to induce ovulation. Reliable and prompt ejaculation becomes the goal of sexual relations, and sexual intimacy at nonfertile times of the month often is abandoned.

Men and women may experience a variety of sexual demands in connection with this "procreative" rather than "recreative" or "relational" sex. Men report feeling the pressure to "get an erection and ejaculate," even when arousal is minimal. For women, some of the particularly gratifying aspects of sex such as sensual caressing and kissing may be abbreviated or abandoned in the pressure to induce ejaculation.

For couples whose sexual adjustment is tenuous to begin with, infertility treatment can negatively impact on sexual response and pleasure. Men with unreliable erections may experience erectile failure and sexual apathy or avoidance. Women with a history of inhibited sexual desire may find themselves becoming sexually avoidant at times other than ovulation.

Not all couples experience all of these difficulties, but most infertile couples experience some of them. The following case illustrates some of the consequences when years have been devoted to the single-minded pursuit of pregnancy.

Case Example

"My own neuroses and rigid personality had to do with some changes in my sexual life but infertility made it worse!"

Barbara and Bob had spent more than a decade trying to conceive and finally agreed on adoption. During their years of infertility treatment, their sexual life deteriorated. Sexual relations occurred only when Barbara had completed a course of ovulation induction medication. Even the expression of physical affection became rare and they became increasingly formal with each other. Barbara was keenly aware of the loss of physical and emotional intimacy.

Throughout her life, Barbara had been a conscientious and anxious woman who obsessed over every decision. She confessed that her entire life had revolved around concerns about procreation. "As soon as I started to menstruate, if I was late in a cycle, I worried that I might be pregnant . . . even if I had only kissed a boy. Then, I did become sexually active and really started worrying about avoiding pregnancy."

In the early years of her marriage, when on oral contraceptives, Betty recalled sex as being lusty and passionate. Then after a year of unsuccessful attempts to become pregnant, infertility evaluations were undertaken. "The doctor said that Bob's sperm could impregnate the world . . . but my situation was more ambiguous."

Barbara underwent an intrusive and frustrating series of infertility evaluations and gynecological treatments: hysterosalpinogram, cryosurgery for cervical dysplasia, laparascopy, laparatomy, and postcoital testing.

She had twelve cycles of intrauterine inseminations (IUIs) as well as three trials of in vitro fertilization (IVF). Barbara laughingly recalled that "We had undergone so many IUIs and IVFs and other fertility procedures that I was afraid to leave a juice cup or plastic cup on the sink; I was afraid Bob would get an erection."

Finally, after suffering an ectopic pregnancy and being rushed to an emergency room doubled over in pain, Barbara and Bob decided to terminate medical interventions. We said, "If it happens, it happens. We can't continue this way. I may die before I get pregnant!"

After several years of therapy during which Barbara felt that she "just couldn't adopt," she finally decided that she could. While still worried about the possibility of having a biological mother return to claim "her" baby, Barbara resolved her ambivalence about adoption. She realized that she could, in fact, develop a loving attachment to a child who was not genetically her own and who did not physically resemble her. "After all," she said, "I love my dog passionately, and he doesn't look like me!"

Despite a variety of misadventures on their road to adoption, Barbara and Bob successfully became the parents of a beautiful baby girl. One year later, when many of the tasks associated with the "transition to parenthood" were completed, Barbara said, "I felt we had gotten back on track. I actually did not know where I was in my menstrual cycle. I could have sex for pleasure and didn't constantly have to be thinking about what day of the month it was. It was a tremendous feeling of relief . . . a burden had been lifted."

On their wedding anniversary, Barbara and Bob planned a romantic cele-bratory dinner, which they both knew would culminate in sex. "I thought to my-self that sex could actually be spontaneous tonight." Later that night when we had sex, I thought, "If I was normal, I could get pregnant tonight." Well, I did get pregnant that night and I didn't want to. And since then, sex has never been the same. I spent the first 10 years of my marriage trying to get pregnant and now I'm spending the next 10 trying to avoid getting pregnant. Now, I don't know if I can or can't."

Barbara now avoids sex because she is phobic about the possibility—which she knows is remote—of conceiving. She is over 40 but says, "Rare things hap-pen and have happened to me. I can't just relax and enjoy sex." At the same time, she misses the closeness and intimacy she had once enjoyed with her husband.

For his part, Bob colludes in avoiding sex. "We haven't done it for so long, I've lost all my sexual desire." Both of them admit to focusing their emotional and physical energy on their child, who has become the center of their marriage. Their relationship has suffered and it has been difficult to reestablish a passionate or physical connection, although neither Barbara nor Bob have sexual performance problems. They are capable of sexual arousal and orgasm, but the years of sex without desire and without joy have taken their toll.

This case poignantly illustrates how sex for procreation, while initially ex-citing and imbued with optimism, can become mechanical and pleasureless. When months of unsuccessful procreative attempts become years of frustra-tion and disappointment, it is not surprising that couples begin to lose sexual de-sire and avoid physical intimacy. Regrettably, if interventions are not taken to correct this situation, couple intimacy suffers.

It should be noted that while infertility can cause sexual problems, sexual problems can be responsible for lack of success in conception. The woman with vaginismus, the involuntary spasmodic contraction of the vaginal introitus, often comes for treatment only when she wants to get pregnant (Leiblum, 1995). Typically, vaginismic "couples" have colluded in avoiding resolution of their sexual problems. Often, these couples have conflicted marriages, in which the husband is angry and disappointed about the lack of intercourse, but is fearful or reluctant to "force the issue." The sexual tension and frustration negatively affects other areas of their relationship and passive-aggressive behavior is typ-ical. These couples need sexual and marital counseling.

Sexual problems other than vaginismus can lead to infertility. The man with erectile failure or ejaculatory delay or inability may be unable to deposit semen in close enough proximity to the vagina so that conception occurs. The couple who engage in infrequent sex or who are unaware of ovulatory days may "miss" the window of opportunity for conception. It is important to take a complete sexual history when dealing with couples who are experiencing infertility. While sexual problems are rarely the primary or single cause of reproductive failure, they may contribute to a reduced probability of conception. And when sexual problems do occur, they are magnified if the couple feel thwarted in their quest for a biological child.

Moreover, it is important to assess the sexual competency of *both* partners in a relationship before assuming that one or the other is responsible for the infertility problem. For example, in a recent case, it was assumed that the vaginismic wife was responsible for the failure to conceive. However, after her gynecologist referred her for sex therapy, it became apparent that her husband played a significant role in maintaining and contributing to the sexual and reproductive problems they were having. He lacked all sexual confidence and was experiencing significant difficulty in getting and maintaining erections. His erectile problems were so humiliating that he avoided sexual contact with his wife. When she protested and begged, cajoled, or pleaded with him to become physically engaged with her, he became angry and withdrawn. Only after she announced that she was leaving the marriage did the husband consent to treatment.

Unsuccessful efforts to conceive—with or without medical intervention—can create marital tension and, over time, can interfere with sexual and marital satisfaction. What can the clinician do to help couples maintain intimacy when coping with infertility?

HELPING COUPLES SUCCESSFULLY SURVIVE INFERTILITY

The mental health clinician can be extremely helpful in assisting couples to survive the frustrations associated with infertility.

By providing support and understanding of the reactions of both partners, the clinician affirms the reality of their distress and normalizes their reactions. Without personally experiencing infertility, few of their friends or family members will be able to provide realistic empathy and support. Banal or trite reassurances that "it will happen when it happens" or "if it's meant to be, it will be" are insulting rather than comforting. The clinician can provide a safe place for expressing irritation and anger at well-meaning but insensitive family members and can counsel couples on how to respond to such statements. Testing apt rejoiners in the privacy of the therapist's office can be extremely useful.

More importantly, the clinician can help couples deal with the insensitivity that may be characteristic of their interaction with each other. Having couples talk about the unique meaning infertility has for them may be revealing and enlightening. A woman who has achieved professional success but who feels that motherhood is her ultimate achievement needs to feel that her husband understands this aspect of her identity. It is validating to articulate the impact infertility may have on one's sense of sexual and physical competency and to feel understood.

For a man, the grief and anger associated with feelings of "impotence"—sexual or otherwise—need to be expressed and examined. The male with "inadequate" sperm often feels emasculated. He may need reassurance from both the therapist and his wife that his potency and desirability reside less in the quality of his semen than in the quality of his love.

When existing "crises" are alleviated, therapy can focus on exploring the impact of infertility on their relationship. Identifying the problems can result in developing realistic treatment goals. A sample list might include too little "fun" time together; too much focus on infertility treatment; too little sex; disagreements about what to tell family and friends; etc. Having identified the sore spots, couples can begin to negotiate solutions.

Even when couples have seemingly resolved the infertility "crisis" and have succeeded in becoming parents—either through adoption or through one of the assisted reproductive procedures—problems may remain. New conflicts arrive with the arrival of a child. The first year of parenthood is stressful for all couples and may be especially difficult for couples who have waited long and worked hard to become parents. It is important that couples not be made to feel ungrateful for "complaining" now that their wish for a child is satisfied.

Even when couples relinquish their efforts to achieve parenthood, old problems can resurface or new problems related to their past experience of infertility can emerge. Unarticulated resentments, misunderstandings, and disappointments can surface at critical times (e.g., when a sibling has a child, family gatherings, menopause). Conflicts over the issue of disclosure may surface when the child conceived via sperm or ovum donation reaches a critical age. If a good relationship has been forged with the clinician, it is not uncommon for couples to return for future counseling when new issues emerge.

KEEPING THE RELATIONSHIP VITAL

If the couple is still actively trying to conceive, it is important that attention be paid toward keeping the relationship vital. Couples need to be reminded that whether they succeed in becoming parents or not, their relationship is ongoing and requires "maintenance." It has been said that "time is the gasoline that keeps relationships running." Planning dates and vacations from the pursuit of infertility treatment can have significant payoffs. Dealing with hurt feelings or misunderstandings promptly rather than burying or avoiding conflict is critical to a well-functioning relationship. Designating some sexual encounters as totally "recreational" rather than "procreational" and planning for them with the same intensity and concern as that paid to "ovulatory sex" can help maintain sexual satisfaction. In recreational sex, the emphasis is on *pleasure* and the chief ingredient is time—time to unwind, to make the transition into physical intimacy, to explore and indulge sensuality for its own sake.

CONCLUSION

Infertility is stressful. Although it need not be a major source of couple conflict, almost invariably, it will cause marital disruptions. The crisis of infertility can strengthen strong relationships or shatter conflicted or uncommitted ones.

Sexual disruption is a common concomitant of infertility treatment, given its long-term nature and intrusive interventions. Most couples cope gracefully with the changes in their sexual script and return to their "normal" sexual life when the infertility dilemma is resolved—either by virtue of becoming parents or by deciding on a life without biological children. However, some couples require assistance in recovering their sexual lives. When sexual dysfunction predates the infertility problems, conjoint sexual counseling is necessary to avoid the further escalation of problems and to resolve the current problems.

REFERENCES

Andrews, F., Abbey, A., & Halman, L. (1992). Is fertility-problem stress different? The dynamics of stress in fertile and infertile couples. *Fertility and Sterility, 57,* 1247–1253.

Beaurepaire, J., Jones, M., Thiering, P., Saunders, D., & Tennant, C. (1994). Psychosocial adjustment to infertility and its treatment: Male and female responses at different stages of IVF/ET treatment. *Journal of Phychosomatic Research, 38,* 229–240.

Benazon, N., Wright, J., & Sabourin, S. (1992). Stress, sexual satisfaction, and marital adjustment in infertile couples. *Journal of Sex and Marital Therapy, 18*(4), 273–284.

Blank, R. (1985). The infertility epidemic. *Futurist, 19,* 177–180.

Collins, A., Freeman, E., Boxer, A., & Tureck, R. (1992). Perceptions of infertility and treatment stress in females as compared with males entering in vitro fertilization treatment. *Fertility and Sterility, 57,* 350–356.

Cook, R., Parsons, R., Mason, B., & Golombok, S. (1989). Emotional, marital and sexual functioning in patients embarking upon IVF and AID treatment for infertility. *Journal of Reproduction and Infant Psychology, 7,* 1–7.

Daniluk, J. C. (1988). Infertility: Intrapersonal and interpersonal impact. *Fertility and Sterility, 49,* 982–990.

Daniluk, J. C., Leader A., & Taylor, P. (1987). Psychological and relationship changes of couples undergoing an infertility investigation: Implications for counseling. *British Journal of Guidance and Counseling, 15,* 29–36.

Fagan, P., Schmidt, C., & Rock, J., (1986). Sexual functioning and psychological evaluation of in vitro fertilization transfer. *Fertility and Sterility, 46,* 668–672.

Freeman, E., Boxer, A., Rickels, K., Tureck, R., & Mastroianni, L. (1985). Psychological evaluation and support in a program of in vitro fertilization and embryo transfer. *Fertility and Sterility, 43,* 48–53.

Freeman, E., Garcia, C., & Rickels, K. (1983). Behavioral and emotional factors: Comparisons of anovulatory infertile women with fertile and other infertile women. *Fertility and Sterility, 40,* 195–201.

Gagnon, J., Rosen, R., & Leiblum, S. (1982). Cognitive and social aspects of sexual dysfunction: Sexual scripts in sex therapy. *Journal of Sex and Marital Therapy, 1,* 44–56.

Golombok, S., & Rust, J. (1986). The Warnock Report and single women: What about the children? *Journal of Medical Ethics, 12,* 182–186.

Leiblum, S. R. (1987). Infertility. In E. Blechman & K. Brownell (Eds.), *Behavioral medicine for women* (pp. 116–125). New York: Pergamon.

Leiblum, S. R. (1994). The impact of infertility on marital and sexual satisfaction. *Annual Review of Sex Research, 4,* 99–120.

Leiblum, S. R. (1995). Relinquishing virginity: The treatment of a complex case of vaginismus. In R. C. Rosen & S. R. Leiblum (Eds.), *Case studies in sex therapy* (pp. 250–263). New York: Guilford Press.

Leiblum, S. R., Kemmann, E., & Lane, M. (1987). The psychological concomitants of in vitro fertilization. *Journal of Psychosomatic Obstetrics and Gynecology, 6,* 166–178.

Leiblum, S. R., Palmer, M., & Spector, I. (1995). Non-traditional mothers: Single heterosexual/lesbian women and lesbian couples electing motherhood via donor insemination. *Journal of Psychosomatic Obstetrics and Gynaecology, 16,* 11–20.

Link P., & Darling, C. (1986). Couples undergoing treatment for infertility: Dimensions of life satisfaction. *Journal of Sex and Marital Therapy, 12,* 46–57.

McEwan, K., Costello, C., & Taylor, P. (1987). Adjustment to infertility. *Journal of Abnormal Psychology, 96,* 108–116.

Morrow, K., Thoreson, R., & Penney, L. (1995). Predictors of psychological distress among infertility clinic patients. *Journal of Consulting and Clinical Psychology, 63,* 163–167.

Nachtigall, R., Becker, G., & Wozny, M. (1992). The effects of gender-specific diagnosis on men's and women's response to infertility. *Fertility and Sterility, 57,* 113–121.

Newton, C., & Houle, M. (1993). Gender differences in psychological response to infertility treatment. In D. Greenfeld (Ed.), *Infertility and reproductive medicine clinics of North America* (pp. 545–558). Philadelphia: W. B. Saunders.

Pakizegi, B. (1990). Emerging family forms: Single mothers by choice—demographic and psychosocial variables. *Maternal-Child Nursing Journal, 19,* 1–19.

Pepe, M., & Bryne, T. (1991). Women's perceptions of immediate and long-term effects of failed infertility treatment on marital and sexual satisfaction. *Family Relations, 40,* 303–311.

Platt, L., & Leiblum, S. R. (1994, November). Infertile men and infertile women: A psychosocial comparison. Poster presented at the meeting of the American Society of Psychosomatic Obstetrics and Gynecology, Washington, DC.

Ravel, H., Slade, P., Buck, P., & Lieberman, B. (1987). The impact of infertility on emotions and the marital and sexual relationship. *Journal of Reproduction and Infant Psychology, 5,* 221–234.

Reading, A. (1993). Sexual aspects of infertility and its treatment. In D. Greenfeld (Ed.), *Infertility and reproductive medicine clinics of North America* (pp. 559–568). Philadelphia: W. B. Saunders.

Schover, L., Collins, R., & Richards, S. (1992). Psychological aspects of donor insemination: Evaluation and follow-up of recipient couples. *Fertility and Sterility, 57,* 583–590.

Ulbrich, P. M., Coyle, A. T., & Llabre, M. M. (1990). Involuntary childlessness and marital adjustment: His and hers. *Journal of Sex and Marital Therapy, 16,* 147–158.

U. S. Center for Health Statistics. (1985). *Fecundity and infertility in the United States: 1965–82* (Advance data No. 104, 11 February). Hyattsville, MD: U. S. Department of Health and Human Services, U. S. Center for Health Statistics.

van Balen, F., & Trimbos-Kemper, T. (1993). Long-term infertile couples: A study of their well-being. *Journal of Psychosomatic Obstetrics & Gynecology, 14,* 53–60.

Wright, J., Duchesne, C., Sabourin, S., Bissonette, F., Benoit, J., & Girard, Y. (1991). Psychosocial distress and infertility: Men and women respond differently. *Fertility and Sterility, 55,* 100–108.

CHAPTER 9

To Tell or Not to Tell: The Issue of Privacy and Disclosure in Infertility Treatment

SUSAN CARUSO KLOCK

Infertility treatment is psychologically as well as physically challenging. Numerous studies have described the psychological stress that infertile couples deal with as they move through the process of trying to have a child on their own, seeking care from an infertility specialist, beginning treatment and waiting each month to find out if the treatment is successful (Daniluk, 1988; Abbey, Halman, & Andrews, 1992). The infertile couple feels as if they are on an emotional roller coaster with times of growing optimism at the beginning of each treatment cycle, followed by disappointment, sadness, and loss if the treatment doesn't work.

As with other stressful life events, infertility can be conceptualized according to the stress and coping model of Lazarus and Folkman (1984), which states that when faced with a threatening situation, people judge how threatening it is to them (appraisal) and then initiate the use of their coping skills to deal with it (coping). This allows them to try to maintain their highest level of functioning as they are coping with the stressful event. Coping strategies are generally categorized as either problem-focused or emotion-focused. Problem-focused coping refers to those behaviors that attempt to change the problem or situation, or to alter the individual's reaction to it. In the infertility situation, an example of problem-focused coping may be to investigate the success rates of various infertility programs, seek information about treatment options, and plan a course of treatment. Emotion-focused coping refers to those behaviors that serve to vent or process the feelings associated with the situation. In the infertility situation, emotion-focused coping would include calling a close friend to discuss a recent treatment failure or to attend a support group to share feelings with others.

When coping with infertility, as with other major life stressors, seeking social support is an important coping mechanism used by couples undergoing infertility treatment. Discussing the diagnosis, workup, and treatment with family and friends can provide important empathy, sympathy, and compassion for the infertile couple. In addition, attending support groups or self-help groups can foster a feeling of "we're all in this together" that can help diminish feelings of social isolation and loneliness. Along with the benefits of social support, there are also some disadvantages to disclosing infertility-related issues to others. First, disclosure can open the door to unsolicited or unwanted advice from others, such as, "Just relax and you'll get pregnant," or "Try adopting, then you'll get pregnant." Although these comments may come from people who are well-meaning, the infertile couple may perceive the remarks as thoughtless and insensitive. In addition to comments like these, disclosure can also bring about repeated intrusion from others regarding the status of the treatment. Comments such as "Are you pregnant yet?" and "Are you having a test-tube baby?" can be heard from the uninformed and are a source of subtle pressure and societal disapproval in many cases. The initial disclosure may be comforting, but it may be followed by unwanted comments or intrusions by others. A fundamental issue in disclosure is trust—can the person who is being told be trusted to react in a supportive way and can they be trusted with the infertility information? In summary, disclosure regarding infertility treatment can be conceptualized from a stress and coping model, with disclosure and the seeking of social support an important coping strategy for the couple. Unfortunately, disclosure to others may also bring about unwanted comments and advice from others.

Throughout this chapter the terms "privacy" and "disclosure" will be used. The term privacy is used instead of "secrecy" because I believe that the term secrecy implies guilt and shame, whereas the term privacy means that the information is not for public knowledge. I also believe that couples can choose to maintain privacy about any or all aspects of infertility treatment without suffering from shame and guilt.

The current chapter focuses on the mental health clinician's evaluation and counseling of an infertile couple around the issues of disclosure.[1] The mental health clinician can be involved with the infertile couple through a variety of routes; as a member of the infertility treatment team, as an external consultant to the infertility team, and as a private practitioner in a therapeutic relationship with a patient in which infertility is a secondary treatment issue. No matter what the route of referral is, the mental health clinician's primary role in this context is to help the couple work through disclosure issues, examine the pros and cons of both privacy and disclosure, and to help the couple come to their *own* decision about a plan that is sensible for them.

DISCLOSURE IN GENERAL INFERTILITY TREATMENT

It is useful to review some basic issues of infertility counseling to set the stage for the discussion of the privacy and disclosure issue. Traditionally, infertility has been a source of shame and guilt, particularly for the partner with the infertility problem (Nachtigall, Becker, & Wozny, 1992). One's ability to reproduce

---

[1] This chapter is based on the author's article, "Issues of Privacy and Disclosure in Infertility Treatment" in *In Session: Psychotherapy in Practice, 2,* 55–71, 1996.

is usually unquestioned until the individual is ready to attempt conception. Therefore, couples are often taken by surprise with a diagnosis of infertility. They may go through stages of shock, denial, anger, and eventual acceptance as they go through with the evaluations and interventions associated with infertility treatment. These stages of working though are complicated by the inequity in infertility diagnoses (in many cases only one partner has an identified problem which affects the couple's fertility). Not only does the infertile person have to deal with his or her own infertility problem, but he or she must also cope with the partner's disappointment. Dealing with the dyadic issues related to infertility can complicate the individual's adjustment to infertility. The infertile partner may be worried that the fertile partner will leave him or her. The fertile partner may feel powerless to help the infertile spouse cope with the diagnosis. The infertile partner may feel a loss of self-esteem and self-value as a healthy sexual and reproductive being.

Throughout the infertility treatment process, there are various points at which couples disclose information to others. Usually couples, in response to questions from family and friends, begin telling close friends that they have started attempting to get pregnant. When these attempts are unsuccessful, the couple often withdraws from others and avoids inquiries concerning whether their efforts have successfully resulted in conception. After six months to a year, they usually decide to seek medical evaluation. The couple may begin infertility assessment or treatment with the woman's gynecologist for several months or years prior to consulting with a reproductive endocrinologist who specializes in infertility. After the couple meets with the reproductive endocrinologist, they will complete a series of several tests to determine the cause of the infertility. In the majority of cases, an identifiable cause for the infertility is found. At this point, many couples begin disclosing to others in order to work through the diagnosis and to begin assimilating the new information. Couples vary greatly in terms of the number of people they talk with and the degree of information that they share. Some couples choose not to tell anyone throughout the treatment process for fear of burdening others or to avoid undesired intrusion into their personal life. Other couples feel free to talk about their infertility to numerous friends, family, and acquaintances. Based on my experience there do not appear to be any systematic ethnic or religious differences between couples who choose to disclose versus those who do not although empirical research on this topic would be interesting. Instead, the differences between couples on the dimension of disclosure seem to be related to the general degree of openness or privacy the couple has regarding other personal information in their lives.

If and when the couple undertakes infertility interventions using the assisted reproductive techniques (ARTs) such as in vitro fertilization (IVF), gamete intrafallopian transfer (GIFT), intracytoplasmic sperm injection (ICSI), or third-party reproduction, e.g., donor insemination (DI), egg donation (ED), donor embryo, or gestational carrier (the creation of an embryo by a couple with the implantation and gestation of the embryo in the uterus of another woman), the level of technology and concomitant psychological reaction to the treatment become more complex. The issues of privacy and disclosure in infertility are more complicated with the use of ARTs particularly third-party reproduction. Donor insemination (DI) and egg donation involve the use of a third party (the egg or sperm donor) and force the couple to deal with the role of the donor in the creation of their child. The complexity of the treatment and its psychological sequelae often prompt a new discussion of who to tell, what to say, when to say it, and what impact it will have on the child.

For the routine ARTs (IVF, GIFT, ICSI), the issues of disclosure are simpler because the husband's sperm and the wife's eggs are used for conception and therefore the biological and psychosocial parenting roles are not divided. In these cases, the primary issues to disclose are: (a) the infertility problem and (b) the use of the ARTs to conceive. When talking to couples at this phase, it is important to determine their attitudes about the acceptability of the ARTs for conception. In addition, it is important to inquire about their social network's attitudes toward the ARTs. For those couples living in a traditional community or who come from an orthodox religion or morally strict family, the use of the ARTs may prompt disapproval. This disapproval can cause a couple to feel guilty and may cause worry and concern about their family's and friends' future acceptance of the child. Surveys of attitudes toward the reproductive technologies indicate that DI and other third-party reproductive technologies do not have wide social approval (Dunn, Ryan, & O'Brien, 1988). Despite some negative attitudes about the ARTs many couples still opt to tell others because the psychological benefit of the social support received from disclosing outweighs the social stigma or negative reaction from others. With the increased use of the ARTs to conceive, society's attitudes toward ART children may become more accepting, thus decreasing the fear of social stigmatization of ART children and increasing the likelihood that couples will disclose to their child(ren).

DISCLOSURE ISSUES IN THIRD-PARTY REPRODUCTION

The issues of disclosure change when one considers third-party reproduction. The critical issue in third-party reproduction is the clarification and understanding of the roles of genetic parenting and psychosocial parenting. In third-party reproduction, the genetic relationship to the offspring is separated from the psychosocial relationship of parenting the child. In the case of egg donation, the egg donor is genetically related to the offspring but the psychosocial mother is not, even though the psychosocial mother gestates and delivers the infant. In the case of sperm donation, the psychosocial father is not the genetic father of the offspring. This separation of the genetic and psychosocial aspects of parenting make third-party reproduction a psychologically complicated treatment. In addition, the inequity of the genetic contribution of the psychosocial parents (e.g., in the case of sperm donation, the mother has the genetic and psychological relationship to the child whereas the father has only the psychological relationship) may cause conflict and differential feelings of "ownership" of the child. The different feelings of ownership may lead to different feelings and concerns about disclosure. The nongenetic parent may feel that disclosure is too risky because it may jeopardize his or her relationship to the child. They may also feel that disclosure will cause social stigma for the child (Klock & Maier, 1991). Alternatively, the genetic parent may feel that the child has a right to know regardless of how the nongenetic parent feels. Parents who plan to disclose often base this decision on the belief that the child has a right to know his or her genetic background. These parents believe that knowledge of one's genetic heritage is crucial to healthy psychological development. Advocates from the adoption field also support the disclosure position based on the child's right to know, although the creation of children via third-party reproduction is different than the transfer of a child from its birth parents to its adoptive parents (Klock, Jacob, & Maier, 1994).

Disclosure in Donor Insemination: A Review of the Literature

The issue of privacy and disclosure that has received the most attention in the infertility literature is the issue of disclosure to the offspring in cases of sperm donation. In brief, sperm donation is used when the husband is oligospermic (low levels of sperm concentration or motility) or azoospermic (no fertile sperm). After the diagnosis of male infertility is made, the couple is told about donor insemination (DI) and decides if they want to pursue it. If they choose to have the treatment, they select or are matched to an anonymous sperm donor. Matches are usually based on the physical and medical characteristics of the husband. The wife then monitors her ovulation and goes to the infertility clinic for insemination when she is ovulating. Medically, the procedure is one of the simplest in reproductive medicine. Psychologically, it is one of the most complex.

Several studies have addressed the psychological issues related to donor insemination, including the critical issue of whether or not the couple plans to tell the child of his or her DI origin. The following is a review of the research on the issue of privacy and disclosure among couples using donor sperm to conceive. A summary of these research findings in regard to parents' attitudes about disclosure is presented in Table 9.1.

Manuel, Chevret, and Cyzba (1980) asked a sample of 72 French couples whether they planned to tell the child of his or her donor insemination origin. Sixty-one percent said they would not tell, whereas 39% reported that they would eventually tell the child. Reasons commonly given for not telling the child included: (a) the child "belongs" more to the couple if he or she does not know; (b) the parents believe the child would be socially stigmatized if others knew of the child's DI origin; (c) the parents fear a negative reaction from the

TABLE 9.1   Studies of Parental Attitudes about Disclosure

Author and Country	Time of Assessment	Tell Child? Response	Percent	Tell Others? Response	Percent
Rowland (1985) Australia	Pretreatment	No	56	No	41
		Yes	9	Yes	59
		DK	35		
Berger et al. (1986) Canada	Pretreatment	No	70	No	68
Cook et al. (1995) England	4–8 yrs posttreatment	No	80	Yes	56
		Yes	4		
		DK	16		
Amuzu et al. (1990) United States	3 yrs posttreatment	No	61	Yes	50
		Yes	18		
		DK	21		
Schover et al. (1992) United States	Pretreatment	No	80 (M) 74 (F)	No	70 (M) 64 (F)
		Yes	20 (M) 26 (F)		
	11 mos posttreatment	No	88 (M, F)	No	63 (M) 60 (F)
Klock & Maier (1991) United States	0–6 yrs posttreatment	No	86	No	40
		Yes	14	Yes	60
Klock et al. (1994) United States	pretreatment	No	47	No	45
		Yes	27	Yes	38
		DK	20	Dis	16
		Dis	5		

Key to symbols: M = male; F = female; DK = don't know; dis = disagreed.

child; and (d) the parents wish to protect the man's self-esteem. Forty-one percent of the subjects in the sample felt that DI was superior to adoption because it allowed the male infertility problem to remain confidential.

Clayton and Kovacs (1982) found that 68% of their sample of 50 Australian couples did not plan to tell the child, 14% planned to tell, and 18% were undecided. These couples were interviewed one to two years after having a child, in contrast to the subjects in Manuel et al.'s study who were assessed prior to conceiving via DI. Rowland (1985) in another study of Australian DI couples found that 56% of her couples planned not to tell the child, 9% planned to tell, and 35% did not know whether or not they would tell. The three most common reasons given for not telling the child were: (a) the couple wanted to protect the man's self-esteem; (b) they feared social stigma to the child; and (c) the couple wanted to feel more "ownership" of the child. In addition to asking couples about whether they planned to tell the child of his or her DI origin, Rowland also asked the subjects whether they had told anyone else about using DI to conceive. It was found that 59% of couples told at least one other person, 41% told no one.

Berger, Eisen, Shuber, and Doody (1986) studied attitudes toward disclosure among Canadian DI couples. They found that among their sample of 76 couples who were beginning DI treatment, 68% of men and 67% of women would not discuss DI with a relative. Seventy percent of both men and women reported that they would not discuss DI with the child. Husbands whose wives had not yet conceived were more willing to discuss their infertility problem with others than were husbands whose wives had already conceived.

Four studies of American couples' attitudes toward disclosure have recently been reported. Amuzu, Laxova, and Shapiro (1990) asked 397 couples who had a child via DI about their attitudes regarding disclosure. They found that 72% had told their obstetricians and 50% had told at least one family member or friend. Sixty-one percent reported that they did not or probably would not plan to tell the child of its DI origin, 18% said they would probably eventually tell the child, and 21% were undecided.

Schover, Collins, and Richards (1992) studied couples' attitudes about confidentiality in a longitudinal study of donor couples. They asked couples about their attitudes before the procedure and 11 months after they had begun treatment. They found that men and women did not differ in their beliefs about privacy, nor were there any differences in beliefs across the two assessment times. Prior to treatment, 80% of men and 74% of women planned not to tell the child; 12% of men and 22% of women would tell the child as soon as the information could be understood; and 8% of men and 4% of women planned to tell the child at some time between the ages of 9 and adulthood. Eleven months after treatment began, 88% of men and women preferred complete privacy unless a medical necessity dictated informing the child. With respect to telling family or friends, initially 70% of men and 64% of women preferred complete privacy. At the 11-month follow-up, the trend was toward openness within the family, with 63% of men and 60% of women preferring complete privacy and 33% of men and 20% of women willing to tell family members about the use of DI. Schover et al. concluded, "The predominant opinion for both spouses over time was that nobody but the spouses should be told about the use of donor insemination." Schover et al. also described how they counsel couples. They advise couples that there is no "right" answer about how to handle the confidentiality issue. They inform the couple of the psychological impact of family secrets but they also share with the couples the available data on DI couples, which indicates that most couples plan not to tell. In addition, Schover et al. also discusses with the couples who plan to tell the child ways to disclose the information that are developmentally appropriate. They recommend adjusting the amount and type of information disclosed to the developmental stage of the child, for example, giving simple, brief answers to toddlers but elaborating on the explanations, using books or other aids, as the child gets older and is cognitively able to understand the information. Pruett (1992) also discusses the disclosure of DI information to a child and stresses that the most important factor regarding the timing of the disclosure is the emotional readiness of the child.

In a retrospective study of 35 couples with donor children between the ages of infancy and 6 years, Klock and Maier (1991) found that 40% had told no one about using DI to conceive and 60% told at least one other person. In descending order of frequency, the most common people to be told were the wive's mother, father, best friend, referring physician, close friend, sister, brother, therapist, and coworker. The most frequently given reasons for telling someone else, in descending order, were: (a) to share confidential information; (b) to help celebrate the pregnancy; (c) to help them make up their mind about using DI; (d) to talk about psychological issues related to DI; (e) to help prepare for childbirth; and (f) to help with child care. The sharing of confidential information referred to the individual's discussion of DI with a person close to him or her. This seems to be an index of closeness between the subject and the person who was confided in. Couples were also asked, "If you had it to do over again, would you tell anyone about using DI to conceive?" Of the total sample, 87% reported that if they had to do it over again, they would tell no one. Of the subjects who had told at least one other person, 81% said that if they had it to do over again, they would tell no one. In terms of telling the child, 86% of the sample planned not to tell the child. The most common reasons given for not telling the child were: (a) it would complicate the child's life unnecessarily; (b) it would complicate the father/child relationship; (c) the husband could be the biological father because the couple had intercourse after the insemination. Of the 14% who planned to tell the child, the most common reasons given for telling were: (a) that the child had a right to know and (b) they did not want the child to find out from someone else.

In the first phase of a prospective, longitudinal study, Klock, Jacob, and Maier (1994) studied the marital adjustment, self-esteem, psychological symptomatology, and attitudes and concerns regarding DI among a group of couples undergoing infertility treatment for male factor infertility. Couples were assessed prior to treatment, at the fifth month of pregnancy, and at yearly intervals after the child was born. The results from the pretreatment assessment indicated that the majority of couples experienced low levels of psychological symptoms, had average levels of self-esteem, and average marital adjustment scores. In terms of the couples' attitudes toward disclosure prior to treatment, 38% had or planned to tell others about using DI to conceive, 45% said they had not or would not tell others, and 16% disagreed with one another about whether they would tell others. The most frequently cited reasons for telling someone were: (a) the sharing of confidential information; (b) having someone to talk to about the procedure; and (c) having someone to help them make up their mind about DI. In terms of telling the child, 27% reported that they planned to tell the child of his or her donor insemination origin, 47% stated that they would not tell, 20% were undecided, and 5% disagreed with one another about whether they would tell. The group that is of greatest clinical concern is the subgroup of couples who disagree with one another about the disclosure issue. When this situation is evident, the clinician should continue to explore with both partners the reasons for their position to see if they can reach some compromise before beginning treatment and thus avoid later conflict during and after pregnancy.

The couples in this study are still being assessed as they become pregnant and at yearly intervals after the child is born. In a preliminary review of the data (Klock, 1994), at the fifth month of pregnancy ($n = 34$) 62% of subjects had told others and 38% planned to tell the child. At the child's first birthday, the number of couples who planned to tell the child dropped to 23%. Although these data are only preliminary and are not representative of the complete sample, they highlight the possibility that couples' attitudes toward disclosure may change over time. Hypothetically, couples may tell others in the excitement of sharing the news of the pregnancy, then once the child is born, they may decide not to tell. This places the couple in a predicament if many other people know about the child's origin and the couple does not plan to tell the child. Counseling couples about this possible scenario may be helpful in creating a plan for disclosure prior to conception that is consistent with their beliefs about what is best for the child over time.

A final study assessing parental attitudes toward disclosure among ART parents was conducted by Cook, Golombok, Bish, and Murray (1995) in the United Kingdom. In this study, the investigators studied four groups of parents and their children: (a) in vitro fertilization (IVF); (b) donor insemination (DI); (c) adoption; and (d) naturally conceived. The children ranged in age from 4 to 8 years. The investigators interviewed the mothers in the families to ask about their attitudes about disclosure. They found that none of the couples who had conceived with DI had told the child yet. Eighty percent said they had definitely decided not to tell, 16% were undecided, and 4% planned to tell their child. This was different from the adoption group in which all but one family had told the child. In the IVF group, 27% told their child, 54% planned to tell, 12% were unsure, and 7% planned not to tell. Similar to the findings of other studies, over half (56%) of the DI couples had told family or friends that they had used DI to conceive, but the majority planned not to tell the child. Ninety-eight percent of the IVF parents had told at least one other person that they had conceived using IVF. When asked why the parents were not planning to tell the child, 70% of the DI mothers reported that they were not going to tell the child in order to protect the child. They were concerned that the child would be devastated that his or her psychosocial father was not the genetic father. Another reason cited for not telling the child was to protect the father. The protection of the father was seen as having two dimensions: (a) to prevent the child from rejecting the father, and (b) to prevent the male infertility from becoming public knowledge. Two difficulties were noted in terms of telling the child, when to tell and how to tell. For the couples who planned to tell the child, this was an issue of concern because they did not know what would be the best age for disclosure and how to discuss the DI origin in a way that the child could understand.

In summary, the studies on disclosure and privacy among DI couples indicate that most couples plan *not* to tell the child about their DI origin. It appears that these attitudes may change over time. Therefore, exploration of the couples' feelings at pretreatment as well at various times throughout the transition to parenthood and beyond may be helpful in the disclosure decision-making process. The couple may find it compelling to tell others during treatment and pregnancy, but after the child is born, they may regret having disclosed. Therefore, clear, direct counseling about disclosure with respect to the use of DI is important. Additionally, the couple may feel that they do not want to tell the child but this position may change after the child's verbal skills develop and the child begins to ask about his or her origin. One of the most compelling findings from the studies of DI couples who wish to tell their child is the absence of research or clinical recommendations regarding how and when to tell the child. It is important to study couples who have disclosed to their child and determine how the timing or method of telling impacts the outcome, such as self-esteem, sense of security, and belonging.

Case Example

The following case illustration focuses on the psychological issues related to privacy and disclosure for a couple considering DI. This is a couple who were seen for a mandatory pre-DI consultation with an infertility team's psychologist. The goals of the pretreatment psychological consultation are to help the couple, particularly the husband, process his feelings about the infertility diagnosis and prepare the couple for treatment. In addition, in some programs, the mental health clinician also screens out couples for whom DI treatment is inappropriate due to psychiatric or cognitive problems. In general, serious Axis I or II diagnoses, active substance abuse or dependence, serious marital discord, and previous legal charges related to child abuse or neglect are reasons for postponing or prohibiting infertility treatment. In the majority of cases, though, these issues are not present and the pre-DI consultation appointment focuses on preparation for treatment. The husband's reaction to and assimilation of the infertility diagnosis need to be discussed. Exploration of the husband's feelings regarding the potential loss of self-esteem, and his sense of himself as a sexual and masculine man must be explored. Some clinicians recommend that the couple wait three to six months from the time of diagnosis until the initiation of DI to allow the couple to react and adjust to the diagnosis of male infertility. This waiting period may be very difficult for the couple to understand because many of them have been trying to conceive for months or years prior to the diagnosis of male infertility. If the couple rushes into beginning treatment, however, they may adjust badly when the woman becomes pregnant. The husband in particular may have a difficult time bonding and forming an attachment to the DI child. The following is a prototypic case based on my experience with numerous DI couples.

Presenting Problem

Sally, aged 28, and Bob, aged 31, are a white, middle-class, college-educated couple who have been married for 4½ years. The couple met through mutual friends 6½ years ago and dated for approximately one year prior to their engagement.

They married the following year. Bob is one of six children in a large, traditional Catholic family. Sally is the youngest of two daughters in a divorced family. Sally was previously treated for depression around the time of her parents' divorce. She is a nonpracticing Protestant. Bob is self-employed as a building contractor and Sally is a real estate agent. They recently built their own home.

Sally and Bob had always planned to start a family after they had been married a few years, became financially stable and had their own home. They began trying to get pregnant over two years ago. They tried on their own for approximately one year. Then Sally went to her gynecologist who performed some preliminary tests. Those tests did not uncover an identifiable fertility problem so the gynecologist prescribed an oral ovulation induction agent and instructed Sally and Bob to have appropriately timed intercourse. After four months, Sally became frustrated and sad so she sought a consultation with a reproductive endocrinologist. The reproductive endocrinologist referred Bob for a semen analysis. Although Bob knew that Sally was anxious to complete all the testing, he was reluctant to go to the infertility clinic to give a semen sample. After much arguing and cajoling, Bob finally agreed to go. The reproductive endocrinologist called the couple back to his office after the results of the semen analysis were known. He explained that Bob's sperm count was very low, less than one million in the sample (normal range 20–100 million) and that the percentage of sperm that were motile was less than 10%. He said that the couple's best chance for successful conception was the use of donor sperm. He then went on to discuss donor selection and screening and the treatment protocol. He also arranged for the couple to have the pre-DI consultation with the team's psychologist to discuss their emotional reaction to Bob's infertility and to discuss their feelings about DI.

Course of Treatment

Sally and Bob were seen for the initial consultation appointment. During that appointment, the psychologist began with a review of the medical treatment thus far. Then the psychologist asked Sally to share her feelings about the infertility. The psychologist began with Sally because it is usually easier for women to express their thoughts and feelings about emotionally laden issues such as infertility. Perhaps Sally would verbalize some of the couple's issues as well as being a role-model for Bob about how to express his feelings.

THERAPIST: Sally, tell me how you felt when Dr. A told you the results of the semen analysis?

SALLY: I couldn't believe it. We had been trying for such a long time and I never even imagined it could be something with Bob. I always felt so responsible and thought that it was something wrong with me. I never thought it would be Bob and now I feel really bad for him because I think he must be going through what I started going through two years ago.

This begins the discussion of the feelings of responsibility, guilt, sadness, and loss inherent in the infertility diagnosis. Also, Sally begins to try to assign blame for the infertility but then ends by expressing her empathy for Bob's feelings.

THERAPIST: Bob, how have you been feeling?

BOB: Uh, . . . well, I feel really bad . . ., like I can't believe that this is really happening to me. You know how you feel like you're really not so much of a man anymore, you know what they say, that I'm shooting blanks now. I just can't believe it. I don't know why this happened to me.

This exchange lets the therapist know that Bob is still in the initial stages of shock and disbelief about his infertility. Therefore, any treatment decision or disclosure decisions are premature. At this point, it is necessary for the therapist to encourage the couple to take time to discuss the infertility diagnosis. The couple may be tempted to share the diagnosis with their family and friends, but the therapist may caution the couple to decide carefully about who they tell now in the event that they decide in the future they do not want to disclose the use of DI. The initial session concludes with a brief social and educational history of both partners. In addition, psychosocial histories are taken with a particular focus on previous stressful life experiences, including other losses and the ways in which the patients coped with them. Description of the couple's social milieu and support network is also obtained. A follow-up appointment is scheduled in two to four weeks to provide the couple time to sort through some of their initial feelings.

Second Appointment

Sally and Bob arrive at the second appointment. Bob begins the hour by stating that they have decided to initiate DI at the beginning of the next cycle. He states that they have "talked it all over" and that they are ready to proceed. The therapist notes that Bob's attitude and demeanor are much more defensive and assertive at this appointment and that Sally is very quiet. The following exchange takes place:

THERAPIST: It sounds like you have come to a lot of decisions about this very rapidly.

BOB: Well, we've been trying to have a child for such a long time that we just figured we might as well get on with it and deal with all that other stuff later.

THERAPIST: Other stuff?

BOB: All the other stuff you mentioned last time we met, like telling people and stuff.

THERAPIST: Well, before we get to plans about telling others, why don't we take a minute and talk about how things have gone with the two of you these past two weeks?

BOB: Everything is fine.

THERAPIST: Sally, is that accurate?

SALLY: Well, we have had some rough spots.

THERAPIST: What kind of rough spots?

SALLY: Well, I really wanted to begin talking about some of this stuff but
                Bob just shuts down when I try to bring it up. I just want to know
                how he's feeling about it but he won't talk to me.

Bob is trying to avoid dealing with his feelings about the infertility diagnosis
and its effect on his self-esteem and sexuality. Attempts by his wife to talk
things through have been unsuccessful and she reveals this to the therapist in
order to cope more openly with the problems. The remainder of the second appointment is spent focusing on Bob's reaction to the infertility and its effect on
his self-esteem and sense of virility. The issues to be addressed at this phase
are: (a) how does the husband feel about his infertility, including its effect on
his self-esteem and sexual functioning, and (b) can the husband imagine fa-
thering a child that is not biologically related to him. Some husbands superfi-
cially state that they are willing to use donor insemination but that they would
like the donor semen to be mixed with their own semen for the insemination.
This suggestion is a sign that the husband has not fully adjusted to the infertility diagnosis, is ambivalent about the use of donor insemination and is not psychologically ready to start treatment. Each of these issues must be addressed
before the couple can begin thinking about the more psychologically complex
issue of disclosure or privacy.

Third Appointment

Bob starts by reporting that he is feeling better and that there have been no problems with his sexual functioning. The couple reports that they have reconsidered
beginning treatment next month and instead will be waiting at least two cycles
to give themselves time to adjust to the idea of using DI. The discussion then
moves to issues related to privacy and disclosure. The therapist begins by discussing with the couple how they handle the disclosure of other emotionally
sensitive issues in their lives. Then the therapist asks if the couple has told others about the infertility workup and/or the intended use of donor insemination.
For example, typically, the wife tells her parents that the couple has been seeking infertility treatment. In addition, she may have told one or two siblings
and/or her best friend. The husband may have told one person, a close friend or
a brother. From the number of people told about the infertility a general index
of the degree of disclosure the couple feels comfortable with is obtained. Other
couples may have told no one that they were seeking infertility treatment and
confirm the decision once they know that a male factor is involved. After learning how many people know about the infertility, the therapist can review the
couple's beliefs about how supportive their family and friends would be if they
knew that Sally and Bob were having a child via DI.
    While the therapist is talking with Bob about his family, the following in-
teraction takes place:

THERAPIST: Bob, how do you think your parents would feel if they knew you
                were using DI to conceive?
BOB: Oh, they'd be fine with it.

SALLY: No, they wouldn't! You know what a problem they had when Joey and his wife couldn't have kids and then talked about adoption. They didn't say anything outright to Joey but they told everyone else that if they couldn't have a baby on their own then God didn't mean for them to be parents. So I think they'd have a fit if they even knew we were thinking about this.

BOB: They are really traditional and my mother is very religious. I think they may be too old to understand all the new ways to have a child.

THERAPIST: Do you think they could love a child conceived with DI?

BOB: Oh yeah, they could love any child but they would always know that the child was different and then they would talk among themselves about it and I would be afraid that our child would hear about it some day.

THERAPIST: So you're not sure you could trust them to keep it confidential if you and Sally choose not to tell.

BOB: Right, but on the other hand, if we told them and the child it might always make them treat our kid differently than their other grandchildren.

THERAPIST: Sally, what do you think?

SALLY: I don't want to tell them because I think they wouldn't understand.

Bob and Sally are frustrated in their efforts to decide whether to tell Bob's parents about the use of DI. The therapist helps try to clarify the dilemma.

THERAPIST: Bob, what would be the advantages of telling your parents?

BOB: Well, we could tell them the whole story without having to make up something. They know we've been trying to have a baby and haven't had any luck yet. Then if we turn around and Sally is pregnant, we'll have to tell them something. It would just be simpler if we could tell them the truth.

THERAPIST: Yes, that would be easier, but on the other hand can you see some disadvantages to telling.

BOB: Yeah, their disapproval and their passing judgment on us. I also think that my family talks a lot so if we told them, they would tell everyone else and I'm not sure I want everyone else to know. Not so much for us, but for the baby. What if some day we're all sitting around my parents' house and the child overhears them talking. That would be the worst!

THERAPIST: Yes, that would not be a good situation.

SALLY: Yeah, and if we told them there would be all that religious stuff that your mother says. She would make it sound like I was having an affair or something with some other guy to have a baby. She wouldn't understand that it's a medical procedure.

THERAPIST: So you think she would pass judgment on you, too, Sally.

SALLY: Oh yeah . . . definitely.

This dialogue illustrates how the couple begins to think in concrete terms of the implications, both pro and con, of disclosing the use of DI to others. The discussion moves on to focus on Sally's family and the couple's perception of their possible reaction. The discussion also touches on the attitudes and perceptions about significant friends, coworkers and others in the couples' lives who may be told with the same pattern of trying to imagine the individual's reaction to the disclosure of DI. This process may be completed in one session or over the course of several sessions, depending on the complexity of the issues and the number of significant others in the couple's life.

After considering others' likely reactions to disclosure of the use of DI, the discussion turns to focusing on the child and whether or not the couple would plan on telling the child of its DI origin. The issues of disclosure to others is inextricably linked to whether the couple plans to tell the child or not. Many couples who have a DI child feel compelled to tell the child only because so many other people already know. In addition, many couples who have told others, regret having done so and if they had it to do over again report that they would tell no one (Klock & Maier, 1991). The only research paradigm available to shed light on this issue is the adoption literature. There is evidence to suggest that adoptees may benefit from being told that they are adopted and the current movement toward openness in adoption reflects a change in the fundamental beliefs about disclosure being best for the child. The use of adoption as a paradigm for decision making in the DI context is not a perfect match because of the numerous differences between adoption and DI. In the case of DI, the psychosocial mother has a genetic relationship to the child and has gestated and delivered the child. The DI child does not have to cope with the psychological issues of having been given up by his or her birth mother. The attitudes toward DI in society are much more negative than they are about adoption and therefore the potential social stigma of telling the child and others may have detrimental effects on the child. In the case of DI, the most important factor in the decision to tell or not tell is the parents' belief about what is best for the child. A couple may feel that it is best not to tell the child to spare the child from the social stigma he or she may receive if it is known that he or she is a DI child. They may also choose not to tell for fear of jeopardizing the father-child bond. In this case, the couple is making the disclosure decision based on *their* beliefs of what is right for their child in their family and in their community.

If a couple feels that it is best for the child to be told and they tell the child in a loving, accepting manner, then the child will understand that even though he or she was created in a nontraditional way, he or she was greatly wanted and loved by the parents. In either situation, it is the mental health clinician's duty to help the couple discover *for themselves* the solution that is best for them. It is a clinical error to persuade the couple to make the decision based on the therapist's bias or beliefs. The technology is too new and there are no outcome data to suggest that one option or another is best for the child. In a generation or two, the issues about disclosure may be vastly different, but for now, it seems best to let the parents decide, as parents do about all other aspects of their child's development and experience. If the clinician forces an opinion, one way or another, it violates the position of neutrality that is necessary for effective therapeutic intervention. Moreover the therapist's suggestion may be completely at odds with the couple's religious, moral or psychological beliefs about what is best for the child or the family.

Fourth Appointment

THERAPIST:	We have talked a lot about how others will respond to DI and whether or not you will tell them. Now we need to talk about what you plan to do in terms of telling or not telling the child. Do either of you have any gut reaction about what you think might be the best?
BOB:	I don't think we should tell.
SALLY:	Neither do I.
THERAPIST:	Why not?
BOB:	Because I think people would think that the child is different in some way and I don't want to put that burden on my child.
SALLY:	Yeah, and you know how mean other kids can get, they would tease him or something and I think that would be really confusing. Anyway, Bob will be his father so I don't see that there is any reason to tell.
BOB:	Besides, I wouldn't want to tell the child and have him start wondering who this guy was who donated the sperm.
THERAPIST:	What are you worried about?
BOB:	Well, that he would think some other guy out there is really his father but that he could never find out who the guy was, so what would be the point of telling him.
THERAPIST:	Well, what would be the advantages of telling the child?
BOB:	I don't know.
SALLY:	Well, I could see that it would be easier to just get it out in the open but then what if the child went around telling everyone before they [the child] knew how other people felt about it.
THERAPIST:	That might be difficult.
BOB:	It might be easier to tell just in case something medical happened to the child and he needed blood or something from me. If he found out I wasn't a biological match then he'd know I wasn't his father and it would be a big mess.
THERAPIST:	Yes that would be a time when telling the child would be better.

The therapist is trying to help the couple clarify the pros and cons of telling or not telling.

BOB:	But I'd still be afraid that if he knew he was conceived with DI that he wouldn't treat me like his real father.
THERAPIST:	Would you feel like his real father?
BOB:	I don't know.
THERAPIST:	What do you think makes someone a real father?
BOB:	Well, mostly that you're there for them, that they know they can count on you to take care of them and to provide for them and to be there for them when they need you.
THERAPIST:	Do you think you could do all those things for this child?
BOB:	Well yeah, of course.
THERAPIST:	Of course. Are there other things that make a man a father?
BOB:	Um, passing on traditions and ideas, teaching them how to do stuff, like playing baseball and showing them how to sail. Doing

all that kind of stuff together and having a good childhood. My parents gave me a really good childhood and I would like to do that for my son or daughter.

The therapist is trying to help Bob explore his beliefs about what makes a father by clarifying the relative importance of the genetic and psychosocial contributions of fatherhood. This is a fundamental issue that both partners have to work through prior to making the decision about telling. Some men, particularly those that are analytically inclined describe the genetic and psychosocial contributions in terms of percentages, such as, "it's 25% genetic and 75% how you raise them." This can give the therapist a rough index of the degree to which the genetic contribution by the donor will be salient for the husband. It is also important for the wife to discuss her feelings about the relative importance of the genetic versus psychosocial contributions of the father in order to reinforce the father's equal role as a parent of the DI child. For many couples, once they become clear regarding the importance of the psychosocial aspects of parenting, they are more likely to disclose to the child because they feel the primary role of the father is the psychosocial role. The remainder of the fourth session is spent discussing the relative importance of the father's role.

Fifth Session

During this session, the therapist reviews the topics covered thus far and helps the couple come to a tentative decision. In the case of Sally and Bob, the couple has decided not to tell anyone except Sally's sister. They will wait until after the child is born to determine whether or not to tell the child. At this time, they are both leaning toward not telling the child.

THERAPIST: So you plan only to tell your sister?
SALLY: Yes, we are so close and I have to tell her. I know she will be really excited for us and she won't tell anyone if we ask her not to.
THERAPIST: How do you feel about this Bob?
BOB: It's okay with me. I trust her.
THERAPIST: And what about telling the child?
BOB: We both think that we probably won't tell but we really can't decide right now so we're not going to tell anyone but Sally's sister. Then if we don't tell the child, we don't have to worry about him finding out from someone else. And if we want to tell, then we can.
THERAPIST: That sounds like a good plan for now. You may find that your thoughts and feelings about this change over time, particularly after your child is born. If there is anything you want to discuss about this decision in the future, please feel free to give me a call and we can talk about it some more.

At the decision-making point in the process, the most significant factor is that the couple arrives at a consensus that they both can live with. If the spouses disagreed with one another, the therapy would continue until they reached consensus. Also, it is important to inform the couple that their attitudes about disclosure may change over time (Klock, Jacob, & Maier, 1994; Schover, Collins, & Richards, 1992). They should be aware of this and plan to discuss it with one another at various points during their child's development. This is another reason why the mental health clinician should not take a rigid stance regarding disclosure or privacy because it may make the couple hesitant to seek out help in the future if their initial experience with a mental health clinician was negative.

Outcome and Prognosis

Sally and Bob conceived after four cycles of donor insemination. Sally had an uneventful pregnancy and gave birth to a healthy daughter. The couple have adjusted well to the demands of new parenthood and are considering having another child using the same donor. Their ability to discuss difficult issues and their shared values and commitment to their marriage facilitated their adjustment to having a child through DI. When their daughter's language developed and later when she began asking questions about where she came from, the couple was seen again in consultation to reconsider their decision about disclosure. They confirmed their decision to remain private. Bob stated that he "is the father" and that there is no reason why their daughter needs to know anything more. Sally stated that she no longer thinks about how their daughter was conceived but instead is enjoying the challenges and rewards of parenting and having the family with Bob that she has always dreamed of.

CLINICAL COMMENTS

For therapists working with couples using the ARTs, particularly third-party reproduction, it is essential to help the couple decide how they will handle issues of privacy and disclosure. After the couple has adjusted to the diagnosis and decides to initiate third-party reproduction techniques, it is important that they have counseling to ease their psychological adjustment to the procedure. One of the major psychological issues is privacy or disclosure to the offspring and to family and friends. The two decisions are obviously closely related in that if the couple decides to tell other people, then they have to tell the child.

In the case example, the couple decided to tell only one other person and not to tell the child. The therapist may want to discuss the logistics of this decision and some possible scenarios in the future that should be considered. The first is the initial visit to the pediatrician and deciding whether to give the donor's medical history as the father's. Also, the couple needs to decide whether they plan to tell the pediatrician or other future physicians. Other scenarios to consider are the comments that family and friends will make about whether the child resembles the father. How to answer questions the child may have about where he or she came from and how to cope with separation and individuation issues when the child is an adolescent are other issues to discuss.

The most negative aspect of the privacy perspective, the potential risk of an unplanned disclosure to the child, needs to be discussed. This concern is largely based on the adoption experience, which has been discussed in the scientific and popular literature. Case stories abound describing a child's discovery that he or she was adopted. The unintentional disclosure leads to a rupture in the child-parent relationship primarily by undermining the trust the child has in the parents. The child may also begin to question whether he or she belongs in the family and may reexamine his or her identity. In the DI context, the most likely scenario would be that the child finds out from someone in the family who is aware of the child's DI origin. Discovery of this information, either accidentally or intentionally, by someone other than the child's parents could cause a devastating breach of trust and feeling of betrayal. This scenario, and its negative implications has to be thoroughly discussed with prospective parents.

Two other conceivable outcomes exist regarding the couple and their decision about disclosure. The couple can agree to tell both others and the child or, the couple can disagree with one another about whether to tell others and the child. In couples where both partners agree to disclose, the psychological issues are much simpler because the couple faces no inconsistency between what they have said to others and what they plan to tell the child. The most common reason for telling the child is the belief that the child has a right to know his or her genetic/medical background. In addition, some parents feel that the genetic information is such an important part of the foundation of the child's sense of self that to not tell is negligent. Helping the couple explore their position regarding disclosure includes discussing how and when to tell the child of his or her donor insemination origin.

When spouses disagree, it is often the case that the wife wants to tell the child and the husband does not. This may be due to a gender difference in attitudes about privacy and disclosure. Or it may be that the wife feels more confident in her connection to the child and is therefore less threatened by the prospect of disclosure. Alternatively, the husband may not want to disclose for fear of jeopardizing his parental connection to the child. In addition, he may not want to acknowledge his infertility publicly. He may fear that the child would be stigmatized by being told that he or she was conceived through donor insemination. The husband may feel that the wife is trying to undermine his role as father if she insists on telling the child. Further exploration with the couple is needed to clarify the different motivations of the partners with respect to disclosure. Ideally, through a process of considering the pros and cons, the couple will come to some consensus about what they will do. If no consensus can be reached, then DI treatment is premature. The mental health professional can recommend that treatment be postponed until the couple has arrived at a consensus and has developed a plan to implement their choice.

When helping couples decide about privacy and disclosure issues, it is important to help them examine the pros and cons of both options in the context of their specific social milieu. Then they need to examine their beliefs about the relative importance of genetics and the environment in the making of a parent. For the husband, emphasizing his role as the child's father can be particularly helpful. If there is disagreement between partners, it is important not to let infertility treatment begin until some consensus can be reached. Until there is some evidence regarding the "best" option for all couples, throughout the discussions with the couple the mental health professional should remain neutral and help the couple come to their own decision regarding disclosure or privacy. Last, the mental health professional should suggest to the couple that their ideas about disclosure may change over time and that the couple may want to reconsider their decision in the future. The mental health professional should be ready to consult with them, if it is needed, because the mental health professional may be one of the few people who is aware of the child's DI origin.

Disclosure Issues in Egg Donation

This discussion has focused on the typical married, heterosexual couple who is presenting for DI. The same issues of disclosure and privacy are relevant for those couples considering egg donation. Although the issues about privacy and disclosure are the same, the context and practice of egg donation make it somewhat different (Braverman, 1993). It is more common in egg donation than in sperm donation for a known donor to be used, usually a sister or close friend. This factor alone will often force a couple to disclose because many members of the immediate family already know that the sister or friend is serving as an egg donor. Therefore, the status of the donor, known versus anonymous, is an important determinant in attitudes about disclosure. The use of known sperm donors is much less common, probably reflecting differences in the ease of obtaining sperm and eggs and also reflecting psychological differences between sperm and egg recipients. Another difference between sperm and egg recipients is based only on my clinical observation that men and women respond differently to infertility. In the case of ovarian failure and the use of donated eggs, women may not feel that their ovarian failure is as great a threat to their femininity as men feel azoospermia is a threat to their masculinity. This may make women's attitudes about disclosure of egg donation different from men's attitudes about disclosure in sperm donation.

Disclosure Issues in Nontraditional Families

Decisions about disclosure for lesbians and single women electing to use DI to create their families differ from those of heterosexual married couples. Jacob, Klock, and Maier (1994), Klock, Jacob, and Maier (1995), and Leiblum, Palmer, and Spector (1995) have reported that 100% of lesbian women and single women choose to tell others and tell the child that the child was conceived through DI. The fact that all lesbians plan to disclose appears to be due to the belief that DI is the best option for family building for lesbian couples, the generally supportive attitudes of the lesbian community, and the absence of a male partner whose infertility has to be kept private. Jacob (1995) provides a thorough overview of the family-building issues among lesbian and single women.

CONCLUSION

Throughout the process of infertility treatment, couples face many decisions about what to disclose and to whom. During treatment, the couple may be compelled to discuss their infertility treatment with others but the rewards of the social support received through disclosure may not outweigh the drawbacks of intrusive comments and unsolicited advice. Issues of privacy and disclosure become more complicated when a third party is used to aid in conception. The clinician's role in helping the couple understand their thoughts and feelings about disclosure is crucial. In addition, the clinician can also help the couple discover for themselves what choice they want to make about disclosure. There are numerous reasons for telling the child, as there are for not telling the child, from both the parents' and child's perspectives. Most studies find that the majority of parents plan not to tell the child. In the final analysis, it is the role of the parents, not the clinician, to decide what path will be taken regarding disclosure based on the parents' beliefs about what is in the best interests of the child and the family. Exploration of the relevant issues in supportive, active therapy can be extremely helpful for the couple. Although several studies have assessed attitudes about disclosure, more research is needed to determine whether choices about disclosure or privacy are related to child development outcomes, such as self-esteem, trust, and feelings of belonging (Klock, 1994). As society becomes more accepting of third-party reproduction and attitudes about the use of donor gametes improve, it will be important to determine whether this improvement prompts greater disclosure among parents.

REFERENCES

Abbey, A., Halman, L. J., & Andrews, F. M. (1992). Psychosocial, treatment, and demographic predictors of the stress associated with infertility. *Fertility and Sterility, 57,* 122–128.

Amuzu, B., Laxova, R., & Shapiro, S. (1990). Pregnancy outcome, health of children, and family adjustment after donor insemination. *Obstetrics and Gynecology, 75,* 899–905.

Berger, D., Eisen, A., Shuber J., & Doody, K. F. (1986). Psychological patterns in donor insemination couples. *Canada Journal of Psychiatry, 31,* 818–823.

Braverman, A. (1993). Survey results on the current practice of ovum donation. *Fertility and Sterility, 59,* 1216–1220.

Clayton, C., & Kovacs, G. (1982). AID offspring: Initial follow-up study of 50 couples. *Medical Journal of Australia, 1,* 338–339.

Cook, R., Golombok, S., Bish, A., & Murray, C. (1995). Disclosure of donor insemination: Parental attitudes. *American Journal of Orthopsychiat, 65,* 549–559.

Daniluk, J. (1988). Infertility: Intrapersonal and interpersonal impact. *Fertil Steril, 49,* 982–990.

Dunn, P., Ryan, I., & O'Brien, K. (1988). College students' acceptance of adoption and five alternative fertilization techniques. *Journal of Sex Research, 24,* 282–287.

Jacob, M. C. (1996). Concerns of single women and lesbian couples considering conception through assisted reproduction. In S. R. Leiblum (Ed.) *Infertility: Psychological Issues and Counseling Strategies* (pp. 189–206). New York: Wiley.

Jacob, M. C., Klock, S. C., & Maier, D. (1994, November 5–10). Lesbian couples as therapeutic donor insemination recipients: Descriptive and psychological factors. Paper presented at the 50th annual meeting of the American Fertility Society, San Antonio, TX.

Klock, S. C. (1994, October 6 & 7). *Psychosocial issues in male infertility and its treatment.* Paper presented at the conference on Psychosocial Aspects of Reproductive System Disorders in Women and Men, National Institute of Mental Health, Office on Special Populations, Washington, DC.

Klock, S. C., Jacob, M. C., & Maier, D. (1994). A prospective study of donor insemination recipients: Secrecy, privacy and disclosure. *Fertility and Sterility, 62,* 477–483.

Klock, S. C., Jacob, M. C., & Maier, D. (1995, October 7–12). A comparison of single and married donor insemination recipients. Paper presented at the 51st annual meeting of the American Society for Reproductive Medicine, Seattle, WA.

Klock, S. C., & Maier, D. (1991). Psychological factors related to donor insemination. *Fertility and Sterility, 56,* 489–495.

Lazarus, R. S., & Folkman, S. (1984). *Stress, appraisal and coping.* New York: Springer.

Leiblum, S., Palmer, M., & Spector, I. (1995). Non-traditional mothers: Single heterosexual/lesbian women and lesbian couples electing motherhood via donor insemination. *Journal of Psychosomatic Obstetrics and Gynecology, 16,* 11–20.

Manuel, C., Chevret, M., & Cyzba, J. (1980). Handling the secrecy by AID couples. In G. David & E. Price (Eds.), *Human artificial insemination and semen preservation* (pp. 419–430). New York: Plenum.

Nachtigall, R. D., Becker, G., & Wozny, M. (1992). The effects of gender specific diagnosis on men's and women's response to infertility. *Fertility and Sterility, 57,* 113–121.

Pruett, K. (1992). Strange bedfellows? Reproductive technology and child development. *Infant Mental Health Journal, 13,* 312–318.

Rowland, R. (1985). The social and psychological consequences of secrecy in artificial insemination by donor (AID) programmes. *Social Science Medicine, 21,* 391–396.

Schover, L., Collins, R., & Richards, S. (1992). Psychological aspects of donor insemination: Evaluation and follow-up of recipient couples. *Fertility and Sterility, 57,* 583–590.

CHAPTER 10

Concerns of Single Women and Lesbian Couples Considering Conception through Assisted Reproduction

MARY CASEY JACOB

This chapter addresses the basic issues about which a clinician will need to be knowledgeable to help single women and lesbian couples who are considering the use of assisted reproduction techniques (ARTs). It is based on extensive familiarity with the literature and also on my own experience as the psychologist on the reproductive endocrinology team at the University of Connecticut Health Center. In our program, all potential recipients of donor gametes see me for mandatory pretreatment counseling. Those with partners are seen as couples. The primary goals of the session are to reassure ourselves that the women and couples have considered this step toward parenthood thoroughly, that the couples are in agreement on all major issues, and that there are no *significant* contraindications to parenthood. Examples of significant contraindications are having had a child taken away previously for abuse or neglect, being in a current episode of a moderate or severe psychiatric illness, or having clear disagreements within the couple about whether or how to proceed. At the University of Connecticut Health Center, we are also conducting a longitudinal study of sperm donor recipients; this work is referred to in this chapter.

The term "single" as used here refers to a heterosexual or lesbian woman without a long-term committed partner, legal or otherwise. Sometimes a woman from a lesbian couple may present as a single woman because she believes it increases the chance she will receive treatment. In my experience, if you routinely ask "And will you be attempting to conceive with a partner, male or female?" the lesbian woman with a partner will tell you, and actually prefers to have her partner involved.

In this chapter, there is an artificial separation of the issues into those facing the single woman (usually presumed to be heterosexual) and those facing the lesbian couple. The situation facing the single lesbian woman is not well addressed in the literature, and may in fact be uncommon. (Although my team would be happy to treat such women, we have not to our knowledge had such a request.) In general, the issues facing the single lesbian desiring parenthood will be a blend of the issues facing single women and lesbian couples.

Assisted conception for single women and lesbian couples generally refers to the use of therapeutic donor insemination (TDI). The donor might be anonymous or known (Wolf, 1984). Anonymous donors can be obtained through a physician or sperm bank, or through a friend serving as a third party. Known donors can be a family member or a friend, who may or may not also serve as a parent (Hornstein, 1984; Pies, 1988). Alternatively, a known donor may be a "professional" who agrees to meet or have identifying information made available to the recipients and/or the potential child. The bulk of this chapter will assume TDI is the treatment under discussion. Some single women and lesbians, however, have difficulty conceiving or may be past childbearing age, and then the issues of experiencing infertility or of using donated oocytes as well as sperm, enter the picture. This latter scenario will be dealt with briefly at the end of the chapter.

BACKGROUND

You may already believe that single women and lesbian couples should have access to assisted reproduction techniques. Some clinicians, however, may have ethical or moral arguments against it, or concerns about the welfare of the unborn children. Lesbians and single women may be doubtful of the wisdom of their own desires too. Like heterosexuals, lesbians have been raised in our homophobic society and naturally, have internalized some homophobic attitudes themselves, including the one that labels lesbians as not fit for parenting (Crawford, 1987; Moses & Hawkins, 1982; Pies, 1987, 1990). Similarly, single women desiring motherhood have always been deemed peculiar and immoral (McGuire & Alexander, 1985; Mechaneck, Klein, & Kuppersmith, 1988) and, of course, the current political climate tends to label all single mothers as unfit. Thus, a brief look at the literature on *adult* lesbian and single mothers (regardless of the circumstances of conception, but excluding teen mothers) will set the stage for the remainder of the chapter.

Lesbian Couples

In contrast to single mothers, who have always been visible in society, discussions of the pros and cons of offering TDI to lesbian women often seem to assume that withholding TDI would prevent lesbians from becoming mothers. This perspective is ignorant, of course, since there have always been lesbian mothers. Estimates vary, but there may be from one to five million children born to lesbian women during previous heterosexual relationships, and from 5,000 to 10,000 children born to lesbian couples through the use of TDI or planned intercourse for the purposes of conception only (Patterson, 1992).

Many concerns have been expressed about the fitness of lesbians as parents. These concerns include a belief that children need two parents, one of each gender; beliefs that homosexuals are maladjusted, that they molest their children, that they will raise their children to be homosexual; beliefs that lesbians cannot be maternal, and that they will reject boy children (Jacob, 1995). In contrast, in the 1970s, the American Psychiatric (American Psychiatric Association, 1973) and Psychological (Task Force on the Status of Lesbian and Gay Male Psychologists, 1979) Associations independently acknowledged the results of empirical studies that found, "Homosexuality per se implies no impairment in judgment, stability, reliability, or general social or vocational capabilities" (Task Force on the Status of Lesbian and Gay Male Psychologists, 1979, p. 2) and that sexual orientation should not be a primary or determining factor in considering fitness for parenting (Task Force on the Status of Lesbian and Gay Male Psychologists, 1979).

Most published studies have compared the children of previously married lesbians with the children of previously or currently married heterosexual women. Numerous reviews have examined this literature (Cramer, 1986; Gibbs, 1988; Golombok & Tasker, 1994; Gottman, 1990; Hutchens & Kirkpatrick, 1985; Jacob, 1995; Moses & Hawkins, 1982; Patterson, 1992; Sears, 1994; Tasker & Golombok, 1991). These reviews cover a range of variables, "including gender role development and sexual identity, separation-individuation, psychiatric evaluations, assessments of social adjustment and behavior problems, personality, self-concept and self-esteem, locus of control, development of moral judgment, and intelligence" (Jacob, 1995, p. 218). The details of this body of work are beyond the scope of this chapter, but the data do not indicate that children of lesbian mothers are disadvantaged in any unique way. (The children of divorced lesbian women suffer the effects of marital strife and divorce, of course, but not apparently differently from the children of divorced heterosexual women.)

Single Women

As with the children of lesbians, the vast majority of published data regarding the children of adult single mothers refers to children conceived in heterosexual unions that later ended in separation or divorce. The bulk of studies of single mothers *by choice* is in dissertation form. To illustrate how single mothers by choice have been ignored in the published literature: The 1988 special issue of *Family Relations* (Hanson & Sporakowski, 1986) on the topic of single-parent families contained 26 articles, and not one pertains to single parents by choice (noted by Potter & Knaub, 1988).

Some studies suggest that children of female-headed families have cognitive abilities similar to those of children in two-parent families, and are likely to be independent and achievement oriented, and have good self-esteem (McGuire & Alexander, 1985). Studies focusing on children of divorce suggest that these children are at risk for reduced educational, occupational, and economic attainment compared with children in two-parent families, for becoming parents themselves at a younger age, and for undergoing separation or divorce themselves (Mueller & Cooper, 1986). Almost certainly these risks are due to the lowered socioeconomic status (Norton & Glick, 1986) and the emotional sequelae of parental divorce, and not the lack of a second parent per se (Adams, Milner & Schrepf, 1984; Golombok & Rust, 1986). The implications for single women seeking parenthood is that finances are an important factor in successful parenting, and single women almost always have less money than couples. Some programs deny TDI to women who cannot demonstrate adequate resources to raise a child (Strong & Schinfeld, 1984).

Successful single-parent, postdivorce families have also been studied. Quality of parent-child communication, social support, and socioeconomic status are important in themselves and also for their contribution to the mental and physical well-being of both single parents and their children (Hanson, 1986). Children of well-educated divorced women who have not suffered a decline in financial circumstances have been reported by their mothers to continue to function well in school and with peers after parental divorce, and to maintain good relationships with their mothers (Tuzlak & Hillock, 1986). Published data suggest that the majority of single women requesting TDI from physicians are well educated and financially stable (Fidell et al., 1989; Leiblum, Palmer, & Spector, 1995; McCartney, 1985; McGuire & Alexander, 1985; Mechaneck et al., 1988; Pakizegi, 1990; Rosenthal, 1990), and thus they may be at reduced risk for the difficulties families face when struggling financially. This is not, however, true of all single candidates for TDI, and even when it is true, single women will generally have fewer financial resources than two-parent families (Pakizegi, 1990). When asked, most single mothers by choice report wanting more than one child but stopping at one for financial reasons (Mechaneck et al., 1988; Pakizegi, 1990).

Single mothers by choice describe the positive aspects of their lives to include self-perceptions of strength, independence, and competence in managing the two roles of provider and parent (Potter & Knaub, 1988). Negative aspects of single motherhood include the financial stress of being the sole income source; social isolation; being chronically fatigued; stress from having the dual roles of provider and parent; increased onset of mood disorders; no adult backup; little time for oneself or for a social life; and negative societal judgments of them and their children (Mack, 1984; Mechaneck et al., 1988; Pakizegi, 1990; Potter & Knaub, 1988).

COUNSELING ISSUES

When assisting single women and lesbian couples in decision making and preparation for conception and parenting, many of the issues that should be discussed are the very same as those addressed with traditional heterosexual couples (Klock & Maier, 1991) and will not be specifically addressed in this chapter.

These "generic" issues include understanding the challenges of parenting, the pros and cons of various reproductive options and of adoption, the expectations of treatment (e.g., success rates, miscarriage, risk of birth defects, etc.), readiness to cope if treatment is unsuccessful, social support, religious and cultural issues, psychiatric history and current status, and legal history as it pertains to child abuse, neglect, or abandonment (including the nonpayment of child support). For couples, general issues include relationship stability, agreement between the partners about their plan for achieving parenthood and how to execute it (including plans for disclosure or privacy), and sexual functioning. Additionally, with the use of donor gametes comes a responsibility to be realistic about the issues that may come up for the child without an identified or available father.

Deciding to Conceive

Deciding to become a parent is a lengthy process for most single women and lesbian couples (Engelstein, Antell-Buckely, & Urman-Klein, 1980; Frank & Brackley, 1989; Leiblum et al., 1995; Martin, 1993; Mechaneck et al., 1988). Reasons for proceeding have been identified as feeling secure in employment, feeling that time is running out, feeling emotionally ready, having worked through ambivalence about parenting, and feeling adequate social support (Leiblum et al., 1995). Ambivalence about parenting, at this stage as well as after becoming a parent, is quite normal for all women, but single women and lesbian couples often find it difficult to acknowledge these feelings. These women may feel obligated to justify their choice (Crawford, 1987).

Reasons given by single women and lesbian couples for wanting to be mothers are similar to those cited by heterosexual couples, including the hope of combating loneliness, confirming one's sexual identity, and fulfilling the expectations of one's family and culture (Rosenthal, 1990).

The reasons offered by lesbian couples and single heterosexual women for wanting to conceive biologically are similar to those offered by heterosexual women: the wish to experience pregnancy, have a biological/genetic link to the child, to control the prenatal environment of the child, or to avoid the cost, hassles, and long process of adoption (Daniels, 1994). Further, lesbian couples and single women will often report they do not want to have paternal emotional or custodial involvement (McCartney, 1985). Additionally, many adoption agencies will not accept single women or lesbian couples, or if they do, they will offer only older or handicapped children (Pakizegi, 1990). Like heterosexual couples, many of these women wish to start their family life with an infant.

In addition to deciding that she *wants* to become a parent, and then, that she *wants* to conceive, each woman can be assisted in examining what she realistically *can* do. Finances, especially, should be self-examined as part of informed consent. As almost every parent can testify, pregnancy, childbirth, and children cost much more than expected. Women should investigate the costs of trying to conceive, of prenatal care and delivery, and of childcare and other child expenses. They should investigate exactly what their medical insurance covers. For example, Mack (1984) wrote of finding that her insurance, which included maternity benefits, did not cover prenatal care.

Lesbian Couples

For some lesbians, the decision to have a child is a fairly straightforward one. Some of these women have always wanted to be parents, but because most states and agencies do not allow lesbians to adopt (see Crockin, 1994 for exceptions), and most lesbians do not want to have sexual intercourse with a man (Wolf, 1984), they may have assumed that parenthood was not possible for them. On learning of TDI and of a doctor and/or sperm bank willing to work with them toward parenthood, it becomes possible. For other lesbian women, however, the decision to become parents is more complicated in that it symbolizes embracing a part of the traditional female role, a concept that may be unpleasant (Muzio, 1993). Just as in heterosexual couples, disagreement between lesbian partners about whether to parent or not can lead to the demise of the relationship (Martin, 1993; Pies, 1990).

An important question in most lesbian relationships is, "Who will bear the child?" Sometimes the answer is clear because only one woman has a burning desire to do so or because only one woman appears biologically able. For other couples, however, a decision must be made (Martin, 1993; Pies, 1990). Some couples agree to have two children, and the older woman tries to conceive first or alternatively, both try simultaneously. Sometimes a decision is based on the anticipated reactions of the extended families (Martin, 1993). That is, the couple may feel that one set of parents will only welcome a grandchild if it is biologically linked to *their* family. Whatever the reasons, if both women would like to bear a child, then the woman who does not will have to deal with feelings such as sadness and perhaps, envy, as well as the reality of being excluded from the physical mother-child relationship. Moreover, it is likely she will not have any legal standing with respect to the child. In counseling, it is important to explore these issues and ascertain if the couple is being realistic about them.

Single Women

Most single women probably would prefer to conceive in the context of a relationship, but advancing age causes them to seek parenthood first (Mechaneck et al., 1988; Pakizegi, 1990). In my clinical experience, a number of divorced women report their husbands didn't want children, and they ended their marriages in order to have a child. Studies suggest that one- to two-thirds of these women were previously married (Engelstein et al., 1980; McCartney, 1985; Mechaneck et al., 1988; Pakizegi, 1990) and that some know they have infertility problems and require a doctor's assistance to conceive (McCartney, 1985). A majority would like to marry or have partners in the future (McCartney, 1985; Mechaneck et al., 1988).

In counseling, each woman should be encouraged to recognize that, whatever her personal reasons for proceeding, people around her may interpret her actions as a statement about "the value of the nuclear family, about the importance of men as fathers, and about her personal need for companionship" (Mack, 1984, p. 58).

Relationships

Lesbian Couples

Lesbian relationships tend to be different from heterosexual couples in that fusion rather than differentiation is the norm (Mencher, 1990). Satisfaction in lesbian relationships has been found to be related to equality of both power and involvement (Peplau, Pedasky, & Hamilton, 1982; Stiglitz, 1990). Having one partner undergo inseminations and become pregnant, deliver a baby, and perhaps nurse it changes the balance of power in the relationship (Pies, 1990). The couple may feel strain as the biological mother focuses more on her bodily changes and on her child. The difficulty of accommodating the biological mother's assumption of a traditional female role may cause such strain that the relationship ends (Stiglitz, 1990). In couples using a known donor, especially one who will be the identified father, the imbalance of power between mothers may be even more problematic (Rohrbaugh, 1992; Wolf, 1984). For example, the comother may feel that the donor/father and the biological mother have formed a special relationship, from which she is excluded. While many of these changes cannot be prevented, they can be expected and normalized. Another way in which changes in the relationship may occur is when the woman trying to conceive miscarries or finds that she is infertile. In these cases, lesbian women generally report all the symptoms and distress commonly reported by heterosexual women, but are also more likely to have to suffer in isolation (Martin, 1993). As the difficulty conceiving or maintaining a pregnancy continues, the comother may begin to feel impatient and isolated, and that the desired pregnancy is more important to her partner than she is.

Single Women

Single women who hope to have a partner in the future should be realistic about the ways that having a child will limit their opportunities. Not only will some potential partners be less interested because of the presence of a child, but the single mother will find it difficult to find time for dating. Often, she already feels guilty about being away from the child while working. To take more time away for "selfish" reasons may be emotionally difficult. The cost of childcare is an additional obstacle. Women should be encouraged, however, to recognize that when they take care of themselves they can do a better job of caring for their children.

Donor Selection

Some women will enter counseling knowing they wish to conceive, but being uncertain how to accomplish this. Some women consider having intercourse with an informed and consenting male, while others consider having unprotected intercourse without securing the man's consent or agreement. The former option may be rejected because the informed woman knows she is asking for repeated liaisons if she does not conceive immediately; because she does not want the male's involvement or desire for involvement; or because she wants to prevent the possibility of a custody suit (Englert, 1994; Frank & Brackley, 1989; Henry, 1993; McCartney, 1985; Pies, 1990; Wolf, 1984). Additionally, lesbians may reject this avenue because it would violate a pledge of fidelity or just be outright distasteful (Englert, 1994). Generally the latter plan is discarded for moral reasons (Englert, 1994; McCartney, 1985), and it may be that women who pursue this course are more likely to have had inadequate parenting and to be less mature psychologically (Engelstein et al., 1980).

Women might decide to use a known donor, but then have to determine whether to do so informally, and outside the medical system, or through a doctor's office. Historically, many lesbian couples managed this on their own, with gay friends as donors (Pies, 1990). The HIV virus makes this a dangerous undertaking, however, and women who desire to use a known donor should be encouraged to do so under a doctor's supervision, using a sperm bank to test the donor for infectious diseases, to quarantine the sperm, and conduct repeat testing in six months. They should also be encouraged to speak frankly and at length with the potential donor about his fantasies and desires regarding this process and the potential child, and the parties should write down their plan and intentions.

Generally, women request a donor of their own race or that of their partner. Single women may sometimes request a donor of a different race. In my clinical experience, they give different reasons for this. One of our recipients described her extended family of origin and its many racial components, and felt a mixed-race child would fit right in. Another recipient was grieving the ending of a relationship with a man of a different race. A third recipient just felt that mixed-race children were beautiful. It is important to educate the woman about the potential life difficulties her child may face if it is of a different race than her own, and make sure she is ready and able to help her child cope.

Disclosure

Disclosure issues encompass not only what the prospective parent(s) choose to tell others and the child about their use of TDI, but also what the child eventually tells others as he or she matures. Many physicians continue to uniformly encourage TDI recipients to keep their actions a secret (Leiblum & Hamkins, 1992). While some heterosexual couples continue to welcome this advice, single women and lesbians generally do not. Counseling should encourage all TDI candidates to consider all the implications of disclosure versus privacy, and should include information about how and when to speak with children should disclosure be planned.

Choices made by the parents about disclosure may limit choices for the child, and this is something potential parents should consider. For example, encourage women to think about what they want to put on the birth certificate regarding the "father." In our culture, birth certificates are used for many reasons, and may be a way others might learn of the child's mode of conception. This may be in keeping with the desire of the mother, but it's an often overlooked issue. Some mothers would like their children to have some choice about how and when to share with others their donor heritage, and they may wish to put something like "undisclosed" in the "father slot" on the birth certificate. Rosenthal (1990) notes that many such birth certificates use the term "unknown," but in the case of a known donor that would not be accurate, and may or may not be the term with which a family will be most comfortable. Recently, in Massachusetts, it has become possible for children of lesbian couples to be given alternative birth certificates with both mothers' names (Crockin, 1994).

All women contemplating the use of donor gametes, and planning to be honest with the child about how he or she was conceived, should be counseled regarding their recognition of the fact that children *really* don't like to be different. Almost certainly, there will be times when the child is unhappy or is treated differently because he or she doesn't have a father, is "illegitimate," or has a lesbian family. These are not reasons not to proceed, and they are not reasons not to disclose, but it will be the mother(s)' job to help a child deal with this aspect of life. Schools, too, play a role in how a child deals with these issues (Sears, 1994). In my experience, lesbian women have considered this rather carefully, and single women have not.

Lesbian Couples

Disclosure issues for lesbian couples are multifaceted. For some, the decision to pursue parenthood has been a stimulus to come out to family for the first time (Pies, 1987). Even when women have previously told their families about their lesbian relationship, having a child may force their families to disclose to others that they have a lesbian daughter. After having a child, each couple will be faced not only with explaining to others and to the child how conception occurred, but they will need to disclose their own relationship to the child as well (if they intend to operate openly as coparents). In our study of lesbian women using TDI, all the couples intend to be fully open with the children, friends, and family about how conception occurred (Jacob, Klock, & Maier, 1994), and other researchers have found this as well (Leiblum et al., 1995). I find that fewer women have considered how they will disclose to the children about their own relationship. This is an important issue as data suggest that children accept this information more readily when it is provided in childhood or late adolescence, rather than early to middle adolescence (Huggins, 1989; Paul, 1986). (Berzon, 1978, and Moses and Hawkins, 1982, are two excellent resources for helping lesbian couples consider how to come out to their children.) Additionally, couples have to decide how they will present themselves to people in the child's world, such as the pediatrician, the school, and the parents of the child's friends, as well as their own employers and more casual acquaintances. These decisions will impact not only the couple but the child as well, especially if the child is asked to hold the parents' "secret" (Rohrbaugh, 1992). Pretreatment counseling should touch on these issues, making certain the couple has talked about them and begun to make decisions about how to proceed.

Single Women

Most single mothers by choice intend to fully inform their children of the circumstances of their conceptions (Jacob et al., 1994; Mechaneck et al., 1988). The majority plan to inform their families as well. Interestingly, our data suggest the reason for this is generally not honesty, but because the alternatives are less desirable.

Social Support

Lesbian Couples

For lesbian couples, social support begins with one another, and in this way, lesbian families have some of the benefits traditionally ascribed to two-parent heterosexual families. Having another adult to share in the practical tasks, the work of worry, as well as the joy, is no small thing. We cannot assume, however, that every lesbian couple intends to operate in this heterosexually conventional way. It is important to discuss the couple's vision of the division of responsibilities, and whether the comother is planning to be a parent rather than "just" another adult in the household. Regardless of the timing of disclosure to one's parents and extended family, the response of family will determine to some extent the kinds of social supports available to this new family. For most women, including lesbian women, the mother-daughter bond is especially important at the time of giving birth. The lesbian coparent may seek this closeness with her mother and family too, but they may have significant difficulty understanding that this planned child will not just be the child of their daughter/sister's "friend," but actually their grandchild or niece or nephew (Pies, 1990).

Social support for most lesbian families must come from the straight world as well as the lesbian community, and prospective parents should recognize this (Crawford, 1987). The lifestyles of lesbians with and without children are very different, and just as heterosexual parents tend to interact mostly with other parents, so will lesbian parents (Muzio, 1993). Children of lesbian women will generally be in community schools, and many of their "fellow parents" will be heterosexual couples and single heterosexual women. The majority of the friends made by a child in a lesbian family will live in heterosexual families.

Additionally, some lesbian communities do not value parenting and will respond negatively to a decision to conceive using TDI or will support the idea but not be accommodating in practice (Clausen, 1987; Lott-Whitehead & Tully, 1993; Rohrbaugh, 1992).

Single Women

Pregnant single mothers by choice report lower levels of tangible social support than pregnant women with partners, although the two groups report equal amounts of emotional and informational social support (Tilden, 1984). Learning to seek and ask for help may be an important developmental task for single mothers by choice, especially the independent, goal-oriented, career woman (Pakizegi, 1990).

Employers are generally neutral or supportive, and more concerned about how the maternity leave will affect the workplace than anything else (Tilden, 1983). Friends are often first to be told of a single woman's plans to conceive, and their reactions are generally supportive, but this may not translate into practical support (Pakizegi, 1990; Tilden, 1983). About half the single mothers by choice report good family support prior to birth, and most report family support after birth (Pakizegi, 1990). Single mothers by choice identify mothers and sisters, first, and friends second, as sources of social support (Tilden, 1983). In considering her readiness to proceed, each potential single mother should inventory her social support network, and also those people who might be willing to offer practical support, such as childcare, money, hand-me-down clothes, or a ride to the hospital if the child is sick.

Male Involvement

Most single women and lesbian couples considering parenthood have thought about whether they want the child to have an active and involved male in his or her life, and if so, how that will be arranged. A number of authors have reported that lesbian mothers acknowledge the importance of providing their children with a variety of role models, including males (Englert, 1994; Hill, 1987; Kirkpatrick, Smith, & Roy, 1981; Lewin, 1994; Moses & Hawkins, 1982). Single women also bring men into their child's lives in a variety of ways, including exposure to relatives, male babysitters, godfathers, male friends, biological fathers, and church members (Frank & Brackley, 1989; McCartney, 1985; Mechaneck et al., 1988).

Coparenting

The lesbian woman who does not conceive and bear the child has been called the comother. This role is quite challenging because of deeply ingrained societal expectations that each child has one mother. Our culture does not have the language for two mothers. I often ask couples what they will have the child call each of them, as a way of getting them to begin to examine these issues if they have not done so already.

Lesbian couples may plan to parent together equally, but the reality is often quite different. The biological mother may find it difficult to share power (Crawford, 1987) (as heterosexual mothers often do). Also, the comother will constantly struggle against invisibility, not only at her child's school or with her pediatrician, but also within the lesbian community. Even her own parents and siblings, as mentioned previously, may not recognize her as a mother. On a practical level, children may be asked to identify their "real" mother (Pies, 1990). Coparents generally have no legal standing (see Crockin, 1994, for exceptions). They may need to carry paperwork giving them legal power to deal with medical emergencies, to take the child from school, and so on.

Legal Issues

Clients should be encouraged to obtain legal counsel. They need to know the laws in their state regarding the use of TDI and the establishment of legal parentage. Many single women and lesbian couples will choose to have anonymous donors if they know that courts have ruled that known donors are legally fathers when the recipient is unmarried (Curry & Clifford, 1989; Pakizegi, 1990; Polikoff, 1990; Yeh & Yeh, 1991). Women who are legally married but separated from their husbands generally should not be offered TDI until their divorces are complete in order to protect all parties (the women, the potential children, the husbands, and the TDI programs) from disputes regarding the legal status of the husband with respect to the child.

A few states have allowed the comother to adopt the child, but this is still not the norm (Crockin, 1994; Curry & Clifford, 1989). The couple should be encouraged to work with a lawyer to at least set down on paper their intentions as they become parents. They should address responsibilities as well as rights (financial and social), within the relationship, if it ends, and if either parent should die. It is useful to state intentions with regard to the rights of the comother's extended family as well, especially if the relationship should end or the comother should die. Single women should clearly establish guardianship for their children.

Resources

Almost every lesbian couple I have counseled has asked if there is a support group for women like themselves. I have located a resource through our local gay and lesbian community center and share this information. Additionally, I have developed a list of couples I have counseled who would like to be in touch with others. Each couple that agrees to have their first names and telephone numbers on the list may have the list for their own use; women who do not wish to share their names and numbers cannot have the list. By using only first names, the women have a degree of control over how much contact they want with others. Some women prefer just telephone contact while others have met and developed relationships.

Single women can benefit from joining *Single Mothers by Choice* (200 East 84th Street, New York, NY 10028) and lesbian women can find like-minded women through the *Gay and Lesbian Parents' Coalition International* (P.O. Box 50360, Washington, DC 20091). In addition, reading can be a helpful way to work through a decision to parent or not, and how to do so. Single women should be referred to Miller (1992) and lesbian women will find Martin (1993), Crawford (1987), and Pies (1988) quite useful.

Couples should seek an obstetrician who will respect their desires with regard to having the comother present for appointments, labor, and delivery, and being treated as a full participant.

Ethics

Physicians are not ethically obligated to assist every woman and couple requesting assistance. This freedom to refuse treatment is based on the autonomy of the doctor rather than on his or her own particular reasons for refusing treatment (Mahowald, 1993) and on the fact that these treatments are not medically necessary (Strong & Schinfield, 1984). Some programs may also refuse treatment if the laws regarding rights to this treatment are unclear. Physicians should be willing to refer women to a practitioner who will help them.

Conception with Donor Oocytes and Donor Sperm

In certain cases of infertility or advanced maternal age, women may seek the option of using both donor eggs and donor sperm to conceive. This is ethically quite a challenging scenario, regardless of recipient. What are the pros and cons of creating a child with no genetic link to his or her parent(s)? How is this different from, and similar to, adoption? In our program, we have been actively discussing this with our ethics committee for several years, and remain undecided. Currently, we do not offer this option for anyone (regardless of sexual orientation or partnership status). If we did, one important issue we would address on a case-by-case basis is maternal age. In our donor oocyte program (currently available only to heterosexual couples), we do not have a specific age cutoff, but our general policy is that we will use donor gametes only when at least one parent is young enough that he or she is statistically likely to be alive when the child turns 18. When the team is uncertain about proceeding, we consult our ethics committee.

Practitioners may also face requests from lesbian couples to harvest the oocytes of one partner, attempt fertilization with donor sperm (known or anonymous), and then transfer the resulting embryos to the other partner. In this way, each woman has a biological link to the child (one genetic, the other gestational). Because our program does not offer surrogacy under any circumstances currently, we have not confronted such requests in any detail.

CONCLUSION

This chapter is meant to be an introduction to working with single women and lesbian couples in the context of an infertility program or a sperm bank. Many issues facing these women are similar to those facing heterosexual couples, but also, many issues are unique. This chapter has been a survey of the unique issues, including factors affecting the decision to pursue parenthood, how that decision can affect love relationships, donor selection, disclosure, social support, male involvement, coparenting, legal issues, and resources. The interested practitioner will need to read further. More importantly perhaps, the neophyte infertility counselor must be comfortable with and knowledgeable about the lifestyle choices discussed here. Most heterosexual practitioners do not have extensive experience in counseling lesbian clients about lesbian issues, and it can be difficult to anticipate all the issues lesbian women will encounter in their pursuit of motherhood without making a point of educating ourselves.

Several important but uncommon issues have not been addressed in this chapter at all. For example, what issues are pertinent in considering the request of a virgin woman requesting TDI (Heywood, 1991; Jennings, 1991)? What are the pros and cons of assisting women in the sex selection of their desired children (Jacob, 1995)?

The vast majority of single women and lesbian couples seeking our help will not be infertile in the traditional medical sense and will not be exhibiting all the emotional characteristics common to women suffering from infertility. Rather, they are fertile women seeking assistance with conception in a medically safe way. While the medical profession has been attempting to control donor insemination for years (Wikler & Wikler, 1991), it is only with the advent of the HIV virus that medically fertile women have begun to seek our services in such numbers. If we prepare ourselves well, one additional benefit to them may be the counseling services many programs offer to all donor recipients.

REFERENCES

Adams, P. L., Milner, J. R., & Schrepf, N. A. (1984). *Fatherless children.* New York: Wiley.

American Psychiatric Association. (1973, December 15). *Resolution.* Washington, DC.

Berzon, B. (1978). Sharing your lesbian identity with your children: A case for openness. In G. Vida (Ed.), *Our right to love: A lesbian resource book* (pp. 69–77). Englewood Cliffs, NJ: Prentice-Hall.

Clausen, J. (1987). To live outside the law you must be honest: A flommy looks at lesbian parenting. In S. Pollack & J. Vaughn (Eds.), *Politics of the heart: A lesbian parenting anthology* (pp. 333–342). Ithaca, NY: Firebrand Books.

Cramer, D. (1986). Gay parents and their children: A review of research and practical implications. *Journal of Counseling and Development, 64*(8), 504–507.

Crawford, S. (1987). Lesbian families: Psychosocial stress and the family-building process. In Boston Lesbian Psychologies Collective (Ed.), *Lesbian psychologies: Explorations and challenges* (pp. 195–214). Urbana: University of Illinois Press.

Crockin, S. L. (1994). Beyond Tammy: Co-parent adoptions in Massachusetts. *Boston Bar Journal, 7–8,* 18–21.

Curry, H., & Clifford, D. (1989). *A legal guide for lesbian and gay couples* (5th ed.). Berkeley, CA: Nolo Press.

Daniels, K. R. (1994). Adoption and donor insemination: Factors influencing couples' choices. *Child Welfare, 73*(1), 5–14.

Engelstein, P., Antell-Buckely, M., & Urman-Klein, P. (1980). Single women who elect to bear a child. In B. L. Blum (Ed.), *Psychological aspects of pregnancy, birthing, and bonding* (pp. 103–119). New York: Human Sciences Press.

Englert, Y. (1994). Artificial insemination with donor semen: Particular requests. *Human Reproduction, 9*(11), 1969–1971.

Fidell, L. S., Marik, J., Donner, J. E., Jenkins-Burk, C., Koenigsberg, J., Magnussen, K., Morgan, C., & Ullman, J. B. (1989). Paternity by proxy: Artificial insemination by donor sperm. In J. Offerman-Zuckerberg (Ed.), *Gender in transition: A new frontier* (pp. 93–110). New York: Plenum.

Frank, D. I., & Brackley, M. H. (1989). The health experience of single women who have children through artificial donor insemination. *Clinical Nurse Specialist, 3*(3), 156–160.

Gibbs, E. D. (1988). Psychosocial development of children raised by lesbian mothers: A review of research. *Women and Therapy, 8*(1/2), 65–75.

Golombok, S., & Rust, J. (1986). The Warnock Report and single women: What about the children? *Journal of Medical Ethics, 12*(4), 182–186.

Golombok, S., & Tasker, F. (1994). Donor insemination for single heterosexual and lesbian women: Issues concerning the welfare of the child. *Human Reproduction, 9*(11), 1972–1976.

Gottman, J. S. (1990). Children of gay and lesbian parents. In F. W. Bozett & M. B. Sussman (Eds.), *Homosexuality and family relations* (pp. 177–196). New York: Haworth Press.

Hanson, S. M. H. (1986). Healthy single parent families. *Family Relations, 35*(1), 125–132.

Hanson, S. M. H., & Sporakowski, M. (Eds.). (1986). The single parent family [Special issue]. *Family Relations, 35*(1).

Henry, V. L. (1993). A tale of three women: A survey of the rights and responsibilities of unmarried women who conceive by alternative insemination and a model for legislative reform. *American Journal of Law & Medicine, 19*(3), 285–311.

Heywood, A. (1991). Immaculate conception? *Nursing Times, 87*(22), 62–63.

Hill, K. (1987). Mothers by insemination: Interviews. In S. Pollack & J. Vaughn (Eds.), *Politics of the heart: A lesbian parenting anthology* (pp. 111–119). Ithaca, NY: Firebrand Books.

Hornstein, F. (1984). Children by donor insemination: A new choice for lesbians. In R. Arditti, R. D. Klein, & S. Minden (Eds.), *Test-tube women: What future for motherhood?* (pp. 373–381). London: Pandora Press.

Huggins, S. L. (1989). A comparative study of self-esteem of adolescent children of divorced lesbian mothers and divorced heterosexual mothers. *Journal of Homosexuality, 18*(1–2), 123–135.

Hutchens, D. J., & Kirkpatrick, M. J. (1985). Lesbian mothers/gay fathers. In D. H. Schetky & E. P. Benedek (Eds.), *Emerging issues in child psychiatry and the law* (pp. 115–126). New York: Brunner/Mazel.

Jacob, M. C. (1995). Lesbian couples and therapeutic donor insemination. *Assisted Reproduction Reviews, 5*(3), 214–221.

Jacob, M. C., Klock, S. C., & Maier, D. (1994). *Lesbian couples as therapeutic donor insemination recipients: Descriptive and psychological factors* [Abstract]. American Fertility Society Program Abstracts, p. S144.

Jennings, S. (1991). Virgin birth syndrome. *Lancet, 337*(8740), 559–560.

Kirkpatrick, M., Smith, C., & Roy, R. (1981). Lesbian mothers and their children: A comparative survey. *American Journal of Orthopsychiatry, 51*(3), 545–551.

Klock, S. C., & Maier, D. (1991). Guidelines for the provision of psychological evaluations for infertile patients at the University of Connecticut Health Center. *Fertility and Sterility, 56*(4), 680–685.

Leiblum, S. R., & Hamkins, S. E. (1992). To tell or not to tell: Attitudes of reproductive endocrinologists concerning disclosure to offspring of conception via assisted reproduction by donor. *Journal of Psychosomatic Obstetrics and Gynaecology, 13*(4), 267–275.

Leiblum, S. R., Palmer, M. G., & Spector, I. P. (1995). Non-traditional mothers: Single heterosexual/lesbian women and lesbian couples electing motherhood via donor insemination. *Journal of Psychosomatic Obstetrics and Gynaecology, 16,* 11–20.

Lewin, E. (1994). Lesbianism and motherhood: Implications for child custody. In T. Darty & S. Potter (Eds.), *Women-identified women* (pp. 163–183). Palo Alto, CA: Mayfield.

Lott-Whitehead, L., & Tully, C. T. (1993). The family lives of lesbian mothers. *Smith College Studies in Social Work, 63*(3), 265–280.

Mack, P. (1984). When baby makes two: Choosing single motherhood. *Ms, 13,* 58–64.

Mahowald, M. B. (1993). *Women and children in health care: An unequal majority.* New York: Oxford University Press.

Martin, A. (1993). *The lesbian and gay parenting handbook: Creating and raising our families.* New York: HarperPerennial.

McCartney, C. F. (1985). Decision by single women to conceive by artificial donor insemination. *Journal of Psychosomatic Obstetrics and Gynaecology, 4*(4), 321–328.

McGuire, M., & Alexander, N. J. (1985). Artificial insemination of single women. *Fertility and Sterility, 43*(2), 182–184.

Mechaneck, R., Klein, E., & Kuppersmith, J. (1988). Single mothers by choice: A family alternative. In M. Braude (Ed.), *Women, power, and therapy: Issues for women* (pp. 263–281). New York: Haworth Press.

Mencher, J. (1990). *Intimacy in lesbian relationships: A critical re-examination of fusion.* Wellesley, MA: Wellesley College, Stone Center.

Miller, N. (1992). *Single parents by choice: A growing trend in family life.* New York: Plenum.

Moses, A. E., & Hawkins, R. O., Jr. (1982). *Counseling lesbian women and gay men: A life issues approach.* St. Louis: C. V. Mosby.

Mueller, D. P., & Cooper, P. W. (1986). Children of single parent families: How they fare as young adults. *Family Relations, 35*(1), 169–176.

Muzio, C. (1993). Lesbian co-parenting: On being/being with the invisible (m)other. *Smith College Studies in Social Work, 63*(3), 215–229.

Norton, A. J., & Glick, P. C. (1986). One parent families: A social and economic profile. *Family Relations, 35*(1), 9–17.

Pakizegi, B. (1990). Emerging family forms: Single mothers by choice—Demographic and psychosocial variables. *Maternal-Child Nursing Journal, 19*(1), 1–19.

Patterson, C. J. (1992). Children of gay and lesbian parents. *Child Development, 63,* 1025–1042.

Paul, J. P. (1986). *Growing up with a gay, lesbian, or bisexual parent: An exploratory study of experiences and perceptions.* Doctoral dissertation, University of California at Berkeley.

Peplau, L. A., Pedasky, C., & Hamilton, M. (1982). Satisfaction in lesbian relationships. *Journal of Homosexuality, 8*(2), 23–35.

Pies, C. (1987). Considering parenthood: Psychosocial issues for gay men and lesbians choosing alternative fertilization. In F. Bozett (Ed.), *Gay and lesbian parents* (pp. 165–174). New York: Praeger.

Pies, C. (1988). *Considering parenthood* (2nd ed.). San Francisco: Spinsters/Aunt Lute.

Pies, C. A. (1990). Lesbians and the choice to parent. In F. W. Bozett & M. B. Sussman (Eds.), *Homosexuality and family relations* (pp. 137–154). New York: Haworth Press.

Polikoff, N. D. (1990). This child does have two mothers: Redefining parenthood to meet the needs of children in lesbian-mother and other nontraditional families. *Georgetown Law Journal, 78*(3), 459–575.

Potter, A. E., & Knaub, P. K. (1988). Single motherhood by choice: A parenting alternative. *Lifestyles: Family and Economic Issues, 9*(3), 240–249.

Rohrbaugh, J. B. (1992). Lesbian families: Clinical issues and theoretical implications. *Professional Psychology: Research and Practice, 23*(6), 467–473.

Rosenthal, M. B. (1990). Single women requesting artificial insemination by donor. In N. L. Stotland (Ed.), *Psychiatric aspects of reproductive technology* (pp. 113–121). Chicago: American Psychiatric Press.

Sears, J. T. (1994). Challenges for educators: Lesbian, gay, and bisexual families. *High School Journal, 77*(1-2), 138–156.

Stiglitz, E. (1990). Caught between two worlds: The impact of a child on a lesbian couple's relationship. *Women and Therapy, 10*(1/2), 99–116.

Strong, C., & Schinfeld, J. S. (1984). The single woman and artificial insemination by donor. *The Journal of Reproductive Medicine, 29*(5), 293–299.

Task Force on the Status of Lesbian and Gay Male Psychologists. (1979). *Removing the stigma: Final report.* Washington, DC: American Psychological Association.

Tasker, F. L., & Golombok, S. (1991). Children raised by lesbian mothers: The empirical evidence. *Family Law, 21,* 184–187.

Tilden, P. V. (1983). Perception of single versus partnered adult gravidas in the midtrimester. *Journal of Obstetric, Gynecologic, and Neonatal Nursing (JOGNN), 12,* 40–47.

Tilden, P. V. (1984). The relation of selected psychosocial variables to single status of adult women during pregnancy. *Nursing Research, 33*(2), 102–107.

Tuzlak, A., & Hillock, D. W. (1986). Single mothers and their children after divorce: A study of those "who make it." *Conciliation Courts Review, 24*(1), 79–89.

Wikler, D., & Wikler, N. J. (1991). Turkey-baster babies: The demedicalization of artificial insemination. *The Milbank Quarterly, 69*(1), 5–40.

Wolf, D. G. (1984). Lesbian childbirth and woman-controlled conception. In T. Darty & S. Potter (Eds.), *Women-identified women* (pp. 185–193). Palo Alto, CA: Mayfield.

Yeh, J., & Yeh, M. U. (1991). *Legal aspects of infertility.* Boston: Blackwell Scientific Publications.

PART THREE

When Medical Treatment Fails

CHAPTER 11

When Is Enough, Enough? Abandoning Medical Treatment for Infertility

ANDREA MECHANICK BRAVERMAN

As recently as a decade ago, medical interventions available to those experiencing infertility were limited. If treatment failed, the couple was quickly advised to pursue adoption. Today, the assisted reproductive technologies (ARTs) offer tremendous advances in the field of infertility treatment and many new options to those facing infertility. By the same measure, the proliferation of therapeutic paradigms has made difficult the decision of when to end treatment should pregnancy not ensue.

The decision may focus on terminating a specific treatment, such as "low-tech" inseminations in favor of high-tech procedures such as in vitro fertilization (IVF), or deciding that "enough is enough" and end the pursuit of genetic parenthood altogether. Often the decision to terminate treatment is made more difficult by conflicting emotions, needs, and information. Pressure to continue treatment may be perceived as coming from partners, parents, cultural expectations, or medical professionals.

When a couple or individual decides to end direct medical treatment, it may be to move on to adoption, surrogacy, or the use of donor gametes (indirect medical treatment). Conversely, the decision to end treatment may be the choice to live child-free. Regardless of what decision is reached, the actual choice to abandon treatment is ultimately bound up in the person's ability to relinquish the hope and dream of having his or her own genetic child.

THE EMOTIONAL IMPACT OF INFERTILITY AND PARENTING CHOICES AVAILABLE

For an estimated 2.4 million infertile couples, technological advances such as in vitro fertilization and new drug therapies have enabled couples to pursue new avenues for achieving pregnancy with minimally invasive therapies that were previously unavailable (Chartland, 1989). These new technologies extend the traditional definition of parenting, pregnancy, motherhood, and fatherhood.

TABLE 11.1   Definitions and Indications for Assisted
Reproductive Techniques

Procedure	Definition	Indication
In Vitro Fertilization (IVF)	The process by which a woman's eggs are collected from her ovaries, fertilized in the laboratory with sperm and transferred to her uterus after normal embryo development has occurred.	Tubal disease or blockage Severe male infertility Endometriosis Unexplained infertility Cervical factor Immunologic infertility
Gamete Intrafallopian Transfer (GIFT)	The process by which oocytes are retrieved from the ovary, placed in a catheter with washed motile sperm, and immediately transferred into the fimbriated end of the fallopian tube(s). Fertilization occurs in the fallopian tube (in vivo) rather than in the laboratory (in vitro).	Same as IVF *except* that there must be normal tubal anatomy, potency, and absence of previous tubal disease Reasonable seminal parameters; i.e., not necessarily normal but not severe impairment
IVF and GIFT with Donor Sperm	The process as previously described except in cases where the husband's fertility is severely compromised and donor sperm may be utilized. If donor sperm is used, the wife must have indications for IVF and GIFT.	Severe male infertility Azoospermia Indications for IVF or GIFT
Donor Oocyte	The process by which eggs are donated by an IVF procedure and the donated eggs are inseminated. The embryos are transferred into the recipient's uterus which is hormonally prepared with estrogen/progesterone therapy.	Premature ovarian failure Surgical removal of ovaries Congenitally absent ovaries Autosomal or sex-linked disorders Lack of fertilization in repeated IVF attempts due to subtle oocyte abnormalities or defects in oocyte/spermatozoa interaction

TABLE 11.1   (Continued)

Procedure	Definition	Indication
Donor Embryo (Embryo Adoption)	Process by which a donated embryo is transferred to the uterus of an infertile woman at the appropriate time (normal or induced) of the menstrual cycle.	Infertility not resolved by less aggressive forms of therapy Absence of ovaries Male partner is azoospermic or is severely compromised
Gestational Carrier (Embryo Host)	The process by which a couple undertakes an IVF cycle and the embryo(s) are transferred to another woman's uterus (the carrier) who has contracted with the couple to carry the child to term. The carrier has no genetic investment in the child, which distinguishes it from surrogate motherhood.	Congenital absence or surgical removal of uterus A reproductively impaired uterus, myomas, uterine synechiae, or other congenital abnormalities A medical condition that might be life threatening during pregnancy such as diabetes, immunologic problems, or severe heart, kidney, or liver disease

Among the available options now widely utilized are cryopreservation, fertilization of donor gametes, IVF in conjunction with the use of a gestational carrier, and the adoption of embryos. (Table 11.1)

In the past 10 years, IVF has gone from being considered an experimental procedure to an accepted treatment modality for infertile couples. Over 15,000 babies have been born worldwide as a result of IVF. IVF's availability and acceptance adds to the burden of choosing to end treatment. According to statistics published by the American Society for Reproductive Medicine/Society for Assisted Reproductive Technology (SART; 1995), there were 27,117 egg retrievals performed for an IVF treatment cycle in 1993 in the United States (Table 11.2). This was an increase of 2,400 cycles from 1992 and 6,544 from 1991.

There were 1,979 canceled cycles in 1993 which represent couples who experienced the tremendous disappointment of canceling an attempt to achieve a pregnancy. These statistics do not begin to represent the financial costs associated with these attempts, time off from work, or the emotional costs associated with these canceled cycles. Finally, there was an overall success rate of 18.8% per retrieval. Therefore, in 1993, 81.2% of couples who attempted to get pregnant were disappointed with each retrieval attempt. For those many couples who have not been successful, the emotional as well as financial cost of repeated unsuccessful cycles is enormous.

There are many couples who experience tremendous disappointments each cycle, whether through cancellation or treatment failure. However, patients are

TABLE 11.2   1993 Society for Assisted Reproductive Technology (SART) Outcomes for All ART Procedures

	IVF	GIFT	ZIFT	Egg	Frozen Embryo
Cycles/Procedures	31,900	4,992	1,792	2,766	6,672
Cancellation (%)	14.0	15.8	13.0	14.4	NA
Pregnancies	6,321	1,472	466	895	984
Pregnancy loss (%)	19.0	20.6	18.5	20.0	19.6
Deliveries	5,103	1,182	380	716	719
Ectopic Pregnancies	288	61	13	21	11

IVF—In Vitro Fertilization
GIFT—Gamete Intrafallopian Transfer
ZIFT—Zygote Intrafallopian Transfer

also aware that the success rate for IVF rose from 15.5% in 1991 to 18.8% in 1993 and for GIFT a rise from 26.5% in 1991 to 28.1% in 1993.

Couples often oscillate between a feeling of optimism generated by reading or hearing about reproductive successes achieved via the new reproductive technologies and the reality of the many unsuccessful or canceled cycles they personally experience. Each unsuccessful cycle takes its emotional and/or physical toll on the couple and influences the decision-making process. Similarly, couples are influenced by the possibility of success suggested by the number of babies born each year (e.g., 8,172 babies born through the ARTs in 1993).

Couples face myriad choices when considering infertility treatment (Tables 11.3 and 11.4). Resulting from these possible roles and choices are families that no longer resemble the traditional nuclear family of only a decade ago. However, families have also been redefined by changes in society and have created new possibilities: blended families from parents who have divorced and remarried, foster families, grandparents who parent, and single-parent families. Any or all of these families may now have children who are genetically related through natural conception or through infertility treatment, result from a gamete donor, adopted either traditionally or at the embryo stage, or are born from a gestational carrier or traditional surrogate.

Since many different factors may bring a couple to choose partial or full nongenetic parenting, these factors may also strongly influence each partner's decision about when to terminate treatment. For example, it is not uncommon for a couple to seek treatment and/or use a donor after one partner has had children from a first marriage. The partner who already has a genetic child may be less willing to expend tremendous financial or emotional resources than the partner who does not have any genetic offspring. Conversely, the partner with the genetic children may feel guilt and be more willing to pursue nongenetic parenting because s/he has already had that opportunity.

Some couples' decision to end treatment may be a result of ambivalence about parenting at an older age than anticipated due to a second marriage or due

TABLE 11.3 Potential Ways for Women to Parent

Player	Role	Title
Mother A	Provides egg and womb	1. Mother 2. Birth mother a. traditional adoption b. surrogate mother
Mother B	Provides egg	1. Genetic mother 2. Donor
Mother C	Provides womb	1. Mother (egg recipient) 2. Gestational carrier 3. Mother (donor embryo)
Mother D	No reproductive role	1. Adoptive mother a. traditional b. surrogate c. egg donor with carrier 2. Foster mother 3. Relative raising child 4. Stepmother 5. Cohabiting and raising partner's child

TABLE 11.4 Potential Ways for Men to Parent

Player	Role	Title
Father A	Provides sperm	1. Biological father a. with partner/wife b. with surrogate c. with carrier d. with donor egg and carrier 2. Sperm donor 3. Embryo donor
Father B	No reproductive role	1. Father (sperm recipient) 2. Adoptive father a. traditional b. embryo donor 3. Foster father 4. Relative raising child 5. Stepfather 6. Cohabiting and raising partner's child

to prolonged infertility treatment. Unresolved feelings, concerns, or issues from previous relationships may also influence the decision-making process.

Other problems may arise due to having families of mixed origins, where one child may be from a donor, one adopted, and another is a biological offspring of both parents. Each of these possible family constellations has particular stresses and issues that may arise as the child(ren) develop, and may influence the couple's decision making about pursuing nonbiological parenting versus choosing to terminate treatment.

EMPIRICAL EVIDENCE ON TREATMENT TERMINATION

There is no true satisfactory resolution to the inability to reproduce, but there are acceptable choices. Whether it is to live child-free, adopt, use surrogacy, or use donor gametes, individuals and couples must grieve the loss of the potential genetically conceived child. It is only after the work of grieving is done that the choices can be explored. The therapist must be able to accompany the patient on this journey through the wasteland of grief and into an uncertain future. Ultimately, the therapist helps the client to hope and to build.

Guilt, anger, and tension can accompany a couple's journey through treatment. Couples who choose to adopt after long-term infertility need to feel that they have resolved their infertility to *the best of their ability.* For some couples, this means minimal medical intervention and for others this means years of financially and emotionally exhaustive treatment.

The literature documents that infertility treatment takes its emotional toll on both individuals and couples. One study (Freeman, Boxer, Rickels, Tureck, & Mastroianni, 1985) revealed that 49% of women and 15% of men reported that infertility was the most upsetting experience of their lives compared with other equally major losses. The stress of daily monitoring injections, semen collection, timing of sexual intercourse, and financial outlay have all been shown to also affect couples (Reading, Chang, & Kerin, 1989; Seibel & Levin, 1987). Other studies (Baram, Tourtelot, Muechler, & Huang, 1988; Leiblum, Kemmann, & Lane, 1987) have demonstrated depressive and grief reactions following failed treatment cycles.

Interestingly, more recent studies have also looked at the interplay between stress and coping. These studies begin to explore the multifactorial approach couples employ when considering whether or not to end treatment. In a recent study (Newton, Hearn, & Yuzpe, 1990), pre-IVF depressive symptoms, in addition to the predisposition of the individual to anxiety, were the best predictor of emotional response to IVF failure.

The ultimate question that has not been answered is whether stress plays a causal role in infertility. Every infertile patient has heard the advice, "Just relax and you'll get pregnant." There are variations on this theme: "Don't try so hard" or "Take a vacation" or "Have a couple glasses of wine before you try" or "Just adopt and you'll get pregnant." In a mind/body program, one study

(Domar, Seibel, & Benson, 1990) showed that there was a statistically significant decrease in anxiety, depression, and fatigue, but failed to answer the question about the causal role of stress in reproduction.

Nonetheless, the folklore surrounding stress and its imagined effects on the reproductive system may subtly influence a couple's choice to end treatment or to "take a break." Friends or family members may exert well-meaning pressure to end treatment with the belief that without "running to the doctors all the time" the patient will conceive because he or she is no longer stressed.

An Australian study (Callan, Kloske, Kashima, & Hennessey, 1988) that looked at women's decisions to continue or end in vitro fertilization treatment related to social, psychological, and background factors suggested that those women who discontinued treatment perceived that their husbands, families, friends, and doctors believed that they should not undergo another IVF cycle. Both women who continued and discontinued treatment held similar beliefs about the value of motherhood, satisfaction of parenting, importance of happy marriages, and the need to be well adjusted. Those women who chose to end treatment were less optimistic about the cycle's success, the potential for parenting making their marriages happier, or improving the quality of their lives.

The assisted reproductive technologies open up a world of hope, joy, and deliberations for families, and appear to fulfill needs to couples who had little prior hope to be genetic parents. Yet, they also create a Pandora's box of choices and, with it, the fear of regret for the road not taken.

FACTORS ENCOURAGING THE DECISION TO TERMINATE TREATMENT

Financial Issues

Couples may be emotionally, physically, and financially depleted by the time they reach the ending treatment stage (Cooper & Glazer, 1994). Insurance coverage may be limited and thus severely restrict treatment options, as many of the assisted reproductive technologies are quite expensive. Hormonal medication used in an IVF cycle costs on average from $1,000 to $3,000 per attempt. Anger about the unfairness of life in presenting infertility problems, combined with restricted resources for helping infertile couples may complicate the decision-making process.

Medical Issues

Couples also may have genuine concern about how all the medication and procedures may ultimately affect their health even though there have not been any conclusive studies to link infertility treatment and ovulation induction medications with health risks. Two recent studies have suggested a relationship between ovulation induction and ovarian cancer, and other articles have begun to examine this possible relationship (Ron & Lunenfeld, 1995; Kaufman, Spirtas, & Alexander, 1995). Thus, couples remain concerned and may factor this into their decision to end treatment.

Women also become less tolerant of side effects experienced as they take these medications. Bloating, bruises, emotional lability, and weight gain can accompany many of the medications taken during infertility treatment. As one woman described, "I can't imagine pumping my body full of this stuff every month can be good for me. I haven't felt like my body has been my own since I started these drugs." Physical and emotional fatigue can be cumulative and can lead some couples to worry about the medical component of infertility treatment.

Emotional Issues

After prolonged treatment attempts, couples may be unwilling to sacrifice their lives for an uncertain future. The emotional, financial, and physical toll that treatment takes can leave some couples exhausted. As one woman who had three miscarriages expressed, "I am 38 years old and I am having my third D&C. I'm just tired of technology messing with me." Women and men both can feel that technology has pushed them to the outer envelope of what they feel comfortable with, even to the point where they may feel they have lost touch with their own bodies.

Feeling "out of control" is the hallmark of infertility treatment, especially for those used to decisive behavior, and ending treatment may be seen as a way for the couple to gain control of their life and future. Since the couple has spent time during treatment being told when to show up for monitoring, have intercourse, take medication, go on vacation, and when to come in for consultations, the decision to end treatment is a way of regaining choices in their lives. As one patient stated, "I can't control whether I'm going to get pregnant. I can control what is going to improve my marriage and myself."

Couple's Reactions

Rarely do both partners share the same emotional reactions about pursuing or discontinuing treatment. It is because there are differences in feelings that the decision to end treatment is so very complicated, whatever the stage. Nonetheless, the couple must be able to negotiate individual needs with that of the partner's needs and feelings.

Pressure to continue treatment, guilt over being the cause of the infertility problem, or fear of stopping treatment too soon can be experienced quite differently by each partner. For example, one woman with blocked fallopian tubes due to exposure to chlamydia, a sexually transmitted disease, felt that she "could not say no" to her husband's wish to continue treatment. The woman believed that her husband would be a father were it not for her earlier sexual behavior. When confronted with the fact that her husband also had sexual relationships prior to the marriage, the woman still insisted that she had no right to refuse treatment, no matter how debilitating she found it.

In another situation, a husband felt unable to refuse his wife's desire to continue medical intervention. The couple had completed years of infertility treatment in four different practices. Despite the lack of success, she felt inadequate without a pregnancy. During the intake, the wife also expressed sadness for her parents who would be unable to be grandparents without her. As an only child, the wife felt burdened by the responsibility of carrying on the "family line," particularly when her parents became evasive when the conversation turned to talk of adoption.

Differences in readiness to end treatment may be compounded by differences in coping styles. Several studies have suggested that women and men handle their reactions to infertility differently (as discussed in another chapter) (Mazure & Greenfeld, 1989). Women may perceive that their male partners are less eager to continue treatment because men tend not to show their feelings or discuss future treatment possibilities as much as their partners would choose. This can lead to misinterpretation between partners of their motivation to continue or abandon medical treatment.

One couple presented for counseling as a result of the wife's depression and panic attacks subsequent to their last unsuccessful insemination cycle. The wife expressed her depression as tremendous feelings of inertia. She felt guilty because her husband was ready to move on to adoption and she was not. When asked whether she had ever directly inquired about her husband's choice whether to adopt or continue treatment, the wife stated that she already knew his answer because he had been bringing home literature on adoption. The husband was startled to hear this and remarked, "Actually, I would prefer to continue treatment. But I felt I couldn't ask you to put your body through any more unless you wanted it. I brought the adoption stuff home because it was something I can do."

Couples can often get caught in the same communication traps that were characteristic of their interaction prior to the infertility. The feelings associated with infertility may magnify any communication flaws, and this can sometimes provoke disagreements or conflict for the couple. One woman stated she would continue treatment only if she could be reassured that her partner would be more supportive of her during the process. The husband was not eager to continue treatment and had been quietly withdrawing from the process. Once the couple realized how they were handling their feelings, the communication improved to the point that they could make a decision about ending treatment based on their real feelings instead of the perceived feelings. The husband was able to state clearly his wish to end treatment and "get our lives back"; the wife was able to ask her husband to work with her on one last different treatment attempt. The husband felt he could be supportive if there was "a definite end in sight" and the wife felt she could stop "if I could use this last cycle for closure."

Intrapersonal Issues

The decision to end medical treatment also interfaces with the individual's intrapersonal relationship. Many individuals have not experienced "failure," e.g., they have never not been able to achieve what they desired. In school, there was always the opportunity to study harder or write the extra credit report. At work, there was always long hours to put in or an opportunity to excel. Choosing to end treatment often sets up tremendous cognitive and emotional dissonance for the individual who has achieved.

Many individuals struggle with the feelings of losing a lifelong dream of biological parenthood. This can precipitate a crisis as the person tries to redefine him- or herself in a brand-new role. One man stated, "I go to work. I come home. On Saturdays, we take care of the house. We go out. Is this all there is for me?" The routine that the individual has found satisfactory before, in part because it was a way of laying a foundation for the planned future, becomes pointless to some individuals. Dissatisfaction grows with his or her achievements because he or she sees them as insignificant compared with the ultimate goal of biological parenthood. Others may feel that they have failed to meet their individual responsibility to their parents of providing grandchildren.

Choosing to end medical treatment may signal a resolution of these feelings, including a redefinition of self and life goals for the individual. Resolution may also need to be made with old intrapersonal issues such as body image, family dynamics, and self-esteem in order to move to end infertility treatment.

There are individuals and couples who cannot end treatment. They are caught in a trap of continuing treatment past the point where it is detrimental to themselves or their partners. Emotional, financial, and time resources are irrelevant compared with the individual's need to achieve a pregnancy. The intrinsic meaning of achieving this pregnancy can be predicated on different issues (e.g., personal worth, status in the family, and fear of losing the "fertile" partner).

These individuals ignore objective data in their decision making and state that they just "know" that they can get pregnant. As one 42-year-old female, who had been through three failed IVF cycles, stated, "But my mother had no fertility problems and my sister conceived at age 43. There's no way I can't get pregnant." This was a second marriage for both partners, and her husband had four children from his previous marriage. The woman went on to state, "It just has to work. I've been a good girl all my life. I've taken care of everyone else, including his kids when they were the most miserable to me. It's my turn. I can't stop."

Relationship Issues

A couple may feel that ending treatment is a positive step toward regaining their independence and privacy. Most couples have been closely subjected to intensive monitored blood tests, ultrasounds, and scheduled sexual relations. As one patient stated, "I feel like there are three people in bed with me every time we make love: my husband, my doctor, and my clinical nurse specialist." The relief of not having to take her temperature in the morning, report coital frequency, have postcoital checks, take medication, and wait for a menstrual period can be a strong inducement to stop infertility treatment. As one husband stated, "It feels so good to stop banging our heads against the wall." However, the patient must weigh the strength of the short-term release from deciding to end treatment against his or her long-term needs and goals.

As couples go through infertility treatment, they may also be surprised to discover that their relationship has grown stronger during their infertility workup. Many couples will find that they can begin to imagine what life will be like with "just the two of us" and find that the thought is not as uncomfortable as they first imagined. Still, they entertain the scenario of life without children with some guilt. Fear that feelings of regret or sadness may arise a decade or two later often creates the counterbalance to the fantasy of living child-free.

It is the work of the therapist to explore all sides of the decision. For example, a 36-year-old woman had been through two IVF cycles which resulted in: (a) an ectopic pregnancy, and (b) no pregnancy. The couple had decided to take six months to consider what they might want to do next: adopt or live child-free. The women came into therapy on an irregular basis to look at family of origin issues and marital issues and wrote the following letter to her therapist:

> We took your suggestion and attended the RESOLVE[1] adoption conference. . . .
> My husband really wanted to go so I found the strength to join him! It was time
> well spent. Although we did not care for the keynote speaker, she made one state-
> ment that hit home, "Do you *need* to be a parent?" (After discussion about that
> question, we both answered—NO!) We attended two workshops on adoption. . . .
> They both provided enough information to reinforce the direction we seem to be
> going in—living child-free. . . . I believe we are slowly coming to a decision.
> The next step is for both of us to meet with you, to verbalize our thoughts, and
> generally make sure we are not missing any important piece to the puzzle.

Thus, therapy can be the start of the exploration process, or it can be a place to consolidate and reach a level of comfort with a decision that has already been made.

Mourning the Loss of Genetic Parenthood

Letting go of a long-held assumption and subsequent dream of genetic parenthood is a mourning process. Couples need support to allow themselves the feelings and the time to work through their grief, regardless of how they choose to move on with their lives. There is, however, no public recognition for these feelings and no ritual mourning process. Couples do not receive sympathy cards

---

[1]RESOLVE is a nonprofit organization dedicated to the education, advocacy, and support for infertility issues.

and no one bakes casseroles for them to help them through their time of grief. Instead, couples are expected to carry on with their lives, letting nothing show of their grief and sadness. Therapy can provide an important structure within which the couple can begin their grief work.

When couples choose to end infertility treatment and pursue nongenetic family building, the therapist often is employed to help them resolve their feelings about never achieving genetic parenthood. The goal of therapy is helping the couple understand what feelings they bring into the process and how these feelings might influence their choices.

Adoption is a wonderful option for many who wish to end treatment and are ready to pursue nongenetic parenting. There is greater social support for couples who choose to adopt as well as many agencies, therapists, books, and support groups available (Carter & Carter, 1989; Cooper & Glazer, 1994; Corson, 1995). Prospective adoptive parents need to be educated about the costs and demands of adoption essential to the decision-making process and preparation for adoptive parenting. Sometimes couples will feel so much pressure to move on to adoption that they do not take the time to fully consider choosing to live child-free.

Couples who are ready to end medical treatment that has been unsuccessful but still wish to be parents may also consider using donor gametes (e.g., donor eggs or sperm). The decision to use donor gametes is inextricably intertwined with each person's feelings about the role of genetics in parenting. The therapist must help the couple, separately and together, to mourn the noncontributing partner's genetic contribution. Examining one's feelings about parenting and genetic ties, whether with donor gametes or adoption, if further complicated by each partner's personal feelings of self-esteem, body image, femininity or masculinity, or family dynamics. Couples who feel that their parents will be disappointed or disapproving need to work through these influences as they try to choose what to do next.

Each couple presenting to a therapist will have a unique set of circumstances leading up to their decision about whether or not to end treatment and what to do next. Therapy can help the couple to identify their feelings and influences in a setting that is free of judgment or prejudice.

THE ROLE OF THE THERAPIST

The role of the therapist during this decision-making process is similar to and different from the usual therapeutic role. As in traditional therapy, the goal is to help the couple explore their thoughts and feelings about the medical infertility treatment process. Evaluation about the decision to end infertility treatment is done through a thorough exploration of all the factors that influence the couple's thoughts and feelings. The therapist needs to take a complete psychological history of each partner as well as marital, sexual, and infertility treatment history.

Unique to infertility counseling is the therapist's need to have a reasonably basic understanding of the treatment options available to the couple; knowledge of insurance coverage, cost of various programs, and the demands of various treatment. This is necessary because all these factors can significantly influence or limit the couple's reproductive choices. The ability to challenge the couple's fears, assumptions, and expectations of infertility treatment are essential to the counseling process.

It is critical that the therapist be as neutral as possible. Couples are acutely aware of the treatment team's opinion and bias about their treatment termination, and this is also true for the therapist's opinion. Couples who choose to end treatment are working against the social bias toward having children. There is little social support for deciding not to become parents, even when this decision is involuntary. Attributions of selfishness, laziness, or inadequacy are often given to couples who do not have children. These attributions are felt even more keenly by couples who wish to parent, but cannot due to medical infertility problems. Furthermore, couples may feel like they already do not "fit in" with the rest of their friends. Concern about the perceptions of others of this decision to live child-free may add to their feelings of being different.

The following case illustration illustrates how a couple negotiates the decision to end infertility treatment. Over the course of psychotherapy treatment, the couple had the opportunity, through individual and couple sessions, to explore their feelings and identify the issues that cause them great pain.

Case Example

Martha and Fred have been married for five years and have been attempting to get pregnant for the last three years. Martha is a 32-year-old white female who works as an office manager in a busy law practice. Fred is a 34-year-old white male who works in sales. Martha and Fred graduated from a state collage and have been working consistently since graduation.

Both Martha and Fred's extended families lived nearby and provided a strong support network for the couple. Martha reported sharing her feelings and experiences more with her siblings than her parents, stating: "My parents are from a different generation and don't understand about infertility. My father would probably faint if I said the word "sperm," and my mother would tell me just to relax and it'll happen." Fred's family is aware that the couple has been trying to conceive, but have elected to remain nonintrusive and noninvolved.

Both Martha and Fred reported that they had a happy, strong relationship. "If anything, this whole infertility experience has brought us closer together," remarked Martha during her first session of therapy. Martha complained of feeling depressed, having no interest in her job, friends, or family. Neither Martha nor Fred considered the possibility of living without children. However, they told their therapist that they could not decide whether or not to pursue more medical treatment or to stop treatment and adopt.

This decision was further complicated by the physician's recommendation that Fred and Martha pursue IVF, a medical treatment that was not covered by either Fred or Martha's medical insurance. The couple reported that they had enough money to either try one IVF procedure or to adopt. They felt completely "stuck" about what to do and Martha stated that she felt she did not have the stamina even to think about the decision.

The couple appeared to be bright, articulate, and motivated to begin treatment. Martha was looking to therapy primarily to make her feel better. Fred was looking to therapy to "fix my wife," but also to help them begin the decision-making process about continuing medical treatment or deciding to adopt. Both had good interpersonal functioning prior to the last cycle, and there did not appear to be any complicating factors in their lives other than the infertility.

Martha felt anxious about her future and pessimism that she would ever find an acceptable solution to her dilemma. She wanted to avoid dealing with the feelings of sadness, self-blame, and failure that the last treatment cycle had engendered. As Fred had taken on the role of the optimist (e.g., that everything would work out and the couple would be parents either through the assisted reproductive technologies or through adoption), Martha had the safety of his optimism to experience her upset, despair, and anger. The strength of the relationship gave Martha her only feeling of a base in the raging storm of her feelings.

Martha's self-esteem issues were common to many patients experiencing treatment failure. Intervention would be focused on identifying these thoughts and feelings about Martha's sense of control, self-worth, and self-blame in conjunction with cognitive/behavioral work. The intrapersonal issues that had arisen during infertility treatment would be explored and a final goal was to normalize the infertility experience by helping them understand where and what feelings arose and to set appropriate family building goals for the future.

Course of Treatment

The first session was spent on gathering family, psychosocial, marital, sexual, and medical history. Martha was tearful throughout most of the session, and Fred was quietly supportive by handing tissues and holding his wife's hand during these crying spells. When particularly agitated, Martha would pull her hand away from Fred's, signaling how deeply alone she felt over that particular feeling or issue. These moments felt like "a black hole" to Martha—a place where Fred could not help her—and she feared she would never negotiate her way clear of these overwhelming feelings.

THERAPIST: When the cycle did not work, this left you feeling pretty bad.

MARTHA: Yeah . . . pretty bad. (Pause) I don't think I've ever felt this bad in my life.

THERAPIST: I wonder if it made you feel other things? (Pause) Maybe defective? Different?

MARTHA: Oh, yes I feel defective! (Tears) I don't get it. On the news, I see mothers hurting their kids, throwing them out the windows, all sorts of things. What is wrong with me that I can't even get pregnant?

FRED: I keep telling you honey that you're okay. Look at all the great things you do.

MARTHA: But I can't even do the most basic, simplest thing as getting pregnant.

THERAPIST: I can see you have had this exchange before. I think it leaves you both frustrated.

Martha had been trying hard not to feel defective. Feeling normal was Martha's goal; she felt badly because she perceived herself as "different" from all her friends who were able to get pregnant easily. Many patients feel that they are being punished through their infertility, which adds to their sense of being bad or defective. Why else would pregnancy be denied to them when undeserving, ill-equipped parents have children? Martha's depression and anxiety gave her a solid reason to pull away from other people; it was easier to blame the depression than her own feelings of being different and wrong.

Martha had to connect her feelings about herself with how she was handling her decisions. It was important that Martha also experience the therapist's empathy, a way of joining her in her isolation and normalizing some of the feelings she was experiencing.

THERAPIST: So maybe this tells you what you should do with your life.

MARTHA: Yeah. Maybe we shouldn't be parents at all. Like this is God telling us to stop, that we'd really mess a kid up and that's why we aren't getting pregnant.

THERAPIST: Well, at least then you can make sense of this whole ordeal even if it makes you feel lousy. But I wonder, what happens if there isn't a reason for you not getting pregnant?

MARTHA: Oh, God. Then there isn't anything I can do about it. I can't be a better person, do more things. I don't know. . . . I guess then I want to have a baby. But I'm afraid to try any more. What if I crack up next time?

At this stage, Martha expressed some of her fears that would play a role in her decision-making ability for the future. Specifically, Martha was afraid that the emotional demands of either a treatment cycle or the adoption process would overwhelm her. Martha began to change her view of herself as she went through infertility treatment from being a warm, strong, and capable woman to a vulnerable, unsure, and depleted person. Consequently, Martha's fears that she was unable to handle either disappointment or anticipation, coupled with the shaken view of herself, left her frightened that she might "crack up." Martha needed to explore how she felt about herself (e.g., that she felt weak or inadequate, and how these feelings related to her feelings of depression).

In later sessions, Martha continued to express a reluctance to "rock the boat" by making any decisions; she feared that making a decision might lead to more emotional distress and dysfunction.

THERAPIST: Martha, you seem to be having a hard time even considering which way you and Fred might go to have a baby.

MARTHA: I start to get real nervous when I think about it. What a basket case I'll be if I start anything.

THERAPIST: So staying put where you are is easier. This might be hard, but not as hard as climbing back onto the emotional roller coaster might be.

MARTHA:	I hadn't thought of it that way. The old me would just have plowed ahead, full steam. But I'm not sure the old me is still around. I still want Fred to have a wife when this is all said and done.
THERAPIST:	And if you make the wrong decision. . . .
MARTHA:	Then we won't have a baby and I'll be locked up somewhere in Happy Acres with the men in the white coats.

In this exchange, Martha was conveying her desire for safety as well as her wish that she did not have to make any decisions. Having dealt with all the choices and reactions so far, Martha was tired of making any more. At this juncture, it was important to bring Fred's joint role into the decision-making process back into the session.

THERAPIST:	I don't think I've heard Fred say he doesn't want to be part of deciding what the future might hold. What do you think Fred wants?
MARTHA:	(Silence) For me to be happy . . . . He'll do anything I ask. Fred is a good man, but I think I scare him now.
THERAPIST:	What scares you now?
MARTHA:	Hope.
THERAPIST:	I think you'll need hope for whatever decision you make. Isn't hope what brought you to marry Fred?

At this point, Martha needed gentle confrontation; she was trying to shut down from the rest of the world on both an emotional and social level. Martha had complained of lack of interest in her friends and family. Partly, this was attributable to her being fearful of careless or thoughtless remarks they might make. However, this was also largely due to Martha's need to abandon hope. Withdrawal offered a "safe" cocoon, where she neither needed to go forward nor backward with her life. This coping strategy did not fully work; Martha was acutely aware that Fred was unhappy being in limbo and that she felt depressed.

Martha eventually began to feel positive about letting go of her dream of having her own biological child. Moreover, Martha began to acclimate to the idea of never being pregnant. It was this tentative trial of considering not being pregnant that allowed her to let go of the idea of using donor eggs.

MARTHA:	I don't think we're going to try donor eggs. We had this terrific discussion and I said to Fred that I just couldn't stand the idea of gambling so much money for so little guarantee. I know there's nothing in life that's guaranteed, but it's an awful lot of money.
THERAPIST:	It's okay not to be pregnant?
MARTHA:	Uh, I guess so. I've joined the gym and am working out. For the first time in years, I feel like I've got my body back. Those drugs did a number on me.
THERAPIST:	So did the hope.
MARTHA:	I guess you're right. I see pregnant women and I still feel a twinge, but not like before. Before I kept thinking that could or should be me. Now I know that it isn't going to be me. I bought a

bathing suit for this summer and didn't think that maybe I shouldn't in case I'm pregnant and need a maternity one.

THERAPIST: That must feel good.

MARTHA: What feels even better is the possibility of being someone's mother. As I looked at what I really wanted, I realized that I want the chance to raise, love, and care for a child. To give as much as I can. . . . To be a family. Somewhere there is a baby that will need us as much as we need him.

At this point in the therapeutic process, Martha was looking for affirmation of her newly acquired feelings. Although Martha attributed some of her relief to the side effects of the medication, it was important that Martha acknowledge how devastating the emotional component (e.g., the hope) was. Martha's resolution about giving up having her own biological child needed to be experienced as a part of the whole emotional process, and not just as the antithetical reaction about the medical treatment.

Following this decision, both Martha and Fred experienced the pleasure and relief from not being in treatment. Fred did not derive the same physical relief as Martha, but vicariously enjoyed the release from scheduled doctor's visits and Martha's internal hypervigilance for signs of pregnancy. Instead, the couple began to read books on adoption and attend seminars. Fred and Martha had made movement in their mourning process for their own genetic child.

Martha and Fred made a private ceremony to mark the occasion in which they chose to read passages from books and poems to each other. They lit a special candle to commemorate the child they had planned and lost together. At the end of the ceremony, they chose to go on a trip to the seashore to watch both the sunset and sunrise, which would symbolize their release of their dreams and their welcome for the future. It was the combination of interventions that created enhanced insight into this very complicated process for the couple. As they described it:

THERAPIST: How did the ceremony feel?

FRED: Like a release. I had carried so much for so long, and now I feel lighter . . . more at peace.

MARTHA: Sad . . . but hopeful, too. On the beach in the morning, I felt in charge for the first time.

THERAPIST: Anything else?

MARTHA: Still a little pissed off. I still say it shouldn't be us. It's not fair. But, I know, I know, so many things aren't. Maybe it's okay for it not to be fair.

THERAPIST: And to feel a little pissed off?

MARTHA: Yeah, and a little pissed off. I'll survive not being Mother Theresa. I even told my mother not to keep cutting things out of the newspaper for me about infertility treatment.

For the first time, Martha was feeling positive about herself and was indicating that she was ready to explore the issues that affected her future. Interestingly, "hope" had become a very loaded term in the therapy. Initially, hope had been a painful, almost punitive term. Others made Martha hope when she did not want to: the doctors, the nurses, family members, and even Fred. Martha carried hope with each treatment cycle to the point where she had exhausted her hope. To be asked to hope was too much for her; an unfair burden in the face of everything else she had to carry.

As Martha moved on in therapy and through the grieving process, hope became less emotionally charged. Hope became a symbol of the possibility that there could be a life after infertility treatment. Eventually, hope also because a multidimensional and complex feeling again; it could be tolerated again.

THERAPIST: You've said that you think that you could go ahead and adopt now. How does that make you feel?

MARTHA: Excited, nervous, jumpy, happy. At this point, I just don't see us not raising kids. Adoption may not be easy. And God knows it's not cheap. But I love that baby already and we haven't even finished the application.

THERAPIST: It sounds like you're on your way to becoming a parent.

MARTHA: If there ever was someone ready to become a parent it's me. And Fred. I don't know of anyone else who has put as much thought into it as us. I still worry whether or not I'll be a good mom, but it doesn't feel so different from what I hear from my girlfriends.

THERAPIST: Maybe you're not so different anymore.

Outcome

Martha and Fred did go on to adopt a baby. It was a long and difficult road for the couple, where one birth mother did change her mind. Martha still has feelings about her infertility; these feelings and reactions are appropriate and do not interfere with her life. The infertility experience demanded that they work on communication. Consequently, Martha and Fred were able to discuss choices, issues, and feelings that arose during the adoption and while they were raising their daughter. Martha kept a journal to share with her daughter, in part to chronicle her daughter's journey into and through their lives and in part to assuage some of Martha's fears that her daughter will have complicated feelings about her adoptive parents. Currently, Martha and Fred are considering adopting another child.

CLINICAL ISSUES

The two most relevant issues when beginning therapy with individuals and couples who are considering ending treatment are: (a) what not having a biological child means to them, and (b) how that makes them feel. In working with couples who are considering terminating medical treatment, it is important that the couple be given sufficient time to grieve and to consider the symbolic meaning that parenthood represents for each of them. Typically, it is not until the unique meaning of biological parenthood is fully understood by both the therapist and the partners that therapy can proceed to a consideration of alternative parenthood options and/or future plans.

Short-term therapy is often indicated in this situation. Whether short- or long-term intervention is indicated, different therapeutic approaches may be needed for different stages of treatment. Cognitive therapy can be very helpful in identifying and challenging the dysfunctional thinking that accompanies the end of treatment. The thoughts of "I'll never be happy again" or "I'm a failure" are very responsive to cognitive intervention. Behavioral therapy can add flexibility into the treatment plan, particularly when other disorders develop concomitant to the treatment closure stage. Finally, psychodynamic therapy is useful when issues are intertwined with intrapersonal dynamic problems.

CONCLUSION

Patients who are terminating infertility treatment are especially vulnerable and fragile. Many are bombarded with opinions and desires of friends and family members. Being able to provide a supportive, neutral, and introspective environment for patients to examine all their feelings as well as the realities of options opened to them is critical.

There is no solution to not being able to have a genetic child, but there are choices. Whether it is to live child-free, adopt, use surrogacy, or use donor gametes, individuals and couples must grieve the loss of the emotionally conceived child. It is only after the grieving work is done that the choices can be explored. The therapist must be able to accompany the patient on this journey through the grief and into an uncertain future. Ultimately, the therapist helps the client to hope and to build.

REFERENCES

American Society for Reproductive Medicine. (1995). Assisted reproductive technology in the United States and Canada: 1993 results generated from the American Society for Reproductive Medicine/Society for Assisted Reproductive Technology Registry. *Fertility & Sterility, 64,* 13–17.

Baram, D., Tourtelot, E., Muechler, E., & Huang, K. (1988). Psychosocial adjustment following unsuccessful in vitro fertilization. *Journal Psychosomatic Obstetrics Gynaecology, 9,* 181–190.

Braverman, A. M. (1994). Oocyte donation: Psychological and counseling issues. *Clinical Consultations in Obstetrics and Gynecology, 6,* 143–149.

Burns, L. H. (1995). An overview of sexual dysfunction in the infertile couple. *Journal of Family Psychotherapy, 6,* 25–46.

Callan, V. J., Kloske, B., Kashima, Y., & Hennessey, J. F. (1988). Toward understanding women's decisions to continue or stop in vitro fertilization: The role of social, psychological, and background factors. *Journal of In Vitro Fertilization and Embryo Transfer, 5,* 363–369.

Carter, J. W., & Carter, M. (1989). *Sweet grapes: How to stop being infertile and start living again.* Indianapolis, IN: Perspectives Press.

Chartland, S. (1989, April 11). Experts assess a decade of in vitro fertilization. *New York Times,* p. 7.

Collins, A., Freeman, E. W., Boxer, A. S., & Tureck, R. (1992). Perceptions of infertility and treatment stress in females as compared with males entering in vitro fertilization treatment. *Fertility and Sterility, 57,* 350–355.

Cooper, S. L., & Glazer, E. S. (1988). *Without child.* New York: Lexington Press.

Cooper, S. L., & Glazer, E. S. (1994). *Beyond infertility: The new paths to parenthood.* New York: Lexington Books.

Corson, S. L. (1995). *Conquering infertility: A guide for couples* (3rd ed.). Vancouver, British Columbia, Canada: EMIS.

Domar, A. O., Seibel, M. M., & Benson, H. (1990). The mind/body program for infertility: A new behavioral approach for women with infertility. *Fertility and Sterility, 53,* 246–249.

Domar, A. O., Broome, A., Zuttermeister, P. C., Seibel, M., & Friedman, R. (1992). The prevalence and predictability of depression in infertile women. *Fertility and Sterility, 58,* 1158–1163.

Freeman, E. W., Boxer, A. S., Rickels, K., Tureck, R., & Mastroianni, L. (1985). Psychological evaluation and support in a program of in vitro fertilization and embryo transfer. *Fertility and Sterility, 43,* 48–53.

Greenfeld, D. A., & Olive, D. L. (1993). Psychospecific treatments in ART. *Assisted Reproduction Reviews, 3,* 190–195.

Kaufman, S. C., Spirtas, R., & Alexander, N. J. (1995). Do fertility drugs cause ovarian tumors? *Journal of Women's Health, 4,* 247–259.

Leiblum, S. R., Kemmann, E., & Lane, M. K. (1987). The psychological concomitants of in vitro fertilization. *Journal of Psychosomatic Obstetrics and Gynaecology, 6,* 165–178.

Mahlstedt, P. P. (1985). The psychological component of infertility. *Fertility and Sterility, 43,* 335–346.

Mahlstedt, P. P., MacDuff, S., & Bernstein, J. (1987). Emotional factors and the in vitro fertilization and embryo transfer process. *Journal of In Vitro Fertilization and Embryo Transfer, 4,* 232–236.

Mazure, C. M., & Greenfeld, D. A. (1989). Psychological studies of in vitro fertilization/embryo transfer participants. *Journal of In Vitro Fertilization and Embryo Transfer, 6,* 242–256.

Menning, B. E. (1979). Counseling infertile couples. *Contemporary Obstetrics and Gynecology, 13,* 101–106.

Newton, C. R., Hearn, M. T., & Yuzpe, A. A. (1990). Psychological assessment and follow-up after in vitro fertilization: Assessing the impact of failure. *Fertility and Sterility, 54,* 879–86.

Reading, A. E., Chang, L. C., & Kerin, J. F. (1989). Attitudes and anxiety levels in women conceiving through in vitro fertilization and gamete transfer. *Fertility and Sterility, 52,* 95–103.

Ron, E., & Lunenfeld, B. (1995). A review of infertility and its treatment in the etiology of female reproductive and other cancers. *Journal of Women's Health, 4,* 261–272.

Seibel, M. M., & Levin, S. (1987). A new era in reproductive technologies: The emotional stages of IVF. *Journal of In Vitro Fertilization and Embryo Transfer, 4,* 135–140.

Seibel, M. M., & Taymour, M. L. (1982). Emotional aspects of infertility. *Fertility & Sterility, 37,* 137–145.

Taylor, P. J. (1990). When is enough enough? *Fertility and Sterility, 54,* 772–774.

CHAPTER 12

Miscarriage and Its Aftermath

ELLEN S. GLAZER

> I had no idea it could be so painful. I have several friends who have had
> miscarriages and I know that my mother had two before I was born.
> Still, the loss of this pregnancy has devastated me. I never anticipated
> that I could feel such longing for someone I never knew.

Miscarriage—the loss of a pregnancy before 20 weeks' gestation—often represents a significant loss. Sadly, the depth of this loss is not always recognized, even by the grieving parents themselves. Because it happens so often—as many as one in four pregnancies ends in miscarriage (Borg & Lasker, 1989)—and because the loss often occurs very shortly after pregnancy is confirmed, there has long been the tendency to minimize the impact of the experience. Medical caregivers, family, and friends attempt to explain away the loss by saying that miscarriage is "nature's way" of ending pregnancies that "were not meant to be." For years, the prevailing societal message has been, "Get on with your lives, plan for another pregnancy and believe that this was all for the best."

In recent years, there has been some increased awareness of the significance of miscarriage. This awareness has been promoted by psychotherapists, who have given voice to the pain of miscarriage (Borg & Lasker, 1989; Friedman & Gradstein, 1982), and by nurses, who are often the ones most involved with patients during and after miscarriage. But perhaps the greatest contribution to public awareness of the impact of pregnancy loss has come from patients themselves (Cooper & Glazer, 1994; Friedman & Gradstein, 1982). Grieving couples speak poignantly of the powerful attachments that they felt to their unborn children and of the depth of sorrow that remained with them, sometimes for many years, following the loss of a pregnancy.

As awareness of the significance of miscarriage has grown, so, also, have the emotional challenges of the experience. With increasingly sophisticated technological options for fostering conception, miscarriage has become a more frequent event for scores of couples who previously might not even have known they were pregnant. Early confirmation of pregnancy promotes early attachment, setting the stage for loss and grief should the pregnancy not progress.

Technological monitoring has also made possible the prediction of pregnancy loss. Miscarriage, once an unanticipated event, can now be predicted when maternal hormone levels do not rise as rapidly as expected or when a fetal heartbeat cannot be detected at six or seven weeks. Although the close monitoring that would lead to such a prediction is usually reserved for women with a history of pregnancy loss or infertility, blood assays and ultrasounds are now widely available and can be used to monitor the course of any new pregnancy. When they are—and when the monitoring reveals that all is not going well—a woman or couple can be in the odd position of awaiting loss.

The assisted reproductive technologies enable countless couples, who once would have been considered barren, to bear children. However, these same technologies are responsible for a significant number of multiple gestations, that is pregnancies that are at increased risk for miscarriage as well as for severe prematurity. Additionally, multifetal reduction, the technique by which a high order multiple gestation (e.g., triplets, quadruplets) is reduced to presumably safer number of fetuses, has led to a new and most often, profoundly difficult, form of early pregnancy loss.

Finally, the assisted reproductive technologies have blurred the definition of pregnancy and hence, of pregnancy loss (Sandelowski, 1994). The old dictim, "you can't be a little bit pregnant," has been replaced—at least in the assisted reproductive technologies (ARTs)—by a series of steps toward pregnancy. Some ART couples consider themselves "a little bit pregnant" when they learn that fertilization has occurred. Others regard the transfer of embryos as the beginning of pregnancy. Still others wait until a first pregnancy test to personally confirm pregnancy. This lack of consensus about when pregnancy begins can lead to a lack of appreciation and respect for the loss that a couple may experience when a pregnancy ends. For example, a couple that has had embryos transferred may feel that they have suffered a miscarriage when the pregnancy test is negative.

This chapter will examine the emotional experience of miscarriage. It will pay particular attention to the ways in which a history of infertility and infertility treatment can complicate and intensify the feelings surrounding this loss. It will focus, also, on the aftermath of miscarriage, offering recommendations for how caregivers—both medical and mental health—can help reduce the long-term pain that accompanies pregnancy loss.

To look at the experience of miscarriage and its aftermath from a psychological perspective, it is necessary first to identify the known and suspected causes of early pregnancy loss.

MEDICAL CAUSES OF MISCARRIAGE

A Historical Perspective

Throughout history, people have tried to understand why many pregnancies end in spontaneous abortion. Explanations have ranged from the ancient Greek belief that women miscarried when they were frightened by a clap of thunder

(Borg & Lasker, 1989), to the belief, in parts of the Philippines, that women will miscarry if their cravings for certain fruits and vegetables are not fulfilled.

Prior to recent advances in reproductive medicine, there were two prevailing suspicions regarding the etiology of miscarriage: physical activity and emotional stress. Physical activities commonly implicated included lifting, sexual intercourse, strenuous exercise, and climbing stairs (ironically, little attention was paid to an activity that has recently been found to increase the incidence of miscarriage: cigarette smoking). Psychological explanations of miscarriage included ambivalence towards motherhood (Deutsch, 1945), marital conflicts, neurosis, or hostility towards ones mother (Borg & Lasker, 1989).

In recent years physicians, biologists, and geneticists have studied miscarriage and concluded that there are medical explanations for the vast majority of miscarriages. Although these findings seldom dissuade grieving women from scrutinizing their recent physical and psychological activities, it is highly unlikely that the "causes" they identify had anything to do with their pregnancy loss.

Current Understanding of Medical Causes

Medical causes of miscarriage fall into two broad categories: fetal and maternal. Chromosomal abnormalities in the fetus account for 60% of miscarriages in the first half of the first trimester and for 15% to 20% of miscarriages in the second half of the first trimester (Semchushyn & Colmar, 1989). Physicians believe that most fetuses with chromosomal abnormality lack the ability to grow and develop beyond a certain point. When they stop growing, the body usually recognizes this event and responds by expelling the fetus.

Problems in the maternal environment are varied. These include uterine factors (such as Asherman's syndrome—a scarring of the uterus that can occur after an abortion or following an infection), hormonal (e.g., progesterone) or nutritional (e.g., folic acid) deficiencies, infections, and systemic disease such as diabetes, thyroid disease, and autoimmune conditions. Endometriosis, a medical condition in which pieces of the uterine lining are found outside the uterine cavity, is also thought to contribute to difficulties in implantation. Finally, there are lifestyle factors such as smoking and exposure to environmental toxins that compromise a maternal environment.

Unlike early miscarriages, which may be caused by either fetal or maternal factors, late miscarriages (those occurring between the 13th and 20th weeks) are usually caused by maternal factors. In addition to those mentioned previously, there may be cervical factors. Sometimes the cervix is too weak and dilates too early. Women whose mothers took DES (diethystilbestrol) when they were pregnant with them are at greater risk. Serious maternal illness can be the cause of late, as well as of early, miscarriage.

Although most miscarriages, especially those occurring in the first trimester, (Semchushyn & Colmar, 1989) are probably random events that do not forecast future pregnancy losses, this is not always the case. Multiple miscarriage can also be caused by any of the aforementioned problems, as well as by immunologic factors. These inappropriate responses to pregnancy can be autoimmune (caused by the mother's contribution to the pregnancy) or alloimmune (caused by the father's contribution to the pregnancy). Research into autoimmune factors has explored the role of anticoagulant antibodies (about 3% of women experiencing recurrent miscarriage will test positive for a lupus-like anticoagulant), antiphospholipid antibodies (about 20% of women experiencing multiple miscarriage will test positive for antiphyospholipid antibodies), and thyroid antibodies (31% of women experiencing recurrent miscarriage will test positive for one or both antithyroid antibodies) (Semchushyn & Colmar, 1989). Current understanding of alloimmune factors focuses on measuring the circulating percentage of white blood cells known as natural killer (NK) cells and on embryotoxicity. Embryo toxic factors have been identified in 30% to 60% of women experiencing recurrent miscarriage (Coulam, 1994).

When a woman has a single miscarriage, its cause is rarely investigated as it is assumed to be a random event. Similarly, a second miscarriage is usually considered "bad luck." However, the woman who suffers three or more miscarriages is typically advised to undergo a series of tests to determine the cause of the losses. Women who experience multiple pregnancy losses are often labeled "habitual aborters," a medical term that does little to enhance these women's positive feelings about themselves. Despite the negativity of the term, women who suffer from recurrent miscarriages are regarded as having a medical problem that requires medical treatment (Harger, Archer, Marchese, Muracco-Clemons, & Garver, 1983).

Current treatment options for women with recurrent miscarriage range from progesterone supplements, for women who are found to have insufficient hormones to support a pregnancy, to baby aspirin, which can facilitate the transmittal of nutrients to the fetus. The effectiveness of some treatments has been well established while others remain experimental.

THE PSYCHOLOGICAL EXPERIENCE OF MISCARRIAGE

Although most women who lose a desired pregnancy (whether planned or unplanned) will experience some emotional pain following their loss, reactions to miscarriage vary considerably. A variety of factors influence the manner in which women and men cope with pregnancy loss:

1. Reproductive history.
2. History of loss.
3. The marital relationship.
4. Social support.
5. Coping style.

Reproductive History

A woman's—and to a lesser extent, a man's—reproductive history affects how she (or he) reacts to miscarriage. Especially vulnerable to pronounced grief are those who have had elective abortions in the past. Old feelings of ambivalence and guilt return, often joined by intense feelings of loss, for the earlier aborted fetus as well as for the wished-for baby. These reactions may be more pronounced for those who have had repeated elective abortions as well as in couples who have aborted a pregnancy that they conceived together. Similarly, those who have had babies and placed them for adoption may fear that they are being punished. They believe they relinquished what may have been their only chance to be parents.

Another group that is especially vulnerable following miscarriage are those with a history of infertility. Their loss is compounded by the fact that most underwent lengthy, exhausting, and costly efforts to conceive and they cannot count on becoming pregnant again. The cost of treatment, their advanced age, or the seriousness of their infertility problem may make another pregnancy unlikely, if not, impossible.

A miscarriage after infertility treatment sometimes prompts a couple to question whether they "are meant to be pregnant." Concerns they may have had about assisted reproduction can resurface after a miscarriage, prompting them to reflect on, and possibly to reconsider, their decision to pursue high-tech treatment. Many find that their self-doubts are intensified by such comments as "This is nature's way" or "If it was meant to be okay, it would be." Some couples even wonder if a miscarriage is their punishment for attempting to bypass nature.

Case Example

Mr. C is a devout Catholic who does not believe in assisted reproductive technology. Although he longs to be a father, he regards the childlessness of his marriage as part of the natural order of things and feels that he and his wife suffer for a reason. He knows that the Catholic Church sanctions GIFT (gamete intrafallopian transfer), but he feels that this process is as "unnatural" as IVF. He states that he cannot understand using a surgical procedure for conception.

Although Mr. C personally opposes all assisted reproduction, he did agree to one GIFT cycle. He felt that if he denied this to his wife, she would never forgive him. To his surprise, the pregnancy test was positive. Initially, Mr. C was delighted with the news but this delight soon turned to pain and worry as he began to reconsider the "unnaturalness" of what they had done. When Mrs. C subsequently miscarried, Mr. C was overwhelmed by a variety of emotions. He was sad to lose the pregnancy, but also relieved, since he had tremendous fears about a baby that could result from "such a bizarre beginning."

Although couples undergoing assisted reproductive technology are informed of the possibility of miscarriage, ectopic pregnancy, or other losses, many believe that if they ever succeed in becoming pregnant, they will be spared the pain of loss. This belief stems from the magical thinking that flourishes during infertility treatment, assigning cause and effect and fairness equations inappropriately. These patients feel that they have "done their time" with infertility and that they have earned an easy and uneventful pregnancy.

Sadly, heroic efforts to conceive do not guarantee a successful pregnancy outcome. In fact, some pregnancies facilitated by assisted reproduction are more vulnerable to loss. These include multiple pregnancies (in some case the loss may be partial) and pregnancies in older women (many women undergoing ART are older). Also, some of the same problems that can cause infertility have also been implicated in miscarriage (embryo toxicity, T-mycoplasma infection).

When an infertile couple miscarries, questions inevitably arise about what this might signify for future pregnancies. Although some will focus on the good news—that they can become pregnant—others will feel tremendous despair. For some, the sheer cost of another ART cycle, makes another pregnancy attempt impossible. For others who took several years and treatment interventions to conceive, it may seem that this one pregnancy was a fluke that is unlikely to happen again. Still others will worry that the miscarriage signals the beginning of a new problem, "Have we moved from the infertile to the 'multiple loss' category?" Frequently, this question resonates with their concerns about "forcing conception" (Sandelowski, 1994): Multiple losses may be regarded as further evidence of what "is not meant to be."

The pain of miscarriage after infertility treatment is heightened by the isolation that couples inevitably experience. When they were in the midst of an IVF (in vitro fertilization) or GIFT (gamete intrafallopian transfer cycle), they were closely connected to their caregivers, and in many instances, to other patients in their program. As difficult as the experience was, there was camaraderie and support. By contrast, pregnancy—and especially, pregnancy loss after assisted reproduction—is an isolating experience. Women report feeling that they have lost important connections. Although they may continue treatment, they are probably not in the active care of their infertility personnel. In addition, the camaraderie they felt with other patients has diminished:

> I found that my relationship with other women changed when I found that I was infertile, and then it changed again when I miscarried. I feel like an infertile woman with a very dark rain cloud over my head. It was as though my burden of infertility was lifted and then returned with even more weight and force. I feel that I am now a walking symbol of the precariousness of good luck.

The isolation of miscarriage after infertility is also intensified because the loss frequently occurs before the couple has told family and friends of the pregnancy. Most often, this is by design. Couples are reluctant to tell others about their pregnancy until they have some confirmation it is viable and likely to continue. However, those who lose a pregnancy that no one knew about feel that their grief is disenfranchised: Others cannot begin to appreciate the magnitude of the loss in part because they had not known that a long-awaited, hard-earned pregnancy had been achieved. Family and friends are likely to respond by saying, "Now you know you can get pregnant," encouraging words that sadly serve to undermine the significance of the loss.

An especially isolated and vulnerable group of infertile couples are those who experience loss in multiple pregnancy. Although all who attempt assisted reproductive treatment are told that it may result in multiple gestations, few are prepared for the significance of the losses that often occur in these pregnancies. These include partial and complete losses.

Partial Loss in Multiple Gestation

When a woman has undergone a cycle of IVF, GIFT, or ZIFT (zygote intrafallopian transfer) and is pregnant, she generally undergoes an ultrasound at six weeks' gestation. The purpose of this ultrasound is not only to see if there is a viable pregnancy, but also to determine if there is more than one fetal sac. It is not uncommon for that first ultrasound to indicate that more than one embryo implanted. However, each sac may not have a beating heart within it. Alternatively, one may have a strong heartbeat and one or two (or more) may appear weaker. A second (or third) ultrasound in early pregnancy following assisted reproduction sometimes reveals that a sac has been reabsorbed or that it is now empty.

When this occurs—when a couple learns that they have lost part, but not all, of a multiple gestation—most find that they are ill prepared for the news. Although blessed with an ongoing pregnancy (and one that may be more likely to proceed uneventfully than it would have if both or all of the fetuses had continued to grow), a loss has occurred. A "wanted" baby has been lost and there is grief involved. Because this grief is minimized by others, who tend to celebrate the success of the conception rather than to acknowledge the significance of the loss, couples are usually confused by their reactions. Some attempt to put their feelings aside, only to reconfront them at a later point:

> Although my pregnancy began as triplets, it was clear, at the six-week ultrasound, that at most two would survive. When I went back at seven weeks, I was not surprised to learn that one sac had vanished. I felt sad for a brief moment, because it was exciting and very special to think about being the mother of triplets, but the doctor was very encouraging. She told me that I now had a much better chance of successfully carrying to term or near term and of delivering healthy babies.
>
> My daughters are now nearly two years old. They are wonderful, active, and thriving children. I know that I have much to be grateful for and I am. Still, at certain moments I feel a tinge of sadness. Sometimes when people ask, "Are they twins?" I feel like saying, "They were almost triplets." Sometimes when I see them playing together, I can't help but wonder what a third would have been like.

Loss of All Multiples

The couple who learns that they have a multiple gestation and then loses the entire pregnancy usually feels a profound sense of grief. Not only are they losing a hard-earned pregnancy, but they are losing the promise of "instant family." For many, who have endured years of "preconception labor" (Sandelowski, 1994), this represents the ultimate reward—the opportunity to begin and complete their family at the same time.

Some couples connect with the "specialness" of being the parents of twins or triplets. While they know that it will be difficult and challenging, they also welcome the opportunity to have public recognition for their efforts:

> Although we were very fortunate to have a healthy son, the loss of our earlier twin pregnancy remains very near to me. When I take my son, now nine months, to a store, people will stop and say, "He's so cute." I like when they notice him, but feel a little sad that people don't know what I went through to have him. I believe that it would have been different with twins. Had I had twins, people would have asked about fertility medications. I know that some mothers want to be private about fertility treatments but I want others to know what hard work it was. And I want other infertile women to have some hope—with twins I could have been visible proof that treatment works.

How a miscarriage occurs will often shape a couple's emotional response to the loss. Those who perceive their pregnancy as proceeding uneventfully, but who suddenly begin to bleed, tend to scrutinize their behavior (especially in the days leading up to the miscarriage), wondering what it is they have done (Friedman, 1993). At the same time, however, they may regard this as a natural event, "nature's way of taking care." Certainly they receive support for this position from caregivers, family, and friends who are generally quick to support the naturalness and inevitability of most miscarriages.

The infertile couple who pursues ART and then has a closely monitored pregnancy, has a very different experience of miscarriage. For them, miscarriage rarely comes as a surprise. They come to anticipate it when they learn that their hormone levels have dropped or when they receive bad news regarding an ultrasound. Unlike those whose hopes and expectations about a pregnancy may be suddenly dashed by the sight of blood or the news that their doctor cannot hear a heartbeat after 11 or 12 weeks, couples pregnant after ART find themselves in a "waiting to lose" position (Harris, Sandelowski, & Holditch-Davis, 1991):

Case Example

Mr. and Mrs. D are a couple who considered themselves "good patients" when they went through three cycles of IVF, but who feel they were transformed into "angry, defiant" patients when their pregnancy was closely monitored. Over the course of three weeks they received a series of confusing predictions about the pregnancy—first, the hormone levels were "a little low," then they were fine, then they dropped again but this drop came simultaneous to a positive ultrasound. Confused by the conflicting information, the D's felt that the monitoring only served to remind them of the lengths they had had to go to to become pregnant and that it reinforced the doubts that they had about "pushing nature." Following the experience, Mrs. D told her doctor that if she ever succeeded in becoming pregnant again, she didn't want to "be subjected to" the monitoring, "I want to be pregnant as long as nature indicates that I am pregnant. If I lose it, I'll let my body give me the news."

It seems that assisted reproduction and the monitoring that follows it have prompted people to perceive that there are actually two categories of miscarriage. One might best be termed the "technological miscarriages," those that are announced by blood test or ultrasound. Included in this group are the losses of those pregnancies that have been labeled "chemical pregnancy," a term which suggests that they are not quite "real" pregnancies. In the second category are what might best be termed "physical miscarriages." These losses are announced by bleeding, cramping, or the sudden loss of pregnancy symptoms.

From an emotional standpoint, a "technological" miscarriage can be more difficult and challenging than a physical miscarriage. Although the latter is painful emotionally as well as physically, women who experience a miscarriage in which there are observable physical changes have some sense that a natural process, however upsetting, is occurring. Their loss is real, concrete, and identifiable.

Women who experience a "technological" miscarriage (especially if it is referred to as "just a chemical pregnancy") are confused by what has happened. Some wonder if they were ever really pregnant at all. Many feel that the close monitoring intruded on a very personal experience and that it spoiled what might otherwise have been a very happy time. Even knowing that the happiness was destined to end does not mitigate their sense of loss: "I feel like I lost not only a baby but the chance to be blissfully, innocently, unknowingly pregnant, if only for two weeks."

History of Loss

As is well documented in the field of psychiatry, new losses often cause people to revisit old ones. This is certainly true of miscarriage.

Case Example

Mrs. A is a 30-year-old married woman and mental health professional, who lost both of her parents when she was 9 years old. Raised by a loving aunt and uncle, but always feeling like an outsider among their children, she longed for the time when she would have children of her own. She especially hoped to have a little girl, believing that her relationship with her daughter would rekindle the love that she had enjoyed so fleetingly with her own mother.

Mrs. A's first pregnancy, achieved with some medical assistance, ended at 16 weeks. Things had gone well until that time, and Mrs. A went to her routine obstetrical appointment without concern. Although she had felt cautious initially, she now felt confident that she was "out of the woods." To her shock and horror, the ultrasound revealed that the fetus—a female—had stopped growing.

In the weeks and months that followed her loss, Mrs. A experienced profound grief. She spoke often of the deaths of each of her parents. Through wells of tears, she told of how she felt her unborn child was connected to her parents and of how bereft she was that her parents and child were now "together in heaven" leaving her to suffer "alone on earth." Her husband's efforts to comfort her, although heartfelt and constant, made little apparent difference as she confronted her grief.

As we see from Mrs. A, a history of loss can make an individual more vulnerable following a miscarriage. However, prior experiences with loss may also help prepare people to cope with new losses. Since many who miscarry are young, and perhaps have never experienced a major loss, miscarriage may represent the first time they are called on to cope with loss. New to serious disappointment and unfamiliar with grief, they may feel ill-equipped to deal with this loss.

Case Example

Mrs. B was 22 when her first pregnancy ended in miscarriage. She had conceived easily and was jubilant when a home pregnancy test confirmed that she was pregnant. Although remotely aware of the possibility of miscarriage, Mrs. B had assumed that it would not happen. She was young and healthy. Furthermore, she was taking good care of herself so she deemed herself unlikely to have problems during the pregnancy. When she began spotting at eight weeks, she was stunned and bewildered, but still hopeful. When the bleeding became heavy, she reacted with disbelief, anger, self-blame, and intense grief. These feelings intensified in the weeks that followed her miscarriage and took many months—and brief, intensive therapy—to subside.

The Marital Relationship

Pregnancy and certainly, pregnancy loss, pose an array of challenges to a couple. First, there is the issue of shared experience: Although they attempt to share the experience, it occurs within one person's body and not the others. Second, there is the question of the meaning and impact of the loss: One member of the couple may have wanted the pregnancy more than the other. Third, there is the issue of guilt: Women tend to blame themselves when they miscarry, and husbands typically stand helplessly by as the cycle of blame unfolds. However, there are also instances in which a woman blames her husband for the miscarriage, feeling that he pushed her to do some activity that she regarded as marginally advisable (this is most charged when he initiated sexual activity at a time when she did not feel they should have intercourse). Finally, there is the issue of attachment: The attachment that a mother feels to her unborn child begins very early, most often before a father can begin to feel attached (Cecil, 1994). Because she feels the attachment earlier, the loss of the pregnancy is likely to be more dramatic and more devastating for her than it is for him.

In the aftermath of a miscarriage, husbands often feel ready to move on sooner than their wives. This can lead to some stress between them, especially when the husband is unclear what to make of his wife's grief. "Why does she remain saddened weeks and months after the loss," he wonders. "Why does she focus on her due date when the pregnancy is long since gone?" "Why does she have such difficulty being around pregnant women?" Behind many of these questions, many husbands are wondering why their wives seem to be disinterested in them, why the women have turned inward, why the pregnancy—and its loss—has formed a gulf between them.

Grieving couples often grapple with feelings of loss in their relationship as well as the shared loss of their unborn child. They have suffered a loss of innocence: The natural process that they anticipated has failed. In addition, they have endured an experience that may raise some questions about their union: "Is there something about us that may create nonviable embryos?" Finally, they may be struggling with feeling out of sync with friends and colleagues who may be having children uneventfully. These losses are cumulative and leave some couples feeling isolated and adrift, unclear of the resiliency of their connection to each other as well as with those around them.

Social Support

Caregivers

The comments and questions of caregivers during and after a miscarriage can profoundly impact the way an individual and/or couple processes the experience. Women react strongly to the question, "Was this a wanted pregnancy?" or to use of the word "fetus" when they would have preferred "baby." They feel soothed by the nurse or physician who appreciates the emotional dimensions of the loss and who does not treat it as a simple physical event.

Perhaps the most helpful thing that caregivers can do is to acknowledge the significance of the loss. Even those couples who suffer a very early miscarriage loss feel that a significant life has been lost. Caregivers, who convey their respect, help give meaning to that life. Statements, such as "The baby really meant a great deal to you" or "You will always remember this pregnancy" (especially if it was a first) or "Your due date will be a difficult but important time for you," all convey sympathy and understanding for the significance of the loss.

Caregivers help grieving couples not only with their kind words but also with their actions. If a woman needs to be in the hospital during or following a miscarriage, she appreciates being away from the visibly expectant mothers and from newborns. Similarly, when she sees her obstetrician for a follow-up visit, it is best that she not be there at a time when she will be surrounded by obviously pregnant women.

Although most caregivers try to be helpful to couples during and after miscarriage, mistakes are unwittingly made. Bearing witness to intense pain is very difficult and some caregivers will mistakenly try to make people feel better. Such statements as "Now you know you can get pregnant" or "The next pregnancy will be a good one" or "It must not have been meant to be" all increase the anguish of grieving parents.

Case Example

Paul and Kathy struggled with infertility for six years before finally achieving pregnancy. They were delighted when the pregnancy test came back positive and ecstatic when the first ultrasound revealed a strong heartbeat. Their joy increased over the next several weeks, as the pregnancy continued uneventfully.

When Kathy was 19 weeks pregnant, she went into labor, apparently due to an incompetent cervix. Her joy and that of her husband, turned to sudden grief as they faced a very early delivery and the inevitable loss of their much cherished baby. However, they felt comforted by the way that the nurses cared for them during and after labor. They were immensely supportive of Kathy and of Paul, taking pictures of the baby and encouraging the couple to hold him.

A month after their loss Kathy and Paul received a follow-up letter from their physician. In it, he presented the autopsy report, indicating that they had lost a healthy "female fetus." Kathy and Paul reacted to this news with distress since the same doctor had announced at delivery, with apparent confidence, that it was a boy. His failure to acknowledge this mistake, even in the letter, made Paul and Kathy feel that he placed no importance on their loss nor on their baby's life. Sadly, this "offhanded" approach to gender, retrospectively undermined the efforts of the nurses to convey respect for the young life that had been lost.

Friends and Family

In the aftermath of miscarriage, grieving couples are keenly aware of the actions and reactions of others. Notes expressing sympathy, verbal expressions of concern, and sometimes, flowers, offer comfort. Each serves as a testimony to the significance of the experience and helps confirm that the early life, now lost, had meaning.

As noted earlier, however, friends and family members are often unable to offer support to a grieving couple. Since many couples lose a pregnancy before they tell others that they are pregnant, friends and family may learn of the pregnancy and its loss simultaneously. Although they may want to offer support and understanding, these efforts may be compromised because without prior knowledge of the pregnancy, they have no foundation on which to base their condolences.

Another handicap for those who would like to offer comfort to a grieving couple is that they have little guidance as to what to say or do. While there are socially and religiously prescribed "rituals" for most kinds of loss, these practices have traditionally applied to the death of an adult or child. Since funerals, burials, wakes, and shiva periods have not traditionally been applied to early pregnancy loss, well-intentioned friends and family have little precedent on which to base their condolences.

Coping Style

Miscarriage, being an "equal opportunity loss," affects people of all personality styles and dispositions. Individuals who tend to blame themselves for everything will be as affected as those who place blame on the shoulders of others. Individuals who are upbeat, optimistic, and relaxed will experience miscarriage as often as those who tend to be anxious, fearful, and pessimistic. And people who live their lives carefully and prudently will probably suffer as many miscarriages as those who "walk on the wild side."

Just as people have different personality styles, so also, do they have different views of their reproductive abilities. Some regard themselves as fertile individuals and do not anticipate problems having children (these are generally women who have had normal periods and who have never had pelvic inflammatory disease or elective abortions). Others anticipate problems and are not surprised when they occur (these may include women who ovulate irregularly or who have suspected—or confirmed—endometriosis).

In the past, miscarriage was not always viewed as an "equal opportunity" loss. Rather, it was regarded as a consequence of a woman's ambivalence about motherhood (Deutsch, 1945) or of her anxiety regarding pregnancy. Alternatively, her activities or lifestyle were indicated (e.g., she "worked too hard" or "did too much physical activity to maintain a pregnancy").

Although the former "blaming the victim" approach to miscarriage has been replaced by a more scientific and compassionate understanding of the experience, women's personality styles continue to impact the way that they experience miscarriage. Women who tend to feel personally responsible when things go wrong blame themselves when they miscarry. Most focus on some action or activity that they now regard as marginally safe during pregnancy and blame it as the cause of their loss. These activities often include sports, sexual intercourse, lifting heavy objects, and engaging in psychologically or physically stressful work. They look back regretfully with a series of "if onlys," scrutinizing their behavior and castigating themselves with "I should have known better."

Case Example

An evening of spontaneous true confessions occurred in a miscarriage support group. It began when one woman painfully revealed that she and her husband had had an abortion soon after they were married. She confessed that she had long felt guilty about the abortion, regarding it as an act of incredible selfishness, and wondered whether she had secretly wished this miscarriage on herself so as to be absolved of her guilt. Following her painful confession, others came forth. One woman "admitted" that she felt her miscarriage was caused by her exercising on a stationary bicycle in order to "get into shape" for pregnancy. Another spoke of her marriage to a man outside her faith and of how this had hurt her elderly parents. She saw her miscarriage as punishment for this transgression. Still another woman told of how she had accepted a new job even though she knew she was pregnant. She believed that travel, which was a frequent requirement of her new position, was the cause of her loss. Finally, there was the poignant account by the woman who had been secretly selecting names for her unborn child. "I knew it was too early but I couldn't resist thinking of names. I'm being punished for my hubris."

Although self-blame is an extremely common reaction to miscarriage, there are those whose personality styles incline them to blame others. Those who externalize blame will focus on physicians, who "did not advise them properly," on employers, who overworked them, and sadly, on husbands, who may have initiated sex or promoted other activities that are later perceived as contributing to miscarriage.

THE AFTERMATH

Many years ago I had a miscarriage. Since that time I have had and raised three wonderful children. I have also had a successful career and a good marriage. I have faced and survived two life-threatening illnesses. I have lost loved ones. It surprises and puzzles me that I still feel the loss of the baby that I never knew. Not always. Not often. But each May, when the flowers are in bloom, I feel the sadness and remember.

A miscarriage marks the end of a beginning. It leaves parents who have no voices nor faces nor movements to remember. Faced with this emptiness, with this loss that has no name nor form, women and men are often surprised by the depth of their sorrow. They are puzzled that they could miss someone they never knew and feel such pain in the absence of memories.

For some, the pain is intense but transient. They go on to have other children, leaving this loss to the recesses of memory. Others may feel less pain at the time of their miscarriage but find that it revisits them in years to come. What the loss of this pregnancy will mean in subsequent years will be determined in part, by future experiences and events. Other losses, successful pregnancies, serious illnesses, and joyous occasions will all help shape the legacy of this loss.

No one can erase the pain of miscarriage. In fact, those who attempt to do so only appear to diminish the significance of the experience. By contrast, caregivers, family, and friends who express sorrow, serve a vital role in the healing process. Their expressions, however awkward or unimaginative, give essential testimony to the importance of lost possibility.

REFERENCES

Borg, S., & Lasker, J. (1989). *When pregnancy fails.* Boston: Beacon Press.

Cecil, R. (1994, May). I wouldn't have minded a wee one running about: Miscarriage and the family. *Social Science and Medicine, 38*(10), 1415–1422.

Cooper, S., & Glazer, E. (1994). *Beyond infertility.* Lexington, MA: Lexington Books.

Coulam, C. (1994, Fall). Immune causes of multiple miscarriage. *Resolve Newsletter, 19*(4), 1, 4–6.

Cuisinier, M. C., Kuispers, J. C., Hoogduin, C., DeGraauw, P., & Jannsen, H. J. (1993, December). Miscarriage and stillbirth: Time since the loss, grief intensity and satisfaction with care. *European Journal of Obstetrics, Gynecology and Reproductive Biology, 52*(3), 163–168.

Deutsch, H. (1945). *The psychology of women* (Vol. 2). New York: Bantam Books.

Friedman, R. (1993). Coping with pregnancy loss: Ectopic pregnancy, recurrent abortion, and stillbirth. In M. M. Seibel, A. A. Kiessling, J. Berstein, & S. R. Levin (Eds.), *Technology and infertility: Clinical, psychosocial, legal and ethical aspects* (pp. 319–327). New York: Springer-Verlag.

Friedman, R., & Gradstein, B. (1982). *Surviving pregnancy loss.* Boston: Little, Brown.

Groll, M. (1984). Endometriosis and spontaneous abortion. *Fertility and Sterility, 41,* 933–935.

Harger, J. H., Archer, D. F., Marchese, S. A., Muracco-Clemons, M., & Garver, K. L. (1983). Etiology of recurrent pregnancy losses and outcome of subsequent pregnancies. *Obstetrics and Gynecology, 62,* 574–581.

Harris, B., Sandelowski, M., & Holditch-Davis, D. (1991, July/August). Infertility . . . and new interpretations of pregnancy loss. *Maternal Child Nursing, 16*(4), 217–220.

Kirk, E. P. (1984). Psychological effects and management of perinatal loss. *Obstetrics and Gynecology, 149,* 46–51.

Lasker, J., & Toedler, L. J. (1991, October). Acute vs. chronic grief: The case of pregnancy loss. *American Journal of Orthopsychiatry, 61*(4), 510–522.

Neugebauer, R., Kline, J., & O'Connor, P. (1992, October). Determinants of depressive symptoms in the weeks after miscarriage. *American Journal of Public Health, 82*(10), 1332–1339.

Ostrofsky, J. (1983). *Advances in clinical and obstetrical gynecology* (Vol. 2). Baltimore: Williams and Wilkins.

Prettyman, R. J., Cordle, C. J., & Cook, C. D. (1993, December). A three month follow-up of psychological morbidity after early miscarriage. *British Journal of Medical Psychology, 66*(4), 363–372.

Sandelowski, M. (1994). *With child in mind.* Philadelphia: University of Pennsylvania.

Seibel, M., & Graves, W. L. (1980). The psychological implications of spontaneous abortion. *Journal of Reproductive Medicine, 25,* 161–165.

Seitz, P., & Warrick, L. (1974). Perinatal death: The grieving mother. *Nursing, 74,* 2028–2033.

Semchushyn, S., & Colmar, C. (1989). *How to prevent miscarriage.* New York: Collier.

CHAPTER 13

Infertility and Adoption Adjustment: Considerations and Clinical Issues

DAVID BRODZINSKY

Becoming a parent is one of the most important developmental milestones in a person's life (Heinicke, 1995). Even more than holding a job, living apart from one's parents, or getting married, achieving parenthood is, for many people, the ultimate indicator of becoming a responsible adult.

The transition to parenthood has often been described as a crisis point in the life of the individual, leading to the attainment of new roles, as well as re- quiring numerous adjustments in role enactment, both within the family and in relation to the workplace and other societal institutions (Grossman, 1988; Rossi, 1968). Parenthood also brings about a new sense of identity, involving feelings of caregiving competence and quality of affective attunement to the child (Barnard & Martell, 1995). In addition, nurturing children is said to offer the individual the opportunity for expressing feelings of generativity and link- ing the self to an intergenerational line (Erikson, 1963). In short, parenting deepens the sense of self, broadens one's connections to the community, and is the bridge to both past and future generations.

There is a strong cultural assumption regarding parenthood in most soci- eties. Typically, children are highly valued, and adults are expected to form families and raise children (Fawcett, 1988). Consequently, lifestyle choices that do not include children tend to be viewed as nontraditional, at the very least. There is also a strong presumption of fertility among most individuals as they enter adulthood, marry, and plan for children (Daly, 1988). Few men or women expect that they will have difficulty conceiving a child. Yet nearly one in six couples must cope with some type of fertility problem (Blank, 1985; Mosher & Pratt, 1990). In light of the importance placed on parenting and fe- cundity in most societies, it is understandable that many couples experience the inability to have a child biologically as a major crisis in their personal and marital life, often leading to increased feelings of anxiety, guilt, anger and de- pression, diminished self-esteem, feelings of having lost control of one's life, and reduced marital well-being (see Leiblum & Greenfeld, Chapter 5; Daniluk, Chapter 6; Epstein & Rosenberg, Chapter 7; and Leiblum, Chapter 8 in this book, for a more complete description of the impact of infertility on individuals and couple relationships).

When faced with a fertility problem, most couples initially seek a medical solution, with nearly 50% eventually being able to have a child biologically (McEwan, Costello, & Taylor, 1987). The remaining couples have two options to choose from: either to remain childless or to seek parenthood through some other means. In the latter category are those individuals who decide to build their family through adoption. It has been estimated that approximately 25% of infertile couples eventually seek to adopt children (Burgwyn, 1981).

How does the experience of infertility affect the decision to adopt a child as well as individual's identity as a parent? Does infertility alter parenting attitudes and practices? What is the legacy of infertility on adoptive family relationships? These questions, and others, will be examined in the current chapter. Before doing so, however, I will describe some of the options available today for individuals and couples who choose to parent through adoption.

CURRENT TRENDS AND OPTIONS IN ADOPTION

In considering the possibility of adopting a child, prospective parents have two types of adoption to choose from: agency adoption and independent (nonagency) adoption. As McDermott (1993) points out, the primary difference between these two types of adoption is the method by which birth parents give their consent to adoption. In both public and private agency adoptions, birth parents legally surrender the child to the agency, which in turn, consents to adoption by specific parents. In independent adoption, on the other hand, birth parents give their consent directly to the adoptive parents.

Currently, there are no accurate statistics on the number of adoptions that take place each year, primarily because the federal government has not collected the data in a consistent and reliable way for some time. In 1986, the most recent year for which national figures are available, a total of 104,088 adoptions occurred, of which 49.1% were unrelated placements (adoptions involving children who were biologically unrelated to the adoptive parents). Of these unrelated adoptions, approximately 39% were handled by public agencies, 29% were sponsored by private agencies, and 31% were independent placements (National Committee for Adoption, 1989).

For most of this century, the vast majority of children placed for adoption have been healthy, white infants. Typically, these adoptions were confidential and involved little, if any, contact or exchange of information between birth parents and adoptive parents. Over the past few decades, however, the demographics of children relinquished for adoption, and the nature of the adoption process itself, have changed dramatically (Cole & Donley, 1990; Stolley, 1993). The growing acceptance of single parenthood in our society has encouraged more and more unmarried women to keep their babies rather than relinquish them for adoption (Bachrach, Stolley, & London, 1992; Weinraub &

Gringlas, 1995). This pattern, coupled with the legalization of abortion and the ready availability of contraception, has resulted in a steady decline in the number of healthy babies, especially white babies, available for adoption (Stolley, 1993).

In response to the limited number of adoptable babies, especially through adoption agencies, an increasing number of couples have chosen to adopt independently or privately. This type of adoption, which is legal in all but six states, involves direct contact between the prospective adoptive parents and birth parents, by means of word of mouth or through advertising, typically *without* intervention by a third party such as an attorney. (The law varies from state to state as to the specific role played by intermediaries such as attorneys. Some states allow attorneys to directly match adoptive parents with birth parents; others only allow the attorney to advise the prospective adoptive parents on methods for locating birth parents.) Today, more infants are placed for adoption through independent means than through adoption agencies (Stolley, 1993). This practice, however, is not without its critics, who caution that independent adoption does not adequately protect the rights of adoptive parents and birth parents, nor prepare them for the realities of adoption, as well as agency based adoption (Emery, 1993; see McDermott, 1993 for a proindependent adoption position).

With fewer white infants available for adoption in this country, many couples have chosen to adopt across racial lines. Typically, this practice involves white parents adopting nonwhite children. Domestic transracial adoption has declined since the 1970s, however, in response to opposition from the African American and Native American communities. In contrast, international adoption is on the rise. In 1991, for example, there were 9,008 intercountry adoptions by U. S. citizens, with the majority of children coming from Pacific Rim countries, Eastern European countries, and Central and South American countries (U.S. Immigration & Naturalization Service, 1991). Finally, with the passage of the Adoption Assistance and Child Welfare Act of 1980 (Public Law 96-272), another source of "adoptable" children has emerged. These "special needs" youngsters include older children who have lingered in foster care, minority children, sibling groups, children with medical problems, and children with physical, mental, and/or emotional handicaps.

The past 20 years have also witnessed some remarkable changes in the adoption process itself. Since the establishment of licensed adoption agencies, in the early part of this century, most adoptions have been confidential, and involved little, if any, contact between birth parents and adoptive parents. In the 1970s, however, some agencies began offering their clients the option of open adoption, in which adoptive parents and birth parents could meet and share information, including the possibility of full disclosure of identity, and, if desired, develop plans for maintaining some type of contact after the child's placement. Although still quite controversial, open adoption has become a fairly common practice, both in agency adoptions and independent adoptions, and offers members of the adoption triad a viable means of meeting their needs in ways that are not always possible with confidential adoption (Baran & Pannor, 1993; Berry, 1993; Brodzinsky, Lang, & Smith, 1995).

Adoption has undergone some remarkable changes over the past few decades, resulting in more options for prospective adoptive parents, as well as greater parenting challenges for those individuals and couples who eventually chose to build their family through adoption (Brodzinsky et al., 1995).

INFERTILITY AND THE DECISION TO ADOPT

Traditional social casework practice has assumed that the decision to adopt a child, as well as the success of the adoption placement, rests largely on the extent to which the adoptive couple have resolved their feelings about infertility. This assumption can be seen in questions used to evaluate couples for their readiness to adopt a child. It is quite common for the adoption caseworker to explore each partner's motivation to adopt, including whether infertility played a role in their decision; whether there is a definitive diagnosis of infertility; what type of medical interventions have been sought and whether the couple is still attempting to conceive biologically; how the couple feels about not having their own biological child; and finally, how each marital partner feels about the child's biological background. But what does it mean to resolve one's feelings about infertility, and is it necessary for this process to be complete before one can successfully take on the role of adoptive parent?

Confronting infertility and eventually deciding to adopt a child is a complex process requiring numerous changes in personal identity and role enactment (Brodzinsky & Huffman, 1988; Daly, 1988, 1990; Kirk, 1964; Matthews & Martin-Matthews, 1986; Reitz & Watson, 1992). The process begins with efforts to have a child biologically. Nearly 95% of newly married couples want and expect to have a biological child during their lifetime (Glick, 1977). When this normative assumption is challenged by the inability to conceive a child, it forces individuals to take stock of themselves and of their lives. For most individuals, the importance of being a parent remains high, and so they seek a medical solution to their problem. Because infertility testing and treatment typically take a long time, with varying degrees of success, depending on the problem, couples are often left in a state of limbo, not knowing whether their goal of biological parenthood will be achieved, and yet not being able to put aside this cherished goal in consideration of other options. In some cases, the inability to arrive at an identifiable diagnosis for the fertility problem only complicates the situation for the couple, leaving them feeling helpless and directionless. Eventually, however, there is a growing recognition and acceptance that biological parenthood may not be achieved. For some, the very process of medical testing and treatment reinforces this possible reality; for others, it is the confirmation of an identifiable diagnosis; for still others, simply the passage of time and the continued failure to conceive bring home the recognition that biological parenthood is problematic (Daly, 1990).

Although not necessarily wanting to relinquish the goal of biological parenthood, couples who continue to experience involuntary childlessness, and for whom parenthood remains a salient part of their identity, begin to consider other options. For many, this means exploring the possibility of adoption. Daly (1988, 1990) points out that while some couples need to "let go" of the biological parenthood identity before they can begin to identify themselves as adoptive parents, others pursue both goals simultaneously. For the latter group, the primary issue is being a parent; it is less important for them whether this goal is achieved through a biological process or through adoption. Daly (1990) reported that of the 68 couples he studied, 65% were characterized by a *sequential* relationship between infertility resolution and adoption readiness. These individuals did not feel ready to identify themselves as adoptive parents until some endpoint was reached with respect to infertility. The attitudes of Mary and Thomas, a couple in their late 30s, reflect this pattern: In a recent counseling session, Mary stated:

> I still have hope of getting pregnant. We've undergone IVF treatment on several occasions, with no luck yet. We're still trying. . . . If we don't succeed with this approach, then we will consider adoption. . . . Until I feel confident that all medical approaches have been exhausted, I can't let myself think about the possibility of adoption. . . . Having my own baby, going through the pregnancy, having my husband there for me during delivery are just too important for me. . . . and for Tom, too.

In contrast, 28% of the couples studied by Daly (1990) were characterized by a *concurrent* relationship between infertility resolution and adoption readiness. For these individuals, the primary commitment was to parenthood per se, regardless of the way it was achieved. Joan and Edward, both 37 years old, typify this pattern. In therapy, Joan reported:

> I cannot think of myself without children. Being a parent has been a lifelong goal . . . Ed and I have been trying to conceive a child for 5 years. We are still trying. Last year we began to realize that maybe we wouldn't have our own child. For some reason we both quickly accepted that if that happened we would adopt a child . . . lately it doesn't seem to matter whether we have a biological child or adopt one . . . in fact, we are pursuing both possibilities now . . . if we are lucky, both will happen.

Finally, the remaining 7% of couples in Daly's (1990) study were characterized by spouses who expressed opposing opinions regarding the relationship between infertility resolution and adoption. Daly (1988) points out that disagreement between spouses in their readiness to adopt represents one of the most critical hurdles in the couple's identification with adoptive parenthood. This has been my experience as well. Alex, 43 years old, and Karen, his 33-year-old wife, are examples of this pattern.

Case Example

For Alex, the fact that he cannot conceive a child biologically has been experienced as a profound narcissistic wound. His deep sense of shame, coupled with rigid "male pride," has prevented him from being able to accept donor insemination as a possible solution to the couple's fertility problem; it also has eliminated adoption as an option for him. Karen reported, ". . . he feels so full of shame . . . as if his very manhood has been taken from him . . . he won't talk about it either . . . that's why he won't come here anymore . . . and he won't even consider the options . . . he just can't accept the idea of having a child who is not his [biologically] . . . when we found out about Alex's problem, I knew that he wouldn't agree to having me impregnated with another man's sperm . . . I hoped he would come around to the idea of adoption. So far he hasn't and I don't know if he will . . . we have a lot of bad feelings between us about this issue."

Other researchers have also noted that infertility resolution is not necessarily a prerequisite for a couple's readiness to adopt. Lorber and Greenfeld (1989) found that 15% of their sample of couples seeking in vitro fertilization (IVF) were pursuing adoption at the same time. In addition, Callan and Hennessey (1986) reported that of the 77 IVF couples interviewed, approximately 50% had already made arrangements to adopt, and another 21% believed that adoption was a strong possibility. Corresponding figures were even higher in a small-scale study reported by Williams (1992), who noted that 12 of 16 couples interviewed were pursuing both IVF and adoption simultaneously. Interestingly, Williams also reported that wives were much more positive about adoption than their husbands (see also Crowe, 1985).

Infertility represents a major crisis in the life of the couple requiring numerous readjustments, both intrapsychically and interpersonally. First, and foremost, the couple must decide whether to remain childless, whether to seek a medical solution for their infertility problem, or to pursue adoption. Recent advances in reproductive technologies have given new hope to couples seeking biological parenthood (see McShane, Chapter 2, in this book, for a complete description of current assisted reproductive options). At the same time, these advances have complicated infertility resolution, as well as the decision-making process regarding adoption (Daly, 1988, 1990; Daniels, 1994; Holbrook, 1990; Williams, 1992). What is becoming increasingly clear, however, is that for many couples it may not be necessary to fully resolve one's feelings about infertility before adopting a child.

IMPACT OF INFERTILITY ON ADOPTIVE
FAMILY LIFE

The transition to adoptive parenthood is characterized by many unique challenges that impact on family members at various stages of the family life cycle

(Brodzinsky, 1987; Brodzinsky & Huffman, 1988; Brodzinsky et al., 1995; Brodzinsky, Schechter, & Henig, 1992; Hajal & Rosenberg, 1991). Prospective adoptive parents, for example, must cope with the uncertainty regarding the timing of the adoption placement, as well as anxiety associated with the adoption evaluation process (the home study) and the uncertainty as to whether the birth parent will change her mind about placing her baby. During this preplacement period, couples also begin to reshape their identity in ways that are synchronous with being adoptive parents (Daly, 1988). They also begin to cope with the social stigma that surrounds adoption in our society (Kirk, 1964). Following the adoption placement, on the other hand, parents must integrate the child into the family and foster the development of mutual family bonds. This process involves not only efforts to facilitate the infant's sense of trust and security, but the parents' sense of commitment and entitlement to the child. As children enter the preschool years, parents are confronted with other tasks, including sharing adoption information with the child, as well as creating a family atmosphere that is conducive to open adoption communication. During the elementary school years, as children's knowledge of adoption deepens, parents must help their youngsters cope with the reality of their relinquishment by birth parents, as well as facilitate the child's grieving in response to adoption-related loss. They must also maintain an atmosphere in which adoption can be freely explored among all family members. Finally, parents of adolescent adoptees not only must continue many of these earlier tasks, but also must help their teenage children develop a stable and secure sense of themselves that incorporates being adopted into their emerging ego identity.

Although most adoptive parents handle these tasks reasonably well, complications often arise leading to adjustment problems in children and parents (Brodzinsky, 1987, 1990, 1993). Some of these problems have been linked by adoption theorists to the legacy of parental infertility. Psychoanalytic writers, for example, have emphasized the unconscious conflicts of adoptive parents as a major factor in the adjustment of their children (Brinich, 1990), especially unresolved conflicts toward parenthood on the part of the mother (Toussieng, 1962), and the defective feelings and disappointments that accompany infertility (Blum, 1983; Schechter, 1970). More specifically, these theorists have argued that the narcissistic wounds experienced by infertile adoptive parents are reencountered when the adoptee begins to explore his or her feelings about the birth family. This deep emotional vulnerability on the part of the parents, coupled with feelings of envy about the child's emerging sexuality and fertility during puberty, are believed to distort their interactions with the child, leading to individual and family adjustment problems.

David Kirk's (1964, 1981) social role theory of the adoptive kinship system also focuses on the impact of parental infertility on the adjustment of the adoptee, as well as other family members. A core assumption of the theory is that adoptive family relationships are built, in part, on a foundation of loss—for the adoptive couple, it is the loss of fertility and the desired biological child;

for the adoptee, it is the loss of his or her birth origins. Kirk argues that the ability of adoptive parents to acknowledge and accept their own loss frees them to be more sensitive to their child's experience of loss. In turn, this sensitivity leads to the creation of a more open, nondefensive family atmosphere, which is likely to facilitate more positive patterns of adjustment. Conversely, when parents are unable to cope with their own sense of loss, they are more likely to create child-rearing conditions that inhibit open adoption communication. In turn, this type of environment increases the risk for distorted family interactions and pathogenic patterns of adjustment.

Parental conflict in dealing with infertility is viewed both by psychoanalytic theory and social role theory as a key factor underlying problems in postplacement adjustment among adoptive family members. The clinical literature has identified at least six specific areas where the legacy of infertility impacts adoptive family life: parental feelings of entitlement to the child, parental attachment to the child, expectations regarding the child, adoption revelation, coping with adoption loss, and adolescent separation and individuation.

Entitlement

Entitlement refers to the adoptive parents' sense of having a right to their child. Recognizing that the child is connected biologically to other people, some adoptive parents question whether they can truly be the child's mother or father. This is more likely to occur, however, when parents are still actively struggling with unresolved infertility issues. Here, the sense of entitlement may be compromised by an overemphasis on biological family ties as the basis for personal and societal recognition of the parent-child relationship. Feelings of being defective, which are often a reaction to infertility, may also undermine self-esteem, leading the adoptive parents to question whether they are sufficiently worthy to raise a child born to another person.

Case Example

A few months after the adoption placement, Marge, the 34-year-old adoptive mother of Jennifer, a healthy 4-month-old infant, began to experience periods of intense anxiety. She questioned her ability to care for her daughter, as well as her right to do so. She stated, "What gives me the right to be her mother . . . I don't know if I can do it . . . I get to feeling this way and waves of anxiety overwhelm me, leaving me drained, uncertain, and depressed." In exploring the issue, Marge focused a great deal on the lack of a biological tie to Jennifer. She expressed a deep conviction that if Jennifer were her [biological] child, she would not feel so unsure of herself as a parent, nor question her right to be the mother.

Entitlement is reinforced through the legal process of adoption, in which all rights and responsibilities for the child are transferred from the biological parents to the adoptive parents. It is also reinforced by caseworkers during the evaluation and placement process through affirming the parenting role of adoptive parents. Supporters of open adoption also argue that a primary benefit of this practice is that the parental role of the adoptive couple is sanctioned directly by the birth parent, which in turn, may enhance their sense of entitlement to the child.

Attachment

Another area in which clinical issues arise in relation to infertility is the adoptive parents' sense of attachment to their child. The ability to claim the child as one's own, and foster a mutually secure and trusting relationship with the child, is a fundamentally important parenting task, enhancing the child's chances for healthy psychological adjustment. In contrast, anything that interferes with the parents' ability to see the child as "belonging" to them, and that weakens the attachment bond, is likely to undermine the child's emotional well-being. When parents overemphasize biological family ties as the basis for a satisfying family life, when their grief regarding the loss of the desired biological child is still strong, and when they have difficulty recognizing similarities between the child and themselves, the process of claiming the child as their own and developing secure family attachments may be compromised.

Case Example

Carla, a 31-year-old mother of a 6-month-old adopted boy, Daniel, sought therapy because of difficulty "feeling close" to her child. Although he was an easy baby to care for, she did not feel the level of satisfaction in being a parent that she had expected. During the course of treatment, she reported that her own mother and grandmother had placed a great deal of pressure on her to have a baby soon after she was married. When she eventually recognized that she would not be able to conceive a child, Carla was greatly disappointed, but eventually decided to adopt a child. Although her mother and grandmother appeared to support her decision, she was not confidant that they fully accepted her son. In turn, she felt unsure of the bond with Daniel. Carla reported frequent fantasies about getting pregnant, followed by bouts of crying and depression when she realized that the fantasies would never come true. As treatment progressed, Carla's mother and grandmother were invited to the sessions. Work on intergenerational relationships not only helped Carla feel more secure about her family's acceptance of Daniel, but gave her more confidence as a parent and fostered a closer and more secure connection to him.

Unfulfilled Expectations

All parents have hopes and expectations for their children and for themselves as caregivers. Adoptive parents are no exception. When these expectations are fulfilled, there is increased satisfaction in relation to the parenting role; when they remain unfulfilled, frustration and disappointment are likely to ensue.

Realistic expectations on the part of parents are more likely to occur when they have reasonable knowledge about the factors that influence their child's growth and development, as well as when they feel in control of these factors. Although adoptive parents have considerable control over their child's environment from the time of adoption placement, they have no input into, and often little knowledge about, their child's biological heritage, and often little information about the child's preplacement history as well. In the absence of reasonable information about the child's biological and social history, adoptive parents are more likely to develop unrealistic expectations about their child, which in turn, could set the stage for significant parenting disappointments. Consider for example, a fairly common situation in which the adoptive couple, because of their own upbringing, place a high value on education, only to find their hopes for their child's academic success and vocational future threatened by the emergence of significant biologically based learning disabilities (see Brodzinsky & Steiger, 1991). In such a situation, parents are likely to feel frustrated and worried. Moreover, in struggling to readjust their parenting expectations and maintain a healthy relationship with their child, parents may find themselves "re-visiting" earlier issues regarding infertility and the lack of a biological tie with their child.

Case Example

Larry, a 44-year-old, corporate vice president was seen for counseling because of difficulty accepting his son's lack of school success. Michael, aged 8 years, had lived in an orphanage in Korea for two years before being placed for adoption with the family. Larry and his wife, Ann, knew very little about Michael's life in the orphanage, and even less about his birth family. Both parents placed a great deal of emphasis on education, and had high hopes that their son would do well in school and go on to college. When Michael was diagnosed as neurologically impaired in first grade, his parents were greatly disappointed and worried about his future. Although his mother was able to adjust her expectations regarding her son's academic abilities, his father was not. As a result, the father-son relationship began to deteriorate as Larry put more and more pressure on Michael. Through the process of therapy, Larry came to realize that he continued to harbor considerable pain about the couple's inability to conceive a biological child. He had hoped that he would be able to share his intellectual and cultural interests with his children as they grew up. When he found out about his son's learning problems, however, he was extremely frustrated and angry. "I feel shortchanged . . . someone should have warned me about this possibility . . . I know that Michael has many strengths, but I can't help seeing the problems . . . I also know that this could have happened with a biological child. At least part of me accepts this fact. The larger part, though, feels that if he was my [biological] son, we wouldn't have to be going through all of this . . . it keeps bringing back all the pain we had when we found out about Ann's [fertility] problem."

Delayed and Conflicted Adoption Revelation

Most couples begin discussing adoption with their child during the preschool years (Brodzinsky et al., 1992). The "telling process" is often difficult for parents, however, because it requires that they openly acknowledge the child's connection to another family. Parents sometimes fear that this knowledge will confuse the child and weaken his or her relationships with adoptive family members. When parents continue to harbor strong feelings about their infertility, it often complicates the adoption revelation process even more. In some cases, parents keep putting off telling the child about his or her adoption. In other cases, some information may be shared, but there also may be an attempt to minimize the child's relationship with his or her birth origins. In either case, parents display heightened anxiety about sharing adoption information with their child.

Case Example

Peter and Beth sought counseling because they could not agree on when and how to tell their 4-year-old daughter about her adoption. Peter had wanted to begin sharing Melissa's adoption story with her for some time. Beth, on the other hand, did not feel ready to begin the process. When the basis for her reluctance was explored, she stated, "[telling] would mean that we would have to talk about the fact that she didn't come from us. We would have to let her know that she has other birth parents . . . I don't think she's ready for that . . . maybe I'm not ready for that. . . . Our relationship is so wonderful now. Won't that information make it different . . . I feel so upset inside when I think that this wouldn't be happening if she were our own child."

Coping with Adoption Loss

As children enter the school-age years, their knowledge of adoption deepens and they become increasingly aware of, and responsive to, adoption-related loss (such as loss of birth parents, birth siblings, and extended birth family; loss of racial and ethnic origins; loss of a genealogical connection; status loss; and loss of self (Brodzinsky, 1987, 1990, 1993; Brodzinsky et al., 1992; Nickman, 1985). One of the major parenting responsibilities for adoptive parents is helping their youngsters cope with the grief experienced in relation to adoption loss (Brodzinsky et al., 1995). In his seminal work, *Shared Fate,* Kirk (1964) was one of the first adoption theorists to point out the potential problems for the adoptive family when parents are unable to acknowledge their child's loss and create an open and nondefensive atmosphere for adoption-related communication. He suggested that this problem was more likely to occur when parents had difficulty acknowledging and accepting their own loss of fertility and the desired biological child. This is a fairly common problem among adoptive parents.

Case Example

Sharon and Bill referred their 10-year-old, Colombian son, Andrew, for therapy because of argumentativeness and defiance at home, particularly in relationship with the mother. The parents also reported that Andrew had been expressing a good deal of anger about his adoption in the past year, occasionally confronting his mother with statements such as, "I don't have to listen to you. You're not my real mother." In the early sessions of therapy, Andrew presented as a reasonably healthy and well-adjusted youngster, who nevertheless was experiencing considerable confusion about his adoption. He acknowledged having frequent fantasies about his birth parents, and wondered what they looked like, and if they ever thought about him. When he occasionally raised issues about his birth parents with his adoptive parents, especially his mother, their response was very upsetting to him. He reported that "they say mean things about her [birth mother] . . . like saying she lived on the streets and probably didn't know anything about raising kids." He further reported that he did not feel comfortable talking about his adoption with his parents; nor did he believe they were very comfortable talking about it either. In a meeting with the adoptive parents, Sharon acknowledged her own discomfort discussing the birth parents, especially the birth mother. She reported having fantasies about Andrew's biological mother giving birth to him. These fantasies, however, were often accompanied by great sadness. She noted, "I can't help thinking that she accomplished what I couldn't . . . it makes me feel like a failure . . . I can't talk about her or anything else associated with Andrew's adoption without thinking that way." As therapy progressed, the focus shifted to the family system, with an emphasis on the shared feelings of grief associated with adoption-related loss experienced by all family members. As Sharon and Bill began to see the connection between their unresolved infertility issues and Andrew's behavior, they were eventually able to create a more receptive and supportive communicative environment for their son, which led to a reduction in his oppositional behavior.

Adolescent Separation and Individuation

Separation and individuation are normal and universal tasks associated with adolescence. This is a period when teenagers seek to create psychological distance between themselves and parents, allowing for the development of their own unique identity. Although a potential problem area in any family, this process is very often a focus of conflict between adoptive parents and their children.

It is especially difficult for adoptive parents to "let go" of their youngsters when they still have unresolved conflicts about the parent-child relationship. Parents sometimes fear that the lack of a biological tie with their children will make it more difficult to maintain strong family relationships once the children move beyond the immediate sphere of their influence. They also worry that in adulthood their children will seek out their birth family, potentially creating even more distance among adoptive family members.

Case Example

Jennifer, an 18-year-old adopted female and her parents were seen in family therapy because of increasing conflict among family members. Mr. and Mrs. T complained that their daughter spent little time with them, was not respectful of their feelings, and seemed unduly moody. Jennifer reported that her parents were "suffocating her" with their love. They monitored wherever she went and required that she call them as soon as she reached her destination. She was not allowed to date anyone whom they had not met, and, from her perspective, required her to be home much too early on weekend evenings. A senior in high school, Jennifer was in the process of applying to college. Mr. and Mrs. T wanted Jennifer to attend a school nearby and live at home, despite having sufficient money to support her at virtually any school where she was accepted. In the course of treatment, Mr. and Mrs. T acknowledged that they were anxious about the possibility of Jennifer leaving home and contacting her birth family. Both parents questioned whether their daughter would still feel close to them, once she had a reunion with her birth family. As therapy progressed, Mr. and Mrs. T came to realize that their concern about Jennifer was grounded in a much earlier conflict related to their own lack of biological connection to their daughter. During the process of applying for adoption, they struggled with the fear that they would not be able to love a child born to other parents. Although they eventually grew more comfortable with the idea of adoption, they now realized that over time, their fear had simply been projected on to their daughter. As Jennifer got older and began to separate from them, they expected that her love for them would weaken because they were not her biological parents. Keeping her close to them was their way of preventing this from happening. In the course of treatment, all family members eventually were able to talk openly about their fears, and with much crying, affirm their love and commitment to one another. At the same time, Mr. and Mrs. T eventually were able to allow Jennifer to begin separating from them in an age-appropriate manner.

CONCLUSION

The transition to adoptive parenthood is a complex process involving a gradual reshaping of identity and role adjustment. For those couples who adopt because of infertility, a primary task involves gradually letting go of the biological parenthood identity in preparation for taking on the identity of adoptive parent. Although traditional social casework models assume that this process occurs in a sequential manner, more recent research and clinical work has shown that, for many couples, it is the pursuit of parenthood per se that is most salient, regardless of the way it is achieved. Consequently, many couples pursue both biological parenthood and adoptive parenthood simultaneously—and they appear to do so without much confusion or ambivalence in their commitment to their children. These findings have important implications both for the meaning of infertility resolution and for adoption casework and counseling.

First, it appears unrealistic to assume that infertility is ever *completely* resolved, or that there is an endpoint to the individual's or couple's "working through" of this deeply personal experience. Instead, the goal of griefwork in dealing with infertility is best understood to be the achievement of a reasonably comfortable way of incorporating this painful loss into a healthy and functional sense of self.

Second, it also appears that resolving one's feelings about infertility is unnecessary for a commitment to adopt a child. Thus, rather than focusing the adoption assessment process on the extent to which the couple has resolved their feelings about infertility, it is likely to be more useful to examine the value of children in the life of the couple, and the significance for them of biological connectedness as a basis for a fulfilling family life (Daly, 1990). From this perspective, couples who *strongly* emphasize biological ties as a foundation for satisfying family relationships probably should be counseled to seek all medical solutions before considering other parenting options, including adoption. In addition, it is likely that these couples would need more in-depth counseling in relation to infertility issues before they could begin to take on the identity of adoptive parents and make a lifelong commitment to an adopted child. On the other hand, for couples who value the social and emotional aspects of parenthood as much, or more, than biological family ties, the pursuit of both adoption and biological parenthood simultaneously is not only understandable, but should be supported by social casework professionals and therapists as a viable option.

Although it may be unrealistic to expect that couples will completely resolve their feelings about infertility prior to adopting a child, research and clinical work do suggest that they need to find a comfortable way of dealing with this issue so that it does not burrow itself into the fabric of adoptive family life, distorting relationships among family members, and creating serious adjustment problems. Consequently, when adoptive families present themselves for clinical services, therapists are well advised to examine the couple's motivation for adoption. If infertility played a role in the decision to adopt, it is important to explore with the couple the meaning of infertility in their lives, and whether the lack of a biological relationship between parent and child has influenced the way the family has handled the many developmental and family life-cycle tasks—especially those associated with adoption—that have been encountered in the course of raising their child.

REFERENCES

Bachrach, C. A., Stolley, K. S., & London, K. A. (1992). Relinquishment of premarital births: Evidence from national survey data. *Family Planning Perspectives, 24,* 27–32, 48.

Baran, A., & Pannor, R. (1993). Perspectives on open adoption. *The Future of Children, 3,* 119–124.

Barnard, K. E., & Martell, L. K. (1995). Mothering. In M. Bornstein (Ed.), *Handbook of parenting: Vol. 3. Status and social conditions of parenting* (pp. 3–26). Mahwah, NJ: Erlbaum.

Berry, M. (1993). Risks and benefits of open adoption. *The Future of Children, 3,* 125–138.

Blank, R. (1985). The infertility epidemic. *Futurist, 19,* 177–180.

Blum, H. P. (1983). Adoptive parents: Generative conflict and generational continuity. *Psychoanalytic Study of the Child, 38,* 141–163.

Brinich, P. M. (1990). Adoption from the inside out: A psychoanalytic perspective. In D. Brodzinsky & M. Schechter (Eds.), *The psychology of adoption* (pp. 42–61). New York: Oxford University Press.

Brodzinsky, D. M. (1987). Children's adjustment to adoption: A psychosocial perspective. *Clinical Psychology Review, 7,* 25–47.

Brodzinsky, D. M. (1990). A stress and coping model of adoption adjustment. In D. Brodzinsky & M. Schechter (Eds.), *The psychology of adoption* (pp. 3–24). New York: Oxford University Press.

Brodzinsky, D. M. (1993). Long-term outcome in adoption. *The Future of Children, 3,* 153–166.

Brodzinsky, D. M., & Huffman, L. (1988). Transition to adoptive parenthood. In R. Palkovitz & M. Sussman (Eds.), *Transitions to parenthood* (pp. 267–286). New York: Haworth Press.

Brodzinsky, D. M., Lang, R., & Smith, D. W. (1995). Parenting adopted children. In M. Bornstein (Ed.), *Handbook of parenting: Vol. 3. Status and social conditions of parenting* (pp. 209–234). Mahwah, NJ: Erlbaum.

Brodzinsky, D. M., Schechter, M. D., & Henig, R. M. (1992). *Being adopted: The lifelong search for self.* New York: Doubleday.

Brodzinsky, D. M., & Steiger, C. (1991). Prevalence of adoptees in special education populations. *Journal of Learning Disabilities, 24,* 484–489.

Burgwyn, D. (1981). *Marriage without children.* New York: Harper & Row.

Callan, V. J., & Hennessey, J. F. (1986). IVF and adoption: The experiences of infertile couples. *Australian Journal of Early Childhood, 11,* 32–36.

Cole, E. S., & Donley, K. S. (1990). History, values, and placement policy issues in adoption. In D. Brodzinsky & M. Schechter (Eds.), *The psychology of adoption* (273–294). New York: Oxford University Press.

Crowe, C. (1985). "Women want it": In vitro fertilization and women's motivations for participation. *Women's Studies International Forum, 8,* 547–552.

Daly, K. (1988). Reshaped parenthood identity: The transition to adoptive parenthood. *Journal of Contemporary Ethnography, 17,* 40–66.

Daly, K. (1990, October). Infertility resolution and adoption readiness. *Families in Society: The Journal of Contemporary Human Services, 71 ,* 483–492.

Daniels, K. R. (1994). Adoption and donor insemination: Factors influencing couples' choices. *Child Welfare, 73,* 5–14.

Emery, L. J. (1993). Agency versus independent adoption: The case for agency adoption. *The Future of Children, 3,* 139–145.

Erikson, E. (1963). *Childhood and society* (2nd ed.). New York: W. W. Norton.

Fawcett, J. T. (1988). The value of children and the transition to parenthood. In R. Palkovitz & M. Sussman (Eds.), *Transitions to parenthood* (pp. 11–34). New York: Haworth Press.

Glick, P. C. (1977). Updating the life cycle of the family. *Journal of Marriage and the Family, 39,* 5–13.

Grossman, F. K. (1988). Strain in the transition to parenthood. In R. Palkovitz & M. Sussman (Eds.), *Transitions to parenthood* (pp. 85–104). New York: Haworth Press.

Hajal, F., & Rosenberg, E. B. (1991). The family life cycle in adoptive families. *American Journal of Orthopsychiatry, 61,* 78–85.

Heinicke, C. M. (1995). Determinants of the transition to parenting. In M. Bornstein (Ed.), *Handbook of parenting: Vol. 3. Status and social conditions of parenting* (pp. 277–304). Mahwah, NJ: Erlbaum.

Holbrook, S. M. (1990). Adoption, infertility, and the new reproductive technologies: Problems and prospects for social work and welfare policy. *Social Work, 35,* 333–337.

Kirk, H. D. (1964). *Shared fate.* New York: Free Press.

Kirk, H. D. (1981). *Adoptive kinship—A modern institution in need of reform.* Toronto, Ontario, Canada: Butterworth.

Lorber, J., & Greenfeld, D. (1989). Couples' experiences with in vitro fertilization: A phenomenological approach. In Z. Ben-Rafael (Ed.), *Proceedings of the Sixth World Congress on In Vitro Fertilization and Alternative Assisted Reproduction* (pp. 965–971). New York: Plenum.

Matthews, R., & Martin-Matthews, A. (1986). Infertility and involuntary childlessness. *Journal of Marriage and the Family, 48,* 641–650.

McDermott, M. T. (1993). Agency versus independent adoption: The case for independent adoption. *The Future of Children, 3,* 146–152.

McEwan, K. L., Costello, C. G., & Taylor, P. J. (1987). Adjustment to infertility. *Journal of Abnormal Psychology, 96,* 108–116.

Mosher, W. D., & Pratt, W. F. (1990). Fecundity and infertility in the United States, 1965–1988. *Advance Data, 192,* 1–9.

National Committee for Adoption (1989). *Adoption factbook.* Washington, DC: Author.

Nickman, S. L. (1985). Losses in adoption: The need for dialogue. *Psychoanalytic Study of the Child, 40,* 365–398.

Reitz, M., & Watson, K. W. (1992). *Adoption and the family system.* New York: Guilford.

Rossi, A. S. (1968). Transition to parenthood. *Journal of Marriage and the Family, 30,* 26–39.

Schechter, M. D. (1970). About adoptive parents. In E. J. Anthony & T. Benedek (Eds.), *Parenthood: Its psychology and psychopathology.* Boston: Little, Brown.

Stolley, K. S. (1993). Statistics on adoption in the United States. *The Future of Children, 3,* 26–42.

Toussieng, P. W. (1962). Thoughts regarding the etiology of psychological difficulties in adopted children. *Child Welfare, 41,* 59–65.

U.S. Immigration and Naturalization Service. (1991). *Statistical yearbook of the Immigration and Naturalization Service.* Washington, DC: U.S. Governmental Printing Office.

Weinraub, M., & Gringlas, M. B. (1995). Single parenthood. In M. Bornstein (Ed.), *Handbook of parenting: Vol. 3. Status and social conditions of parenting* (pp. 65–88). Mahwah, NJ: Erlbaum.

Williams, L. S. (1992). Adoption actions and attitudes of couples seeking in vitro fertilization. *Journal of Family Issues, 13,* 99–113.

About the Contributors

Andrea Mechanick Braverman, PhD, Director of Psychological Services, Pennsylvania Reproductive Associates, Pennsylvania Hospital, Philadelphia, PA.

David Brodzinksy, PhD, Department of Psychology, Rutgers—The State University, New Brunswick, NJ.

Susan Cooper, EdD, Psychologist, Reproductive Science Center of Boston, and Co-Director, Focus Counseling and Consultation, Inc., Cambridge, MA.

Judith C. Daniluk, PhD, Department of Counselling Psychology, Faculty of Education, University of British Columbia, Vancouver, BC.

Alice D. Domar, PhD, Division of Behavioral Medicine, Deaconess Hospital, and Mind/Body Medical Institute, Harvard Medical School, Boston, MA.

Yakov M. Epstein, PhD, Department of Psychology, Rutgers—The State University, New Brunswick, NJ.

Ellen S. Glazer, LICSW, Reproductive Medicine Center, Boston Regional Medical Center, Stoneham, MA.

Dorothy A. Greenfeld, MSW, Director of Psychological Services, Center for Reproductive Medicine, Yale University School of Medicine, New Haven, CT.

Mary Casey Jacob, PhD, Departments of Psychiatry and Obstetrics/Gynecology, University of Connecticut School of Medicine, Farmington, CT.

Susan Caruso Klock, PhD, Northwestern University School of Medicine, Department of Obstetrics/Gynecology, Division of Reproductive Endocrinology, Chicago, IL.

Sandra R. Leiblum, PhD, Department of Psychiatry, University of Medicine and Dentistry of New Jersey—Robert Wood Johnson Medical School, Piscataway, NJ.

Patricia M. McShane, MD, Program Medical Director, Reproductive Science Center of Boston, Deaconess Waltham Western Hospital, Waltham, MA.

Helane S. Rosenberg, PhD, Department of Learning and Teaching, Graduate School of Education, Rutgers—The State University, New Brunswick, NJ.

Author Index

Subject Index